Queen Marguerite

The Heptameron of Margaret, Queen of Navarre

Translated from the French.

Queen Marguerite

The Heptameron of Margaret, Queen of Navarre
Translated from the French.

ISBN/EAN: 9783337132156

Printed in Europe, USA, Canada, Australia, Japan

Cover: Foto ©ninafisch / pixelio.de

More available books at **www.hansebooks.com**

BOHN'S EXTRA VOLUME.

THE HEPTAMERON

OF

MARGARET, QUEEN OF NAVARRE.

THE

HEPTAMERON

OF

MARGARET, QUEEN OF NAVARRE.

Translated from the French.

WITH A MEMOIR OF THE AUTHOR.

BY

WALTER K. KELLY.

LONDON:
HENRY G. BOHN, YORK STREET, COVENT GARDEN.
1864.

PREFACE.

MARGARET OF ANGOULÊME, Duchess of Alençon, Queen of Navarre, only sister of Francis I., is certainly the author of the collection of tales which bears her name, though the fact has been doubted by some French writers. La Croix du Maine, for instance, says: "I question whether the princess composed this book; forasmuch as it is full of bold discourses and ticklish expressions." But, against this surmise, we may set the positive testimony of Brantôme. The Queen of Navarre, he says, "composed most of these novels in her litter as she travelled; for her hours of retirement were employed in affairs of importance. I have heard this account from my grandmother, who always went with her in her litter, as her lady of honour, and held her standish for her; and she wrote them down as quickly and readily, or rather more so, than if they had been dictated to her." Besides, as Bayle remarks, La Croix du Maine could never have entertained a doubt on the matter if he had read Claude Gruget's dedication of the second edition of the work to

Joan d'Albret, only daughter of Queen Margaret. Had the work been supposititious, it is incredible that Gruget should have thus addressed the princess: "Such a present will not be new to you; you will only recognise it as your mother's heiress. However, I persuade myself that it will be acceptable to you to see it by this second impression restored to its primitive state; for (as I have heard) the first displeased you; not but that he who undertook it was a learned man, and had taken pains with it, and, as is easy to believe, would not have thus disguised it without some reason for doing so; yet his labour proved disagreeable."

The history of the Heptameron is singular. It is the best known and the most popular of all the old collections of tales in the French language. It has been the delight of the unlearned, scholars have warmly commended it, and men of talent and genius have borrowed from its pages. Brantôme speaks of it with enthusiasm, and quotes it repeatedly; Lafontaine, the *conteur par excellence*, acknowledges his obligations to it; Montaigne calls it *un gentil livre pour son étoffe*—"a nice book for its matter;" and Bayle says it is, "after the manner of Boccace's novels," and "has some beauties in that kind which are surprising." The book, too, has had its enemies as well as its admirers, for it abounds with reflections on religious topics which accord with the author's known leaning to the cause of the Reformers; and through the whole work the monks, especially the Cordeliers, are treated with much severity, and are represented as committing, and sometimes with impunity even when discovered, the most cruel, deceitful, and immoral actions. From all this, would it not seem reasonable to presume that the world had long possessed a tolerably correct text of this celebrated book—one at least which has not been seriously falsified both by omissions and interpolations? But such is not the fact. The genuine Heptameron, after remaining in manuscript for more than three hundred years from the Queen of Navarre's death, was only published two years ago by the Société des Bibliophiles Français.

Margaret died in 1549. In 1558, Pierre Boaistuau published the first edition of her novels under the title of Histoire des Amans Fortunés, which he dedicated to Margaret of Bourbon, the deceased queen's niece. He took strange liberties with the original, inverting the order of the stories, and suppressing several of them, as well as many names of real personages, numerous passages that seemed to him too bold, and nearly the whole series of conversations by which one tale is followed and the next introduced. Now these conversations occupy almost one-half of the work, and comprise some of its most characteristic matter: no wonder, therefore, that Joan d'Albret was dissatisfied with Boaistuau's editorial labours. In 1559, Claude Gruget replaced the novels in their original order, restored most of the suppressed prologues and epilogues, and gave to the whole the title of Heptameron, instead of Decameron, which Margaret had intended to call it; for she had modelled it upon the Decameron of Boccaccio, but died before she had completed more than two novels of the eighth day. So far the second editor's work was a great improvement on that of his predecessor; but Gruget did not venture to restore the proper names, or the passages which Boaistuau had suppressed as objectionable; while, on the other hand, he foisted into the work tales and dialogues of his own composition, without a word of warning to the reader, and left them to pass as the genuine productions of the Queen of Navarre.

All this was bad enough, but worse followed. The Heptameron having grown very scarce, the booksellers of Amsterdam reprinted it in 1698. "They published two editions of it," says Bayle, "one from that of Claude Gruget, the other metamorphosed into new French: the latter will please foreigners who only understand the modern language, and many ignorant and lazy Frenchmen, who care not to be at the pains of informing themselves how they spoke in the reign of Francis I. The other edition is the only one which will be used by Frenchmen of good taste and judgment." The majority of readers, however, not being persons of that description, the modernised edition quickly supplanted the antique one; and for the last hundred and fifty years the Heptameron has scarcely been known in any other form than that given to it by the literary cobbler by whom it was *mis en beau language, et accommodé au goût de ce temps* — "put into fair language, and accommodated to the taste of the age." It is no exaggeration of his demerits to say, that he neither understood old French rightly, nor could write modern French passably. His "beau language" is mere slipslop; he mistakes the meaning of his original a thousand times; and by way, no doubt, of "accommodating it to the taste of the age," he patches it with paltry scraps from the common repertory of the "fast school" of his day.

Mal sur mal n'est pas santé, says a French proverb. The work which survived all this accumulated ill-usage must have possessed no ordinary stock of vitality. It has at last been reproduced in its original form from MSS., of which there are twelve in the Bibliothèque Nationale of Paris, all belonging to the second half of the sixteenth century. From this edition (L'Heptameron des Nouvelles de très haute et très illustre Princesse Marguerite D'Angoulême, Reine de Navarre. Nouvelle edition, publiée sur les manuscrits par la Société des Bibliophiles Français. A Paris, 1853. 3 vols.) the present translation has been made.

W. K. K.

CONTENTS.

INTRODUCTION 1

FIRST DAY.

NOVEL I.

A woman of Alençon having two lovers, one for her pleasure and the other for her profit, caused that one of the two to be slain who was the first to discover her gallantries—She obtained her pardon and that of her husband, who had fled the country, and who afterwards, in order to save some money, applied to a necromancer—The matter was found out and punished . . 11

NOVEL II.

Chaste and lamentable death of the wife of one of the Queen of Navarre's muleteers 18

NOVEL III.

A king of Naples, having debauched the wife of a gentleman, at last wears horns himself 22

NOVEL IV.

Presumptuous attempt of a gentleman upon a Princess of Flanders, and the shame it brought upon him 27

NOVEL V.

A boatwoman escapes from two Cordeliers, who wanted to force her, and exposes them to public derision 34

NOVEL VI.

Stratagem by which a woman enabled her gallant to escape, when her husband, who was blind of an eye, thought to surprise them together 37

NOVEL VII.

Trick put by a mercer of Paris upon an old woman, to conceal his intrigue with her daughter 40

NOVEL VIII.

A man having lain with his wife, believing that he was in bed with his servant, sends his friend to do the same thing; and the friend makes a cuckold of him without the wife being aware of it 42

NOVEL IX.

Deplorable death of a lover in consequence of his knowing too late that he was beloved by his mistress 43

NOVEL X.

The loves of Amadour and Florida, wherein are seen several stratagems and dissimulations, and the exemplary chastity of Florida 54

SECOND DAY.

NOVEL XI.

A nasty adventure which befel Madame de Roncex at the Franciscan Monastery of Thouars 83

Facetious sayings of a Cordelier in his sermons 85

NOVEL XII.

Incontinence and tyranny of a Duke of Florence—Just punishment of his wickedness 88

NOVEL XIII.

A captain of a galley, under the cloak of devotion, fell in love with a demoiselle—What happened in consequence . . . 95

NOVEL XIV.

Subtlety of a lover who, counterfeiting the real favourite, found means to recompense himself for his past troubles . . . 104

NOVEL XV.

A lady of the court, seeing herself neglected by her husband, whose love was bestowed elsewhere, retaliated upon him . 110

NOVEL XVI.

A Milanese lady tested her lover's courage, and afterwards loved him heartily 122

NOVEL XVII.

King Francis gives a signal proof of his courage in the case of Count Guillaume, who designed his death 127

NOVEL XVIII.

A lady tests the fidelity of a young student, her lover, before granting him her favours 131

NOVEL XIX.

Two lovers, in despair at being hindered from marrying, turn monk and nun 136

NOVEL XX.

A gentleman finds his cruel fair one in the arms of her groom, and is cured at once of his love 144

THIRD DAY.

NOVEL XXI.

Virtuous love of a young lady of quality and a bastard of an illustrious house—Hinderance of their marriage by a queen—Sage reply of the demoiselle to the queen—Her subsequent marriage 148

NOVEL XXII.

A hypocritical prior tries every means to seduce a nun, but at last his villany is discovered 166

NOVEL XXIII.

A Cordelier is the cause of three murders, that of husband, wife, and child 176

NOVEL XXIV.

Ingenious device of a Castilian in order to make a declaration of love to a queen, and what came of it 183

NOVEL XXV.

Cunning contrivance of a young prince to enjoy the wife of an advocate of Paris 19

NOVEL XXVI.

By the advice and sisterly affection of a virtuous lady the lord of Avannes was weaned from his dissolute amours with a lady of Pampeluna 197

NOVEL XXVII.

A secretary had the impudence to solicit the favours of his host's wife, and had only the shame for his pains 210

NOVEL XXVIII.

A secretary, thinking to dupe a certain person, was himself duped 212

NOVEL XXIX.

A villager, whose wife intrigued with the parish priest, suffered himself to be easily deceived 215

NOVEL XXX.

Notable example of human frailty in a lady who, to conceal an evil, commits a still greater one 217

FOURTH DAY.

NOVEL XXXI.

A monastery of Cordeliers was burned and the monks in it, in perpetual memory of the cruelty of one of them who was in love with a lady 225

NOVEL XXXII.

A husband surprises his wife in flagrante delicto, and subjects her to a punishment more terrible than death itself . 230

NOVEL XXXIII.

Incest of a priest who got his sister with child under the cloak of sanctity, and how it was punished 235

NOVEL XXXIV.

Two over-inquisitive Cordeliers had a great fright, which had like to cost them their lives 238

NOVEL XXXV.

Contrivance of a sensible husband to cure his wife of her passion for a Cordelier 243

CONTENTS.

NOVEL XXXVI.

A president of Grenoble, becoming aware of his wife's irregularities, took his measures so wisely, that he revenged himself without any public exposure of his dishonour 249

NOVEL XXXVII.

Judicious proceedings of a wife to withdraw her husband from a low intrigue with which he was infatuated 255

NOVEL XXXVIII.

Memorable charity of a lady of Tours with regard to her faithless husband 259

NOVEL XXXIX.

Secret for driving away the hobgoblin 262

NOVEL XL.

The Count de Jossebelin has his brother-in-law put to death, not knowing the relationship 264

FIFTH DAY.

NOVEL XLI.

Strange and novel penance imposed by a Cordelier confessor on a young lady 271

NOVEL XLII.

Chaste perseverance of a maiden, who resisted the obstinate pursuit of one of the greatest lords in France—Agreeable issue of the affair for the demoiselle 275

NOVEL XLIII.

Hypocrisy of a court lady discovered by the dénouement of her amours, which she wished to conceal 285

NOVEL XLIV.

A Cordelier received a double alms for telling the plain truth . 290

How two lovers cleverly consummated their amours, the issue of which was happy 293

NOVEL XLV.

A husband giving the Innocents to his servant girl, plays upon his wife's simplicity 300

NOVEL XLVI.

A sanctimonious Cordelier attempts to debauch the wife of a judge, and actually ravishes a young lady, whose mother had foolishly authorised him to chastise her for lying too late in bed . . 305

A Cordelier's sermons on the subject of husbands beating their wives 308

NOVEL XLVII.

A gentleman of the Pays du Perche, distrusting his friend, obliges him to do him the mischief of which he has falsely suspected him 311

NOVEL XLVIII.

A Cordelier took the husband's place on his wedding-night, while the latter was dancing with the bridal party . . . 315

NOVEL XLIX.

Of a countess who diverted herself adroitly with love sport, and how her game was discovered 317

NOVEL L.

A lover, after a blood-letting, receives favours from his mistress, dies in consequence, and is followed by the fair one, who sinks under her grief 324

SIXTH DAY.

NOVEL LI.

Perfidy and cruelty of an Italian duke 328

NOVEL LII.

A nasty breakfast given to an advocate and a gentleman by an apothecary's man 332

NOVEL XLIII.

Madame de Neufchastel, by her dissimulation, forced the Prince of Belhoste to put her to such a proof as turned to her dishonour 335

NOVEL LIV.

A lady laughed to see her husband kissing her servant, and being asked the reason, replied that she laughed at her shadow. . 342

NOVEL LV.

Cunning device of a Spanish widow to defraud the Mendicant Friars of a testamentary bequest made to them by her husband 344

CONTENTS.

NOVEL LVI.

A pious lady having asked a Cordelier to provide a good husband for her daughter, he marries another Cordelier to the young lady, and possesses himself of her dowry—The cheat is discovered and punished 347

NOVEL LVII.

Of a ridiculous milord who wore a lady's glove on his dress-coat 353

NOVEL LVIII.

How a lady of the court pleasantly revenged herself on her faithless lover 356

NOVEL LIX.

The same lady, whose husband was jealous of her without just cause, contrives to detect him in such a position with one of her women that he is obliged to humble himself, and allow his wife to live as she pleases 359

NOVEL LX.

A woman of Paris quits her husband for one of the king's chanters, counterfeits death, and is buried, but secretly disinterred alive and well—Her husband marries another wife, and fifteen years afterwards is obliged to repudiate her, and take back his first wife 365

SEVENTH DAY.

NOVEL LXI.

A husband became reconciled to his wife after she had lived fourteen or fifteen years with a canon 370

NOVEL LXII.

A lady recounting an adventure of gallantry that had occurred to herself, and speaking in the third person, inadvertently betrayed her own secret 377

NOVEL LXIII.

Notable chastity of a French lord . . . . .

NOVEL LXIV.

A gentleman having been unable to marry a person he loves, becomes a Cordelier in despite—Sore distress of his mistress thereat. . . . .

NOVEL LXV.

Simplicity of an old woman who presented a lighted candle to Saint Jean de Lyon, and wanted to fasten it on the forehead of a soldier who was sleeping on a tomb—What happened in consequence 387

NOVEL LXVI.

Amusing adventure of Monsieur de Vendôme and the Princess of Navarre 389

NOVEL LXVII.

Love and extreme hardships of a woman in a foreign land . . 392

NOVEL LXVIII.

A woman gives her husband powder of cantharides to make him love her, and goes near to killing him 395

NOVEL LXIX.

An Italian suffered himself to be duped by his servant maid, and was caught by his wife bolting meal in place of the girl . . 398

NOVEL LXX.

The horrible incontinence and malice of a Duchess of Burgundy was the cause of her death, and of that of two persons who fondly loved each other 400

EIGHTH DAY.

NOVEL LXXI.

A woman at the point of death flew into such a violent passion at seeing her husband kiss her servant, that she recovered . 421

NOVEL LXXII.

Continual repentance of a nun who had lost her virginity without violence and without love 424

MEMOIR OF
LOUISE OF SAVOY, DUCHESS OF ANGOULÊME,

AND OF HER DAUGHTER

MARGARET, QUEEN OF NAVARRE.

Two children were born of the marriage of Charles of Orleans, Count of Angoulême, a prince of the blood royal of France, and Louise, the daughter of Philip Duke of Savoy, and Margaret of Bourbon. The elder of the two was Margaret, the principal subject of this memoir, born on the 11th of April, 1492; the younger, born on the 12th of September, 1494, was the prince who succeeded Louis XII. on the throne of France, February, 1515, under the name of Francis I.

Married when she was little more than eleven years old, Louise of Savoy was left a widow before she had completed her eighteenth year, and thenceforth devoted herself with exemplary assiduity to the care of her children, who repaid her solicitude by the warm affection they always felt for their mother and for each other. She was a woman of remarkable beauty and capacity, and her character and conduct were deserving, in many respects, of the eulogies which her daughter never wearied of lavishing upon them; but less partial writers have convicted her of criminal acts, which brought disasters upon her son and her country. In the first year of his reign, Francis I. committed the regency of the kingdom to his mother, and set out on his expedition to Italy. He was absent but a few months; nevertheless, this first regency enabled Louise of Savoy to fill the most important offices with men entirely devoted to her interests, and even to her caprices, and to gratify by any and every means the insatiable thirst for money with which she was cursed.

In the beginning of the year 1522, Lautrec, one of the king's favourites, who commanded his forces in Italy, lost in a few days all the advantages which Francis had gained by the victory of Marignano. He returned to Paris with only two attendants, and sought an audience of the king, who refused at first to receive him. Finally, at the intercession of the Constable of Bourbon, Francis allowed Lautrec to appear before him, and after loading him with reproaches, demanded what excuse he could offer for himself. Lautrec calmly replied, "The troops I commanded not having been paid, refused to follow me, and I was left alone."—"What!" said the king, "I sent you four hundred thousand crowns to Genoa, and Semblançay, the superintendent of finance, forwarded you three hundred thousand."—"Sire, I have received nothing." Semblançay being summoned to the presence, "Father," said the king (who addressed him in that way on account of his great age), "come hither and tell us if you have not, in pursuance of my order, sent M. de Lautrec the sum of three hundred thousand crowns?"—"Sire," replied the superintendent, "I am prepared to prove that I delivered that sum to the duchess your mother, that she might employ it as you say."—"Very well," said the king, and went into his mother's room to question her. Louise of Savoy threw the whole blame on Semblançay, who was immediately confronted with her. He persisted in his first statement, and the duchess was forced to confess that she had received the greater part of the sum in question, but she alleged that the money was due to her by the superintendent, and she did not see why her private income should be applied to the Italian expedition. Francis most bitterly upbraided his mother for thus embezzling the money of the state, but his wrath fell more heavily on the minister, whom she found to have been guilty of culpable complaisance towards her. The unfortunate Semblançay was arrested; commissioners were appointed to examine his accounts, and being condemned by their report, he was hung on the gibbet at Montfaucon on the 9th of August, 1527.

Louise of Savoy was deeply implicated in a still fouler

transaction, which was attended with the most terrible consequences: this was the iniquitous lawsuit brought against the Constable of Bourbon, which was followed by his desertion and treason. According to all historians, the insensate love of the Duchess of Angoulême, then aged forty-four, for the constable, who was but thirty-two, was the sole cause of this suit; but her cupidity, and the secret jealousy with which Francis I. regarded one of the handsomest, wealthiest, and bravest men in his kingdom, also contributed to that result. The object of the suit was to wrest from the constable the lordships bequeathed to him by Suzanne de Beaujeu, one of the richest heiresses in Europe, and to which Louise of Savoy laid claim as next of kin to the deceased. She did so at the instigation of the Chancellor Duprat, whose reasonings on this subject we are enabled to give in his own words, as follows:

"The marriage of M. Charles de Bourbon with Madame Suzanne was nothing else than a mere shift to stop the action at law which the said lord was ready to move against Madame de Bourbon and her daughter, on account of the estates of appanage and others entailed on the marriage of Jean de Bourbon and Maria of Berry. The mere apprehension of this contest made the said Madame de Bourbon condescend thereto, and to that end she dissolved the contract passed between M. d'Alençon and Madame Suzanne. Hence there is a likelihood that a similar apprehension of a suit to be promoted for the whole inheritance of the house by two stronger parties than was then the said Lord of Bourbon, who was neither old enough nor strong enough to prosecute it, as the king and his mother will be, may cause some overtures to be made on the one side or the other to compromise and allay this difference.

"M. de Bourbon is now but thirty-two, and Madame, the king's mother, cannot be more than forty at most, which is not too disproportioned an age for so great a lady, handsome, rich, and so highly qualified. Should the said Lord of Bourbon agree to this marriage, why there she is at the point she desires, Duchess of Bourbonnais and Auvergne, and lady of that great heritage. If, on the contrary, he refuses, it will be necessary to bring this action, prosecute it vigorously, employ in it the authority of the king and my lady his mother, and spare nought to further it. This will make him bethink himself, however intractable he may be, and he will be very glad to return into favour by this means. If not, as he is a courageous prince, when he finds himself threatened with the loss of all his possessions, titles, and dignities, he will do something extraordinary, and will choose rather to abandon his country (as M. du Bellay says) than to live in it in a necessitous condition. He will withdraw out of the realm; and by so doing he will confiscate all. So that he cannot fail to do what is desired, be it how it may."*

The Constable of Bourbon having rejected, and even it is said with disdain, the offer of marriage made to him, the suit was brought before the parliament, and was decided in favour of the Duchess of Angoulême. But the pleasure brought her by this triumph over her haughty adversary was not of long duration. A few months after he was despoiled of all his estates, Charles of Bourbon quitted France, and entered the service of Charles V. In the following year, 1524, he drove the French out of Italy, and on the 24th of February, 1525, he defeated them in the famous battle of Pavia, in which Francis I. was taken prisoner, after receiving five wounds. The Duchess of Angoulême, as Regent of France, displayed great courage and ability under this heavy calamity. She soon received from her captive son the letter containing that memorable phrase: *De toutes choses ne m'est demeuré que l'honneur, et la vie qui est sauve*—" I have lost all but honour and life." This letter was a great joy to her. Margaret wrote respecting it to her brother, " Your letter has had such an effect of Madame, and of all those who love you, that it has been to us a Holy Ghost after the sorrow of the Passion. . . . Madame has felt her strength so greatly redoubled, that all day and evening not a minute is lost for your affairs, so that you need not have any pain or care about your realm and your children."

After taking all necessary measures for the internal defence of the kingdom, the regent and her daughter took up their residence at Lyon, for the purpose of the more readily receiving news from Italy. There they learned that Charles V. had removed his prisoner to Madrid, and that he was

---

* *Histoire de Bourbon*, p. 226 r°· *Des desseins des professions nobles et publiques*, &c., &c. Par Ant. de Laval. Paris, 1605.

becoming more and more exacting in the conditions for his
release. Francis I. wrote to his mother that he was very ill,
and begged her to come to him; but, in spite of her love for
her son, she felt that she could not comply with his request,
for it would have been risking the fate of the monarchy to
put the regent along with the King of France into the
Emperor's hands. Sacrificing, therefore, her feelings as a
mother to the requirements of the state, she sent her
daughter Margaret instead of herself to Madrid.

After she had done her part to the utmost for her son's
release, and in the negotiations for the treaty of peace which
was concluded at Cambrai on the 5th of August, 1529, the
Duchess of Angoulême took no further share in the government
of the realm. She had repaired, as far as it was possible
for her, the misfortunes earned by her conduct with regard
to the constable. Her labours as regent, during her son's
captivity, had completely ruined her health, which had begun
to fail before that event. In September, 1531, she was at
Fontainebleau with her daughter and all the other ladies of
her court; the plague was raging in the neighbourhood, and
Louise, who had a great dread of death, was incessantly occupied with medicine and new receipts against disorders of
all kinds. Her spirits were very low, and her countenance
so changed as scarcely to be recognised by her daughter.
"If you would like to know her pastime," Margaret writes
to her brother, "it is that, after dinner, when she has given
audience, instead of doing her customary works, she sends
for all those who have any malady, whether in the legs, arms,
or breasts, and with her own hand she dresses them, by way
of trying an ointment she has, which is very singular." This
horror at the thought of death was common to both mother
and daughter. Brantôme says of the former, "She was in
her time, as I have heard many say who have seen and
known her, a very fine lady, but very worldly withal, and was
the same in her declining age, and hated to hear discourse of
death, even from preachers in their sermons: as if, said she,
we did not know well enough that we must all die some time
or other; and these preachers, when they have nothing else
to say in their sermons, like ignorant persons, fall to talking
of death. The late Queen of Navarre, her daughter, liked no

more than her mother these repetitions and preachings concerning death."*

A few days after the date of the letter quoted in the last paragraph, Louise of Savoy quitted Fontainebleau for change of air, but was obliged to stop at Grès, a little village of the Gâtinais, where she died on the 22nd of September, 1531. We now turn to her daughter's history.

Charles of Austria, Count of Flanders, afterwards the Emperor Charles V., was residing at the court of Louis XII. when Margaret of Angoulême appeared there, accompanying her brother on his entrance into public life. The Count of Flanders was much struck by her appearance and her accomplishments, and eagerly sought her in marriage. But Louis XII. refused to bestow upon him the sister of the heir presumptive of the throne of France, and chose rather to marry her in the following year, December, 1509, to Charles, Duke of Alençon, a prince of the royal family.

Historians have treated the memory of Margaret's first husband with excessive severity. He had the misfortune to escape unwounded from the fatal battle of Pavia, while endeavouring to save the remains of the routed army; and it has been alleged that, on his arrival at Lyon, where he found his wife and mother-in-law, he was received by them both with the most contumelious reproaches, and that, unable to endure his shame and remorse, he died a few days after. That is not true. The battle of Pavia was fought on the 24th of February, 1525, and the Duke of Alençon did not die until the 11th of April, that is to say, more than a month after his arrival in Lyon. It appears from the testimony of an eye-witness, brought to light by the last editors of the Heptameron, that he was carried off by a pleurisy in five days, that he was comforted on his death-bed by his wife and her mother, that he spoke with profound regret of the king's misfortune, but that nothing escaped his own lips or those of the two ladies to indicate the faintest idea on either side that he had not done his duty at Pavia.

The first five years of Margaret's wedded life were passed in privacy in her duchy of Alençon, but from the date of her brother's accession to the throne, in January, 1515, her

* *Dames Galantes.*

talents were employed with advantage in affairs of state. "Such was her discourse," says Brantôme, "that the ambassadors who addressed her were extremely taken with it, and gave a high character of it to their countrymen on their return, and by this she became a good assistant to the king her brother; for they always waited on her after their principal audience, and frequently, when he had affairs of importance, he referred them entirely to her determination, she so well knowing how to engage and entertain them with her fine speeches, and being very artful and dexterous in pumping out their secrets: these qualifications the king would often say made her of great use to him in facilitating his affairs. So that I have heard there was an emulation between the two sisters, who should serve her brother best; the one—the Queen of Hungary—her brother the emperor, the other, her brother King Francis; but the former by war and force, the latter by the activity of her fine wit and complaisance." . . . "During the imprisonment of the king her brother, she was of great assistance to the regent her mother in governing the kingdom, keeping the princes and grandees quiet, and gaining upon the nobility; for she was of a very easy access, and won the hearts of all people by the fine accomplishments she was mistress of."*

The death of her husband, without children, six weeks after the battle of Pavia, left Margaret free to act as became her intense affection for her mother and her brother, who both had the most urgent need of her help. With the emperor's permission she embarked at Aigues Mortes for Spain, in spite of contrary winds, on the 27th of August, 1525; hastened to Madrid, "and found her brother in so wretched a condition, that had she not come he had died; because she understood his temper and constitution better than all his physicians could do, and caused him to be treated accordingly, which entirely recovered him: so that the king would often say that without her he must have died; and that he was so much obliged to her for it that he should for ever acknowledge it, and love her (as he did) to his dying day."†

The task which Margaret had to accomplish at Madrid was one of great difficulty. In spite of the apparent cor-

* Brantôme, *Dames Illustres*. † *Ibid.*

diality with which she was universally treated at the imperial court, and the very favourable disposition Charles V. always evinced in words, she soon perceived the hollowness of his friendly protestations. "Every one tells me that he likes the king," she says in one of her letters, "but the experience thereof is small. If I had to do with good men, who understood what honour is, I should not care; but it is the reverse." Fortunately, she was not one to give way before the first difficulties. She tried in the beginning to win over some great personages of the imperial court, but afterwards perceiving that the men always avoided talking with her upon any serious topic, she took care to address herself to their mothers, wives, or daughters. In a letter to Marshal de Montmorency she says of the Duke de Infantado, who had invited her to his castle of Guadalaxara, "You will tell the king that the duke has been warned from the court that as he desires to please the emperor, neither he nor his son is to speak to me; but the ladies are not forbidden me, and I shall speak to them doubly."

As for Margaret's behaviour towards Charles V., let us again have recourse to Brantôme, whom we shall quote as often as we can: "She spoke so bravely and so handsomely to the emperor concerning his bad treatment of the king her brother, that he was quite astonished, setting before him his ingratitude and felony wherewith he, the vassal, dealt towards his lord on account of Flanders; then she reproached him with the hardness of his heart for being so devoid of pity with regard to so great and so good a king; and said that acting in that manner was not the way to win a heart so noble and royal and so sovereign as that of the king her brother; and that should he die in consequence of his rigorous treatment, his death would not remain unpunished, for he had children who would be grown up some day, and would take signal vengeance. These words, pronounced so bravely, and with so much passion, made the emperor bethink himself, so that he moderated his behaviour, and visited the king, and promised him many fine things, which he did not, however, perform for that time. But if this queen spoke so well to the emperor, she did still more so to those of his council, here she had audience, and where she triumphed with her fine speaking and graceful manner, of which she had no lack."

Margaret took great pains to hasten the conclusion of the marriage between Francis I. and Eleonore of Austria, widow of the King of Portugal, rightly regarding that alliance as the surest means of a prompt deliverance. Though the royal widow had been promised to the Constable of Bourbon, the emperor did not hesitate to sacrifice his engagement with the illustrious deserter to the interests of his policy. He himself, fascinated by Margaret's talent and graces, entertained for a moment the idea of a union with her, and sent a letter to the regent containing a distinct proposal to that effect. In the same letter the emperor said, with reference to the Constable of Bourbon, that "there were good marriages in France, and quite enough for him; naming Madame Renée, with whom he might content himself." These words have been understood to imply that there had been some question of a marriage between the Duchess of Alençon and the constable, but there is no evidence to warrant such a conjecture. There is no mention of anything of the sort in any of the diplomatic pieces exchanged between France and Spain on the subject of the king's liberation. They stipulate that the constable shall be restored to all his possessions, and even that a wife shall be procured for him in France; but Margaret's name nowhere appears in them, nor does she herself ever speak of the constable in any of her numerous letters. The story of an amour between those two persons, which is told by Varillas in his Histoire de François I., and which forms the main subject of a fictitious Histoire de Marguerite, published in 1696, is totally without foundation.

After three months and a half of negotiations, Margaret and her brother saw the necessity of providing for the safety of the crown and government of France in case the king's captivity should be perpetual, and Francis signed an edict, in 1525, by which he ordained that the young dauphin should be immediately crowned, that the regency should remain in his mother's hands, but that in case of her being disabled by sickness or other impediment, or by death, from exercising it, then it should devolve upon his "most dear and most beloved only sister, Margaret of France, Duchess of Alençon and Berry."

It has been erroneously asserted that Margaret carried with her this act of abdication when she quitted Spain, and that because the emperor was aware of this fact he gave orders that she should be arrested the very moment her safe-conduct expired. It was Marshal de Montmorency who carried the act of abdication to France, and in designing to seize the person of the princess, Charles V. had no other object in view than to secure to himself a fresh hostage in case the treaty should not be executed. At her brother's instance Margaret applied to the imperial court for permission to quit Spain; it was granted her, but in such a manner as plainly showed her there was more wish to retard her journey than to speed her upon it. She left Madrid in the beginning of December, and travelled at first by easy stages, until word was sent her by her brother that she should hasten, for the emperor, hoping that on the 25th of the month, on which day her safe-conduct was to expire, she would be still in Spain, had given orders for her arrest. Thereupon she quitted her litter, got on horseback, and making as much way in one day as she had previously done in four, she arrived at Salses, where some French lords awaited her, one hour before the expiry of the safe-conduct.

In return for all Margaret's pains to hasten his deliverance, Francis I. could not do less than procure for her a fit husband. Negotiations were opened on the subject with Henry VIII. of England, but happily they came to nothing. There was at the court of France a young king—one, indeed, who was without a kingdom, but not without eminent advantages both of mind and person. This was Henri d'Albret, Count of Béarn, legitimate sovereign of Navarre, which was withheld from him by Charles V., contrary to treaty. Henri had been taken prisoner at the battle of Pavia, and had made his escape after a captivity of about two months, by letting himself down from the window by means of a rope. Having lived some time at the court of France, he was well known to Margaret, and there is every reason to believe that the marriage was one of inclination, on her side at least. It was celebrated, therefore, notwithstanding a considerable disparity of age, at Saint Germain en Laye, in January, 1527.

Henri d'Albret received as his wife's portion the duchies of Alençon and Berry, and the counties of Armagnac and

Perche, which Francis entailed on his sister's issue, whether male or female. He also pledged himself in the marriage contract to force the emperor immediately to restore Navarre to his brother-in-law. Margaret repeatedly urged him to fulfil this promise, and she speaks of it in many of her letters; but political exigencies always prevailed against her, and there was even a clause inserted in a protocol relative to the deliverance of the children of France, which ran thus: "Item, the same king promises not to assist or favour the King of Navarre to reconquer his kingdom, albeit he has married his most beloved and only sister."

The indifference of Francis I. with regard to the political fortunes of his brother-in-law, notwithstanding the numerous and signal services the latter had rendered him, disgusted the young prince, and he resolved to quit the court, where Montmorency, Brion, and several other persons, his declared enemies, were in the ascendant. He put his design into execution in 1529, after the conclusion of the treaty of Cambrai, and Margaret retired with him to Béarn, where she diligently applied herself, in conjunction with her husband, to all measures capable of raising their dominions to a more flourishing condition, as we learn from Hilarion de la Coste. "This country," he says, "naturally good and fruitful, but lying in a bad state, uncultivated and barren, through the negligence of its inhabitants, quickly changed its face by their management. They invited husbandmen out of all the provinces of France, who occupied, improved, and fertilised the lands; they caused the towns to be adorned and fortified; houses and castles to be built, that of Pau among others, with the finest gardens which were then in Europe. After having fitted up a handsome place of residence, they gave orders about laws and good government; they established, for the differences of their subjects, a court to determine them without appeal; and they reformed the common law of Oléron, which was used in that country, and which, since its last reformation in 1288, had been greatly corrupted. By their conversation and court they greatly civilised the people. And to guard themselves against a new usurpation from Spain, they covered themselves with Navarrins, a town upon one of the Gaves, which they fortified with strong ramparts, bastions, and half-moons, according to the art then in use." "This," says Bayle, "is one of the finest encomiums that could be bestowed on the Queen of Navarre."

After the death of her first husband, Margaret retained full possession of the duchy of Alençon, not only as regarded its revenues, but also its civil and political administration. She always watched over that principality with great solicitude. As she never could reside in it except for very brief intervals, she was careful to commit its government to able men, whose conduct fully justified her choice.

It was chiefly during her frequent and long residences in her principality of Béarn that the Queen of Navarre had opportunities of conferring with the advocates of the Reformation, and there many of them, including Andrew Melanchthon, Gérard Roussel, Lefèvre d'Etaple, Pierre Calvi, Charles de Sainte Marthe, and Calvin himself, found a refuge with her from persecution. The question whether or not Margaret ever seriously entertained the thought of abjuring the Church of Rome has been much debated by historians, but that she very much inclined to the opinions of the Reformers is not disputed either by Protestant or Catholic writers; both sides confess the fact. Florimond de Remond says, in his History of the Birth and Progress of Heresy, "It is particularly observed by all the historians of both parties that this princess was the sole cause, without designing any ill, of the preservation of the French Lutherans, and that the Church, which afterwards took the name of Reformed, was not stifled in its cradle; for besides that she lent an ear to their discourses, which at first were specious, and not so bold as afterwards, she with a good intention maintained a great many of them in schools at her own expense, not only in France but also in Germany. She took a wonderful care to preserve and secure those that were in danger for the Protestant religion, and to succour the refugees at Strasburg and Geneva. Thither she sent to the learned at one time a benefaction of four thousand livres. . . . . In short, this good-natured princess had nothing more at heart for those nine or ten years than to procure the escape of such as the king exposed to the rigour of justice. She frequently talked to him of it, and by little touches endeavoured to impress on his soul some pity for the Lutherans."

Margaret's influence would perhaps have induced Francis to favour the Reformation if the extravagance of some hot-headed people, who posted up certain placards in the year 1534, had not exasperated him to such a degree as to make him become afterwards a violent persecutor of Lutheranism—the name then given in France to what has since been called Calvinism. She was obliged, from that time, to act with great caution, and to conduct herself in such a manner as the Calvinists have highly condemned, and which gave occasion to the Papists to say that she perfectly renounced her errors. Brantôme, after saying that this queen was suspected of Lutheranism, adds, that "out of respect and love to her brother, who loved her entirely, and always called her his darling, she never made any profession or appearance of it; and if she believed it, she always kept it to herself with very great secrecy, because the king violently hated it, declaring that this and every new sect tended more to the destruction of kingdoms, monarchies, and dominions, than to the edification of souls." Others believe that it was not possible for Francis I. to be ignorant that the Queen of Navarre was a Lutheran in her heart; her attachments to the party, and the protection she gave the fugitives for this cause, were not such things as could be concealed from the King of France; he only affected not to know them. "The Constable de Montmorency, discoursing . . . one day with the king, made no difficulty or scruple to tell him, that if he would quite exterminate the heretics of this kingdom he must begin with his court and with his nearest relations, naming the queen his sister. To this the king answered, 'Let us not speak of that; she loves me too much; she will never believe but what I believe, or take up a religion to the prejudice of my state.'"[*]

Catholic writers assert that some years before her death the Queen of Navarre acknowledged her religious errors and De Remond even goes so far as to imply that she denied on her death-bed having ever swerved from the standard of Roman orthodoxy. Bayle comments on the remarks of this writer in a singularly earnest and noble passage.

[*] Brantôme, *Dames Illustres*.

"I do not examine," he says, "whether Florimond de Remond has it from good authority that she protested at her death that what she had done for the followers of the new opinions proceeded rather from compassion than from any ill-will to the ancient religion of her fathers. But, granting her protestation to be sincere, I maintain that there was something more heroic in her compassion and generosity than there would have been had she been persuaded that the fugitives she protected were orthodox. For a princess or any other woman to do good to those whom she takes to be of the household of the faith, is no extraordinary thing, but the common effect of a moderate piety. But for a queen to grant her protection to people persecuted for opinions which she believes to be false; to open a sanctuary to them; to preserve them from the flames prepared for them; to furnish them with a subsistence; liberally to relieve the troubles and inconveniences of their exile, is an heroic magnanimity which has hardly any precedent; it is the effect of a superiority of reason and genius which very few can reach to; it is the knowing how to pity the misfortune of those who err, and admire at the same time their constancy to the dictates of their conscience; it is the knowing how to do justice to their good intentions, and to the zeal they express for truth in general; it is the knowing that they are mistaken in the hypothesis, but that in the thesis they conform to the immutable and eternal laws of order, which require us to love the truth, and to sacrifice to that the temporal conveniences and pleasures of life; it is, in a word, the knowing how to distinguish in one and the same person his opposition to particular truths which he does not know, and his love for truth in general; a love which he evidences by his great zeal for the doctrines he believes to be true. Such was the judicious distinction the Queen of Navarre was able to make. It is difficult for all sorts of persons to arrive at this science; but more especially difficult for a princess like her, who had been educated in the communion of Rome, where nothing has been talked of for many ages but fagots and gibbets for those who err. Family prejudices strongly fortified all the obstacles which education had laid in the way of this princess; for she entirely loved the king her brother, an implacable persecutor of those they called heretics, a people whom he caused to be burned without mercy wherever the indefatigable vigilance of informers discovered them. I cannot conceive by what method this Queen of Navarre raised herself to so high a pitch of equity, reason, and good sense: it was not through an indifference as to religion, since it is certain she had a great degree of piety, and studied the Scriptures with singular application. It must therefore have been the excellence of her genius, and the greatness of her soul, that discovered a path to her which scarcely any one knows. It will be said, perhaps, that she needed only to consult the primitive and general ideas of order, which most clearly show that involuntary errors hinder not a man who entirely loves God, as he has been able to discover him after all possible inquiries, from being reckoned a servant of the true God, and that we ought to respect in him the rights of the true God. But I might immediately answer, that this maxim is of itself subject to great disputes; so far is it from being clear and evident; besides, that these primitive ideas hardly ever appear to our understanding without limitations and modifications which obscure them a hundred ways, according to the different prejudices contracted by education. The spirit of party, attachment to a sect, and even zeal for orthodoxy, produce a kind of ferment in the humours of our body; and hence the medium through which reason ought to behold those primitive ideas is clouded and obscured. These are infirmities which will attend our reason as long as it shall depend on the ministry of organs. It is the same thing to it as the low and middle region of the air, the seat of vapours and meteors. There are but very few persons who can rise above these clouds, and place themselves in a true serenity. If any one could do it, we must say of him what Virgil said of Daphnis:

> Candidus insuetum miratur lumen Olympi,
> Sub pedibusque videt nubes et sidera Daphnis."

We have seen how the Constable de Montmorency endeavoured to poison the mind of Francis I. against his sister. Margaret heard of this, and resented it the more strongly, as she had always behaved to Montmorency as a friend, and especially she had espoused his interests in opposition to those of his rival, Admiral Brion. The sequel of this affair, as related by Brantôme, is curious : " She never afterwards liked the constable, and she helped greatly towards his disgrace and banishment from court: insomuch that the day on which Madam the Princess of Navarre" (Margaret's only daughter) " was married to the Duke of Cleves at Chasteleraud, as she was to be led to church, being so heavily laden with jewels, and cloth of gold and silver, that by reason of the weakness of her body she could not walk" (she was but twelve years old), " the king commanded the constable to take his little niece in his arms and carry her to the church ; at which the whole court was very much surprised, as being an office not suitable or honourable enough in such a ceremony for the constable, and which might have been given to some other; wherewith the Queen of Navarre seemed not at all displeased, and said, 'There is a man who would ruin me with the king my brother, and who serves at present to carry my daughter to church.' I have this story from the person I have mentioned, and also that the constable was much displeased with this office, and greatly mortified to be made such a spectacle to all the company, and said, ' There is an end of all my favour; farewell, host.' And so it happened; for after the entertainment and the wedding dinner, he was dismissed, and departed immediately."

Judging from several original portraits of Margaret which are preserved in the libraries of France, her last editors infer that her beauty, so much celebrated by the poets of her time, consisted chiefly in the dignity of her deportment, and the sweet and cheerful expression of her countenance. Her eyes, nose, and mouth were large. She retained no marks of the small-pox with which she was attacked before middle age, and she preserved the freshness of her complexion to a late period. Like her brother, to whom she bore a strong likeness, she was tall and stately; but her imposing air was tempered by extreme affability and a merry humour. Her enthusiastic panegyrist, Sainte Marthe, says of her, " Seeing her humanely receive everybody, refuse none, and patiently listen to each, thou wouldst have promised thyself an easy access to her ; but if she cast her eyes on thee, there was in her face I know not what divinity, that would have so confounded thee, that thou wouldst have been unable, I do not say to walk one step, but even to stir one foot to approach her." Though conforming on special occasions to her brother's sumptuous tastes, Margaret's personal habits were remarkably simple. She dressed plainly, and, after the loss of her infant son, almost always in black. Brantôme, speaking of the extravagant pomp displayed by Cæsar Borgia when he visited France, remarks, that the great Queen of Navarre never had more than "three sumpter mules and six for her litters, though she had three or four chariots for her ladies." Her biographers have generally asserted that this frugality was imposed on Margaret by the precarious state of her fortune; but it is rather to be attributed to her sober character and her munificent charity. The supposition that her means were inadequate to her rank is manifestly erroneous; for at the very time when they are said to have been lowest, we find her declining to receive from Henry II. payment of a considerable sum lent five-and-twenty years before to his predecessor in a moment of financial difficulty, and desiring that the amount should be given to the sisters of her first husband, the Duke d'Alençon.

Distinguished as Margaret was by her mental powers and graces, she was still more admirable for the warmth and tenderness of her affections. These, it is to be feared, were but inadequately requited, and would have been a source of unhappiness to her, were it not for that precious prerogative which loving natures enjoy, to find pleasure in self-sacrifice and suffering. There was little community of feeling between her and the Duke d'Alençon, and their marriage was childless. The husband of her choice, Henry of Navarre, was a handsome, brave cavalier, of respectable capacity, and passably good-humoured; but he had little sympathy with his wife's literary and theological tastes, and the difference in their ages was not favourable to connubial concord. It is even said that he treated her at times with a roughness unworthy of a *preux chevalier*. Hilarion de la Coste says that Henry, "having been informed that there was used in his wife's chamber some form of prayer and instruction contrary to that of his fathers, entered it, with a resolution to punish the minister, but finding they had contrived his escape, the weight of his anger fell upon the queen, to whom he gave a box on the ear, saying to her, 'Madam, you want to be too knowing;' and immediately gave advice of it to King Francis." Brantôme, having given some instances of matrimonial discord between princes, adds this: "And lately King Henry d'Albret, with Queen Margaret of Valois, as I have it from good hands, who treated her very ill, and would have done still worse had it not been for King Francis, her brother, who spoke home and roughly to him, and charged him with threats to honour the queen his sister in regard to the rank she bore." The whimsical behaviour of this King of Navarre on the occasion of the birth of his grandson, afterwards Henry IV. of France, may enable us to guess how far he was capable of tenderness and delicacy of feeling in his conduct to his wife. On hearing that his daughter was pregnant, he recalled her from Picardy, where she was residing with her husband. The princess arrived in Pau on the 4th of December, after a journey of twenty days, and nine days afterwards her child was born. Her father had promised that he would put his will into her hands as soon as she should be delivered, but on condition that in her labour she should sing a song; "to the end," said he, "that you may not bring me a crying and ill-humoured child." The princess promised that she would, and had so much courage and resolution, that, in spite of the pains of labour, sang as she heard him enter her chamber a Bearnish ditty, the burden of which was, *Noste Donne deou cap deou pon, adjouda mi en aqueste houre;* that is, "Our Lady of the bridge-end, help me at this hour." As soon as the child was born, his grandfather took him out of the midwife's hands, carried him into his cabinet, and there plentifully rubbed his lips and gums with garlic, by which horrible treatment the poor infant very narrowly escaped suffocation.

The intense affection which Margaret bestowed on her brother he returned as fully as it was in his nature to do. His conduct towards her was marked by that imperious egotism of which he gave so many unfortunate proofs in the most important circumstances of his life. He always called her *ma mignonne*, but he exacted unsparingly from " his darling" the surrender of her opinions, inclinations, and feelings to the claims of his policy or his caprice. He even took from her her only surviving child when it was but two years old, and had it brought into the château of Plessis les Tours, where the poor mother saw it only at long intervals during her unfrequent journeys in France. But Margaret was never weary of making sacrifices for the brother she idolised; and it is remarkable, not less as a characteristic of the age than of herself, that notwithstanding the propriety of her personal conduct and her ardent piety, she was more than tolerant of the illicit amours to which her splendid brother openly addicted himself. She composed the devices for the jewels which Francis I. presented to Madame de Chateaubriant; she maintained a most friendly intercourse with Madame d'Etampes, and to her she presented her poem of *Le Coche*, or the *Débat d'Amour*, in which she pronounced a most pompous eulogy on the beauty and the virtues of that royal mistress.

The death, in April, 1547, of that brother whom she had loved so much, and to whose glory and welfare she had devoted her existence, was a heavy blow to Margaret.* She survived him but two years, and that brief remnant of her life was spent chiefly in seclusion and religious abstraction from the concerns of the world. Nevertheless, it is not correctly stated by a recent English writer,† that during that period "no solicitations could induce the queen to emerge from her seclusion, or interest herself as formerly in literature or politics." In the very next paragraph the same writer contradicts this loose assertion, by saying that Margaret "often solaced her grief by composing elegies and plaintive songs on her misfortune." Besides this, it is cer-

---

* "In his last sickness," says Brantôme, "I have heard that she spoke to this purpose: 'Should the courier who brings me news of the king my brother's recovery, be he ever so tired, harassed, mud-spattered and dirty, I would embrace and kiss him as the finest prince and gentleman of France; and should he want a bed and not be able to find one to repose himself, I would give him mine, and gladly lie on the ground for sake of the good news he brought.'"

† *The Life of Marguerite d'Angoulême, Queen of Navarre*, &c. By Martha Walker Freer. 2 vols. London, 1854.

tain that the Queen of Navarre was occupied but a few months before her death in the composition of her book of tales; for the 66th novel of her Heptameron recounts a ludicrous adventure which befel her daughter, Joanne d'Albret, and the Duke de Vendôme, shortly after their marriage in October, 1548. Margaret's health began to decline in the summer of the following year, and she expired at the château of Audos, in Bigorre, on the 21st of December, 1549, in her fifty-seventh year.

Amidst the multifarious occupations of her well-filled life, the Queen of Navarre found leisure to compose a great number of literary works, besides carrying on a voluminous correspondence with her brother, his ministers, and many other persons. Her productions in verse, the greater part of which have been printed, consist of eight long poems on sacred, amorous, or historical subjects; eight dramatic pieces, including four mysteries, two moralities, and two farces; poetical epistles to her brother, her mother, and the King of Navarre; and rondeaux, dixains, songs, and other small pieces. According to the last editors of the Heptameron, some of Margaret's fugitive pieces, published by them for the first time, are superior as literary works to her more serious compositions, and in them alone are to be found the gaiety and grace for which she has been so much celebrated by her contemporaries. There is one among them of a graver character, which appears to us so remarkable for its impassioned force and its full and flowing rhythm, that we gladly lay it before the reader:

> "Souvieigne vous des lermes respandues,
> Qui par regret très grand furent rendues
> Sur vostre tant amyable visaige;
> Souvieigne vous du dangereux oultraige
> Que vous cuida faire mon povre coeur,
> Pressé par trop d'une extreme douleur,
> Quand il força la voix de satisfaire
> Au très grand mal où ne sçavois que faire,
> Tant qu'à peu près la pleur fut entendu;
> Souvieigne vous du sens qui fut perdu,
> Tant que raison, parolle & contenance
> N'eurent pouvoir, ny force, ny puissance,
> De desclairer ma double passion,
> Ny aussi peu ma grand affection;

Souvieigne vous du cœur qui bondissoit
Pour la tristesse en quoy il perissoit ;
Souvieigne vous des souspirs très ardens
Qui à la foule en despict de mes dentz
Sortoient dehors, pour mieulx me soulaiger ;
Souvieigne vous du peril & danger
Où nous estions, dont nous ne tenions compte,
Car vraye amour ne congnoist paour ny honte ;
Souvieigne vous de nostre amour honneste,
Dont ne devons pour nul baisser la teste,
Car nous sçavons tous deux certainement
Qu'honneur & Dieu en sont le fondement ;
Souvieigne vous du très chaste embrasser
Dont vous ne moy ne nous pouvions laisser ;
Souvieigne vous de vostre foy promise
Par vostre main dedans la mienne mise ;
Souvieigne vous de mes doubtes passées,
Que vous avez en une heure effassées,
Prenant en vous si grande seureté,
Que je m'asseure en vostre fermeté ;
Souvieigne vous que vous avez remis
Du plus parfaict de voz meilleurs amys
Le cœur, l'esprit & le corps en repos,
Par vostre honneste & vertueux propos,
Auquel je veulx adjouster telle foy,
Que plus n'aura doubte pouvoir sus moy ;
Souvieigne vous que je n'ay plus de paine,
Que ceste là que avecques moy je maine :
C'est le regret de perdre vostre veue,
Par qui souvent tant de joye ay receue ;
Souvieigne vous du regard de vostre œil,
Dont l'esloingner me faict mourir de dueil
Souvieigne vous du lieu très mal paré
Où fust de moy trop de bien separé ;
Souvieigne vous des heures qui sonnoyent,
Et du regret qu'en sonnant me donnoient,
Voyant le temps & l'heure s'advancer
Du despartir où ne fays que penser ;
Souvieigne vous de l'adieu redoublé
A chascun pas, de l'esperit troublé,
Du cœur trancy & du corps affoibly,
Et ne mectez le triste œil en oubly ;
Souvieigne vous de la parfaicte amour,
Qui durera sans cesser nuyet & jour,
Qui a dens moy si bien painct vostre ymaige,
Que je n'ay riens sinon vostre visaige,
Vostre parler, vostre regard tant doulx
Devant mes yeulx ; bref, je n'y ay que vous,
Vous suppliant, o amye estimee,
Plus que nulle aultre & de moy tant aymée,

> Souvieigne vous d'immortel souvenir
> De vostre amy, & le vueillés tenir
> Dens vostre coeur seul amy & parfaict,
> Ainsi que vous dedens le sien il faict."

On the whole, the Queen of Navarre has been far more successful in the poetical treatment of secular than of sacred subjects, and for obvious reasons. We cannot speak from personal knowledge of her efforts in the latter field, but we are very well disposed to accept the judgment pronounced upon them by the Bibliophiles Français, that they are barren of poetry and brimful of tediousness, consisting as they do of long paraphrases of Scripture, theological dissertations, and metaphysico-devotional rhapsodies. One of them, however, deserves more special mention, as marking the author's dissent from the religion of Rome. "The mirror of the sinful soul" (*Miroir de l'ame pecheresse*) "was composed in a strain very unusual in the Church of Rome, there being no mention made in it either of male or female saints, or of merits, or of any other purgatory than the blood of Jesus Christ."* The work was consequently assailed with fierce denunciations from the orthodox pulpits; a comedy was acted by the students of the College of Navarre, in which the queen was represented as a Fury of Hell, and the Sorbonne decreed at least, if it did not promulgate, a censure upon her heretical production. Margaret complained to her brother, and the result was that Nicolas Cop, rector of the Sorbonne, expressly disowned the censure pronounced by the body over which he presided; the student-comedians, and the most intemperate of the preachers, were committed to prison; and Noël Beda, syndic of the faculty of theology, who had been the most ardent promoter of the attacks on the king's sister, died in confinement at Mont Saint Michel.

The Heptameron is, of all Margaret's works, the one on which her literary reputation has mainly rested since her death. We have sketched its bibliographical history in our preface, and it now remains for us to speak of its composition. Dunlop, who may be considered as expressing the general opinion of literary historians, says that "few of the tales composed in it are original; for, except about half a dozen which are historically true, and are mentioned as having

---

* Beza, *Hist. Ecclesiast* book i. p. 5.

fallen under the knowledge and observation of the Queen of Navarre, they may all be traced to the Fabliaux, the Italian Novels, and the Cent Nouvelles Nouvelles." On the contrary, the last editors of the Heptameron allege that "its distinctive character is, that it reproduces, under a tolerably transparent veil, real events which happened at the court of France, especially in the reigns of Louis XI., Charles VIII., Louis XII., and Francis I. Of the seventy-two tales which compose the Heptameron, we know but five or six which are evidently borrowed from the French *conteurs* of the thirteenth, fourteenth, and fifteenth centuries. This character of truth, which has not even been suspected by the majority of those who have spoken of this collection, may be demonstrated in the most evident manner." This opinion very nearly agrees with the Queen of Navarre's own statement in her prologue, that all the tales she was about to relate were founded on fact, and it is corroborated by many evidences, direct and indirect. Brantôme, for instance, tells us that "his mother knew some secrets of the novels, and that she was one of the confabulators" (*une des devisantes*). He analyses many of the tales in the Heptameron, certifies the authenticity of some of them, and makes known to us the real names of certain persons whom Margaret has introduced into them. From him we learn, that under the title of a Princess of Flanders the Queen has portrayed herself, and related the audacious attempt made upon her chastity by Admiral de Bonnivet. Another notable verification of the Heptameron is supplied by the Bibliophiles Français. The first novel relates a murder committed by a proctor at Alençon, and mentions that the murderer obtained letters of pardon from the King of France at the intercession of the King of England. The Bibliophiles have discovered these very letters in the French archives, and found them to agree perfectly with the Queen of Navarre's narrative.

The more closely to imitate her Florentine model, she introduces her tales by describing a remarkable accident of nature, by which the supposed narrators are thrown together for a season, and driven to seek for some device to while away the time. Certainly there is no comparison between the fine description of the plague at Florence which opens the Decameron, and that multiplicity of little events which the

Queen has accumulated in her prologue; nevertheless, the contrivance of the latter is sufficiently ingenious, and bears a considerable resemblance to the frame of the Canterbury Tales. Ten French ladies and gentlemen, intercepted by a perilous inundation on their return from the baths of Cauterets, take shelter in a monastery of the Pyrenees, where they are forced to remain till a bridge should be thrown over an impassable stream, and amuse themselves meanwhile by relating stories in a beautiful meadow on the banks of the Gave. As to the persons into whose mouths Margaret has put her stories, it is natural enough to suppose that she chose them from her own family, and from among the lords and ladies who were usually about her. Madame Oisille, for instance, appears to be Margaret's mother, that name being almost an anagram of Louise. She is represented as an aged widow of great experience, who is as a mother to the other ladies. The rest of the company call each other simply by their respective names, but in addressing Oisille they always say *Madame*. Many of the novels which turn on the debauchery and wickedness of the Franciscans or Cordeliers are related by Oisille. The tone in which she speaks of them accords with the concluding passage of the journal of Louise of Savoy: "In the year 1522, in December, my son and I, by the grace of the Holy Ghost, began to know the hypocrites white, black, grey, smoky, and of all colours, from whom God in His infinite mercy and goodness preserve and defend us, for if Jesus Christ is not a liar, there is not among all mankind a more dangerous generation."

Hircan, another of the ten interlocutors, may very probably represent one of Margaret's two husbands, but which of the two we are not prepared to say. The Bibliophiles infer that it is the Duke d'Alençon, from the deference with which he is treated by the rest of the gentlemen; but surely this would apply quite as well to the King of Navarre. In the prologue, Hircan says to Simontault, "Since you have been the first to speak, it is right that you should take the lead, *for in sport we are all equal.*" Hircan's wife, Parlamente, who was never idle or melancholy, is no doubt Margaret herself; and if Hircan is the Duke d'Alençon, then Simontault is probably the King of Navarre, or *vice versâ*. With respect to the other six persons, the Bibliophiles Français offer no conjectures, or only such as seem to us of little weight.

The conversations in the Heptameron on the characters and incidents of the last related tale, and which generally introduce the subject of the new one, are much longer than in the Italian novels, and indeed occupy nearly one-half the work. Some of the remarks are quaint and comical, others are remarkable for their *naïveté*, while a few breathe the conceits of the Italian sonneteers; for example, "It is said that jealousy is love, but I deny it; for though jealousy be produced by love as ashes are by fire, yet jealousy extinguishes love, as ashes smother the flame." These epilogues are well worthy of attention, as embodying the author's personal views on sundry important topics, such as friendship, love, and conjugal fidelity; and also as a curious model of conversation among persons of quality in the first half of the sixteenth century. Especially curious is it to observe in them how stories and comments of a very ticklish character are mingled with reflections imbued with the most exalted piety; how the company prepare themselves by devotional exercises for telling tales which are often anything but edifying; and how, when the day's work is done, they duly praise the Lord for giving them the grace to spend their time so pleasantly. Margaret's contemporaries were by no means shocked at these incongruities, as our more sceptical age would be. The causes of this difference would be an interesting subject of inquiry, but here we can only note the fact. To give another instance of it: When Clement Marot published his poetical versions of some of the Psalms, they quickly superseded all other songs throughout the country. The press could not throw off copies fast enough to supply the demand. Each of the princes and courtiers appropriated a psalm, and sang it to such a tune as he thought fit. Henry II. chose the psalm, *Ainsi qu'on oyt le cerf braire*, and made a hunting song of it. His mistress, Diane de Poitiers, jigged out *Du fond de ma pensée* to the popular dance tune, *Le branle de Poitou;* and Catherine de Medici, in allusion to her husband's infidelities, profanely appropriated *Ne veuillez pas, ô Sire*, set to the air, *Des bouffons*.

We have alluded to the questionable morality of the Heptameron, and certainly we will not endorse the argument of its new editors, who combat the common opinion that it should be classed among licentious books, upon the plea that "the Queen of Navarre excels in winding up a tale of extreme gallantry with moral reflections of the most rigorous kind." The best apology for the book is that its author has not exceeded the allowed licence of good society in her own age, and that she is not to be judged by the standard of ours. Free as her language must often appear to us, it will be found, upon closer scrutiny, to be always controlled by certain conventional rules of propriety. Some grossly obscene passages, for which she has incurred unmerited censure, prove now to have been the work of those manifold offenders, her first editors.

INTRODUCTION.

On the 1st of September, when the baths of the Pyrenees begin to have efficacy, several persons from France, Spain, and other countries were assembled at those of Cauterets, some to drink the waters, some to bathe in them, and others to be treated with mud; remedies so marvellous, that patients given over by physicians go home cured from Cauterets. My intention is not to speak to you either of the situation or the virtue of the baths; but only to recount what is pertinent to the matter I am about to write. The patients remained at these baths until they found themselves sufficiently improved in health; but then, as they were preparing to return home, there fell such excessive and extraordinary rains, that it seemed as though God had forgotten his promise to Noah that he would never again destroy the world with water. The houses of Cauterets were so flooded that it was impossible to abide in them. Those who had come from Spain returned over the mountains the best way they could, such of them as knew the roads coming best off. But the French lords and ladies, thinking to return to Tarbes as easily as they had come from it, found the rivulets so swollen as to be scarcely fordable; and when they came to the Bearnese Gave, which was not two feet deep when they crossed it on their way to the baths, they found it so enlarged and so impetuous that they were forced to turn out of their direct course and look for bridges. These, however, being only of wood, had been carried away by the violence of the current. Some attempted to break its force by crossing it several together in one body; but they were swept away with such rapidity that the rest had no mind to follow them. They separated, therefore, either to look for another route, or because they were not of the same way of thinking. Some crossed the mountains, and passing through Aragon, arrived in the county of Roussillon, and thence in Narbonne. Others went straight to Barcelona, and crossed over by sea to Marseilles or to Aigues-mortes.

But a widow of long experience, named Oisille, resolved to banish from her mind the fear of bad roads, and repair to Notre Dame de Serrance; not that she was so superstitious as to suppose that the glorious Virgin would quit her place at her son's right hand to come and dwell in a desert land, but only because she wished to see the holy place of which she had heard so much; and also because she was assured that if there were any means of escaping from a danger, the monks were sure to find it out. She met with no end of difficulties; but at last she arrived, after having passed through places almost impracticable, and so difficult to climb and descend, that notwithstanding her age and her weight, she was compelled to perform the greater part of the journey on foot. But the most piteous thing was that most of her servants and horses died on the way, and that she arrived with one man and one woman only at Serrance, where she was charitably received by the monks.

There were also among the French two gentlemen who had gone to the baths rather to accompany the ladies they loved than for any need they themselves had to use the waters. These gentlemen, seeing that the company was breaking up, and that the husbands of their mistresses were taking them away, thought proper to follow them at a distance, without acquainting any one with their purpose. The two married gentlemen and their wives arrived one evening at the house of a man who was more a bandit than a peasant. The two young gentlemen lodged at a cottage hard by, and hearing a great noise about midnight they rose with their varlets, and inquired of their host what was all that tumult. The poor man, who was in a great fright, told them it was some bad lads* who were come to share the booty that was in the house of their comrade the bandit. The gentlemen instantly seized their arms and hastened with their varlets to the aid of the ladies, holding it a far happier fate to die with them than to live without them. On reaching the bandit's house they found the first gate broken open and

---

* *Mauvays garsons*, the name given to a gang of masked robbers, who ravaged Paris, even by day, in the reign of Francis I.

the two gentlemen and their servants defending themselves valorously; but as they were outnumbered by the bandits, and the married gentlemen were much wounded, they were beginning to give way, having already lost a great number of their servants. The two gentlemen, looking in at the windows, saw the two ladies weeping and crying so hard, that their hearts swelled with pity and love, and falling on the bandits like two enraged bears from the mountains, they laid about them with such fury, that a great number of the bandits fell, and the rest fled for safety to a place well known to them. The gentlemen having defeated these villains, the owner of the house being among the slain, and having learned that the wife was still worse than himself, despatched her after him with a sword-thrust. They then entered a room on the basement, where they found one of the married gentlemen breathing his last. The other had not been hurt, only his clothes had been pierced and his sword broken; and seeing the aid which the two had rendered him, he embraced and thanked them, and begged they would continue to stand by him, to which they assented with great good-will. After having seen the deceased buried, and consoled the wife as well as they could, they departed under the guidance of Providence, not knowing whither they were going.

If you would know the names of the three gentlemen, that of the married one was Hircan, and his wife's Parlamente. The widow's name was Longarine. One of the young gentlemen was called Dagoucin, and the other Saffredent. They were in the saddle all day, and towards evening they descried a belfry, to which they made the best of their way, not without toil and trouble, and were humanely welcomed by the abbot and the monks. The abbey is called St. Savin's. The abbot, who was of a very good house, lodged them honourably, and on the way to their lodgings begged them to acquaint him with their adventures. After they had recounted them, he told them they were not the only persons who had been unfortunate, for there were in another room two ladies who had escaped as great a danger, or worse, inasmuch as they had encountered not men but beasts; for these poor ladies met a bear from the mountain half a league this side of Peyrchite, and fled from it with such speed that their horses dropped dead under them as they entered the abbey gates; and two of their women, who arrived long after them, reported that the bear had killed all their men-servants. The two ladies and the three gentlemen then went into the ladies' chamber, where they found them in tears, and saw they were Nomerfide and Ennasuite. They all embraced, and after mutually recounting their adventures, they began to be comforted through the sage exhortations of the abbot, counting it a great consolation to have so happily met again; and next day they heard mass with much devotion, and gave thanks to God for that he had delivered them out of such perils.

Whilst they were all at mass, a man came running into the church in his shirt, and shouting for help, as if some one was close at his heels. Hircan and the other gentlemen hastened to him to see what was the matter, and saw two men pursuing him sword in hand. The latter would have fled upon seeing so many people, but Hircan and his party were too swift for them, and they lost their lives. On his return, Hircan discovered that the man in his shirt was one of their companions named Geburon. His story was, that being at a cottage near Peyrchite, he had been surprised in his bed by three men. Springing out in his shirt he had seized his sword, and mortally wounded one of them; and whilst the two others were busy succouring their comrade, Geburon, seeing that the odds were two to one against him, and that he was naked whilst they wore armour, thought his safest course was to take to his heels, especially as his clothes would not impede his running. He too praised God for his deliverance, and he thanked those who had revenged him.

After the company had heard mass and dined they sent to see if it were possible to pass the Gave river, and were in consternation at hearing that the thing was impracticable, though the abbot entreated them many times to remain with him until the waters had abated. This they agreed to for that day, and in the evening, when they were about to go to bed, there arrived an old monk who used to come regularly every September to Our Lady of Serrance. Being asked news of his journey, he stated that, in consequence of the flood, he had come by the mountains, and travelled over the worst roads he had ever seen in his life. He had beheld a very sad spectacle. A gentleman named Simontault, tired of waiting till the river should subside, had resolved to attempt the passage, relying on the goodness of his horse, and had made his domestics place themselves round him to break the force of the current; but when they reached the middle of the stream the worst mounted were swept away and were seen no more. Thereupon the gentleman made again for the bank he had quitted. His horse, good as it was, failed him at his need; but by God's will this happened so near the bank, that the gentleman was able at last to scramble on all fours to the hard, not without having drunk a good deal of water, and so exhausted that he could hardly sustain himself. Happily for him a shepherd, leading back his sheep to the fields in the evening, found him seated on the stones, dripping wet, and not less sad for the loss of his people who had perished before his eyes. The shepherd, who understood his need both from his appearance and his words, took him by the hand and led him to his cabin, where he made a little fire, and dried him as well as he could. That same evening Providence conducted to the cabin the old monk, who told him the way to Our Lady of Serrance, and assured him that he would be better lodged there than elsewhere, and that he would find there an aged widow named Oisille, who had met with an adventure as distressing as his own.

The company testified extreme joy at hearing the names of the good dame Oisille and the gentle knight Simontault; and every one praised God for having saved the master and mistress after the loss of the servants. Parlamente especially gave hearty thanks to God, for she had long had a most affectionate servant in Simontault. They inquired carefully about the road to Serrance, and though the good old man represented it to them as very difficult, nothing could stop them from setting out that very day, so well provided with all things necessary that nothing was left them to wish for. The abbot supplied them with the best horses in Lavedan, good Bearnese cloaks, wine, and plenty of victuals, and a good escort to conduct them in safety across the mountains. They traversed them more on foot than on horseback, and arrived at last, after many toils, at Our Lady of Serrance. Though the abbot was churlish enough, he durst not refuse to lodge them, for fear of disobliging the lord of Bearn, by whom he knew they were held in consideration; but like a true hypocrite as he was, he showed them the best possible countenance, and took them to see the lady Oisille and the gentleman Simontault. All were equally delighted to find themselves so miraculously reassembled, and the night was spent in praising God for the grace he had vouchsafed them. After taking a little rest, towards morning they went to hear mass, and receive the holy sacrament of union, by means of which all Christians are united as one, and to beg of God, who had reassembled them through his goodness, the grace to complete their journey for his glory.

After dinner they sent to know if the waters were fallen, but finding, on the contrary, that they were still higher, and that it would be a long time before they could pass safely, they resolved to have a bridge made, abutting on two rocks very near each other, and on which there still are planks used by people on foot, who coming from Oleron wish to pass the Gave. The abbot, very well pleased at their incurring an expense which would increase the number of pilgrims, furnished them with workmen; but he was so miserly that he would not contribute a farthing of his own. The workmen, however, having declared that it would take at least ten or twelve days to construct the bridge, the company began to grow tired. Parlamente, the wife of Hircan, always active and never melancholy, having asked her husband's permission to speak, said to old dame Oisille, "I am surprised, madam, that you, who have so much experience that you fill the place of a mother to the rest of us women, do not devise some amusement to mitigate the annoyance we shall suffer from so long a delay; for unless we have something agreeable and virtuous to occupy us, we are in danger of falling sick."

"What is still worse," said Longarine, the young widow, "we shall grow cross, which is an incurable malady; the more so as there is not one of us but has cause to be extremely sad, considering our several losses."

"Every one has not lost her husband like you," said Ennasuite, laughing. "To have lost servants is not a matter to break one's heart about, since they can easily be replaced. However, I am decidedly of opinion that we should pass the time away as agreeably as we can."

Nomerfide, her companion, said it was a very good idea, and that if she passed one day without amusement, she should be dead the next. The gentlemen all warmly approved of the proposal, and begged dame Oisille to direct what was to be done.

"You ask a thing of me, my children," replied the old lady, "which I find very difficult. You want me to invent an amusement which shall dissipate your ennui. I have been in search of such a remedy all my life long, and I have never found but one, which is the reading of Holy Writ. It is in such reading that the mind finds its true and perfect joy, whence proceed the repose and the health of the body. If you ask me what I do to be so cheerful and so healthy at so advanced an age, it is, that as soon as I rise I read the Holy Scriptures. I see and contemplate the will of God, who sent his Son on earth to announce to us that holy word and that good news which promises the pardon of all sins, and the payment of all debts, by the gift he has made us of his love, passion, and merits. This idea affords me such joy, that I take my psalter, and sing with my heart and pronounce with my lips, as humbly as I can, the beautiful canticles with which the Holy Spirit inspired David and other sacred authors. The pleasure I derive from them is so ravishing, that I regard as blessings the evils which befal me every day, because I have in my heart through faith Him who has suffered all these evils for me. Before supper I retire in like manner to feed my soul with reading. In the evening I review all I have done in the day; I ask pardon for my faults; I thank God for his graces, and lie down in his love, fear, and peace, assured against all evils. This, my children, is what has long been my amusement, after having searched well, and found none more solid and more satisfying. It seems to me, then, that if you will give yourselves every morning for an hour to reading, and say your prayers devoutly during mass, you will find in this solitude all the charms which cities could afford. In fact, he who knows God finds all things fair in him, and without him everything ugly and disagreeable. Take my advice, therefore, I entreat you, if you wish to find happiness in life."

"Those who have read the Holy Scriptures," said Hircan,

"as I believe we have done, will confess, madam, that what you have said is true. But you must also consider that we are not yet so mortified but that we have need of some amusement and corporeal pastime. When we are at home we have the chase and hawking, which make us forget a thousand bad thoughts; the ladies have their household affairs, their needlework, and sometimes dancing, wherein they find laudable exercise. I propose, then, on the part of the men, that you, as the eldest lady, read to us in the morning the history of the life of our Lord Jesus Christ, and of the great and wondrous things he has done for us. After dinner until vespers we must choose some pastime which may be agreeable to the body and not prejudicial to the soul. By this means we shall pass the day cheerfully."

Dame Oisille replied, that she had so much difficulty in forgetting vanities, that she was afraid she should succeed ill in the choice of such a pastime; also, that the matter should be referred to the majority of voices. "And you, monsieur," she said to Hircan, "shall give your opinion first."

"If I thought," replied Hircan, "that the diversion I should like to propose would be as agreeable to a certain lady in this company as to myself, my choice would be soon announced; but as I am afraid this would not be the case, I have nothing to say, but will submit to the decision of the rest."

His wife Parlamente coloured up at these words, believing they were meant for her. "Perhaps, Hircan," she said, "a little angrily and half laughing, "that the lady you think hardest to please could find means to content herself if she had a mind. But let us say no more of the pastime in which only two can take part, and think of one in which everybody can share."

"Since my wife has so well comprehended my views," observed Hircan to the other ladies, "and a private diversion is not to her taste, I believe she is the best person to invent an amusement which will give satisfaction to us all. I declare, therefore, beforehand, that I assent to her proposal."

The whole company spoke to the same effect, and Parlamente, seeing that she was appointed mistress of the sports, thus addressed the company: "Were I conscious of possessing as much capacity as the ancients who invented the arts, I would contrive an amusement which should fulfil the obligation you lay upon me; but as I know myself, and am aware that I find it difficult even to recollect the ingenious inventions of others, I shall think myself lucky if I can closely follow those who have already done what you desire. I believe there is not one of you but has read the novels of Boccaccio recently translated into French, and which the most Christian King, Francis I. of that name, Monseigneur le Dauphin, Madame la Dauphine, and Madame Marguerite, prized so highly, that if Boccaccio could hear them, the praises bestowed on him by those illustrious persons would surely raise him from the dead. I can certify that the two ladies I have named, and several other personages of the court, resolved to imitate Boccaccio, except in one thing—namely, in writing nothing but what was true. Monseigneur and the two ladies arranged at first that they would each write ten tales, and that they would assemble a party of ten persons, selecting for it those whom they thought most capable of telling a story with grace, and expressly excluding men of letters; for Monseigneur did not wish that there should be any intrusion of art into the matter, and was afraid lest the flowers of rhetoric should be in some manner prejudicial to the truth of history. But the great affairs in which the king afterwards became involved, the peace concluded between the sovereign and the King of England, the accouchement of Madame la Dauphine, and several other affairs of a nature to occupy the whole court, caused this project to be forgotten; but as we have time to spare we will put it into execution whilst waiting for the completion of our bridge. If you think proper, we will go from noon till four o'clock into that fine meadow along the Gave river, where the trees form so thick a screen that the sun cannot pierce it, or incommode us with its heat. There, seated at our ease, we will each relate what we have seen or been told by persons worthy of belief. Ten days will suffice to make up the hundred. If it please God that our work prove worthy of being seen by the lords and ladies I have named, we will present it to them on our return, in lieu of images and paternosters, and I am convinced that such an offering will not be displeasing to them. At the same time, if any one can suggest something more agreeable, I am ready to fall in with his ideas."

The whole company declared they could not imagine anything better, and every one looked forward with impatience for the morrow. As soon as the morning broke they all went to the chamber of Madame Oisille, whom they found already at prayers. She read to them for a good hour, after which they heard mass, and at ten o'clock they went to dinner. Every one then retired to his own chamber, and attended to what he had to do. At noon all were punctually assembled in the meadow, which was so beautiful and agreeable, that it would need a Boccaccio to depict all its charms: enough for us to say that there never was its like.

The company being seated on the green turf, so soft and delicate that no one had need of floor or carpet, " Which of us," said Simontault, " shall have the command over the rest ?"

" Since you have been the first to speak," said Hircan, " it is right you should have the command; for in sport all are equals."

" God knows," replied Simontault, " I could desire nothing better in the world than to command such a company."

Parlamente, who knew very well what that meant, began to cough, so that Hircan did not perceive she had changed colour, and told Simontault to begin his tale, for all were ready to hear him. The same request being urged by the whole company, Simontault said: " I have been so ill-requited for my long services, ladies, that to revenge myself on love and on the fair one who treats me with so much cruelty, I am about to make a collection of misdeeds done by women to men, in the whole of which I will relate nothing but the simple truth."

THE HEPTAMERON

or

THE QUEEN OF NAVARRE.

NOVEL I.

A WOMAN OF ALENÇON HAVING TWO LOVERS, ONE FOR HER PLEASURE AND THE OTHER FOR HER PROFIT, CAUSED THAT ONE OF THE TWO TO BE SLAIN WHO WAS THE FIRST TO DISCOVER HER GALLANTRIES—SHE OBTAINED HER PARDON AND THAT OF HER HUSBAND, WHO HAD FLED THE COUNTRY, AND WHO AFTERWARDS, IN ORDER TO SAVE SOME MONEY, APPLIED TO A NECROMANCER—THE MATTER WAS FOUND OUT AND PUNISHED.

In the lifetime of the last Duke Charles, there was at Alençon a proctor named St. Aignan, who had married a gentlewoman of that country more handsome than virtuous, who, for her beauty and her levity, was much courted by the Bishop of Sées. In order to accomplish his ends, this prelate took care to amuse the husband so well, that not only he took no notice of the doings of either of the pair, but even forgot the attachment he had always felt towards his masters. He passed suddenly from fidelity to perfidy, and finally went the length of practising sorceries to cause the death of the duchess. The prelate maintained a long correspondence with this unlucky woman, who intrigued with him rather from motives of interest than of love; whereto she was also solicited by her husband. But she entertained such a passion for the son of the Lieutenant-General of Alençon, named Du Mesnil, that it half crazed her; and she often made the prelate give her husband some commission or another, that she might see the lieutenant-general's son at her ease. This affair lasted a long while, the prelate being entertained for her purse, and the other for her pleasure. She vowed to Du Mesnil that if she received the bishop well, it was only that she might be the more free to continue her caresses to himself; and that whatever she did, the bishop got nothing but words, and he might be assured nobody but himself should ever have anything else of her.

One day when her husband had to wait upon the bishop, she asked leave of him to go to the country, alleging that the air of the city did not agree with her. No sooner had she arrived at his farm, than she wrote to the lieutenant's son, bidding him not fail to visit her about ten o'clock at night. The poor young man did so, but on his arrival the servant woman who usually let him in, met him and said, "Go elsewhere, my friend; for your place is filled." Du Mesnil, supposing that the husband had returned, asked the servant how all was going on. Seeing before her a handsome, well-bred young man, the girl could not help pitying him to think how much he loved, and how little he was loved. With this feeling, she resolved to acquaint him with her mistress's behaviour, believing that it would cure him of loving her so much. She told him that the Bishop of Sées had but just entered the house, and was in bed with her mistress, who had not expected him till the following day; but having detained the husband at his own residence, he had stolen away by night to visit her. The lieutenant's son was thunderstruck at this disclosure, and could hardly bring himself to believe it. To clear up his doubts, he secreted himself in a neighbouring house, where he remained on sentry till three o'clock in the morning, when he saw the bishop come out, and recognised him but too well, in spite of his disguise.

The young man returned in despair to Alençon, where his wicked mistress arrived soon after. Never doubting but that she should dupe him as usual, she lost no time in coming to see him, but he told her that since she had touched sacred things, she was too holy to talk to a sinner like him, but a sinner so repentant, that he hoped his sin would soon be forgiven. When she found she was detected, and that excuses and promises never to offend in that way again were of no avail, she went off and complained to her bishop. After long pondering over the matter, she told her husband that she could no longer reside in Alençon, because the lieutenant's son, whom he thought so much his friend, was incessantly importuning her; and she begged that in order to prevent all suspicion, he would take a house at Argentan. The husband, who let himself be led by her, easily consented.

They had been but a few days settled in Argentan, when this wretched woman sent word to the lieutenant's son that he was the most wicked of men, and that she was not ignorant that he publicly maligned her and the prelate; but that she would yet find means to make him repent of this. The young man, who had never spoken to any one but herself, and who was afraid of involving himself in a quarrel with the prelate, mounted his horse and rode to Argentan, attended only by two of his servants. He found the lady at the Jacobins, where she was hearing vespers. "I am come, madam," he said, "to protest to you before God, that I have never complained of you to any but yourself. You have behaved so vilely to me, that what I have said to you is not half what you deserve. But if any one says that I have publicly spoken ill of you, I am here to give that person the lie in your presence."

The proctor's wife, seeing that there were many people in the church, and that he was accompanied by two stout men, put constraint upon herself, and spoke to him as civilly as she could. She told him she did not doubt the truth of what he said; that she believed him too upright to speak ill of anybody, and still less of her, who always loved him; but as something had come to her husband's ears, she begged he would say before him that he had never spoken as had been said, and that he did not believe a word of such tales. To this he readily consented, and took her by the arm to conduct her home; but she begged him not to do so, lest her husband should suppose that she had schooled him as to what he should say. Then taking one of his servants by the sleeve, she said, "Let this man come with me, and when it is time he shall come and fetch you. Meanwhile you may remain quietly in your lodging." He, never dreaming of a conspiracy against him, made no objection to what she proposed.

She gave the servant she took home with her his supper, and when the man frequently asked her when would it be time to go for his master, she always replied that he would come soon enough.

At night she privily sent off one of her own domestics to fetch Du Mesnil, who, having no suspicion, accompanied the man to St. Aignan's house, having with him only one of his servants, the other being with the mistress of the house. As he entered the door his guide told him his mistress would be glad to say a few words to him before he spoke to her husband; that she was waiting for him in a room with only one of his servants, and that he had better send away the other by the front door. This he accordingly did; and as he was going up a narrow and very dark flight of stairs, the proctor, who had set men in ambush, hearing a voice, called out to know what it was. Some one replied it was a man who was making his way secretly into the house. Upon this one Thomas Guerin, an assassin by profession, and hired by the proctor for the occasion, fell upon the poor young man, and gave him so many sword-wounds that at last he fell dead. Meanwhile his servant who was with the lady said to her, "I hear my master's voice on the stairs. I will go to him." But she stopped him, saying, "Don't trouble yourself, he will come soon enough." Soon afterwards, hearing his master cry out, "I am a dead man! my God have mercy on me!" he wanted to go to his aid, but again she stopped him. "Be quiet," she said; "my husband is chastising him for his pranks. Let's go see." Leaning over the stairhead, she called out to her husband, "Is it done?" "Come and see," replied the husband; "you are avenged on him who put you to such shame." And so saying, he struck his dagger ten or twelve times into the dead body of a man whom when living he durst not have looked askance upon.

After the deed was done, and the two servants of the murdered man had fled with the news to his poor father, St. Aignan began to consider what steps he should next take. The servants of the murdered man could not be admitted to give evidence, and no one else had seen the deed besides the murderers, an old woman-servant, and a girl of fifteen. He endeavoured to secure the old woman; but she found means of escape, and took refuge in the Jacobins. Her testimony was the best that was had respecting this crime. The young chambermaid remained some days in St. Aignan's house; but contriving to have her suborned by one of the assassins, he had her taken to Paris, and placed in a house of ill-fame, in order to hinder her from being believed as a witness. That nothing else might remain to prove his guilt, he burned the body; and the bones which the fire could not consume he had mixed with mortar, for he was then building. All this being done, he sent to the court to sue for his pardon, and set forth that having ascertained that the deceased was endeavouring to dishonour his wife, he had often forbid him his house; that he had come notwithstanding by night, under suspicious circumstances, to speak with her, and that having found him at the door of his wife's chamber, he had killed him more in the heat of anger than deliberately. But in spite of his haste, before he had despatched his letter, the duke and duchess learned the whole truth, which they had from the father of the unfortunate young man, and made it known to the chancellor in order to hinder St. Aignan from obtaining his pardon. Upon this the wretch fled to England with his wife and several of her relations. Before his departure, he told the assassin he had employed that he had express orders from the king to arrest him and have him put to death; but that, in consideration of the service he had rendered him, he would save his life. He gave him ten crowns to quit the realm, and the man has never been heard of since. The murder, however, was so well authenticated by the servants of the deceased, by the old woman who had fled to the Jacobins, and by the bones which were found in the mortar, that the criminal process was completed in the absence of St. Aignan and his wife, who were condemned to death as contumacious, to pay their victim's father fifteen hundred crowns for the costs of the process, and to have the rest of their property confiscated to the sovereign.

St. Aignan being in England, and finding himself condemned to death in France, so managed by his services to gain the good-will of several great lords, and set his wife's relations to work to such purpose, that the King of England entreated the King of France to pardon him and to restore him to his possessions and his honours. The king having been informed of the atrocity of this affair, sent the details of the process to the King of England, and begged him to consider if the crime was one which could be pardoned; adding, that throughout his realm none but the Duke of Alençon alone had the privilege of granting grace in his duchy. The King of England did not yield to these representations, but so urgently solicited St. Aignan's pardon, that at last he obtained it.

On his return home, to fill up the measure of his wickedness the proctor made acquaintance with a sorcerer named Gallery, hoping to be put by him in a way to escape payment of the fifteen hundred crowns due by him to his victim's father. To this end he and his wife went in disguise to Paris; but the wife, seeing how he often shut himself up for a long time with Gallery without saying a word to her, watched them one morning, and saw Gallery set before her husband five wooden images, three of which had their hands hanging down, and two had them raised. "We must have waxen images made like them," said Gallery to St. Aignan; "those which shall have their arms hanging down will be for the persons we shall cause to die; and those with raised arms will be for the persons whose good-will we seek."

"Very well," said the proctor. "This one, then, shall be for the king, by whom I would be favoured, and this one for Monsieur Brinon, Chancellor of Alençon."

"The images," said Gallery, "must be put under the altar, where they will hear mass, with certain words which I will teach you."

The proctor coming then to the images with pendent arms, said that one was for Maître Gilles du Mesnil, father of the deceased, for he knew well, that as long as the old man lived, he would not cease to pursue the murderer of his son. One of the female figures with pendent arms was for my lady the Duchess of Alençon, the king's sister, because she was so fond of her old servant Du Mesnil, and had on so many occasions known the wickedness of the proctor, that unless she died he could not live. The second female figure of the same sort was for his wife, who, he said, was the cause of all his misfortunes, and who, he well knew, would never amend. His wife, who was peeping through the keyhole, and saw herself thus devoted by him to death, thought it high time to anticipate him. She had an uncle, named Neaufle, who was referendary to the Duke of Alençon, and going to him under the pretence of borrowing money, she related to him all she had seen and heard. The uncle, a good old servant of the duke's, went to the Chancellor of Alençon, and communicated to him what he had learned from his niece. As the duke and duchess were not that day at court, the chancellor waited on Madame la Régente, the mother of the king and the duchess, who as soon as she was informed of the matter set La Barre, the Provost of Paris, to work at once. The provost did his duty so promptly and so well, that the proctor and his necromancer were both arrested. Neither torture nor constraint was required to make them avow their guilt, and on their own confession their judgment was completed and laid before the king. Some persons who wished to save the lives of the culprits represented to the king that they had no other intention in performing their enchantments than to secure his good graces; but the king, to whom his sister's life was as dear as his own, commanded that they should be sentenced just as though they had been guilty against his own person. His sister, the Duchess of Alençon, nevertheless entreated the king to spare the proctor's life, and condemn him to a severe corporal punishment. Her request was granted, and St. Aignan and Gallery were sent to Saint Blancart's galleys at Marseilles, where they ended their days, and had leisure to reflect on the atrocity of their crimes. The proctor's wicked wife, after the loss of her husband, conducted herself worse than ever, and died miserably.*

* The events related in this novel, and the names of the persons, are all real. The last editors of the Heptameron (la Société des Bibliophiles Français, 1853) have published the writ of pardon granted by Francis I. to St. Aignan, the original of which is preserved in the Archives Nationales. The writ, as usual, recites the statement of the case made by the petitioner for pardon, and this agrees closely with the

Consider, ladies, I beseech you, what disorders a wicked woman occasions, and how many mischiefs ensued from the sin of the one you have just heard of. Since Eve made Adam sin, it has been the business of women to torment, kill, and damn men. For my part, I have had so much experience of their cruelty, that I shall lay my death to nothing but the despair into which one of them has plunged me. And yet I am crazed enough to confess this hell is more agreeable to me, coming from her hand, than the paradise which another might bestow upon me.

Parlamente, affecting not to understand that it was of herself he spoke, replied, " If hell is as agreeable as you say, you can't be afraid of the devil who put you into it."

" If my devil," replied Simontault in a pet, "were to become as black as it has been cruel to me, it would cause this company as much fright as I feel pleasure in looking upon it. But the fire of love makes me forget the fire of that hell. So I will say no more about it, but call upon Madame Oisille, being assured that if she would speak of women as she knows them, she would corroborate my opinion."

The whole company turned to the old lady and begged her to begin, which she did with a smile, and with this little preamble:—" It seems to me, ladies, that the last speaker has cast such a slur upon our sex by the true story he has narrated of a wretched woman, that I must run back through all the past years of my life in order to call to my mind one woman whose virtue was such as to belie the bad opinion he has of our sex. Happily I recollect one such woman who deserves not to be forgotten, and will now relate her story to you."

NOVEL II.

CHASTE AND LAMENTABLE DEATH OF THE WIFE OF ONE OF THE QUEEN OF NAVARRE'S MULETEERS.

THERE was at Amboise a muleteer who served the Queen of Navarre, sister of Francis I. This princess being at Blois,

Queen of Navarre's narrative—allowance, of course, being made for the peculiar colouring which it was the murderer's interest to give to the facts.

where she was delivered of a prince, the muleteer went thither to receive his quarterly payment, and left his wife at Amboise, in a house beyond the bridges. For a long time one of her husband's men had felt such a passion for her, that at last he could not help declaring it; but she being a virtuous woman, reproved him so sharply, threatening to have him beaten and dismissed by her husband, that he never afterwards durst address her with such language. Nevertheless, the fire of his love, though smothered, was not extinguished. His master then being at Blois, and his mistress at vespers at St. Florentin, which is the church of the castle, very remote from the muleteer's house, in which he was left alone, he resolved to have by force what he could not obtain either by prayers or services. To this end he broke an opening through the boarded partition between his mistress's chamber and that in which he himself slept; and this was not perceived, being covered by the curtains of the master's bed on one side, and by those of the men's bed, on the other.

When the poor woman had gone to bed with a little girl of twelve years old, and was sleeping soundly, as one usually does in the first sleep, the man entered the room through the opening, in his shirt, with his sword in his hand, and got into the bed with her. The moment she felt him she sprang out of bed, and addressed such remonstrances to him as would occur to any woman of honour in the like case. He, whose love was but brutality, and who would better have understood the language of his mules than such virtuous pleadings, appeared more insensible to reason than the brutes with which he had long associated. Seeing that she ran so fast round a table that he could not catch her, and that although he had twice laid hands on her she had strength enough both times to break from his grasp, he despaired of ever taking her alive, and stabbed her in the loins, to see if pain would make her yield what fear and force had failed to extort from her. But it was quite the reverse; for as a brave soldier when he sees his own blood is the hotter to revenge himself on his enemies and acquire honour, so her chaste heart gathering new strength, she ran faster than ever to escape falling into the hands of that wretch, at the same time remonstrating with him in the best way she could, thinking by that means to make him conscious of his fault. But he was in such a frenzy that he was incapable of profiting by good advice. In spite of the speed with which she ran as long as her strength lasted, she received several more wounds, till at length, weakened by loss of blood and feeling the approach of death, she raised her eyes and her clasped hands to heaven, and gave thanks to God, whom she called her strength, her virtue, her patience, and her chastity, beseeching him to accept the blood which, according to his commandment, was shed through respect for that of his son, wherein she was thoroughly assured that all sins are washed out, and effaced from the memory of his wrath. Then exclaiming, "Lord, receive my soul which thy goodness has redeemed," she fell on her face and received several more wounds from the villain, who, after she had lost the power of speech and motion, satisfied his lust, and fled with such speed that, in spite of all efforts to track him, he was never heard of afterwards.

The little girl who had been in bed with the poor woman had hid herself beneath it in her fright; but as soon as she saw that the man was gone, she went to her mistress, and finding her speechless and motionless, she called out through the window to the neighbours for help. Esteeming and liking the muleteer's wife as much as any woman in the town, they all hurried at once to her aid, and brought with them surgeons, who found that she had received twenty-five mortal wounds. They did all they could for her, but she was past saving. She lingered, however, for an hour, making signs with her eyes and hands, and showing thereby that she had not lost consciousness. A priest having asked her in what faith she died, she replied by signs as unequivocal as speech, that she put her trust in the death of Jesus Christ, whom she hoped to see in his heavenly glory. And so with a serene countenance and eyes uplifted to heaven, she surrendered her chaste body to the earth, and her soul to her Creator.

Her husband arrived just as they were about to carry her to the grave, and was shocked to see his wife dead before he had heard any news of her; but double cause he had to grieve when he was told how she had died; and so poignant was his sorrow, that it had like to cost him his life. The martyr of chastity was buried in the church of St. Florentin, being attended to the grave by all the virtuous women of the place, who did all possible honour to her memory, deeming it a happiness to be the townswomen of one so virtuous. Those, too, who had led bad lives, seeing the honours paid to the deceased, amended their ways, and resolved to live better for the time to come.*

There, ladies, you have a true tale, and one which may well incite to chastity, which is so fine a virtue. Ought we not to die of shame, we who are of good birth, to feel our hearts full of the love of the world, since, to avoid it, a poor muleteer's wife did not fear so cruel a death? Therefore we must humble ourselves, for God does not bestow his graces on men because they are noble or rich; but, according as it pleases his goodness, which regards not the appearance of persons, he chooses whom he will. He honours with his virtues, and finally crowns with his glory, those whom he has elected; and often he chooses low and despised things to confound those which the world esteems high and honourable. Let us not rejoice in our virtues, as Jesus Christ says, but let us rejoice for that we are enrolled in the Book of Life.

The ladies were so touched by the sad and glorious death of the muleteer's wife, that there was not one of them but shed tears, and promised herself that she would strive to follow such an example should fortune expose her to a similar trial. At last, Madame Oisille, seeing they were losing time in praising the dead woman, said to Saffredent, "If you do not say something to make the company laugh, no one will forgive me for the fault I have committed in making them weep." Saffredent, who was really desirous to say something good and agreeable to the company, and especially to one of the ladies, replied that this honour was not due to him, and that there were others who were older and more capable than himself who ought to speak before him. "But since you will have it so," he said, "the best thing I can do is to despatch the matter at once, for the more good speakers precede me, the more difficult will my task be when my turn comes."

* The tragedy here related must have occurred after August, 1530, when Margaret was delivered of a son named Jean, who lived only two months.

NOVEL III.

A KING OF NAPLES, HAVING DEBAUCHED THE WIFE OF A GENTLEMAN, AT LAST WEARS HORNS HIMSELF.

As I have often wished I had shared the good fortune of one about whom I am going to tell you a tale, I must inform you that in the time of King Alfonso, the sceptre of whose realm was lasciviousness, there was at Naples a handsome, agreeable gentleman, in whom nature and education had combined so many perfections, that an old gentleman gave him his daughter, who for beauty and engaging qualities was in no respects inferior to her husband. Great was their mutual love during the first months of their marriage; but the carnival being come, and the king going masked into the houses, where every one did his best to receive him well, he came to this gentleman's, where he met with a better reception than anywhere else. Confections, music, concerts, and other amusements were not forgotten; but what pleased the king most was the wife, the finest woman, to his thinking, he had ever seen. After the repast she sang with her husband, and that so pleasingly, that she seemed still more beautiful. The king, seeing so many perfections in one person, took much less pleasure in the sweet harmony of the husband and wife than in thinking how he might break it. Their mutual affection appeared to him a great obstacle to his design; therefore he concealed his passion as well as he could; but to solace it in some manner, he frequently entertained the lords and ladies of Naples, and did not forget the husband and his wife.

As one readily believes what one desires, the king thought that the lady's eyes promised him something agreeable, if only those of the husband were not in the way. To put his conjecture to the proof, he sent the husband to Rome with a commission which would occupy him a fortnight or three weeks. When he was gone, his wife, who never before had lost sight of him, so to speak, was in the deepest affliction. The king went to see her frequently, and did his best to console her by obliging words and presents. In a word, he played his part so well, that she was not only consoled, but even very well pleased with her husband's absence. Before the end of three weeks she was so much in love with the king, that she was quite as distressed at her husband's return as she had been at his departure. That she might not be deprived of the king's presence, it was settled between them, that whenever the husband went to the country she should give notice to the king, who then might come to see her in perfect security, and so secretly, that her honour, which she respected more than her conscience, should not be hurt; a hope which the fair lady dwelt on with great pleasure.

The husband, on his return, was so well received by his wife, that even had he been told that the king fondled her during his absence, he never could have believed it. But in course of time this fire, which such pains were taken to conceal, began gradually to make itself visible, and became at last so glaring, that the husband, justly alarmed, set himself to observe, and with such effect, that he had scarcely any room left for doubt. But as he was afraid that he who wronged him would do him a still worse mischief if he made any noise about the matter, he resolved to dissemble, thinking it better to live with grief at his heart, than to expose his life for a woman who did not love him. Nevertheless, he longed, in the bitterness of his resentment, to retaliate on the king, if it were possible; and as he knew that spite will make a woman do more than love, especially such as are of a great and honourable spirit, he took the liberty one day to say to the queen how grieved he was that the king her husband treated her with indifference. The queen, who had heard of the king's amour with his wife, replied that she could not have honour and pleasure both together. "I know well," she added, "that I have the honour whereof another receives the pleasure; but then she who has the pleasure has not the same honour as is mine."

Well knowing to whom these words applied, the gentleman responded, "Honour is born with you, madam. You are of so good a lineage, that the rank of queen or empress could add nothing to your nobility; but your beauty, your graces, and your winning deportment, merit so much pleasure, that she who robs you of that which is your due does more harm to herself than to you, since for a glory which turns to shame she loses as much pleasure as you or any woman in the kingdom could enjoy. And I can tell you, madam, that the king, the crown apart, is not more capable than I of contenting a woman. Far from it, I am certain that to satisfy a woman of your merit the king ought to wish that he was of my temperament."

"Though the king is of a more delicate complexion than you," replied the queen, laughing "the love he has for me gratifies me so much, that I prefer it to any other thing."

"If that be so, madam," returned the gentleman, "I no longer pity you. I know that if the king had for you a love as pure as that you have for him, you would literally enjoy the gratification you speak of; but God has determined that it should be otherwise, in order that, not finding in him what you desire, you should not make him your god on earth."

"I own to you," said the queen, "that the love I have for him is so great, that no heart can love with such passion as mine."

"Allow me, if you please, to tell you, madam, that you have not fathomed the love in every heart. I dare assure you, madam, that there is one who loves you with a love so perfect and impassioned, that what you feel for the king cannot be compared with it. His love grows stronger as that of the king grows weaker, and it only rests with yourself, madam, if you think proper, to be more than compensated for all you lose."

By this time the queen began to perceive, both from the gentleman's words and his manner, that his tongue was the interpreter of his heart. She now recollected that for a long time past he had been seeking opportunities to do her service, and seeking them with such eagerness that he had become quite melancholy. At first she had supposed that his wife was the cause of his sadness; but now she made no doubt that it was all on her own account. As love never fails to make itself felt when it is real, the queen had no difficulty in unriddling what was a secret for every one else. The gentleman, therefore, appearing to her more amiable than her husband, considering, besides, that he was forsaken by his wife, as she was by her husband, and animated with resentment and jealousy against her husband, "My God!" she exclaimed with a sigh, and with tears in her eyes, "must it be that vengeance shall effect upon me what love has never been able to effect?"

"Vengeance is sweet, madam," observed the now hopeful suitor, "when, instead of killing one's enemy, one bestows life on a real friend. It is high time, methinks, that the truth should cure you of an unreasonable love you entertain for a person who has none for you; and that a just and well-founded love should expel the fear which is very ill-lodged in a heart so great and so virtuous as yours. Let us put out of consideration, madam, your royal quality, and let us contemplate the fact that you and I, of all persons in the world, are the two who are most basely duped and betrayed by those whom we have most perfectly loved. Let us avenge ourselves, madam, not so much for sake of retaliation as for the satisfaction of love, which on my side is such that I could not bear more and live. If your heart is not harder than adamant, you must feel some spark of that fire which augments in proportion as I labour to conceal it, and if pity for me, who am dying for love of you, does not incite you to love me, at least you should do so out of resentment. Your merit is so great, that it is worthy of the love of every honest heart; yet you are despised and abandoned by him for whom you have abandoned all others."

These words caused the queen such violent transports, that in order to conceal the commotion of her spirits, she took the gentleman's arm, and went with him into a garden adjoining her chamber, where she walked up and down a long while without being able to speak a single word to him. But the gentleman, seeing her half-conquered, no sooner reached the end of an alley where no one could see them, than he plied her to good purpose with his long-concealed passion. Being both of one mind, they revenged themselves together; and it was arranged between them that whenever the king went to visit the gentleman's wife, the gentleman should visit the queen. Thus, the cheaters being cheated, four would share the pleasure which two imagined they had all to themselves. When all was over, the queen retired to her chamber, and the gentleman went home, both of them so well contented, that they thought no more of their past vexations. The gentleman, far from dreading lest the king should visit his wife, on the contrary desired nothing better; and to afford him opportunity for doing so, he went to the country oftener than he had been used. When the king knew that the gentleman was at his village, which was but half a league from the city, he went at once to the fair lady; whilst the gentleman repaired by night to the queen's chamber, where he did duty as the king's lieutenant so secretly that no one ever perceived it.

Things went on in this way for a long while; but whatever pains the king took to conceal his amour, all the world was aware of it. The gentleman was much pitied by all good-natured people, and ridiculed by the ill-natured, who used to make horns at him behind his back. He knew very well that they did so, and he laughed in his sleeve, for he thought his horns were as good as the king's crown. One day when the royal gallant was at the gentleman's, casting his eyes on a pair of antlers hung up in the hall, he could not help saying, with a laugh, in presence of the master of the house himself, "These antlers very well become this place." The gentleman, who had as much spirit as the king, had this inscription put up beneath the antlers after the king was gone:

> Io porto le corna, ciascun lo vede;
> Ma tal le porta, chi no lo crede.
>
> I wear the horns as all men know;
> He wears them too who thinks not so.

On his next visit the king observed this inscription, and asked the meaning of it. "If the stag," replied the gentleman, "does not know the king's secret, it is not just that the king should know the stag's secret. Be satisfied with knowing, sire, that it is not every one who wears horns who has his cap lifted off his head by them; some horns are so soft that a man may wear them without knowing it."

It was plain to the king from this reply that the gentleman knew something of his own affair, but he never suspected either him or the queen. That princess played her part extremely well; for the more pleased she was with her husband's conduct, the more she pretended to be dissatisfied. So they lived as good friends on both sides until old age put an end to their mutual pleasures. This, ladies, is a story which I have great pleasure in proposing to you by way of example, to the end that when your husbands give you horns you may do the same by them.*

* The king who figures in this novel appears to be Alfonso V., King of Aragon and Sicily, who supplanted King René on the throne of

"I am very well assured, Saffredent," said Ennasuite, laughing, "that if you were as much in love as you have formerly been, you would endure horns as big as oaks for the sake of bestowing a pair as you pleased; but now that your hair is beginning to turn grey, it is time to put a truce to your desires."

"Though she whom I love, mademoiselle, allows me no hope," replied Saffredent, "and age has exhausted my vigour, my desires remain still in full force. But since you reproach me with so seemly a passion, you will, if you please, relate to us the fourth novel; and we shall see if you can find some example which may refute me."

One of the ladies present, who knew that she who had taken Saffredent's words to herself was not the person he loved so much as to be willing to wear horns of her making, could not help laughing at the manner in which she had taken them up. Saffredent, who perceived that the laughing lady had guessed right, was very glad of it, and let Ennasuite talk on. "To prove, ladies," she said, "to Saffredent and all the company that all women are not like the queen of whom he has told us, and that the audacious are not always successful, I will relate to you the adventure of a lady who deemed that the vexation of failing in love was harder to bear than death itself. I shall not name the persons, because the story is so recent that I should be afraid of offending some of the near relations if I did so."

NOVEL IV.

PRESUMPTUOUS ATTEMPT OF A GENTLEMAN UPON A PRINCESS
OF FLANDERS, AND THE SHAME IT BROUGHT UPON HIM.

THERE was in Flanders a lady of such good family that there was none better in the country. She was a widow, had

Naples in 1443, and remained in possession of it until his death in 1438. He married, in 1415, Maria, daughter of Henry III., King of Castile, and lived on very bad terms with that princess, who, according to the authors of *l'Art de vérifier les Dates*, never set foot in Italy. Queen Mary, who was married in 1415, must have been long past her bloom in 1443. For this reason the Bibliophiles Français are inclined to believe that the Queen of Navarre has here related under borrowed names a true story of her own times.

been twice married, but had no children living. During her second widowhood she resided with her brother, who loved her much, and who was a very great lord, being married to one of the king's daughters. This young prince was much addicted to pleasure, and was fond of the chase, amusements, and the ladies, as usual with young people. He had a very ill-tempered wife, who was by no means well pleased with her husband's diversions; wherefore as his sister was the most lively and cheerful companion possible, she accompanied the prince to every place to which he took his wife. There was at the prince's court a gentleman who surpassed all the others in height, figure, and good looks, and who, seeing that his master's sister was a lively lady, and fond of laughing, thought he would try if a well-bred lover would be to her taste. But the result was quite contrary to what he had expected; although she pardoned his audacity in consideration of his good looks and good breeding, and even let him know that she was not angry that he had spoken to her, only she desired she might never hear the same language from him again. He promised this, that he might not lose the honour and pleasure of her society, but as his passion increased with time, he forgot his promise. He did not, however, have recourse to words, for experience had taught him that she knew how to make chaste replies; but he flattered himself that being a widow, young, vigorous, and good-humoured, she would, perhaps, take pity on him and on herself if he could find her in a convenient place.

To this end he acquainted the prince that he had a house admirably situated for the chase, and that if he would come thither and hunt three or four stags in the month of May, he would have excellent sport. The prince promised he would do so, and he kept his word. He found a handsome house prepared for his reception, in the best order, as belonging to the richest nobleman in the country. Its owner lodged her whom he loved better than himself in an apartment opposite to that which he assigned to the prince and princess. Her bedroom was so well tapestried above and so well matted below, that it was impossible to perceive a trap-door he had contrived in the alcove, and which led down into the room occupied by his aged and infirm mother. As the good old lady coughed a great deal, and was afraid of disturbing the princess, she exchanged bedrooms with her son. Not an evening passed that the old lady did not carry confections to the princess, on which occasions her son failed not to accompany her; and as he was much liked by the brother, he was allowed to be present at the sister's *coucher* and *lever*, when he always found cause for the increase of his passion.

One night he stayed so late with the princess, that seeing she was falling asleep he was obliged to leave her and return to his own chamber. He took the handsomest and best perfumed shirt he had, and a nightcap of the choicest kind; then, looking at himself in the glass, he was so satisfied with his own appearance, that he thought no lady could possibly withstand his good looks. Promising himself marvels therefore from his enterprise, he lay down on his bed, where he did not think he should stay long, for he expected to exchange it for one more honourable.

No sooner had he dismissed his attendants, than he rose and locked the door, and listened for a long time to hear whether there was any noise in the princess's chamber, which, as already said, was above his own. When he had satisfied himself that all was quiet, he began to put his fine project in execution, and gradually let down the trap-door, which was so well made and so well covered with cloth, that it did not make the least noise. Then stealing up into the alcove where the princess was fast asleep, he got into bed to her without ceremony, regardless of her high birth and the obligations he was under to her, and without having in the first instance obtained her consent. The first intimation she had of his arrival was to find herself in his arms; but being a strong woman she broke loose from his grasp, and, demanding who he was, made such good use of her hands and nails that he tried to stuff the quilt into her mouth for fear she should cry out. But he never could accomplish his purpose, for as she found that he was doing his best to dishonour her, she did her best to defend herself, and called out to her lady of honour, an aged and very prudent woman who slept in the same room, and she hastened in her shift to her mistress's aid.

The gentleman finding he was discovered, was so much afraid of being recognised, that he hurried away through his trap-door as fast as he could, no less overcome at the plight in which he returned from his enterprise than he had been keen-set and confident when he entered upon it. The candle was still burning on the table before his mirror, which showed his face all scratched and bitten, and the blood streaming from it over his fine shirt. "Thou art rightly served, pernicious beauty!" he said, apostrophising his own lacerated visage. "Thy vain promises set upon an impossible enterprise, and one which, far from increasing my good fortune, will, perhaps, bring upon me a world of trouble. What will become of me if she knows that I have committed this folly in violation of my promise? The least that can happen to me will be to be banished from her presence. Why did I employ fraud to steal what my birth and my good looks might have obtained for me by lawful ways? Could I expect to make myself master of her heart by violence? Ought I not to have waited till love put me in possession of it in recompense for my patience and my long service? For without love, all the merits and power of man are nothing."

The rest of the night was spent by the discomfited gallant in such reflections as these, mingled with tears, groans, and wailings indescribable. In the morning he feigned illness, to conceal the mangled state of his countenance, pretending all the while the company remained in the house that he could not endure the light. The lady, who was convinced that there was no one at the court capable of so audacious an act except the man who had had the boldness to declare his love to her, searched the chamber with the lady of honour; but not finding a passage through which any one could have entered, she broke into a towering passion. "Be assured," she said to the lady of honour, "that the lord of this mansion is the man, and that I will make such a report to-morrow morning to my brother, that the culprit's head shall bear witness to my chastity."

"I am delighted, madam," said her wary attendant, who saw what a transport of rage she was in—"I am delighted that honour is so precious in your eyes, that for its sake you would not spare the life of a man who has put it in jeopardy through excess of love. But in this, as in every other matter, one may fall backwards when thinking to advance.

Therefore, tell me, madam, the plain truth. Has he had anything of you?"

"Nothing, I do assure you," replied the princess, "besides scratches and cuffs; and unless he has found a very clever surgeon, I am sure he will show the marks of them to-morrow."

"That being the case, madam, it strikes me you ought rather to praise God than think of vengeance. Since he has had the heart to make such an attempt, the vexation of having failed in it will be more poignant than even death itself. If you would be avenged on him, leave him to his love and to his shame, which will make him suffer more than anything you can do. Do not fall, madam, into the blunder he has committed. He promised himself the sweetest of all pleasures, and he has brought upon himself the most miserable torment. Profit by his example, madam, and do not diminish your glory in thinking to augment it. If you complain of the adventure, you will publish what is known to nobody; for you may be sure that on his part it will remain an everlasting secret. Suppose even my lord your brother does you the justice you demand, and that it costs the poor gentleman his life, people will say that he has had his will of you; and most people will find it hard to believe that he would have made such an attempt if you had not given him encouragement. You are handsome, young, and lively. All the court knows that you are graciously familiar with the gentleman you suspect; and so every one will conclude that he only made this attempt because it was your wish that he should do so. Your honour, which has hitherto sustained no blemish, will become at least questionable wherever this story is told."

The princess yielded to the force of these judicious representations, and asked the lady of honour what she should do. "Since you are pleased to receive my counsel, madam," replied the lady, "seeing the affection from which it proceeds, I must say, that in my opinion, you ought to be heartily rejoiced that the handsomest and best-bred man I know has neither by fair means nor by foul been able to make you swerve from the path of virtue. For this, madam, you should feel bound to humble yourself before God, and acknowledge that it is his work, and not your own. Many a woman, indeed, has maintained a more imposing air of gravity than you, who yet has yielded to a man less worth loving than this gentleman. You ought to be more on your guard than ever against everything in the shape of soft speeches, and bethink you that many have resisted a first attack who have yielded to a second. Remember, madam, that love is blind, and that he makes people blind, so that they think they have nothing to fear when they are most in danger. It is my opinion, then, madam, that you ought not to tell any one what has occurred to you, and that even if he should think of speaking to you on the subject, you should affect not to understand him. Thereby you will avoid two bad things: one is vainglory for the victory you have achieved; the other, the pleasure you might take in remembering things so agreeable to the flesh; for the chastest of our sex can hardly prevent themselves, strive as they will, from feeling something of the sort. Furthermore, madam, that he may not believe that what he has done accords in any way with your inclinations, I advise you to make him feel his folly by gradually withdrawing something of that friendly countenance you have been used to show him. He will also feel at the same time that you manifest great goodness of heart in contenting yourself with your victory and renouncing vengeance. God grant you the grace, madam, to persist in the virtue with which he has endowed you, and to love and serve him better than you have hitherto done, knowing that he is the source of all good things."

The princess followed her lady of honour's sage counsels, and slept calmly through the rest of the night, whilst the gentleman lay awake in bitter anguish of spirit. Next day, the prince being about to take his departure, asked after his host, and was told he was so ill he could not bear to see the light or hear any one speak. Surprised at this sudden malady, the prince would have gone to see him, but hearing that he was asleep, and not wishing to disturb him, he went away with his wife and sister without bidding him farewell. His sister, concluding that the gentleman's illness was only a pretence to avoid showing the marks she had left upon his face, was now assured beyond all doubt that it was he who had been her nightly assailant. The prince repeatedly sent word to him to return to court, but he did not obey until he had been thoroughly cured of all his wounds, except those which love and vexation had made in his heart. On his return to court, he could not sustain the presence of his victorious enemy without blushing. Though he had been possessed of more assurance than any man at court, he was so disconcerted that he often appeared before her quite abashed—a new proof that her suspicions were well founded. She broke with him, therefore, little by little. Adroitly as she did this, he failed not to perceive it, but durst not remonstrate for fear of worse. He kept his love concealed, and endured patiently a disgrace he had well merited.*

There, ladies, is a story which should strike fear into those who would seize what does not belong to them, and which should inspire ladies with courage, considering the virtue of the young princess and the good sense of her lady of honour. Should a similar thing befal one of you, here you see how it is to be remedied.

"To my thinking," said Hircan, "the tall gentleman you have been telling us of had such a faint heart that he did not deserve the honour of having his adventure talked of. Having such a fine opportunity, nothing should have prevented him from profiting by it. His love, it must be owned, was not very great, since the fear of death and of shame found a place beside it in his heart."

"And what could the poor gentleman have done against two women?" said Nomerfide.

"He should have killed the old one," replied Hircan, "and

---

* The princess and the gallant spoken of in this novel are none other than the Queen of Navarre herself and Guillaume de Bonnivet, Admiral of France, as we are informed by Brantôme (*Dames Galantes*, Discours iv. t. vii.). He states the fact upon the authority of his grandmother, who, as well as his mother, Anne de Vivonne, was about Margaret's person, and it is generally regarded as true. It is to be observed, however, that Margaret has purposely introduced into her narrative several circumstances calculated to disguise her own identity: the second widowhood, for instance, for the King of Navarre survived her, and the absence of children by both marriages, for Margaret had a surviving daughter by her second husband. The handsome and gallant Bonnivet figures repeatedly in the Heptameron.

the young one, seeing herself alone, would have been half vanquished."

"Killed!" exclaimed Nomerfide; "you would turn a lover into a murderer! It would be a terrible thing to fall into your hands, I see."

"If I had pushed matters so far," continued Hircan, "I should think myself ruined in reputation unless I went the whole way to the end."

"Do you think it matter for wonder," said Geburon, "that a princess trained to virtue proves too much for one man? What would you say, then, to one woman in low life escaping from two men?"

"Geburon," said Ennasuite, "I call upon you for the fifth novel. If I am not mistaken, you know one about this poor woman which will not be displeasing to the company."

"Be it so, then," said Geburon; "I will tell you a story which I know to be true, having examined into it on the spot. You will see from it that princesses are not the only prudent and the only virtuous of their sex, and that often those who are reputed very amorous and very sly are less so than is supposed.

NOVEL V.

A BOATWOMAN ESCAPES FROM TWO CORDELIERS, WHO WANTED TO FORCE HER, AND EXPOSES THEM TO PUBLIC DERISION.

THERE was in the port of Coulon, near Niort, a boatwoman, who did nothing day and night but convey people from point to point. Two Cordeliers of Niort crossed the river alone with her. As it is one of the widest ferries in France, they took it into their heads to make love to her, for fear she should grow dull by the way. She gave no more ear to them than they deserved; but the good fathers, who were neither fatigued by the labour of the passage, nor chilled by the coldness of the water, nor abashed by the woman's refusal, resolved to force her, or throw her into the river if she was refractory. But she was as good and as shrewd as they were wicked and witless, and said to them, "I am not so ill-natured as you might suppose; only grant me two things I have to beg of you, and you will see I am not more willing to satisfy you than you are to be satisfied. The Cordeliers swore by their good St. Francis there was nothing they would not grant her to have from her what they wanted. "Well, then," said she, "I ask you, in the first place, to promise and vow that living man shall never know from you what passes between us." This they did with great readiness. "The second thing I ask is, that you will have to do with me one by one, for I should be too much ashamed if it was done in presence of you both. Settle between yourselves which is to have me first." The Cordeliers thought that fair enough, and the younger of them yielded precedence to the elder.

Running the boat ashore at a little island, she said to the younger one, "Say your prayers there whilst your comrade and I go to another island. If he is satisfied with me when we come back, we will leave him, and you and I will go away together." The younger friar jumped ashore at once, and the boatwoman rowed away with his companion to another island. When they reached it, she pretended to be making her boat fast, whilst she said to the monk, "See if you can find a convenient spot." The Cordelier, like a booby, stepped out of the boat to do as she told him, and no sooner was he ashore, than setting her foot against a tree, she shot the boat out into the stream, and left the two good fathers in the lurch. "Wait there, my masters," said she, "till God's angel comes to console you, for you will get nothing from me." The duped Cordeliers went down on their knees, and begged her, for Heaven's sake, not to serve them so, but take them to the port, upon their solemn oath they would ask nothing of her. "A pretty fool I should be," she replied, still rowing away, "to put myself into your hands again once I have got out of them."

When she got home to the village, she told her husband what had occurred, and applied to the ministers of justice to come and capture those two wolves from whose fangs she had contrived to escape. The ministers of justice set out for the purpose, well accompanied, for there was no one, great or small, but was bent on taking part in this hunt. The poor friars, seeing such a multitude coming after them, hid themselves each on his island, as Adam did from the sight of God when he had eaten the apple. Half dead with shame and the fear of punishment, they were caught and led away prisoners, amid the jeers and hootings of men and women. "These good fathers," said one, "preach chastity to us, and want to foul our wives." "They dare not touch money," said the husband, "but they are ready enough to handle women's thighs, which are far more dangerous." "They are sepulchres," said others, "whitened without, but full of rottenness within." "By their fruits you shall know the nature of these trees." In short, all the passages of Scripture against hypocrites were cast in the teeth of the poor prisoners. At last the warden came to the rescue. They were given up to him at his request, upon his assuring the magistrate that he would punish them more severely than secular justice itself could do, and that by way of reparation to the offended parties, they should say as many masses and prayers as might be desired. As he was a worthy man, they were chaptered in such a manner, that they never afterwards passed over the river without crossing themselves, and beseeching God to keep them out of all temptation.

If this boatwoman had the wit to trick two such bad men, what should they do who have seen and read of so many fine examples? If women who know nothing, who scarcely hear two good sermons in a year, and have no time to think of anything but earning their bread, do yet carefully guard their chastity, what ought not others of their sex to do who, having their livelihood secured, have nothing to do but to read the Holy Scriptures, hear sermons, and exercise themselves in all sorts of virtues? This is the test by which it is known that the heart is truly virtuous, for the more simple and unenlightened the individual, the greater are the works of God's spirit. Unhappy the lady who does not carefully preserve the treasure which does her so much honour when well kept, and so much dishonour when she keeps it ill!

"It strikes me, Geburon," said Longarine, "that it does not need much virtue to refuse a Cordelier. On the contrary, I should rather think it impossible to love such people."

"Those who are not accustomed to have such lovers as you have," replied Geburon, "do not think so contemptuously of Cordeliers. They are well-made, strapping fellows, can talk like angels, and are for the most part importunate as devils.

Accordingly, the *grisettes* who escape out of their hands may fairly be called virtuous."

"O by my faith!" exclaimed Nomerfide, raising her voice, "you may say what you will, but for my part I would rather be flung into the river than go to bed with a Cordelier."

"You can swim, then," retorted Oisille, laughing.

Nomerfide was piqued at this, and said with warmth, "There are those who have refused better men than Cordeliers, without making any flourish of trumpets about it for all that."

"Or yet beating the drum about what they have done and granted," rejoined Oisille, who laughed to see her vexed.

"I perceive that Nomerfide has a mind to speak," said Geburon, "and I give my voice in her favour, that she may unburden her heart upon some good novel."

"The remarks which have just been made," said Nomerfide, "concern me so little, that they can give me neither pain nor pleasure. But as I have your voice I beg you to hear mine, while I show you that if one is sly for a good purpose, others are so for a bad one. We are vowed to speak the truth, and therefore I will not conceal it; for just as the boatwoman's virtue is no honour to other women if they do not resemble her in it, so the vice of another cannot dishonour them. Listen, then.

NOVEL VI.

STRATAGEM BY WHICH A WOMAN ENABLED HER GALLANT TO ESCAPE, WHEN HER HUSBAND, WHO WAS BLIND OF AN EYE, THOUGHT TO SURPRISE THEM TOGETHER.

Charles, the last Duke of Alençon, had an old valet-de-chambre who was blind of an eye, and who was married to a woman much younger than himself. The duke and duchess liked this valet better than any other domestic of that order in their household, and the consequence was that he could not go and see his wife as often as he could have wished, whilst she, unable to accommodate herself to circumstances, so far forgot her honour and her conscience as to fall in love with a young gentleman of the neighbourhood. At last the affair got wind, and there was so much talk about it, that it reached the ears of the husband, who could not believe it, so warm was the affection testified to him by his wife. One day, however, he made up his mind to know the truth of the matter, and to revenge himself if he could on the person who put this affront upon him. With this view he pretended to go for two or three days to a place at some little distance; and no sooner had he taken his departure, than his wife sent for her gallant. They had hardly been half an hour together when the husband came and knocked loudly at the door. The wife knowing but too well who it was, told her lover, who was so astounded that he could have wished he was still in his mother's womb. But while he was swearing and confounding her and the intrigue which had brought him into such a perilous scrape, she told him not to be uneasy, for she would get him off without its costing him anything; and that all he had to do was to dress himself as quickly as possible.

Meanwhile the husband kept knocking and calling to his wife as loud as he could bawl, but she pretended not to know him. "Why don't you get up," she cried to the people of the house, "and go and silence those who are making such a noise at the door? Is this a proper time to come to honest people's houses? If my husband was here he would make you know better." The husband, hearing her voice, shouted louder than ever. "Let me in, wife; do you mean to keep me at the door till daylight?" At last, when she saw that her lover was ready to slip out, "Oh, is that you, husband?" she said; "I am so glad you are come! I was full of a dream I had that gave me the greatest pleasure I ever felt in my life. I thought you had recovered the sight of your eye." Here she opened the door, and catching her husband round the neck, kissed him, clapped one hand on his sound eye, and asked him if he did not see better than usual. Whilst the husband was thus blindfolded the gallant made his escape. The husband guessed how it was, but said, "I will watch you no more, wife. I thought to deceive you, but it is I who have been the dupe, and you have put the cunningest trick upon me that ever was invented. God mend you! for it passes the act of man to bring back a wicked woman from her evil ways by any means short of putting her to death. But since the regard I have had for you has not availed to make you behave better, perhaps the contempt with which I shall henceforth look upon you will touch you more, and have a more wholesome effect." Therefore he went away, leaving her in great confusion.

At last, however, he was prevailed upon by the solicitations of relations and friends, and by the tears and excuses of his wife, to cohabit with her again.*

You see from this example, ladies, with what adroitness a woman can get herself out of a scrape. If she is prompt at finding an expedient to conceal a bad deed, I believe she would be still more prompt and ingenious in discovering means to hinder herself from doing a good one; for, as I have heard say, good wit is always the stronger.

"You may boast of your cunning as much as you will," said Hircan, "but I believe, if the same thing had happened to you, you could not have concealed it."

"I would as soon you told me flatly," said Nomerfide, "that I am the most stupid woman in the world."

"I do not say that," replied Hircan, "but I look upon you as more likely to be alarmed at a rumour against you than to find an ingenious way of putting an end to it."

"You think that every one is like yourself, who to get rid of one rumour set another afloat. You pass for a very cunning man, but if you think that you surpass woman in that way, I will give up my turn to you, that you may tell us some story in point. Of course you know plenty, of which you are yourself the hero."

"I am not here to make myself appear worse than I am," returned Hircan, "though there are some who give me a worse character than I desire or deserve," he added, looking at his wife.

"Don't let me hinder you from speaking the truth," said she. "I would rather hear you relate your sly tricks than see you play them. But be assured that nothing can diminish the love I have for you."

"For that reason," said Hircan, "I do not complain of the injustice with which you often judge me. And so, since we understand each other, there will be so much the more peace and quiet for the future. But I am not the man to tell a story of myself, the truth of which may be displeasing to you, but shall relate one of a person who was an intimate friend of mine."

* Although Margaret asserts that this is a true story, and that th actors in it belonged to the household of her first husband, it is to b

NOVEL VII.

TRICK PUT BY A MERCER OF PARIS UPON AN OLD WOMAN, TO CONCEAL HIS INTRIGUE WITH HER DAUGHTER.

THERE was a mercer in Paris who was enamoured of a girl in his neighbourhood, or, to speak more properly, who was loved by her, rather than she by him, for he only pretended to be attached to her in order to conceal another amour with a more exalted object. For her part, she was very willing to be deceived, and loved him so much that she forgot all the usual coyness of her sex. After the mercer had long taken the trouble of going in search of her, he used afterwards to make her come to him wherever he pleased. The mother, who was a respectable woman, perceived this, and forbade her daughter ever to speak to the mercer, under pain of being sent to a convent; but the girl, who loved the mercer more than she feared her mother, behaved worse than ever. One day the mercer, finding her alone in a convenient place, began to entertain her on matters that ought not to be discussed before witnesses; but a servant who had seen him come in, ran and told the mother, who hastened to the spot to put an end to the conversation. The daughter hearing her footsteps, said, with tears in her eyes, "My love for you will cost me dear; here comes my mother, and she will now be convinced of what she has always feared." The mercer, without losing his presence of mind, instantly quitted the girl, ran to meet her mother, threw his arms round the old woman's neck, hugged her with all his might, threw her on a little bed, and began to expend upon her all the rage her daughter had excited within him. The poor old woman, quite confounded at being treated in this way, could only exclaim, "What are you about? Are you mad?" But he no more desisted than if she had been the handsomest young girl in the world; and if her screams had not brought the servant men and maids to her assistance, she would have suffered the fate she apprehended so much for her daughter. The servants dragged the good woman by

---

found in many previous collections; as, for instance, the *Cent Nouvelles Nouvelles*, where it occurs as the 16th novel, entitled *Le Borgne Aveugle*. It is the sixth fable of the first book of the Pantcha Tantra, a collection of Hindoo stories.

force out of the mercer's hands, without the poor creature ever knowing why she had been so worried. During the scuffle, the daughter escaped to a neighbour's house, where there was a wedding going on; and she and the mercer often afterwards laughed at the expense of the old woman, who never detected their intercourse.

Here you have, ladies, an instance of a man's having been cunning enough to deceive an old woman, and save the honour of a young one. If I were to name the persons, or if you had seen the countenance of the mercer and the surprise of the old woman, you must have had very tender consciences to keep from laughing. I have sufficiently proved to you by this example that men are not less ingenious than women in inventing at need expedients upon the spot; and so, ladies, you need not be afraid of falling into their hands, for, should your own wit fail, you will find theirs ready to screen your honour.

"I own, Hircan," said Longarine, "that the story is comical and the stratagem well invented; but, for all that, it does not follow that the example is one which ought to be imitated by girls. I have no doubt there are plenty whom you would wish to approve of it; but you have too much sense to wish that your wife and your daughter, whose honour is dearer to you than pleasure, should play at such a game. I believe there is no one who would watch them more closely, and put a stop to such doings more promptly, than yourself."

"Upon my conscience," replied Hircan, "if my wife had done the same thing, I should not esteem her the less, provided I knew nothing about it. I don't know if some one has not played as good a trick at my expense, but, fortunately, as I know nothing, I give myself no concern."

"The wicked are always suspicious," said Parlamente; "but happy are they who give no cause for suspicion."

"I can't say I ever saw a fire without some smoke," said Longarine; "but I have certainly seen smoke without any fire. Those who have bad hearts suspect alike where there is mischief and where there is none."

"You have so well supported the cause of ladies unjustly suspected," said Hircan to Longarine, "that I call upon you for your novel. I hope you will not make us weep as

Madame Oisille has done by too much praise of honest women."

"Since you would have me make you laugh," said Longarine, laughing with all her heart, "it shall not be at the expense of our sex. I will let you see how easy it is to cheat jealous wives who think they are wise enough to cheat their husbands."

NOVEL VIII.

A MAN HAVING LAIN WITH HIS WIFE, BELIEVING THAT HE WAS IN BED WITH HIS SERVANT, SENDS HIS FRIEND TO DO THE SAME THING; AND THE FRIEND MAKES A CUCKOLD OF HIM WITHOUT THE WIFE BEING AWARE OF IT.

THERE was in the county of Allez a person named Bornet, who had married a virtuous wife, and held her honour and reputation dear, as is the case, I suppose, with all the husbands here present. Though he desired that his wife should be faithful to him, he did not choose to be equally bound to her; in fact, he made love to his servant, though all the good he could get by the change was the pleasure attending a diversity of viands. He had a neighbour, much of his own sort, named Sandras, a tailor by trade, with whom he was on terms of such close friendship, that everything was common between them except the wife. Accordingly Bornet declared the design he had formed upon the servant-girl to his friend, who not only approved of it, but did what he could for its success, in hopes of having a finger in the pie. But the servant would not hear of such a thing, and finding herself persecuted on all sides, she complained to her mistress, and begged to be allowed to go home to her relations, as she could no longer endure her master's importunity. The mistress, who was very fond of her husband, and who even before this had been jealous of him, was very glad to have this opportunity of reproaching him, and showing that it was not without reason she had suspected him. With this view she induced the servant to finesse with her master, give him hopes by degrees, and finally promise to let him come to bed to her in her mistress's wardrobe. "The rest you may leave to me," she said.

"I will take care that you shall not be troubled at all, provided you let me know the night he is to come to you, and that you do not breathe a syllable of the matter to any one living."

The girl faithfully obeyed her mistress's instructions, and her master was so delighted that he hastened at once to impart this good news to his friend, who begged that, since he had been concerned in the bargain, he should also partake of the pleasure. This being agreed to, and the hour being come, the master went to bed, as he supposed, with the servant; but the mistress had taken her place, and received him, not as a wife, but as a bashful and frightened maid; and she played her part so well that he never suspected anything. I cannot tell you which of the two felt the greater satisfaction, he in the belief that he was cheating his wife, or she in the belief that she was cheating her husband.

After he had remained with her not so long as he wished, but as long as he could, for he showed symptoms of an old married man, he went out of doors to his friend, who was younger and more vigorous, and told him what a fine treat he had just had. "You know what you promised me," said the friend. "Well, be quick then," said the master, "for fear she gets up, or my wife wants her." The friend lost no time, but took the unoccupied place beside the supposed servant, who, thinking he was her husband, let him do whatever he liked without a word said on either side. He made a much longer business of it than the husband, greatly to the surprise of the wife, who was not accustomed to be so well regaled. However, she took it all patiently, comforting herself with the thought of what she would say to him in the morning, and how she would make game of him. The friend got out of bed towards daybreak, but not without taking the stirrup cup. During this ceremony he drew from her finger the ring with which her husband had wedded her, a thing which the women of that country preserve with great superstition, thinking highly of a woman who keeps it till death; on the other hand, one who has had the mischance to lose it, is looked upon as having given her faith to another than her husband.

When the friend had rejoined the husband, the latter asked him what he thought of his bedfellow. "Never was a better," replied the friend; "and if I had not been afraid of being surprised by daylight, I should not have come away from her so soon." That said, they went to bed, and slept as quietly as they could. In the morning, when they were dressing, the husband perceived on his friend's finger the ring, which looked very like that he had given his wife when he married her. He asked who had given him that ring, and was astounded to hear that he had taken it from the servant's finger. "Oh Lord! have I made a cuckold of myself, without my wife's knowing it?" cried the husband, knocking his head against the wall. The friend suggested for his consolation that possibly his wife might have given the ring overnight to the servant to keep.

Home goes the husband, and finds his wife looking handsomer and gayer than usual, delighted as she was to have hindered her servant from committing a sin, and to have convicted her husband without any more inconvenience to herself than having passed a night without sleeping. The husband, seeing her in such good spirits, said to himself, "She would not look so merry if she knew what has happened." Falling into chat with her upon indifferent matters, he took her hand, and saw that the ring she always wore was not on her finger. Aghast, and with a trembling voice, he asked her what she had done with it. This gave her the opportunity she was on the watch for to let loose upon him, and she seized it with avidity:

"O, you most abominable of men!" she said, "from whom do you suppose you took it. You thought you had it from the servant. You thought it was for her you did more than you ever did for me. The first time you came to bed to her, I thought you made as much of her as it was possible to do; but after you left the room and came again the second time, it seemed as though you were the very devil of incontinence. What infatuation has possessed you to praise me so much, you wretch? You have had me long enough, and never cared about me. Is it the beauty and plumpness of your servant that made the pleasure seem so sweet to you? No, base man, it is the fire of your own disorderly lust that makes you so blindly and madly in love with the servant, that in the furious fit you were in, I believe you would have taken a she-goat with a nightcap on for a fine girl. It is high time, husband, that you should mend your ways, and content yourself with me who am your wife, and, as you know, an honest woman, as much as you did when you mistook me for a vicious woman. My only object in the matter has been to withdraw you from vice, so that in our old days we may live in amity and repose of conscience; for if you choose to continue the life you have led hitherto, I would rather we should separate than that I should see you daily treading the path that leads to hell, and at the same time using up your body and your substance. But if you resolve to behave better, and to fear God and keep his commandments, I am willing to forget the past, as I trust God will forgive the ingratitude I am guilty of in not loving him as much as I ought."

If ever a man was utterly confounded and horrified, it was the poor husband. It was bad enough to think that he had forsaken his wife, who was fair, chaste, and virtuous, and overflowing with affection for him, for a woman who did not love him; but it was infinitely worse when he represented to himself that he had been so unlucky as to make her quit the path of virtue, in spite of herself and without knowing it, to share with another the pleasures which should have been his alone, and to have forged for himself the horns of perpetual mockery. Seeing, however, that his wife was already angry enough about his intended intrigue with the servant, he did not dare to tell her of the villanous trick he had played upon herself. He implored her pardon, promised to make amends for the past by the strictest propriety of conduct in future, and gave her back her ring, which he had taken from his friend, whom he begged not to say a word of what had happened. But as everything whispered in the ear is by-and-by proclaimed from the house-top, the adventure became public at last, and people called him a cuckold, without any regard for his wife's feelings.*

It strikes me, ladies, that if all those who have been guilty of similar infidelity to their wives were punished in the same way, Hircan and Saffredent would have great cause for fear.

"Why, Longarine?" said Saffredent. "Are Hircan and I the only married men in the company?"

"You are not the only married men," she replied, "but you are the only ones capable of playing such a trick."

* This tale is taken from the fabliau of *Le Meunier d'Alens*, and also occurs in the facetiæ of Poggio, in Sacchetti, and in the *Cent Nouvelles Nouvelles*.

"Who told you," returned Saffredent, "that we have sought to debauch our wives' servant-maids?"

"If those who are interested in the matter," she answered, "were to speak the truth, we should certainly hear of servant-maids dismissed before their time."

"This is pleasant, truly," observed Geburon; "you promised to make the company laugh, and instead of that you vex these gentlemen."

"It comes to the same thing," replied Longarine; "provided they do not draw their swords, their anger will not fail to make us laugh."

"If our wives were to listen to this lady," said Hircan, "there is not a married couple in the company but she would set at variance."

"Nay," said Longarine, "I know before whom I speak. Your wives are so prudent, and love you so much, that though you were to make them bear horns as big as those of a deer, they would believe, and try to make others believe, that they were chaplets of roses."

The whole company, including even the ladies concerned, laughed so heartily, that the conversation would have ended there if Dagoucin, who had not yet spoken, had not taken it into his head to say, "A man is surely very unreasonable who cannot content himself when he has the means. I have often known people who, thinking to better themselves, only made themselves much worse off because they could not be satisfied in reason. Such people deserve no pity; for, after all, inconstancy is unpardonable."

"But what would you do," inquired Simontault, "with those who have not found their true half? Would you call it inconstancy on their part to seek it wherever it might be found?"

"As it is impossible to know," replied Dagoucin, "where is that half so exactly like its counterpart that there is no difference between them, one should hold fast where love has once attached him, and change neither in heart nor will, happen what may. For if she you love is like you, and has but one will with you, it is yourself you will love and not her."

"You would fall into a false opinion, Dagoucin," said Hircan; "as though we ought to love our wives without being loved."

"When one loves a woman, Hircan," said Dagoucin, "only because she has beauty, charming manners, and fortune, and the end he proposes to himself is pleasure, honours, or riches, such a love is not of long duration; for when the principle that inspired it ceases, the love itself vanishes at once. I am then convinced that he who loves, and has no other end and desire than to love well, will die rather than cease to love."

"In good faith, Dagoucin," said Simontault, "I do not believe you have ever been really in love. Had you known what it is to be so, like other men, you would not now be picturing to us Plato's Republic, founded on fine phrases, and on little or no experience."

"You are mistaken," replied Dagoucin; "I have been in love; I am so still, and shall be so as long as I live. But I am so much afraid that the demonstration of my passion would do injustice to the perfection of my love, that I shrink from making it known to her by whom I would be loved in equal measure. I dare not even think how I love her, lest my eyes should betray the secret of my heart; for the more I conceal my flame, the more pleasure I feel in the consciousness that I love perfectly."

"Yet I suppose you would be very glad to be loved in return?" said Geburon.

"I own I should; but as nothing could diminish my love, though I love much and am not loved, so it could not be augmented, even were I loved as much I love."

"Take care, Dagoucin," said Parlamente, who disapproved of this fantastic sentiment; "I have known others who chose rather to die than to declare themselves."

"And they were happy, doubtless," returned Dagoucin.

"Yes," retorted Saffredent, "and worthy, moreover, of being classed with those innocents for whom the Church chants *Non loquendo, sed moriendo confessi sunt*. I have heard much of these languishing lovers, but I never yet saw one of them die for love. Since I myself have recovered, after much tribulation, I do not believe that any other man can ever die from that cause."

"Ah, Saffredent!" said Dagoucin, "how can you expect to be loved? I know many instances of lovers who have died from nothing else than the intensity of their passion."

"Since that is the case, tell us one of those stories, and let it be a good one," said Longarine.

"Yes," said he, "to confirm my doctrine by signs and miracles, I will tell you a story that happened three years ago."

NOVEL IX.

DEPLORABLE DEATH OF A LOVER IN CONSEQUENCE OF HIS KNOWING TOO LATE THAT HE WAS BELOVED BY HIS MISTRESS.

On the confines of Dauphiné and Provence there lived a gentleman who was much better endowed with the gifts of nature and education than with those of fortune. He was passionately enamoured of a demoiselle whose name I will not mention, on account of her relations, who are of good and great houses; but you may rely on the reality of the fact. Not being of as good family as she was, he durst not declare his passion; but though his inferior birth made him despair of ever being able to marry her, nevertheless the love he bore her was so pure and respectful that he would have died rather than ask of her anything which could compromise her honour. He loved her then only because he thought her perfectly lovable, and he loved her so long that at last she had some inkling of the fact. Seeing, then, that his love for her was founded on virtue only, she deemed herself fortunate in being loved by so upright a man; and she treated him with such affability that he, who aspired to nothing better than this, was transported with delight. But envy, the enemy of all quiet, could not suffer so innocent and so sweet an intercourse to continue. Some one told the girl's mother he was surprised the gentleman went so often to her house, that people saw it was her daughter's beauty that attracted him, and that they had often been seen together. The mother, who was thoroughly assured of the gentleman's probity, was greatly annoyed at finding that a bad interpretation was put upon his visits; but in the end, dreading scandal and malicious gossip, she begged he would for some time cease to frequent her house. The gentleman was the more mortified at this, as the proper and respectful manner in which he had always behaved towards the daughter had deserved very different treatment. However, to put an end to the gossip about him, he withdrew, and did not renew his visits until it had ceased.

Absence, meanwhile, by no means diminished his love; but one day, when he was paying a visit to his mistress, he heard talk of her being married to a gentleman not richer than himself, and whom consequently he thought no better entitled to have her. He began to take heart, and employed his friends to speak on his part, in the hope that if the lady was allowed to choose, she would prefer him to his rival; but as the latter was much the wealthier man, the young lady's mother and relations gave him the preference. The gentleman, who knew that his mistress was a loser as well as himself, was so grieved at being rejected, that, without any other malady, he began by degrees to waste away, and became so changed, that one would have said he had covered his handsome face with the mask of death, to which from hour to hour he was gaily hastening. Still he could not refrain from going as often as he could to see her whom he loved so well; but at last, his strength being worn out, he was compelled to keep his bed, but would never let his mistress know of it for fear of distressing her. So entirely did he give himself up to despair, that he neither ate, drank, slept, nor rested; and became so lean and wan that he was no longer to be recognised. Some one made his state known to the mother of the demoiselle, who was very kind-hearted, and had besides so much esteem for the gentleman, that if the relations had been of the same mind as herself and her daughter, the personal merit of the invalid would have been preferred to the alleged wealth of the other suitor; but the paternal relations would not hear of it. However, she went with her daughter to see the poor gentleman, whom she found more dead than alive. As he knew that his end was near, he had confessed and communicated, and never expected to see any more visitors; but on beholding again her who was his life and his resurrection, his strength returned, so that he at once sat up in the bed, and said, "What brings you hither, madam? How come you to visit a man who has already one foot in the grave, and of whose death you are the cause?"

"What!" exclaimed the lady. "Is it possible we should cause the death of a person we love so much? Tell me, I entreat, why you speak in this manner?"

"Madam, I concealed my love for your daughter as long as I could; my relations, however, who have asked her of you in marriage, have gone further than I wished, since I have thereby had the misfortune to lose hope. I say misfortune, not with reference to my individual satisfaction, but because I know that no one will ever treat her so well or love her so much as I would have done. Her loss of the best and most faithful friend and servant she has in the world touches me more sensibly than the loss of my life, which I wished to preserve for her alone. Nevertheless, since henceforth it can be of no use to her, I gain much in losing it."

The mother and daughter tried to comfort him. "Cheer up, my friend," said the mother; "I promise you, that if God restores you to health, my daughter shall never have any other husband than you. She is present, and I command her to make you the same promise."

The daughter, weeping sorely, assured him of what her mother said; but he, knowing that although God were to restore him to health, he should not have his mistress, and that it was only to cheer him that these hopes were held out, replied, "Had you spoken in this manner three months ago, I should have been the healthiest and happiest gentleman in France; but this succour comes so late, that I can neither believe it nor rest any hope upon it." Then, as they strove to overcome his incredulity, he continued, "Since you promise me a blessing which can never be mine even if you would grant it, I will ask you to confer on me one much less, which I have never ventured to demand of you." They both vowed that they would grant his request, and that he might declare it boldly. "I implore you," said he, "to put into my arms her whom you promise me for a wife, and to bid her embrace and kiss me."

The daughter, who was not accustomed to such caresses, was on the point of making objections: but her mother expressly commanded her to comply, seeing that there was no longer in him either the feeling or the power of a living man. After such a command, the daughter no longer hesitated, but going up to the bedside, " Cheer up, my friend," she said ; " cheer up, I conjure you." The poor dying creature, notwithstanding his extreme weakness, stretched out his emaciated arms, embraced with all his might her who was the cause of his death, and laying his cold pale lips to hers, clung there as long as he could.

" I have loved you," he said at last, " with a love so intense and so pure, that, marriage excepted, I have never desired any other favour of you than that which I now receive. But as God has not been pleased to unite us in marriage, I gladly surrender up my soul to him who is love and perfect charity, and who knows how much I have loved you, and how pure my desires have been, beseeching him, that since I hold the dear object of my desires within my arms, he will receive my soul in his." So saying, he clasped her again in his embrace with such vehemence, that his enfeebled heart, being unable to sustain the effort, was abandoned by all his spirits ; for joy so dilated them, that the seat of the soul gave way and fled to its Creator.

Though it was already some time since the poor gentleman had expired, and could not retain his hold, the love she had felt for him, and which she had always concealed, broke forth at this moment in such wise, that the mother and the servants had much difficulty in detaching the almost dead survivor from the corpse. The poor gentleman was honourably interred ; but the greatest triumph in his obsequies was the tears and cries of that poor demoiselle, who as openly displayed her feelings after his death as she had concealed them during his life, as if she would make amends for the wrong she had done him. And I have been told, that for all they gave her a husband to console her, she never afterwards knew real joy.*

* It is possible that this may be, as Margaret asserts, a true story of her own day, but it very closely resembles the history of the troubadour Geoffroi Rudel of Blaye, who lived in the latter part of the twelfth century. Merely upon hearsay of the moral and personal perfections of the Countess of Tripoli, he fell so desperately in love with her that he pined away, and embarked in an advanced stage of illness to go and see her. When the vessel reached the port of Tripoli he was too weak to quit it. Moved by so extraordinary a display of love, the countess

Does it not strike you, gentlemen, who refused to believe me, that this example must force you to confess that intense love, too much concealed and too little known, brings people to the grave? There is not one of you but knows the relations on both sides; therefore you cannot question the fact. But this is one of those things which no one believes until he has experienced it.

"Well," said Hircan, who saw that the ladies were weeping, "a greater fool I never heard of. Now, in good faith, is it reasonable that we should die for women who are made only for us, and that we should be afraid of asking of them what God commands them to give us? I do not speak for myself, or for others who are married; for as for me, I have as much as I want in that way, or more; but I say it for those who stand in need. They are, to my thinking, great blockheads to fear those who ought to fear them. Don't you see that this girl repented of her imprudence? Since she embraced the dead man—a thing repugnant to nature—rely upon it she would still better have embraced the living man if he had been as bold as he was pitiable on his deathbed."

"By the very conduct for which you upbraid him," said Oisille, "he showed that he loved honestly, and for that he deserves eternal praise; for chastity in an enamoured heart is a thing more divine than human."

"Madam," replied Saffredent, "to confirm what Hircan has just said, I beg you to believe that fortune favours those who are bold, and that no man who is loved by a lady fails to obtain from her at last what he demands, either in whole or in part, provided he knows how to set about it sagely and amorously; but ignorance and timidity make men lose many a good fortune. What is singular is, that they attribute the loss of them to the virtue of their mistress, which they have never put to the least proof. Be assured, madam, that no fortress was ever well attacked but it was taken at last."

"I am shocked at you two," said Parlamente, "that you

---

visited him on board, took his hand, and spoke graciously and cheeringly to him. Geoffroi could hardly falter out his thanks, and overcome by emotion, instantly expired.

dare to hold such language. Those whom you have loved have little reason to be obliged to you; or else you have employed your address upon such easy conquests, that you have concluded all others are like them."

"For my part, madam," said Saffredent, "I have the misfortune to have nothing to boast of; but this I attribute much less to the virtue of the ladies than to the fault I have committed in not having conducted my enterprises with sufficient sagacity and prudence. In support of my opinion, I shall cite no other authority than that of the old woman in the 'Romance of the Rose,' who says: 'Without question, fair sir, we are all made for each other; every she for every he, and every he for every she.' In short, I am persuaded that if a woman is once in love, her lover will compass his end unless he be a booby."

"Now if I should name a lady," returned Parlamente, "who loved well, was strongly solicited, pressed, and importuned, and yet remained a virtuous woman, victorious over her love and her lover, would you own that this fact, which is truth itself, was possible?"

"Why, yes," replied Saffredent.

"Then you are very incredulous if you do not believe the example adduced by Dagoucin."

"As I have given you," said Dagoucin, "an authentic instance of virtuous love on the part of a gentleman which continued to his last gasp, if you, madam, know any story that is to the honour of some lady, I beg you will be good enough to finish the day by relating it. Never mind the length; for there is time enough still to say many good things."

"Since I am to finish the day," said Parlamente, "I will not make you a long preamble, my story being so good, so beautiful, and so true, that I long to put you in possession of it. I have not been an eye-witness to the facts; but I have them from an intimate friend of the hero, who related them to me on condition that if I repeated them I should conceal the names of the persons. Everything, then, which I am about to tell you is true, except the names, the places, and the country.

NOVEL X.

THE LOVES OF AMADOUR AND FLORIDA, WHEREIN ARE SEEN SEVERAL STRATAGEMS AND DISSIMULATIONS, AND THE EXEMPLARY CHASTITY OF FLORIDA.

There was in the county of Aranda, in Aragon, a lady who, while still quite young, was left a widow by Count Aranda, with one son and one daughter, named Florida. She spared no pains to bring up her children according to their quality in virtue and good breeding, so that her house was considered to be one of the most honourable in all the Spains. She often went to Toledo, where the King of Spain then resided; and when she came to Saragossa, which was not far from her own house, she used to remain a long time at the queen's court, where she was as much esteemed as any lady could be. Going one day, according to her custom, to pay her court to the king, who was then in Saragossa, she passed through a village belonging to the Viceroy of Catalonia, who did not quit the frontiers of Perpignan, on account of the wars between the Kings of France and Spain. But as peace was then made, the viceroy, accompanied by several officers, had come to pay his devoirs to the king. The viceroy having been apprised that the countess was to pass through his domains, went to meet her, as well by reason of the old friendship he bore her, as to do her honour as the king's kinswoman. He was accompanied by several gentlemen of merit, who had acquired so much glory and reputation during the wars that every one thought it a good fortune to enjoy their society. There was one among them named Amadour, who, notwithstanding his youth (he was not more than eighteen or nineteen), had such an air of self-possession, and a judgment so ripe, that one would have chosen him among a thousand as a fit man to govern a state. It is true that besides good sense he had so engaging a mien, and graces so vivid and natural, that one never tired of gazing upon him. His conversation so well corresponded with all this, that it was hard to say whether nature had been more bountiful in regard to corporeal or to mental endowments. But what gained him most esteem was his great daring, far exceeding what was common with persons of his age. He had on so many occasions shown what he was capable of, that not only the Spains, but France and Italy also, highly esteemed his virtues, for he had never spared himself in any of the wars in which he had been engaged. When his country was at peace he went in search of war among foreigners, and won the respect and love of friends and enemies.

This gentleman was among those who accompanied his captain to the domain at which the countess had arrived. He could not behold with indifference the beauty and the charms of her daughter, who was then but twelve years old. He had never, he thought, seen a being so beautiful and of such high breeding, and he believed that if he could have her good grace he should be happier than if he possessed all the wealth and all the pleasures he could receive from another. After having long regarded her, he finally resolved to love her, in spite of all the insurmountable obstacles to success which reason presented to his view, whether on account of disparity of birth, or as regarded the extreme youth of the beautiful girl, who was not yet of an age to listen to tender speeches. Against all these obstacles he set a resolute hope, and promised himself that time and patience would bring all his toils to a happy end. To remedy the greatest difficulty, which consisted in the remoteness of his residence and the few opportunities he had of seeing Florida, he resolved to marry, contrary to what he had resolved in Barcelona and Perpignan, where he was in such favour with the ladies that they hardly refused him anything. He had lived so long on those frontiers during the war, that he had the air of a Catalan rather than of a Castilian, though he was born at Toledo, of a rich and distinguished family. Being a younger son, he had not much patrimony; but love and fortune seeing him ill provided by his parents, resolved to make him a *chef-d'œuvre*, and gave him by means of his valour what the laws of the country refused him. He was thoroughly versed in the art of war, and princes and lords esteemed him so highly, that he oftener refused their good offices than took the trouble to solicit them.

The Countess of Aranda arrived then in Saragossa, and was extremely well received by the king and the whole court. The Governor of Catalonia paid her frequent visits, in which Amadour failed not to accompany him, for the sole pleasure of seeing Florida, for he, in order to make himself known in such good company, attached himself to the daughter of an old knight, his neighbour. Her name was Aventurada. She had been brought up from childhood with Florida, and knew all the secrets of her heart. Whether it was that Amadour found her to his taste, or that her dowry of three thousand ducats a year tempted him, he made her an offer of marriage. She listened to him with pleasure; but as he was poor, and the old knight was rich, she was afraid he would never consent to the marriage, except at the solicitation of the Countess of Aranda. She addressed herself, therefore, to Florida, and said, "I believe, madam, that this Castilian gentleman, who as you are aware often speaks to me here, intends to seek me in marriage. You know what sort of man my father is, and you must be sure he will never give his consent unless the countess and you have the goodness to press him strongly." Florida, who loved the damsel like herself, assured her she would make the business her own; whereupon Aventurada presented Amadour to her, who on kissing her hand had like to faint for joy. Though he was considered one of the men who spoke best in all the Spains, he could not find a tongue in presence of Florida. She was greatly surprised at this, for though she was but twelve years old, she nevertheless well remembered to have heard that there was not in Spain a man who could deliver what he had to say more fluently, or with a better grace. Seeing then that he uttered not a word, she broke silence.

"You are so well known by reputation all over the Spains," she said, "that it would be surprising, Señor Amadour, if you were unknown here; and all who know you desire to have an opportunity to serve you. So if I can be of use to you in any way, I beg you will employ me." Amadour, who was gazing on Florida's charms, was so rapt and transported, that he could hardly say grammercy. Though Florida was surprised at his silence, she attributed it to some caprice rather than to its true cause, and retired without saying more. "Do not be surprised," said Amadour to her he wished to marry, "if I was tongue-tied in presence of the Lady Florida. She speaks so discreetly, and so many virtues are latent under her great youth, that admiration made me dumb. As you know her secrets, I beg you will tell me, Aventurada, how is it possible that she does not possess the hearts of all the gentlemen of this court, for those who shall know her and love her not must be stones or brutes." Aventurada, who already loved Amadour above all men, and could conceal nothing from him, told him that Florida was loved by everybody; but that, in accordance with the custom of the country, she spoke to few; and that as yet she was aware of only two persons who made much show of love for Florida, and those were two young Spanish princes, who desired to marry her. One was son of the Fortunate Infante, and the other was the young Duke of Cardona.

"Tell me, pray," said Amadour, "which of the two do you think she likes best?"

"She is so good and virtuous, that all she can be prevailed on to say is, that she has no choice but as her mother pleases. As far, however, as we can judge, she likes the son of the Fortunate Infante better than the young Duke of Cardona. I believe you to be a man of such good sense, that you may, if you like, come to a right surmise upon the matter at once. The son of the Fortunate Infante was brought up at this court, and is the handsomest and most accomplished young prince in Europe. If the question were to be decided by the votes of us maidens, this match would take place, in order that the most charming couple in all Spain might be united. You must know, that although they are both very young, she being but twelve and he fifteen, they have loved each other these three years. If you wish to have her good grace, I advise you to become his friend and servant."

Amadour was very glad to hear that Florida loved something, for he hoped, with the help of time, to become, not her husband, but her lover; for her virtue caused him no uneasiness; his only fear being lest she should not love at all. He had little difficulty in introducing himself to the son of the Fortunate Infante, and still less in gaining his good-will, for he was expert in all the exercises which the young prince was fond of. He was, above all, a good horseman, skilled in feats of arms, and in all sorts of exercises befitting a young man. As war was then beginning again in Languedoc, Amadour was obliged to return with the governor; but it was not without keen regret, for there was no prospect of his returning to the place where he could see Florida. Before his departure he spoke to his brother, who was majordomo to the Queen of Spain, told him the good match he had in the Countess of Aranda's house in the Lady

Aventurada, and begged him to do his best during his
absence to further his marriage, and to procure on his
behalf the influence of the king, the queen, and all his
friends. The brother, who loved Amadour not only as a brother but for his great worth, promised to do all he could,
and bestirred himself so well, that Aventurada's miserly old
father forgot his avarice, and suffered himself to be moved
by Amadour's virtues as they were represented to him by
the Countess of Aranda, the beautiful Florida, and the
young Count of Aranda, who was beginning, as he grew up,
to love people of merit. After the marriage had been agreed
on between the relations, the major-domo made his brother
return to Spain under favour of a truce then pending between
the two kings. During this truce the King of Spain withdrew to Madrid, to avoid the bad air which was in several
places, and at the request of the Countess of Aranda gave his
sanction to the marriage of the heiress-Duchess of Medinaceli
with the little Count of Aranda. The wedding was celebrated at the palace of Madrid. Amadour was present, and
turned the occasion to such account, that he married her
whom he had inspired with more love than he felt for her,
and whom he made his wife only that he might have a plausible pretext for frequenting the place where his mind incessantly dwelt.

After his marriage he became so bold and so familiar in
the family of the Countess of Aranda, that no more distrust
was entertained of him than if he had been a woman.
Though he was then but twenty-two years old, he was so
prudent that the countess communicated all her affairs to
him, and commanded her daughter and her son to converse
with him and follow all his advice. Having gained this
capital point, he conducted himself so discreetly and with
such address, that even she whom he loved never suspected
it. As she was very fond of Amadour's wife, she had such
confidence in the husband that she concealed nothing from
him, and even declared to him all the love she felt for the
son of the Fortunate Infante; and Amadour, whose views
were all directed to gaining her entirely, talked to her incessantly of the young prince; for he cared not what was the
subject on which he spoke to her provided he could hold
her long in conversation.

He had hardly been a month married when he was obliged

to go to the wars again, and it was more than two years
before he could return to his wife, who all the while continued to reside where she had been brought up. He wrote
frequently to her in the interval; but the chief part of his
letters consisted of compliments to Florida, who on her
part failed not to return them, and often even wrote with
her own hand some pretty phrase in Aventurada's letters.
This was quite enough to induce the husband to write frequently to his wife; yet in all this Florida knew nothing but
that she loved him like a brother. Amadour went and came
several times, and during five years he saw Florida not more
than two months altogether. Yet, in spite of distance and
long absence, his love not only remained in full force, but
even grew stronger.

At last Amadour, coming to see his wife, found the
countess far away from the court. The king had gone into
Andalusia, and had taken with him the young Count of
Aranda, who was already beginning to bear arms, and the
countess had retired to a country-house of hers on the fron-
tier of Aragon and Navarre. She was very glad of the
arrival of Amadour, whom she had not seen for nearly three
years. He was welcomed by everybody, and the countess
commanded that he should be treated as her own son.
When he was with her, she consulted him on all the affairs
of her house, and did just as he advised. In fact, his influence in the family was unbounded; and so strong was the
belief in his discernment, that he was trusted on all occasions
as though he had been a saint or an angel. As for Florida, who loved Aventurada, and had no suspicion of her
husband's intentions, she testified her affection for him without reserve. Her heart being free from passion, she felt
much pleasure in his society, but she felt nothing more. He,
on the other hand, found it a very hard task to evade the
penetration of those who knew by experience the difference
between the looks of a man who loves and of one who does
not love; for when Florida talked familiarly with him in her
frank simplicity, the hidden fire in his heart blazed up so
violently, that he could not help feeling it in his face, and
letting some sparks from it escape from his eyes.

To baffle observation, therefore, he entered into an intrigue
with a lady named Paulina, who was considered in her time
so beautiful, that few men saw her and escaped her fascina-

tious. Paulina being aware how Amadour had made love in Barcelona and Perpignan, and won the hearts of the handsomest ladies in the country, especially that of a certain Countess of Palamos, who was reputed the finest woman in all Spain, told him one day that she pitied him for having, after so many good fortunes, married a wife so ugly as his own. Amadour, who well knew that she had a mind to supply his wants, talked to her in the most engaging terms he could use, hoping to conceal a truth from her by making her believe a falsehood. As she had experience in love she did not content herself with words, and plainly perceiving that Amadour's heart was not her own, she made no doubt that he wanted to use her as a stalking-horse. With this suspicion in her mind, she observed him so narrowly, that not a single glance of his eyes escaped her; but he managed, though with the utmost difficulty, to regulate them so well, that she could never get beyond conjectures. Florida, who had no notion of the nature of Amadour's feelings towards her, used to speak to him so familiarly before Paulina, that he could hardly prevent his eyes from following the movements of his heart. To prevent bad consequences, one day, as Florida and he were talking together at a window, he said to her, "My dear, I beseech you to advise me which of the two is better, to speak or to die?"

"I shall always advise my friends to speak," she replied without hesitation; "for there are few words which cannot be remedied; but from death there is no return."

"You promise me, then, that not only you will not be angry at what I want to tell you, but even that you will not give way to surprise until I have laid my whole mind open to you?"

"Say what you please," replied Florida, "for if you surprise me there is no one who can reassure me."

"Two reasons, madam, have hindered me hitherto from declaring the strong passion I feel for you: one is, that I wished to make it known to you by long services, and the other, that I was afraid you would regard it as a great vanity that a simple gentleman like myself should raise his desires so high Even though my birth were as illustrious as your own, a heart so true as yours would take it ill that any other than he on whom you have bestowed it, the son of the Fortunate Infante, should talk to you of love. But, madam, as in war necessity often compels the belligerent to destroy his own property, and ruin his standing crops that the enemy may not profit by them, so I venture to forestal the fruit which I hoped to gather in time, lest your enemies and mine profit by our loss. Know, madam, that from the first moment I had the honour of seeing you, I so wholly consecrated myself to your service, though you were very young, that I have forgotten nothing whereby I could hope to acquire your good grace. It was to that end alone that I married her whom I thought you loved best; and knowing the love you bore to the son of the Fortunate Infante, I took pains to serve him and be about him; in short, whatever I thought could please you, I have tried with all my might to do. You see that I have had the good fortune to win the esteem of the countess your mother, of the count your brother, and of all those whom you love, and that I am regarded here not as a servant, but as a son of the family. All the pains I have taken for five years have had no other object than to procure me the happiness of passing my whole life with you. I crave no favour or pleasure of you which is not consistent with virtue. I know that I cannot wed you, and if I could I would not do so to the prejudice of the love you bear to him whom I would gladly see as your husband. To love you with a criminal love, like those who presume to think that a lady's dishonour should be the recompense of their long services, is a thought I am so far from entertaining, that I would rather see you dead than know that you were less worthy of love, and that your virtue should suffer the least blemish for sake of any pleasure whatever to myself. I ask but one thing of you in recompense for my long services, and that is, that you will deign to become a mistress so loyal as never to remove me from your good grace, but let me continue on my present footing, and trust in me more than in any one besides. Furthermore, madam, do me the honour to be well assured that, be the matter what it may, should you have need of the life of a gentleman, you may count on mine, which I would sacrifice for you right gladly. I beseech you to believe, likewise, madam, that whatever I shall do that is honourable and virtuous shall be done for love of you. If, for sake of ladies inferior to you, I have done things which have been thought well of, what shall I not do for a mistress like you? Things which I found difficult or impossible will seem easy to me. But if you will not permit me to be wholly devoted to you, my resolution is to forsake the career of arms, and renounce the virtue which shall not have helped me at need. I entreat you, then, madam, to grant me the just grace which I ask, and you cannot refuse in conscience and with honour."

Florida changed colour at a speech so novel to her. Surprise made her cast down her eyes; nevertheless, her good sense prompted her to reply, " Does it need so long an harangue, Amadour, to ask of me what you have already? I fear so much, that under your seemingly courteous and modest language there is some lurking mischief to deceive my unpractised youth, that I know not how to reply to you. Were I to reject the virtuous friendship you offer me, I should do contrary to what I have done hitherto; for you are the person in whom I have reposed most confidence. My conscience and my honour do not revolt either against your request, or against the love I bear to the son of the Fortunate Infante, since it rests on marriage, to which you do not aspire. There is nothing, then, to hinder me from replying in accordance with your desires, except a fear I have in my heart, proceeding from the little occasion you have for speaking to me as you do; for if you already have what you ask, how comes it that you ask for it again with so much eagerness?"

"You speak very prudently, madam," replied Amadour, who had his answer ready, "and you do me so much honour and so much justice in putting the confidence in me you say, that if I were not content with such a blessing, I were unworthy of all others. But consider, madam, that he who wants to build a durable edifice must begin by laying a good and solid foundation. As I desire to remain for ever in your service, I think not only of the means of being near you, but also of hindering my attachment to you from being perceived. Though this attachment, madam, is quite pure, yet those who do not know the hearts of lovers often judge ill of them, and this gives occasion for scandal as much as if their conjectures were well founded. What makes me speak of this is, that Paulina, who knows well that I cannot love her, suspects me so much, that wherever I am she has her eyes continually upon me. When you speak to me before her with so much kindness, I am so much afraid of making some gesture on which she may rest a surmise, that I fall into the very thing I wish to avoid. I am, therefore, constrained, madam, to request you will not for the future address me so suddenly before her, or before those whom you know to be as malicious as she is, for I would rather die than that any creature living should perceive it. If your honour was less dear to me, I should not have been in haste to say this to you, since I am so happy in the love and the confidence you manifest towards me, that I desire nothing more than their continuance."

Florida was so gratified that she could hardly contain herself, and thenceforth she felt in her heart emotions that were new to her. "Virtue and good breeding reply for me," she said, "and grant you what you request."

That Amadour was transported with joy will not be doubted by any who love. Florida followed his advice better than he could have wished; for as she was timid not only in presence of Paulina, but everywhere else too, she no longer sought his society as she had been used to do. She even disapproved of his intercourse with Paulina, who seemed to her so handsome that she could not believe he did not love her. Florida vented her grief with Aventurada, who was beginning to be very jealous of her husband and Paulina. She poured out her lamentations to Florida, who being sick of the same distemper, consoled her as well as she could.

Amadour, soon perceiving the change in Florida's conduct, believed not only that she was reserved, as he had advised her to be, but even that she had conceived unfavourable sentiments with regard to him. One day, as he was escorting her home from a convent where she had heard vespers, "What sort of countenance do you show me, madam?" he said.

"Such as I believe you wish me to show," she replied.

Suspecting the truth then, he continued, "I have taken such means, madam, that Paulina no longer suspects you."

"You could not do better for yourself and for me," she replied; "for while doing yourself pleasure, you do me honour."

Amadour, inferring from this that she believed he took pleasure in talking with Paulina, was so incensed, that he could not help saying in anger, "You begin betimes, madam, to make me suffer. I am more to be pitied than blamed, and the most cruel mortification I have ever endured in my life, is the painful necessity I am under of speaking to a woman I do not love. Since you put a bad interpretation on what I have done for your service, I will never speak more to Paulina, happen what may. To hide my sorrow as I have hidden my joy, I will retire to some place in the neighbourhood, and wait there until your caprice has passed away. But I hope I shall receive news from my captain, and be obliged to return to the army, where I will remain so long as will prove to you, I hope, that nothing keeps me here but you."

So saying, he went away without awaiting her reply, which caused Florida an anxiety it is impossible to express. Thus love began to make its strength felt through its opposite. Finding on reflection that she had been wrong, Florida wrote to Amadour begging him to return, which he did after his anger had somewhat subsided. I cannot tell you in detail what they said to each other to destroy these prejudices of jealousy; but the result was, that he justified himself so well that she promised not only that she would never believe he loved Paulina, but that she would remain convinced that it was a most cruel martyrdom for him to speak to her, or any other woman, except only with a view to render her service.

After love had dissipated this cloud, and when the lovers were beginning to take more pleasure than ever in each other's society, news came that the King of Spain was sending his whole army to Salces. Amadour, whose custom it was to be among the first to join the royal standards, would not miss this new opportunity of acquiring glory; but it must be owned that he set out with unwonted regret, as well on account of the pleasure he lost, as because he was afraid of finding a change on his return. He reflected that Florida was now fifteen, that many princes and great lords were seeking her hand, and that if she married during his absence he would have no more opportunity of seeing her, unless the Countess of Aranda should give her Aventurada for her companion. Accordingly, he managed so adroitly, that the countess and Florida both promised him that wherever the latter resided after her marriage, his wife should never leave her; and as there was a talk then of her being married in Portugal, it was resolved that Aventurada should accompany her to that country. Upon this assurance Amadour took his departure, not without extreme regret, and left his wife with the countess.

Florida, left lonely by her lover's departure, lived in such a manner as she hoped would gain for her the reputation of the most perfect virtue, and make the whole world confess that she merited such a servant as Amadour. As for him, on arriving at Barcelona, he was cordially welcomed by the ladies; but they found him so changed, that they never could have believed that marriage could have such an effect upon a man. In fact, he was no longer the same; he was even vexed at the sight of what he formerly desired; and the Countess of Palamos, of whom he had been so enamoured, could never find means to make him even visit her. Being impatient to reach the spot where honour was to be gained, he made as short a stay as possible in Barcelona. He was no sooner arrived at Salces than war broke out with great fury between the two kings. I will not enter into details of the campaign, nor enumerate the heroic actions performed in it by Amadour, for then, instead of telling a tale, I should have to compose a great book. It is enough to say that his renown overtopped that of all his comrades in arms. The Duke of Nagyeres, who commanded two thousand men, arrived at Perpignan, and took Amadour for his lieutenant. He did his duty so well with his little corps, that in every skirmish no other cry was heard than that of Nagyeres!

Now the King of Tunis, who had long been at war with the Spaniards, learning that Spain and France were waging mutual hostilities about Perpignan and Narbonne, thought it a good opportunity to harass the King of Spain, and sent a great number of ships to pillage and destroy every ill-guarded point they found on the coasts of Spain. The people of Barcelona, seeing so many strange sail pass by, sent word to the viceroy, who was then at Salces, and who immediately despatched the Duke of Nagyeres to Palamos. The barbarians, finding the place so well defended, made a feint of sheering off; but they returned in the night, and landed so many men that the Duke of Nagyeres, who had let himself be surprised, was taken prisoner. Amadour, who was very vigilant, hearing the noise, assembled instantly as many of his men as he could, and made so stout a resistance that the

F

enemy, however superior in numbers, were for a long time held at bay. But at last, learning that the Duke of Nagyeres was a prisoner, and that the Turks were resolved to burn Palamos and the house in which he withstood them, he thought it better to surrender than to cause the loss of those who had followed him. Besides, by paying for his ransom, he expected to see Florida again. He surrendered then to a Turk named Dorlin, Viceroy of Tunis, who presented him to his master, in whose service he remained nearly two years, honoured and well treated, but still better guarded; for, having him in their hands, the Turks thought they had the Achilles of all the Spains.

The news of this event having reached Spain, the relations of the Duke of Nagyeres were greatly affected at his disaster; but those who had the glory of the country at heart thought the loss of Amadour still more grievous. It became known to the Countess of Aranda, in whose house poor Aventurada lay dangerously ill. The countess, who had great misgivings as to the tender feelings which Amadour entertained for her daughter, but concealed and tried to suppress them, in consideration of the virtues which she recognised in him, called her daughter aside to communicate this painful intelligence to her. Florida, who could dissemble well, said it was a great loss for their whole house, and that, above all, she pitied his poor wife, who, to make the matter worse, was on her sick bed; but seeing that her mother wept much, she let fall a few tears to keep her company, for fear that the feint should be discovered by being overdone. The countess often talked with her again on the subject, but could never draw from her any indication on which she could form a definite conclusion. I will say nothing of the pilgrimages, prayers, orisons, and fasts which Florida regularly performed for Amadour's safety. Immediately on his reaching Tunis, he sent an express to Florida to acquaint her that he was in good health and full of hope that he should see her again, which was a great consolation to her. In return, she corresponded with him so diligently, that Amadour had not leisure to grow impatient.

At this period the countess received orders to repair to Saragossa, where the king was. The young Duke of Cardona was there, and bestirred himself so effectually with the king and the queen, that they begged the countess to conclude the marriage between him and Florida. The countess, who neither could nor would refuse their majesties anything, consented to it the more willingly, as she believed that her daughter would at those years have no other will than hers. All being settled, she told her daughter she had chosen for her the match she thought would be most advantageous; and Florida submitted, seeing no room was left her for deliberation, the business being already settled. To make matters worse, she heard that the Fortunate Infante was at the point of death. She never suffered the least evidence of her mortification to escape in presence of her mother or any one else; and so strongly did she constrain her feelings, that instead of shedding tears she was seized with a bleeding at the nose so copious as to endanger her life. By way of re-establishing her health, she married the man she would willingly have exchanged for death. After the marriage she went with her husband to the duchy of Cardona, and took with her Aventurada, whom she acquainted, in confidence, with her mother's harshness towards her, and her regret for the loss of the Fortunate Infante; but with regard to Amadour, she spoke of him only to console his wife. Resolutely setting God and honour before her eyes, she so well concealed her sorrows, that none of those who were most intimate with her ever perceived that she disliked her husband. For a long time did she continue this life, which was hardly better than death. She failed not to make all known to Amadour, who, knowing the greatness of her heart, and how she had loved the Fortunate Infante, thought it impossible she could live long, and mourned for her as one whom he looked upon as worse than dead. This affliction augmented that under which he already laboured. Gladly would he have been a slave all his life, so Florida had found a husband after her own heart; for the thought of his mistress's sorrows made him forget his own. Meanwhile he learned from a friend he had made at the court of Tunis, that the king was resolved to give him his choice, either to renounce his faith or be impaled, for he wished to keep him in his service if he could make a good Turk of him. To prevent this, Amadour prevailed upon his master to let him go upor his parole without speaking to the king; and his ransom was set so high that the Turk calculated that a man who had so little wealth could never raise the amount.

On his return to the court of Spain he made but a short stay there, and went away to seek his ransom in the purses of his friends. He went straight to Barcelona, whither the young Duke of Cardona, his mother, and Florida, were gone on some business. Aventurada was no sooner apprised of her husband's return, than she imparted the news to Florida, who rejoiced at it as if for her sake. But for fear lest the joy of again beholding Amadour should produce a change in her countenance which might be noticed by those who did not know her, and therefore would misjudge her, she placed herself at a window, in order to catch sight of him at a distance, and the moment she perceived him, running down a staircase so dark that it was impossible to discern if she changed colour, she embraced him, took him up to her chamber, and then presented him to her mother-in-law, who had never seen him. He had not been there two days before he was as great a favourite as he had been in the house of the Countess of Aranda. I will say nothing of the conversations between Florida and Amadour, nor all she told him of the afflictions she had incurred during his absence. After many tears wrung from her eyes by her grief at having married contrary to her inclination, and at having lost him whom she loved so passionately, and whom she never hoped to see again, she resolved to console herself with the love and confidence she had in Amadour. However, she durst not avow her intentions; but Amadour, who suspected them, lost neither time nor opportunity to make known to her how much he loved her.

Just when Florida could hardly refrain from advancing Amadour from the condition of an expectant to that of a favoured lover, a distressing and very inopportune accident occurred. The king summoned Amadour to the court upon an affair of importance. His wife was so shocked by this news that she fainted, and falling down a flight of stairs, hurt herself so much that she never recovered. Florida, whom her death bereaved of all her consolation, was as much afflicted as one who had lost all her good friends and relations. Amadour was inconsolable, for, on the one hand, he lost one of the best of wives, and, on the other hand, the means of being again with Florida; and so overwhelming was his grief that he was near dying suddenly. The old Duchess of Cardona was constantly at his bedside, repeating the arguments of the philosophers to console him; but it was of no avail, for if his grief for the dead was great, his love for the living made him a martyr.

Amadour's wife being interred, and the king's orders being pressing, he could find no pretext to prolong his stay; which so augmented his anguish that he had like to lose his senses. Florida, who, thinking to console him, was his very desolation, passed a whole afternoon in conversing with him in the most gracious manner, thinking to comfort him by the assurance that she would always find means to see him, oftener than he supposed. As he was to depart on the following day, and was so weak that he could not quit his bed, he entreated her to come again in the evening to see him, after every one else had left him. She promised to do so, not knowing that excessive love knows no restraint of reason; whilst he, despairing for the future of seeing her whom he had so long loved, and of whom he had never had but what you have seen, was so racked by his love and his despair, that he resolved to play, as it were, at double or quits—that is to say, to win or lose all, and to pay himself in one hour for what he thought he had merited. He had his bed hung with such good curtains that he could not be seen by persons in the room, and he complained more than usual, so that everybody in the house thought he had not four-and-twenty hours to live.

After every one else had visited him in the evening, Florida came at the request of her husband himself to see him, her mind made up to console him by a declaration of her affection, and to tell him, without disguise or reserve, that she was resolved to love him as much as honour could allow her. Seated on a chair beside the head of his bed, she began her consolations by weeping with him; seeing which, Amadour fancied that in this great agitation of her mind he could the more easily accomplish his purpose, and he sat up in his bed. Florida, thinking he was too weak to do this, offered to prevent him. "Must I lose you for ever?" he exclaimed, on his knees; and saying this he let himself fall into her arms like a man whose strength suddenly failed him. Poor Florida embraced and supported him a long while, doing her best to comfort him; but the remedy she applied to assuage his pain increased it greatly. Still counterfeiting the appearance of one half dead, and saying not a word, he set himself in quest of what the honour of ladies prohibits. Florida, seeing his bad intention, but unable to believe it after the laudable language he had always addressed to her, asked him what he meant. Amadour, fearing to provoke a reply which he knew could not be other than chaste and virtuous, went straight to his mark without saying a word. Florida's surprise was extreme, and choosing rather to believe that his brain was turned than that he had a deliberate design upon her virtue, she called aloud to a gentleman who she knew was in the room; whereupon Amadour, in an agony of despair, threw himself back on his bed so suddenly that the gentleman thought he was dead. Florida, who had risen from her chair, sent the gentleman to fetch some vinegar, and then said to Amadour, "Are you mad, Amadour? What is this you have thought of doing?"

"Do such long services as mine merit such cruelty?" replied Amadour, who had lost all reason in the violence of his love.

"And where is that honour you have so often preached to me?" she retorted.

"Ah, madam," said he, "it is impossible to love your honour more than I have done. As long as you were unmarried I so well mastered my passion that you never were aware of it; but now that you are married and your honour is shielded, what wrong do I do you in asking of you what belongs to me? For have I not won you by the force of my love? The first who had your heart has so little coveted your body that he deserved to lose both. He who possesses your body is unworthy to have your heart, and consequently your body even does not belong to him. But I have taken such pains for your sake during the last five or six years, that you cannot but be aware, madam, that to me alone belong your body and your heart, for which I have forgotten my own. If you think to excuse yourself on the ground of conscience, doubt not that when love forces the body and the heart, sin is never imputed. Those even who are so infuriated as to kill themselves, cannot sin; for passion leaves no room for reason. And if the passion of love is the most intolerable of all others, and that which most blinds all the senses, what sin would you attribute to him who lets himself be led by an invincible power? I am constrained to go away without the hope of ever seeing you again. But if I had from you before my departure that assurance which my love deserves, I should be strong enough patiently to endure the pains of that long absence. If, however, you will not grant me what I ask, you will soon learn that your rigour has caused me to perish miserably."

Florida, equally astonished and grieved at hearing such language from a man whom till then she had never distrusted, replied, in tears, "Is this, Amadour, the end of all the virtuous speeches you made me during my youth? Is this the honour and the conscience you have often counselled me to prize more than my own life? Have you forgotten the good examples you have given me of virtuous ladies who have withstood criminal love, and the scorn you have always expressed for the wanton? I cannot believe, Amadour, that you are so different from yourself that God, your conscience and my honour, are dead in you. But if what you say is true, I thank God for having prevented the misfortune into which I had nearly fallen, by causing your tongue to make known to me the bottom of your heart, which I have never fathomed till now. After losing the son of the Fortunate Infante, not only by my marriage, but also because I know he loves another, and seeing myself wedded to a man I cannot love in spite of all my efforts, I had resolved to love you with my whole heart, basing my affection on that virtue which I thought I discerned in you, and which I think I have attained through your means, which is to love my honour and my conscience more than my very life. With these laudable views I had come, Amadour, to lay a good foundation for the future; but you have convinced me that I should have built on a drifting sand, or rather on loathsome mud; and though a great part of the house was already built, in which I hoped perpetually to abide, you have knocked it all down at a blow. So never more expect anything of me; and never think of speaking to me wherever I may be, either with your tongue or your eyes and be assured that my sentiments will never change. I say this to you with extreme regret. If I had plighted you a perfect friendship, I am sure my heart could not have borne this rupture and lived; though, indeed, the amazement into which I am cast at having been deceived is so intense and poignant, that if it does not cut short my life, it will at least render it very unhappy. I have no more to say but to bid you an eternal farewell."

I will not attempt to describe the anguish of Amadour at hearing these words. It would be impossible not only to depict it but even to imagine it, except for those who have been in a similar position. As Florida turned to depart, he caught her by the arm, well knowing that he should lose her for ever unless he removed the bad opinion his conduct had caused her to entertain of him. "It has been the longing of my whole life, madam," he said, with the most sanctimonious countenance he could assume, "to love a woman of virtue; and as I have found few such, I wished to know if you were as estimable in that respect as you are for beauty; whereof I am now, thanks be to God, fully convinced. I congratulate myself on having given my heart to such an assemblage of perfections; and I entreat you, madam, to pardon my caprice and my audacity, since the dénouement is so glorious for you, and yields me such pleasure."

Florida was beginning to have her eyes opened to the wiles of men; and as she had been slow to believe evil where it existed, she was still slower to believe good where it was not. "Would to God," she said, "that your words were true; but I am not so ignorant but that my married experience shows me clearly that the force and infatuation of passion have made you do what you have done. Had God suffered me to slacken the reins, I am quite sure you would not have tightened them. No one would think of looking for virtue in that sort of way. But enough of this. If I too lightly gave you credit for some goodness, it is time I should know the truth, which now delivers me out of your hands."

So saying, she left the room, and passed the whole night in tears. The anguish she felt from the change was so great that she could hardly bear it. Reason told her she should cease to love, but her heart told her quite another thing, and who can master the heart? Unable, then, to overcome her love, she resolved to cherish it as warmly as ever, but to suppress all tokens of it for the satisfaction of her honour.

Amadour went away the next day, in such a state of mind as you may imagine. His great heart, however, instead of letting him yield to despair, suggested to him a new device whereby he might again see Florida and regain her goodwill. Taking the road then to Toledo, where the King of Spain was residing, he passed through the county of Aranda, arrived late one evening at the countess's mansion, and found the countess sick with grief at the absence of Florida. She kissed and embraced Amadour as though he were her own son, both because she loved him, and because she suspected that he loved Florida. She asked news of her, and he gave her as much as he could, but not all true. He avowed the friendship which subsisted between them, which Florida had always concealed, begged her mother often to send him news of her, and to bring her soon to Aranda. He passed the night at the countess's, and continued his journey next day.

Having despatched his business with the king, he joined the army, but looked so melancholy and so changed, that the ladies and the captains with whom he was intimate could hardly believe he was the same man. He wore only black clothes, and those of a much coarser nap than was requisite for the mourning he wore ostensibly for his wife, whose death served as a convenient pretext for his sadness. Amadour lived in this way for three or four years, without returning to court. The Countess of Aranda, hearing that her daughter was piteously changed, wanted her to come back to her, but Florida would not; for when she learned that Amadour had acquainted her mother with their mutual friendship, and that her mother, though so discreet and virtuous, had so much confidence in Amadour that she approved of it, she was in marvellous perplexity. On the one hand, she considered that if she told her mother the truth, it might occasion mischief to Amadour, which she would not have done for her life, believing that she was quite able to punish his insolence without any help from her relations. On the other hand, she foresaw that if she concealed his misconduct, her mother and her friends would oblige her to speak with him and show him a fair countenance, and thereby, as she feared, encourage his evil intentions. However, as he was far away, she said nothing of what was past, and wrote to him when the countess desired her to do so; but it was plain, from the tone of her letters, that they were written not from her spontaneous impulses, but in obedience to her mother, so that Amadour felt pain in reading them instead of the transports of joy with which he had formerly received them.

Having during two or three years performed so many fine exploits that all the paper in Spain could not contain them, he devised a grand scheme, not to regain Florida's heart, for he believed he had lost it wholly, but to vanquish his enemy, since such she declared herself. Setting aside reason, and even the fear of death to which he exposed himself, he adopted the following course. He made such interest with the governor-in-chief that he was deputed to go and report to the king respecting certain enterprises that were in hand against Leucate; and without caring for the consequences, he communicated the purport of his journey to the Countess of Aranda before he had mentioned it to the king. As he knew that Florida was with her mother, he posted to the countess's, under pretence of wishing to take her advice, and sent one of his friends before him to apprise her of his coming, begging she would not mention it, and would do him the favour to speak with him at night unknown to every one. The countess, very glad of this news, imparted it to Florida, and sent her to undress in her husband's room, that she might be ready when she should send for her after every one was in bed. Florida, who had not recovered from her first fear, said nothing of it, however, to her mother, and went to her oratory to commend herself to God, and pray that he would guard her heart from all weakness. Remembering that Amadour had often praised her for her beauty, which had lost nothing by her long illness, she chose rather to impair it with her own hand than to suffer it to kindle so criminal a fire in the heart of so worthy a man. To this end she took a stone, which she found opportunely, and gave herself such a great blow with it on the face, that her mouth, eyes, and nose were quite disfigured. That it might not appear she had done it designedly, when the countess sent for her she let herself fall on coming out of her oratory. The countess hearing her cries hurried to her, and found her in that sad condition. Florida raised herself up and told her mother she had struck her face against a great stone. Her wounds were immediately dressed and her face bandaged, after which her mother sent her to her own chamber, and begged her to entertain Amadour, who was in her cabinet, until she had got rid of her company. Florida obeyed, supposing that Amadour had some one with him; but when she found herself alone with him, and the door closed, she was as much vexed as Amadour was delighted, fancying that he should achieve, by fair means or by force, what he had so long coveted.

After a brief conversation, finding her sentiments unchanged, and hearing from her lips a protestation that, though it were to cost her her life, she would never swerve from the principles she had professed at their last meeting, he exclaimed desperately, " By God, Florida, your scruples shall not deprive me of the fruit of my toils. Since love, patience, and entreaties are of no avail, I will employ force to have that without which I should perish."

Amadour's visage and his eyes were so changed that the handsomest complexion in the world was become red as fire, and the mildest and most agreeable aspect so horrible and furious, that it seemed as though the fire in his heart blazed out through his eyes. In his rage he had seized both Florida's delicate hands in his strong gripe, and finding herself deprived of all means of defence or flight, she thought the only chance left her was to try if his former love was so extinct that it could not disarm his cruelty. " If I must now look upon you as an enemy, Amadour," she said, " I conjure you, by the virtuous love with which I formerly believed your heart was animated, at least to hear me before you do me violence. What can possess you, Amadour," she said, seeing that he listened to her, " to desire a thing that can give you no pleasure, and would overwhelm me with grief? You have so well known my sentiments during my youth and my prime, which might have served as an excuse for your passion, that I wonder how, at my present age, and ugly as you see I am, you seek for that which you know you cannot find. I am sure you do not doubt that my sentiments are still the same, and, consequently, that nothing but violence can enable you to obtain your wishes. Look at the state of my face, forget the beauty you have seen in it, and you will lose all desire to approach me. If there is any remnant of love in your heart, it is impossible but that pity shall prevail over your rage. It is to your pity, and to the virtue of which you have given me so many proofs, that I appeal for mercy. Do not destroy my peace of mind, and make no attempt upon my honour, which, in accordance with your counsel, I am resolved to preserve. If the love you had for me has degenerated into hate, and you design from vindictiveness rather than affection to make me the most miserable woman on earth, I declare to you that it shall not be so, and that you will force me to complain openly of your vicious conduct to her who is so prejudiced in your favour. If you reduce me to this extremity, consider that your life is not safe."

"If I must die," replied Amadour, "a moment will put an end to all my troubles; but the disfigurement of your face, which I believe is your own work, shall not hinder me from doing what I have resolved; for though I could have nothing of you but your bones, I would have them close to me."

Finding that entreaties, arguments, and tears were useless, Florida had recourse to what she feared as much as the loss of life, and screamed out as loudly as she could to her mother. The countess, on hearing her cries, at once suspected the truth, and hastened to her with the utmost promptitude. Amadour, who was not so near dying as he said, let go his hold so quickly that the countess, on opening the cabinet, found him at the door, and Florida far enough away from him. "What is the matter, Amadour?" said the countess. "Tell me the truth." Amadour, who was prepared beforehand, and was never at a loss for an expedient at need, answered, with a pale and woebegone countenance, "Alas! madam, I no longer recognise Florida. Never was man more surprised than I am. I thought, as I told you, that I had some share in her good-will, but now I see plainly I have no longer any. Methinks, madam, that whilst she lived with you she was neither less discreet nor less virtuous than she is now; but she had no squeams of conscience to hinder her from talking to people and looking them in the face. I wanted to look at her, but she would not allow it. Seeing this, I thought I must be in a dream or a trance, and I asked leave to kiss her hand, according to the custom of the country, but she absolutely refused it. It is true, madam, I have done wrong, and I crave your pardon for it, in taking her hand and kissing it in a manner by force. I asked nothing more of her, but I see plainly that she is resolved upon my death, and that, I believe, is why she called you. Perhaps she was afraid I had some other design upon her. Be that as it may, madam, I acknowledge I was wrong; for though she ought to love all your good servants, such is my ill-luck, that I have no part in her good-will. My heart will not change for all that, with regard either to her or to you; and I entreat you, madam, to let me retain your good-will, since I have lost hers without deserving it."

The countess, who partly believed and partly doubted, asked her why she had called out so loudly. Florida replied that she did so because she was frightened. The countess asked her many other questions, and never got any but the same reply; for having escaped from her enemy, Florida thought him sufficiently punished by the disappointment. After the countess had conversed a long time with Amadour, she let him talk again with Florida in her presence, in order to see how he would look; but he said little to her, and contented himself with thanking her for not having told her mother, and begging her that at least, since he was banished from her heart, another might not profit by his disgrace. "If I could have defended myself in any other way," said Florida, "all would have passed between our two selves. You shall be let off with this, unless you force me to do worse. Do not be afraid that I shall ever love; for since I have been deceived in my judgment of a heart which I thought was full of virtue, I shall never believe that a man exists who is worthy to be trusted. This misfortune will make me banish for ever from my breast all passions which love can occasion." So saying, she took leave of him.

Her mother, who had been watching them, could come to no conclusion, except that she saw clearly that her daughter had no longer any friendship for Amadour. She thought this unreasonable, and that it was enough for herself to like any one to make Florida conceive an aversion for that person. From that moment she was so displeased with her, that for seven years she never spoke to her but with asperity, and all this at the solicitation of Amadour. Florida, who had formerly shunned nothing so much as her husband's presence, resolved to pass all her life by his side, to avoid her mother's harshness; but seeing that nothing succeeded with her, she made up her mind to deceive Amadour. To this end she pretended to be more tractable, and advised him to attach himself to a lady who she said she had spoken of their mutual love. This lady, who was in the queen's household, and whose name was Loretta, delighted at having made such a conquest, was so little mistress of her transports, that the affair became noised abroad. The Countess of Aranda herself, being at court, became aware of it, and afterwards treated Florida with more gentleness. Loretta's husband, who was a captain, and one of the King of Spain's great governors, was so incensed, that he was resolved to kill Amadour at all hazards; but Florida, who heard of this, and, in spite of herself, still loved Amadour, instantly gave him warning. Eager as he was to return to her, he replied, that if she would grant him every day three hours' conversation, he would never speak another word to Loretta; but she would do nothing of the sort. "Since, then, you do not wish me to live," said Amadour, "why would you hinder me from dying, unless you hope to make me suffer more in living than the pain of a thousand deaths. Let death fly me as it will, I will seek it, so that at last I shall find it, and then only I shall be at rest."

Meanwhile news arrived that the King of Grenada had begun hostilities against the King of Spain, which obliged the king to send his son thither with the Constable of Castile and the Duke of Alva, two old and sage lords. The Duke of Cardona and the Count of Aranda desired to take part in the campaign, and begged the king to give them some command. The king gave them appointments suitable to their quality, and desired they should act under the advice of Amadour, who performed during the war such astonishing acts as testified as much desperation as valour. His desperate rashness at last cost him his life. The Moors having offered battle, gave way before the charge of the Spaniards, and made a feint of flying, in order to draw on the Christian army to pursue them. Their stratagem succeeded. The old Constable and the Duke of Alva, suspecting it, detained the Prince of Spain against his will, and hindered him from passing the river; but the Count of Aranda and the Duke of Cardona crossed it in defiance of orders to the contrary. The Moors, finding themselves pursued only by a small body, wheeled round. The Duke of Cardona was killed with a seymetar, and the Count of Aranda was so dangerously wounded, that he was left for dead on the field. Amadour, coming up, cleft his way through the *mêlée* with such fury, that one would have said he was a maniac, and had the bodies of the duke and the count carried to the camp of the prince, who regretted them as if they had been his own brothers. On examining their wounds, it was found that the Count of Aranda was not dead. He was laid on a litter and carried home, where he lay ill for a long time. The body of the young duke was transported to Cardona. After rescuing the two bodies, Amadour took so little care of his own person that he let himself be surrounded by a great number of Moors. Knowing, then, that if he fell into the hands of the King of Grenada he should die a cruel death, unless he renounced the Christian religion, he resolved not to give his enemies the glory of his death or his capture, but to surrender up his body and his soul to God; and kissing the cross of his sword he plunged it into his body with such force that no second blow was needed.

Thus died poor Amadour, as much regretted as his virtues deserved. The news instantly spread from mouth to mouth all over Spain. Florida, who was then at Barcelona, where her husband had formerly directed that he should be buried, after having caused his obsequies to be performed with pomp, retired into the convent of Jesus, without saying a word to her mother or her mother-in-law, taking for her spouse and lover him who had delivered her from a love so violent as that of Amadour, and from the distress caused her by the society of such a husband. Her sole subsequent occupation and care was to love God so perfectly that, after having been a long time a nun, she surrendered up her soul to him with the joy with which a bride meets her husband.*

I am afraid, ladies, you have found this long story tedious; but it would have been still longer if I had given it as it was told to me. Imitate Florida's virtues, ladies, but be not so cruel; and never esteem men so highly, lest, when you are undeceived, you bring upon them a miserable death, and a life of sorrow upon yourselves.

"Do you not think," said Parlamente, turning to Hircan, "that this lady was tried to the utmost, and that she resisted virtuously?"

* "We have every reason to believe that this novel was suggested to the Queen of Navarre by some actual occurrence at the court of Charles VIII. and Louis XII. Whilst disguising the names of the principal actors, the princess has yet intermingled real events with her narrative. The beginning of the novel might even lead us to surmise that Margaret alludes in it to something in which she was personally concerned. The Countess of Aranda, left a very young widow, with a son and daughter, is very like Louise of Savoy and her two children. This, however, is a mere conjecture of ours, on which we by no means insist.

"For those who would like to attempt the solution of this little historical problem, we subjoin a list of some facts which occurred at the period in which the Queen of Navarre places her story.

"Taking of Salces by the French in 1496. Don Henry of Aragon, Count of Ribagorce, was then Viceroy of Catalonia, and Don Henry Henriquez governor of Roussillon.—Truce between France and Spain in 1497.—Revolt at Grenada in 1499.—In 1500 revolt of the Moors in the Alpujarras; King Ferdinand marches against them in person.—In 1501 defeat of the Spaniards, in which were killed Don Alfonso de Aguilar, Pedro de Sandoval, &c., &c. The Duke of Najera is sent against him.—In 1503 a Moorish fleet, consisting of ten *flustes*, ravages the coasts of Catalonia. That same year King Ferdinand burns Leucate.—In 1513 the King of Spain, to appease the feud existing between the Count of Ribagorce and the Count of Aranda, commissions Father Juan de Estuniga, provincial of the order of Saint Francis, to effect an agreement between them by means of a marriage between the eldest daughter of Count Aranda and the eldest son of the Count of Ribagorce. The latter refuses, and is banished the realm. As for the son of the Fortunate Infante, this must be Don Alfonso of Aragon, Count of Ribagorce, Duke of Segovia, sole male heir of the house of Castile, proposed in 1506 as husband for Jane the Crazed. His father, Henry of Aragon, Duke of Segovia, was surnamed the *Infante of Fortune*, because he was born in 1445, after the death of his father.

"Such are the events which the Queen of Navarre has mixed up with a narrative in which she declares that she has changed *names, places, and countries.*"—*Bibliophiles Français.*

"No," he replied; "for the least resistance a woman can decently make is to cry out. But what would she have done if she had been in a place where she could not be heard? Besides, if Amadour had not been more swayed by fear than by love, he would not so easily have given up. So I still maintain that no man ever loved heartily and was loved in return, who did not obtain what he sought if he went the right way about it. I must, however, applaud Amadour for having in part done his duty."

"Duty?" said Oisille. "Do you think that a servant does his duty, in offering violence to his mistress, to whom he owes all respect and obedience?"

"When our mistresses, madam," replied Saffredent, "hold their rank in chamber or hall, seated at their ease as our judges, we are on our knees before them; we timidly lead them out to dance, and serve them with so much diligence that we anticipate their commands; we have so much fear of offending them, and so much desire to serve them well, that no one can look upon us without compassion. We are often thought more witless than brutes, and people praise the proud spirit of our ladies, who look so imperious, and speak with so much good breeding, that they make themselves feared, loved, and esteemed by those who see only the outside. But in private, where there is no other judge than love, we know very well that they are women and we are men. The name of mistress is then changed to that of friend, and he who was a servant in public becomes a friend in a *tête-à-tête*. Thence comes the old proverb—

> Well to serve and loyal to be,
> Raiseth a servant to mastery.

Of honour they have as much as men, who can give it them and take it away; and as they see we suffer with patience, it is just that they should indemnify us when they can do so without damage to their honour."

"You do not speak," said Longarine, "of that true honour which is the most perfect contentment that can be had in this world. Though all the world believed me a virtuous woman, and I alone knew the contrary, the praises of others would but increase my shame and my secret confusion. On the other hand, were all mankind to condemn me, whilst my conscience was free from all reproach, I should derive a sort of pleasure from calumny, so true it is that virtue is never wholly unhappy."

"Though you have left nothing to say," observed Geburon, "you will permit me to remark that I regard Amadour as the most worthy and most virtuous of cavaliers. Though he has been given a feigned name, I think, nevertheless, that I recognise him; but since others have not named him, neither will I. I will only say that if he is the same as I suppose, never was his heart susceptible of fear, or exempt from love."

"It strikes me," said Oisille, "that this day has passed so agreeably, that if this continues, our time will seem very short. The sun is already low, and vespers have been rung at the abbey this long time. I did not tell you so before, because I was less desirous to hear vespers than to know the end of the story."

Hereupon everybody rose, and proceeding to the abbey they found that the monks had been waiting for them for more than an hour. After vespers they supped. The evening was not passed without discussing the tales that had been told in the day, and reviewing in memory the means of making the next day pass as agreeably as the first. After no end of sports in the meadow, every one went to bed highly gratified by the way in which their first day had been spent.

SECOND DAY.

In the morning they rose early, eager to return to the spot where they had had so much pleasure. Every one had his tale ready, and was impatient to bring it forth. After having heard Madame Oisille's reading and attended mass, dinner was the next affair, during which they also recalled to mind many a story.

After dinner they went to rest in their chambers, and at the appointed hour every one repaired to the meadow, where it seemed that the weather and the day expressly favoured their design. After they were all seated on verdant couches prepared by nature's own hands, Parlamente said, "Since I was the last speaker yesterday, it is for me to select the lady who shall begin this day's proceedings. Those of yesterday having been opened by Madame Oisille, the sagest and eldest lady present, I give my vote to-day to the youngest,—I do not say to the most light-witted, for I am sure that if we all follow her example, the monks will not have to wait so long to say vespers as they did yesterday. I call upon you, Nomerfide, but I beg you will not make us begin the day with tears."

"There was no need to give me that caution," said Nomerfide; "for one of our companions has made me choose a tale which I have set so fast in my head that I could not tell any other; and if it engenders sadness in you, why then your nature must be very melancholy."

NOVEL XI.

A NASTY ADVENTURE WHICH BEFEL MADAME DE RONCEX AT THE FRANCISCAN MONASTERY OF THOUARS.

IN the household of Madame de La Tremouille there was a lady named Roncex, who one day when her mistress had gone to the Cordeliers, had a pressing need to go to the place to which she could not send her waiting-woman. She took with her a girl named La Mothe to keep her company, but from bashfulness and desire of secrecy, left her in the chamber, and entered alone into a very dark privy, which was common to all the Cordeliers; and they had rendered such good account there of all their victuals, that the whole place, the seat and the floor, were covered with must of Bacchus and Ceres, passed through the bellies of the Cordeliers. The poor woman, who was so hard pressed that she had scarcely time to tuck up her skirts to sit down, unluckily seated herself on the filthiest spot in the whole place, and there she stuck as if she had been glued to it, and her poor buttocks, garments, and feet were so bewrayed, that she durst not step or turn any way for fear of making herself still worse. Thereupon she began to cry out, as loud as she could, "La Mothe, my dear, I am undone and dishonoured!" The poor girl, who had heard sundry tales of the wickedness of the Cordeliers, suspecting that some of them were hid there, and wanted to violate the lady, ran as fast as she could, saying to every one she met, "Come and help Madame de Roncex; the Cordeliers want to ravish her in that privy." They ran to the place with all speed, and found the poor dame De Roncex crying for help, desiring to have some woman who could clean her, and with her hinder parts all uncovered, for she was afraid to touch them with her garments lest she should befoul them. Rushing in at her cries, the gentlemen beheld that fine spectacle, and found no Cordelier molesting her, but only the ordure with which all her posteriors were glued. This did not pass without laughter on their part or great shame on hers; for instead of having women to clean her, she was waited on by men, who saw her naked in the worst condition in which a woman could show herself. Thereupon she dropped her clothes, and so dirtied what was still clean, forgetting the filth she was in for the shame she felt at seeing men. When she was out of that nasty place, it was necessary to strip her stark naked, and change all her clothes before she left the monastery. She was very much disposed to resent the help which La Mothe had brought her, but understanding that the poor girl believed her case was still worse, she forgot her anger and laughed like the rest.

Methinks, ladies, this story has been neither long nor melancholy, and that you have had from me what you expected.

The company laughed heartily at her story, and Oisille said to her, "Though the tale is nasty and dirty, we cannot object to it, knowing the persons to whom it happened. Well, I should have been very glad to see the faces worn by La Mothe and by her to whom she brought such good aid. But since you have ended so soon, give your voice to some one who does not think with such levity."

"If you would have my fault repaired," replied Nomerfide, "I give my voice to Dagoucin, who is so discreet that for his life he would not utter a folly."

Dagoucin thanked her for the favourable opinion she entertained of his good sense, and said, "The story I propose to relate will serve to show how love infatuates the greatest and worthiest hearts, and how difficult it is to overcome wickedness by dint of kindness."

[The preceding novel and epilogue, which are found in all the manuscripts consulted by the Bibliophiles Français, are the nineteenth of the edition of 1558. They are suppressed in that of 1559 and in all the subsequent editions except that of 1853, and the following substituted for them.]

FACETIOUS SAYINGS OF A CORDELIER IN HIS SERMONS.

Near the town of Bleré, in Touraine, there is a village named Martin le Beau, where a Cordelier of Tours was called on to preach the Advent and Lent sermons. This Cordelier, who had more gabble than learning, finding himself sometimes short of matter, would contrive to eke out his hour by telling tales which were not altogether disagreeable to the good villagers. Preaching on Holy Thursday on the Pascal Lamb, when he had to state that it was eaten by night, seeing among the congregation some handsome young ladies newly arrived from Amboise with the intention of spending Easter at the village, he wished to surpass himself, and asked all the women if they knew what it was to eat raw meat at night. "If you don't, I will tell you, ladies," said he. The young men of Amboise, who had come, some with their wives, others with their sisters and nieces, and who were not acquainted with the pilgrim's humour, began to be scandalised; but after having heard him further, instead of being shocked, they laughed, especially when he told them that to eat the Pascal Lamb it was necessary to have one's loins girt, one's feet in one's shoes, and a hand on one's staff. The Cordelier seeing them laugh, and guessing why, immediately corrected himself. "Well, then, shoes on one's feet, and one's staff in his hand," said he. "Buttered bread, and bread buttered—is it not all one?" How this was received I leave you to guess. The Cordelier, perceiving that his hour was nearly out, made new efforts to divert the ladies, and gave them reason to be pleased with him. "By-and-by, ladies," he said to them, "when you are chatting with your gossips, you will ask them, 'Who is this master friar who speaks so boldly? He is a jovial companion, I warrant.' I tell you ladies, be not astonished—no, be not astonished if I speak boldly, for I am of Anjou, at your service." So saying he ended his sermon, leaving his audience more disposed to laugh at his absurdities than to weep over the Passion of our Lord, the commemoration of which they were then celebrating.

His other sermons during the holidays were pretty much of the like efficacy. You know that the brethren of that order do not forget to go about making their collections to get them their Easter eggs, as they say. Not only have they no lack of these, but people give them besides many other things, such as linen, yarn, chitterlings, hams, chines, and so forth. On Easter Tuesday, when he was making his exhortations to charity, of which people of his sort are no niggards, he said, "I am bound, ladies, to thank you for the charities you have bestowed on our poor convent, but I cannot help remarking to you that you have not duly considered our wants. You have given us, for the most part, nothing but chitterlings, of which, thanks be to God, we have no scarcity, the convent being choke-full of them. What shall we do, then, with such lots of chitterlings? Do you know what we shall do with them? It is my advice, ladies, that you mix your hams with our chitterlings, and you will make a fine alms."

Then continuing his sermon, he contrived to introduce the subject of scandal. After having expatiated upon it and adduced some examples, he cried out, with warmth, "I am surprised, ladies and gentlemen of St. Martin, that you are scandalised at a thing that is less than nothing, and that you make a talk of me everywhere without reason, saying, 'Who would have thought it of the father, that he should have got his landlady's daughter with child?' That is a thing to be astonished about, truly. A monk has got a girl with child. What a wonder! But hark you, fair ladies, would you not have reason to be much more surprised if the girl had got the monk with child?"

Such, ladies were the precious viands with which this good shepherd fed the Lord's flock. So shameless was he, that after the commission of his sin, he had the impudence to speak of it in the pulpit, where nothing should be uttered but what is edifying to one's neighbour, and tends, in the first place, to the glory of God.

"That was what you may call a master-monk," said Saffredent. "I should be at a loss to choose between him and Friar Angebaut, at whose door were laid all the facetious things that were said in good company."

"I see no matter for laughter in all this," said Oisille, "nor is the circumstance of the time to the monk's advantage."

"You omit to say, madam," observed Nomerfide, "that at that time, although the thing happened not very long ago, your honest villagers, nay, most of the people even of the good towns, who think themselves cleverer than the others, had more regard for such preachers than for those who preached to them the holy gospel purely and simply."

"Be that as it may," said Hircan, "he was not far wrong in asking for hams in exchange for chitterlings, for there is a great deal more eating in them. If any devout dame had understood the thing amphibologically, as I believe the monk intended, neither he nor his brethren would have been badly off, any more than the young wench who had her bag full."

"What effrontery!" exclaimed Oisille, "to pervert the sense of the text according to his caprice, thinking he had to do with people as brutalised as himself, and impudently endeavouring to corrupt silly women, in order to teach them to eat raw meat at night."

"Ay," said Simontault, "but then he had before him those young tripesellers of Amboise, in whose tub he would fain have washed his—— Shall I say what? No, you understand me. He would gladly have given them a taste of it, not roasted, but all stirring and frisking, to give them the more pleasure."

"Gently, gently, Seigneur Simontault," said Parlamente; "you forget yourself. Where is your usual modesty, of which you can make such good use at need?"

"True, madam; but the foul-mouthed monk made me equivocate. To return to our first proceedings, I beg that Nomerfide, who is the cause of my error, will give her voice to some one who will make us forget our common fault."

"Since you will have it that I am a sharer in the fault," said Nomerfide, "I will choose one who will set all right again; and that is Dagoucin, who is so well behaved that he would rather die than say anything improper."

Dagoucin thanked her for her good opinion. "The story I am going to relate," he said, "is calculated to show you how love infatuates the greatest and the best, and how difficult it is to overcome wickedness by dint of kindness."

NOVEL XII.

INCONTINENCE AND TYRANNY OF A DUKE OF FLORENCE—JUST PUNISHMENT OF HIS WICKEDNESS.

Ten years ago there was at Florence a duke of the house of Medicis, who had married Madame Margaret, natural daughter of the Emperor Charles the Fifth. As the princess was still very young, and the duke would not sleep with her until she was of more mature age, he treated her very tenderly; and to spare her he amused himself with some other ladies of the city, whom he used to visit by night whilst his wife slept. Among others, he took a fancy to a lady as beautiful as she was good and virtuous, the sister of a gentleman whom the duke loved as himself, and to whom he conceded such authority, that he was obeyed like the duke himself. The latter had no secrets which he did not communicate to him, so that, in a manner, he might be called his second self. The duke, knowing that the gentleman's sister was a lady of the highest virtue, durst not at first speak to her of his passion; but after having tried every other expedient, he at last addressed his favourite on the subject.

"If there was anything in the world, my friend," he said, "which I would not do for you, I should be afraid to tell you what is in my thoughts, and still more to ask your aid. But I have so much friendship for you, that if I had a wife, a mother, or a daughter who could save your life, you may be assured you should not die. I am persuaded that you love me as much as I love you. If I, who am your master, have such an affection for you, that which you should have for me should be no less. I have a secret, then, to tell you. Through trying to conceal it, I have fallen into the state in which you now see me, from which I have no hope of escaping but by death, or by the service you may render me, if you will."

Touched by these representations on the part of his master, and seeing his face bathed in tears, the gentleman felt so much pity, that he said: "I am your creature, my lord; it is from you I hold all my wealth and honours, and you may speak to me as to your own soul, being sure that whatever I can do is at your command."

The duke then declared the passion with which he was possessed for his favourite's sister, and told him it was impossible he should live long unless the brother enabled him to enjoy her; for he was quite sure that prayers or presents would be of no avail with her. "If, then," said the duke, in conclusion, "you love my life as much as I love yours, find means to secure to me a bliss I can never obtain but through your aid." The gentleman, who loved his sister and the honour of his house more than his master's pleasure, remonstrated with him, and implored him not to reduce him to the horrible necessity of soliciting the dishonour of his family, protesting there was nothing he would not do for his master, but that his honour would not suffer him to perform such a service as that. The duke, inflamed with intolerable anger, bit his nails, and replied furiously, "Since I find no friendship in you, I know what I have to do." The gentleman, who knew his master's cruelty, was alarmed, and said, "Since you absolutely insist on it, my lord, I will speak to her." "If you set store by my life, I will set store by yours," were the duke's last words as he went away.

The gentleman knew well what this meant, and remained a day or two without seeing the duke, pondering over the means of extricating himself from so bad a dilemma. On the one hand he considered the obligations he was under to his master, the wealth and honours he had received from him; on the other hand, he thought of the honour of his house, and the virtue and chastity of his sister. He knew very well that she never would consent to such infamy, unless she were overcome by fraud or violence, which he could not think of employing, considering the shame it would bring upon him and her. In fine, he made up his mind that he would rather die than behave so vilely to his sister, who was one of the best women in Italy; and he resolved to deliver his country from a tyrant who was bent on disgracing his house; for he saw clearly that the only means of securing the lives of himself and his kindred was to get rid of the duke. Reso.ved, then, without speaking to his sister, to save his life and prevent his shame by one and the same deed, he went after two days to the duke, and told him that he had laboured so hard with his sister, that at last, with infinite difficulty, he had brought her to consent to the duke's wishes; but on condition that the affair should be kept secret, and that no one should know of it but they three. As people readily believe what they desire, the duke put implicit faith in the brother's words. He embraced him, promised him everything he could ask, urged him to hasten the fulfilment of his good tidings, and appointed a time with him for that purpose.

When the exulting duke saw the approach of the night he so longed for, in which he expected to conquer her whom he had thought invincible, he retired early with his favourite, and did not forget to dress and perfume himself with his best care. When all was still, the gentleman conducted him to his sister's abode, and showed him into a magnificent chamber, where he undressed him, put him to bed, and left him, saying, "I am going, my lord, to bring you one who will not enter this room without blushing; but I hope that before day dawns she will be assured of you." He then went away to his own room, where he found one trusty servant awaiting him by his orders. "Is thy heart bold enough," he said to him, "to follow me to a place where I have to revenge myself on the greatest of my enemies?" "Yes, my lord," replied the man, who knew nothing of the matter in hand, "though it were upon the duke himself." Thereupon, without giving the man time for reflection, the gentleman hurried him away so abruptly that he had not time to take any other weapon than a poniard with which he was already armed.

The duke, hearing his favourite's footsteps at the door believed that he was bringing him the object of his passion, and threw open the curtains to behold and welcome her; but instead of her he saw her brother advance upon him with a drawn sword. Unarmed, but undaunted, the duke started up, seized the gentleman round the middle, saying, "Is this the way you keep your word?" and for want of other weapons used his nails and his teeth, bit his antagonist in the thumb, and defended himself so well that they fell together beside the bed. The gentleman not feeling confident in his own strength, called his man, who, seeing his master and the duke grappling each other so desperately that he could not well distinguish which was which in that dark spot, dragged them both out by the heels into the middle of the room, and then set about cutting the duke's throat with his poniard. The duke defended himself to the last, until he was exhausted by loss of blood. Then the gentleman and his man laid him on the bed, finished him with their poniards, drew the curtains upon the body, and left the room, locking the door behind them.

Having slain his enemy and liberated the republic, the gentleman thought that his exploit would not be complete unless he did the same by five or six near relations of the duke. To this end he ordered his man to go and fetch them one by one; but the servant, who had neither vigour nor boldness enough, replied, "It strikes me, my lord, that you have done enough for the present, and that you had much better think of saving your own life than of taking that of others. If every one of them should take as long to despatch as the duke, it would be daylight before we had finished, even should they be unarmed." As the guilty are easily susceptible of the contagion of fear, the gentleman took his servant's advice, and went with him alone to a bishop, whose place it was to have the gates opened and to give orders to the postmasters. The gentleman told the prelate he had just received intelligence that one of his brothers was at the point of death; that the duke had given him leave to go to him, and therefore he begged his lordship would give him an order to the postmasters for two good horses, and to the gate-keepers to let him pass. The bishop, to whom his request seemed almost equivalent to a command from the duke his master, gave him a note, by means of which he at once obtained what he required; but instead of going to see his brother, he made straight for Venice, where he had himself cured of the bites inflicted by the duke, and then passed over into Turkey.

Next morning the duke's servants, not seeing or hearing anything of him, concluded that he had gone to see some lady; but at last becoming uneasy at his long absence, they began to look for him in all directions. The poor duchess, who was beginning to love him greatly, was extremely distressed at hearing that he could not be found. The favourite also, not making his appearance, some of the servants went for him to his house. They saw blood at his chamber door, but no one could give any account of him. The trace of blood led the duke's servants to the chamber where he lay, and finding the door locked, they broke it open at once, saw the floor covered with blood, drew the curtains, and beheld the poor duke stark dead on the bed. Picture to yourselves the affliction of these poor servants, as they carried the body to the palace. The bishop arrived there at the same time, and told them how the gentleman had fled in the night under pretence of going to see his brother. This was enough to lead every one to the conclusion that it was he who had done the deed. It clearly appeared that his sister had known nothing about it. Though she was surprised at so unexpected an event, she loved her brother for it, since, without regard to his own life, he had delivered her from a tyrant who was bent on the ruin of her honour. She continued always to lead the same virtuous life; and though she was reduced to poverty by the confiscation of all the family property, her sister and she found husbands as honourable and wealthy as any in Italy. Both of them have always lived subsequently in the best repute.*

Here is a fact ladies, which should make you beware of that little god, who delights in tormenting princes and private persons, the strong and the weak; and who so infatuates them that they forget God and their conscience, and even the care of their own lives. Princes and those who are in authority ought to fear to outrage their inferiors. There is no man so insignificant but he can do mischief when it is God's will to inflict vengeance on the sinner, nor any so great that he can do hurt to one whom God chooses to protect.

This story was listened to by the whole company, but with very different sentiments. Some maintained that the gen-

* The historical fact related in this novel is one of the most celebrated in the annals of Florence. The duke was Alessandro, natural son of Lorenzo de Medicis, and the murderer was his cousin, Lorenzo de Medici. Historians state that the latter decoyed the duke to his house under pretence of affording him an interview with a Florentine lady, but they do not mention that she was Lorenzo's sister.

tleman had done well in securing his own life and his sister's honour, and delivering his country from such a tyrant. Others, on the contrary, said that it was enormously ungrateful to take the life of a man who had loaded him with wealth and honours. The ladies said he was a good brother and a virtuous citizen; the gentlemen, on the contrary, maintained that he was a traitor and a bad servant. It was amusing to hear the opinions and arguments delivered on the one side and on the other; but the ladies, as usual, spoke more from passion than from judgment, saying that the duke deserved death, and that blessed was the brother who had slain him. "Ladies," said Dagoucin, who saw what a lively controversy he had excited, "pray do not put yourselves in a passion about a thing that is past and gone; only take care that your beauties do not occasion murders more cruel than that which I have related."

"'The Fair Lady without Compassion,'"* said Parlamente, "has taught us to say that people hardly ever die of so agreeable a malady."

"Would to God, madam," rejoined Dagoucin, "that every lady here knew how false is this notion. They would not then, I imagine, desire the reputation of being pitiless, or like to resemble that incredulous fair one who let a good servant die for want of responding favourably to his passion."

"So then," said Parlamente, "to save the life of a man who says he loves us, you would have us violate our honour and our conscience?"

"I do not say that," replied Dagoucin, "for he who loves thoroughly would be more afraid of hurting the honour of his mistress than she herself. Hence it seems to me, that a gracious response, such as is called for by a seemly and genuine love, would only give more lustre to the honour and conscience of a lady. I say a seemly love, for I maintain that those who love otherwise do not love perfectly."

"That is always the upshot of your orisons," said Ennasuite. "You begin with honour, and end with its opposite. If all the gentlemen present will tell us the truth of the matter, I will believe them on their oaths."

* *La Belle Dame sans Merci* is the title of a poem by Alain Chartier, in the form of a long metaphysical dialogue between a lady and her lover.

Hircan swore that he had never loved any one but his wife, and that it was far from his wish to make her offend God. Simontault spoke to the same effect, and added that he had often wished that all women were ill-natured except his own wife. "You deserve that yours should be so," retorted Geburon; "but for my part, I can safely swear that I loved a woman so much that I would rather have died than have made her do anything capable of diminishing the esteem in which I held her. My love was so founded upon her virtues, that I would not have seen a stain upon them for the most precious favours I could have obtained from her."

"I thought, Geburon," said Saffredent, laughing, "that the love you have for your wife, and the good sense with which nature has endowed you, would have saved you from playing the lover elsewhere; but I see I was mistaken, for you use the very phrases which we are accustomed to employ to dupe the most subtle of dames, and under favour of which we obtain a hearing from the most discreet. Where is the lady, indeed, who will not lend us an ear when we begin our discourse with honour and virtue? But if we were all to lay open our hearts before them just as they are, there is many a man well received by the ladies, whom then they would not condescend so much as to look upon. We hide our devil under the form of the handsomest angel we can find, and so receive many a favour before we are found out. Perhaps, even, we lead the ladies so far, that thinking to go straight to virtue, they have neither time nor opportunity to retreat when they find themselves face to face with vice."

"I thought you quite a different sort of man," said Geburon, "and imagined that virtue was more agreeable to you than pleasure."

"Why," said Saffredent, "is there any greater virtue than to love in the way God has ordained? To me it seems much better to love a woman as a woman, than to make her one's idol, as many do. For my part, I am convinced that it is better to use than to abuse."

All the ladies coincided in opinion with Geburon, and bade Saffredent hold his tongue. "Very well," said he; "I am content to say no more on the subject, for I have fared so badly with regard to it that I don't want to have any more to do with it."

"You may thank your own bad thoughts for having fared badly," said Longarine; "for where is the woman with a proper sense of decorum who would have you for a lover after what you have just said?"

"There are those," he retorted, "who did not think me intolerable, and who would not have exchanged their own sense of decorum for yours. But let us say no more about it, in order that my anger may shock no one, and may not shock myself. Let us think to whom Dagoucin will give his voice."

"I give it to Parlamente," he replied at once, "persuaded as I am that she must know better than any one what is honourable and perfect friendship."

"Since you elect me to tell a story," said Parlamente, "I will relate to you one which occurred to a lady who had always been one of my good friends, and has never concealed anything from me."

NOVEL XIII.

A CAPTAIN OF A GALLEY, UNDER THE CLOAK OF DEVOTION, FELL IN LOVE WITH A DEMOISELLE. WHAT HAPPENED IN CONSEQUENCE.

THERE was in the household of the regent, mother of King Francis, a very devout lady, married to a gentleman of the same character. Though her husband was old, and she young and fair, nevertheless she served him and loved him as though he had been the handsomest young man in the world. To leave him no cause of uneasiness, she made it her care to live with him like a woman of his own age, shunning all company, all magnificence in dress, all sorts of dances and diversions such as women are usually fond of, and making the service of God her sole pleasure and recreation. One day her husband told her that from his youth upwards he had longed to make the journey to Jerusalem, and he asked her what she thought of the matter. She, whose only thought was how to please him, replied, "Since God has deprived us of children, my dear, and has given us wealth enough, I should be strongly inclined to spend a part of it in performing that sacred journey; for, whether you go to Jerusalem or elsewhere, I am resolved to accompany, and never forsake you." The good man was so pleased with this reply, that he fancied himself already standing on Mount Calvary.

Just at this time there arrived at court a gentleman who had served long against the Turks, and who was come to obtain the king's approval for a projected enterprise against a fortress belonging to the Ottomans, the success of which was likely to be very advantageous to Christendom. The old devotee talked with him about his expedition, and learning from him that he was resolved upon it, asked him if he would be disposed, after it was accomplished, to make another journey to Jerusalem, which himself and his wife had a great desire to see. The captain highly approving of so good a design, promised to accompany him, and to keep the thing secret. The old gentleman was impatient to see his wife, to tell her what he had done. As she had scarcely less longing than her husband to perform the journey, she talked of it often to the captain, who, paying more attention to her person than to her words, became so much in love with her, that in talking to her of the voyages he had made by sea, he often confounded the port of Marseilles with the Archipelago, and said horse when he meant to say ship, so much was he beside himself. He found her, however, of so singular a character that he durst not let her see that he loved her, much less tell her so in words. The fire of his passion became so violent by dint of his concealing it, that it often made him ill. The demoiselle, who regarded him as her guide, took as much care of him as of the cross, and sent to inquire after him so often, that the interest she evinced for him cured the patient without the aid of physic. Several persons who knew that the captain had always had a better reputation for valour than for devotion, were surprised at the great intercourse between him and this lady; and seeing that he had changed from white to black, that he frequented the churches, attended sermons, and performed all the devoirs of a devotee, they doubted not that he did so to ingratiate himself with the lady, and could not even help hinting as much to him. The captain, fearing lest this should come to the ears of the lady, withdrew from society, and told her husband and her that, being on the point of receiving his orders and quitting the court, he had many things to say to them; but that for the greater secrecy he would only confer with them in private, to which end he begged they would send for him when they had both retired for the night.

This proposal being quite to the old gentleman's liking, he failed not to go to bed early every night and make his wife undress. After everybody had gone to rest he used to send for the captain to talk about the journey to Jerusalem, in the course of which the good man often fell asleep devoutly. On these occasions, the captain seeing the old gentleman sleeping like the blessed, and himself seated in a chair at the bedside, close to her whom he thought the most charming woman in the world, felt his heart so hard pressed between his fear and his desire to declare himself, that he often lost the use of his tongue. But that she might not perceive his perplexity, he launched out upon the holy places of Jerusalem, where are to be seen the memorials of the great love which Jesus Christ had for us. What he said of that love was only uttered to conceal his own; and while he expatiated upon it he kept his eyes fixed on the lady, wept and sighed so *à propos*, that her heart was quite penetrated with piety. Believing from this outward appearance of devotion that he was quite a saint, she begged him to tell her how he had lived, and how he had come to love God with such fervour? He told her he was a poor gentleman, who to acquire wealth and honours had forgotten his conscience, and married a lady who was too nearly related to him; one who was rich, but old and ugly, and whom he did not love at all; that after having drawn all his wife's money from her, he had gone to seek his fortune at sea, and had sped so well that he had become captain of a galley; but that since he had had the honour of her acquaintance, her holy converse and her good example had so changed him, that he was resolved, if by God's grace he came back alive from his expedition, to take her and her husband to Jerusalem, there to do penance for his great sins which he had forsaken, after which it would only remain for him to make reparation to his wife, to whom he hoped soon to be reconciled. This account which he gave of himself was very pleasing to the pious lady, who congratulated herself much on having converted a sinner of such magnitude.

These nocturnal confabulations continued every night until the departure of the captain, who never ventured to declare himself. Only he made the fair devotee a present of a crucifix from Our Lady of Pity, beseeching her, whenever she looked upon it, to think of him. The time of his departure being come, and having taken leave of the husband, who was falling asleep, he had last of all to take leave of the fair one, in whose eyes he saw tears, drawn forth by the kind feeling she entertained for him. His impassioned heart so thrilled at the sight, that he almost fainted as he bade her farewell, and burst into such an extraordinary perspiration, that he wept, so to speak, not only with his eyes, but with every part of his body. Thus he departed without any explanation, and the lady, who never before had seen such tokens of regret, was quite astonished at his emotion. She had not the less good opinion of him for all that, and her prayers accompanied him on his way. A month afterwards, as she was returning to her own house one day, she was met by a gentleman, who delivered a letter to her from the captain, begging her to read it in private, and assuring her that he had seen him embark, fully resolved to perform an expedition which should be pleasing to the king and advantageous to the faith. At the same time the gentleman mentioned that he was going back to Marseilles to look after the captain's affairs. The lady went to the window and opened the letter, which consisted of two sheets of paper written all over. It was an elaborate declaration of the feelings which the writer had so carefully concealed, and in it was enclosed a large handsome diamond mounted in a black enamelled ring, which the lady was supplicated to put on her fair finger.

Having read the enormously long letter from beginning to end, the lady was the more astonished as she had never suspected the captain's love for her. The diamond caused her much perplexity, for she knew not what to do with it. After thinking over the matter all that day, and dreaming of it at night, she rejoiced that she could abstain from replying for want of a messenger, saying to herself, that as the bearer of the letter had taken such pains on the writer's behalf, she ought to spare him the mortification of such a reply as she had resolved to give him, but which she now thought fit to reserve till the captain's return. The diamond was still a cause of much embarrassment to her, as it was not her custom to adorn herself at any one's expense but her husband's. At last her good sense suggested to her that she could not employ it better than for the relief of the captain's conscience, and she instantly despatched it by the hands of one of her servants to the captain's forlorn wife, to whom she wrote as follows, in the assumed character of a nun of Tarrascon:

"Madam,—Your husband passed this way a little before he embarked. He confessed, and received his Creator like a good Christian, and declared to me a fact which lay heavy on his conscience, namely, his regret for not having loved you as he ought. He begged me at his departure to send you this letter with this diamond, which he begs you to keep for his sake, assuring you that if God brings him back safe and sound, he will make amends for the past by all the love that you can desire. This diamond will be for you a pledge of his word. I ask of you on his behalf the aid of your good prayers; for all my life he shall have part in mine."

When the captain's wife received this letter and the diamond, it may well be imagined how she wept with joy and sorrow: joy at being loved by her husband, and sorrow at being deprived of his presence. She kissed the ring a thousand times, washing it with her tears, and praised God for having restored her husband's affection to her at the close of her days, and when she least expected it. The nun who under God had wrought such a blessing for her was not forgotten in her grateful acknowledgments. She replied to her by the same man, who made his mistress laugh heartily when he told her how the captain's wife had received her communication. The fair devotee congratulated herself on having got rid of the diamond in so pious a manner, and was as much rejoiced at having re-established the good understanding between the husband and wife as though she had gained a kingdom.

Some time afterwards news arrived of the defeat and death of the poor captain. He had been abandoned by those who ought to have supported him, and the Rhodians, who had most interest in concealing his design, were the first to make it known. Nearly eighty men who had made a descent on the land were cut off almost to a man. Among them there was a gentleman named Jean and a converted Turk, for whom the fair devotee had been godmother, and whom she had given to the captain to accompany him on his expedition. Jean fell along with the captain; the Turk, wounded in fifteen places with arrows, escaped by swimming to the French vessels, and it was from his report that it was known exactly how the thing had happened. A certain gentleman whom the captain believed to be his friend, and whose interests he had advanced with the king and the greatest personages in France, after the captain had landed stood off shore with his vessels. The captain, seeing that his scheme was discovered, and that he was opposed by four thousand Turks, set about retreating. But the gentleman in whom he put such confidence, considering that after his death he himself would have the command and the profit of that great fleet, represented to the officers that it was not right to risk the king's vessels and the lives of so many brave men on board them in order to save eighty or a hundred persons. The officers, as spiritless as himself, coincided with him in opinion. The captain, seeing that the more he called to them the more they drew off from the shore, faced round against his foes, and though he was up to his knees in sand, he defended himself so valiantly, that it almost seemed as if his single arm would defeat the assailants. But at last he received so many wounds from the arrows of those who durst not approach him within less than bowshot distance, that he began to grow weak from loss of blood. The Turks, seeing that the Christians were nearly spent, fell upon them with the scimitars; but notwithstanding the overwhelming numbers of the foe, the Christians defended themselves as long as they had breath. The captain called to him the gentleman named Jean, and the Turk whom the devotee had given him, and planting his sword in the ground, kissed and embraced the cross on his knees, saying, "Lord, receive the soul of him who has not spared his life for the exaltation of thy name." Jean, seeing him droop as he uttered these words, took him and his sword in his arms, wishing to succour him; but a Turk cut both his thighs to the bone from behind. "Come, captain," he cried, as he received the stroke, "let us go to Paradise to see him for whose sake we die." As he had been united with the captain in life, so was he also in death. The Turk, seeing that he could be of no use to either of them, and that he was pierced with arrows, made his way to the vessels by swimming; and though he was the only one who had escaped out of eighty, the perfidious commander would not receive him. But being a good swimmer, he went from vessel to vessel, till at last he was taken on board a small one, where in the course of a little time he was cured of his wounds.

It was through this foreigner that the truth became known respecting this event, glorious to the captain, and shameful to his companion in arms. The king, and all good people who heard of it, deemed the act of the latter so black towards God and man, that there was no punishment too bad for him. But on his return he told so many lies, and made so many presents, that not only did his crime remain unpunished, but he succeeded to the post of him whose lackey he was not worthy to be. When the sad news reached the court, the regent-mother, who highly esteemed the captain, greatly mourned his loss. So did the king and all who had known him. When she, whom he had so passionately loved, heard of his strange, piteous, and Christian end, the obduracy she had felt towards him melted into tears, and her lamentations were shared by her husband, whose pilgrim hopes were frustrated by the catastrophe.

I must not forget to mention that a demoiselle belonging to this lady, who loved the gentleman Jean better than herself, told her mistress the very day the captain and he were killed, that she had seen in a dream him whom she loved so much, that he had come to her in white raiment to bid her farewell, and told her that he was going to Paradise with his captain. But when she learned that her dream was true, she made such piteous moans that her mistress had enough to do to console her. Some time after the court went into Normandy, of which province the captain was a native, and his wife failed not to come and pay her respects to the regent-mother, intending to be introduced by the lady with whom her husband had been so much in love. Whilst waiting for the hour when she could have audience, the two ladies entered a church, where the widow began to laud her husband, and make lamentations over his death. "I am, madam, the most unhappy of women," she said. "God has taken my husband from me at the time when he loved me more than ever he had done." So saying, she showed her the diamond she wore on her finger as a pledge of his perfect affection. This was not said without a world of tears; and the other lady, who saw that her good-natured fraud had produced so excellent an effect, was so strongly tempted to laugh in spite of her grief, that not being able to present the widow to the regent, she handed her over to another, and retired into a chapel, where she had her laugh out.*

Methinks, ladies, that those of our sex to whom presents are made, ought to be glad to employ them as usefully as did this good lady; for they would find that there is pleasure and joy in doing good. We must by no means accuse her of fraud, but praise her good sense which enabled her to extract good out of a bad thing.

"You mean to say, then," said Nomerfide, "that a fine diamond worth two hundred crowns is a bad thing? I assure you, if it had fallen into my hands, neither his wife nor his relations would ever have set eyes on it. Nothing is more one's own than a thing that is given. The captain was dead, no one knew anything of the matter, and she might well have abstained from making the poor old woman cry."

"Good faith, you are right," said Hircan, "for there is many a woman who, to show that she is better than others, does acts contrary to her nature. In fact, do we not all know that nothing is more covetous than a woman? Yet vanity often prevails with them over avarice, and makes them do things in which their hearts have no share. In my opinion, the lady who set so little store by the diamond did not deserve it."

"Gently, gently," said Oisille; "I think I know her, and I pray you not to condemn her unheard."

---

* The incidents related in this novel appear to be real, but it is impossible to discover the names of the actors. M. Paul Lacroix supposes the hero of the novel to be a Baron de Malleville, Knight of Malta, who was killed at Beyrout in an expedition against the Turks, and whose death has been celebrated by Clement Marot. But the Bibliophiles Français remark that the conjecture is untenable, De Malleville being styled *Parisien* by the poet, whereas the captain was a Norman. He was a married man, too, which a Knight of Malta could not be.

"I do not condemn her, madam," replied Hircan; "but if the gentleman was so gallant a man as he has been represented to have been, it was a glorious thing for her to have a lover of such merit and to wear his ring. But perhaps some one less worthy to be loved held her so fast by the finger that the ring could not be placed on it."

"Truly," said Ennasuite, "she might fairly keep it, since no one knew anything about it."

"What!" exclaimed Geburon, "is everything allowable for those who love, provided nobody knows of it?"

"I have never," said Saffredent, "seen anything punished as a crime except imprudence; in fact, no murderer, robber, or adulterer, is ever punished by justice, or blamed amongst men, provided they are as cunning as they are wicked. But wickedness often blinds them so that they become witless. Thus it may be truly said that it is only fools who are punished and not the vicious."

"You may say what you will," said Oisille, "but it is for God to judge the heart of the lady; for my part, I see nothing in her conduct but what is comely and virtuous, and to put an end to this dispute, I beg you, Parlamente, to call on some one to follow you."

"I have great pleasure in calling on Simontault," replied Parlamente, "and I am mistaken if, after these two sad novels, he will not give us one which will not make us weep."

"That is almost as good as saying that I am a buffoon," said Simontault. "By way of revenge, I will let you see that there are women who make a show of being chaste with regard to certain people, or for a certain time; but the end unmasks them, as you will see by this true story."

NOVEL XIV.

SUBTLETY OF A LOVER WHO, COUNTERFEITING THE REAL FAVOURITE, FOUND MEANS TO RECOMPENSE HIMSELF FOR HIS PAST TROUBLES.

In the time when the grand-master of Chaumont was governor of the duchy of Milan, there was a gentleman named Bonnivet, whose merits afterwards raised him to the rank of admiral of France. As his rare endowments made him liked by everybody, he was often a welcome guest at banquets and entertainments where ladies were present, and he was better received by them than ever was Frenchman before or since, both because he was a handsome, agreeable man, and spoke well, and because he had the reputation of being one of the ablest and most resolute soldiers of his time. One day during the carnival, when he was among the maskers, he danced with a lady, one of the handsomest and finest women in Milan. At every pause in the music he failed not to entertain her with the language of love, in which no one was such an adept as he; but the fair one, not thinking herself bound to respond to his most humble supplications, cut him short, told him flatly that she neither loved nor ever would love any one but her husband, and that he had better address his tender speeches elsewhere. Nothing daunted by this reply, which he would by no means take for a refusal, Bonnivet stuck to the lady, and continued to press his suit with great vivacity until Mid-Lent. In spite of all his endeavours he found her steadfast in the resolution she had expressed, yet could not persuade himself that all this was real earnest, seeing the hard favour of the husband and the beauty of the wife.

Convinced, then, that she practised dissimulation, he resolved to have recourse to the same art, and thenceforth desisted from his solicitations. He narrowly inquired into her conduct, and found that she loved an Italian gentleman of good parts and accomplishments. Bonnivet gradually insinuated himself into the Italian's acquaintance, and did so with such adroitness that the latter never suspected his motive, but conceived such an esteem for him, that next to his fair one he was the person he loved best in the world.

In order to extract the Italian gentleman's secret from his breast, Bonnivet pretended to unlock his own, and told him that he loved a lady, naming one whom he scarcely ever thought of; at the same time begging him to keep the secret, that they might both have but one heart and one thought. The Italian, in return for the confidence which Bonnivet reposed in him, informed him, without reserve, of his passion for the lady before mentioned, on whom Bonnivet wanted to be revenged. The two friends met every day, and mutually recounted the good fortunes of the last four-and-twenty hours, with this difference, however, that one lied and the other told the truth. The Italian confessed that he had loved the lady in question for three years, without ever having obtained from her more than fair words and assurances that he was loved. Bonnivet gave him his very best advice; the Italian acted upon it, and prospered by it so well, that in a few days the lady consented to fulfil all his desires. Nothing remained now but to contrive means for their meeting; but as Bonnivet was fertile in expedients, this was soon done.

"I am more obliged to you than to any man living," said the Italian to him one evening before supper, "for, thanks to your excellent advice, I expect this night to enjoy what I have been longing for so many years."

"Pray let me know the nature of your enterprise," said Bonnivet, "so that if there is any risk in it, or it requires any artifice, I may aid and serve as your friend."

He then learned that the lady had an opportunity for leaving the great door of the house open, under the pretext of enabling one of her brothers, who was ill, to send out at any hour of the night for what he might require. The Italian was to enter the court-yard through that door, but was not to ascend the main staircase. He was to turn to the right to a small staircase, go up it to the first gallery, on which the chambers of her father-in-law and her brother-in-law opened. He was to take the third door from the stairs, push it gently, and if he found it locked, he was to go away at once, for he might conclude for certain that her husband had returned, though he was not expected back for two days; but if he found the door open, he was to come in softly, and lock the behind him, being assured that there was no one in the room but herself. Above all, he was to wear felt shoes that he might make no noise, and not leave home till two hours after midnight, for her brothers-in-law, who were much addicted to play, never went to bed till past one o'clock. Bonnivet congratulated his friend, wished him good speed, and bade him not hesitate to command his services if he could be of any use to him. The Italian thanked him, said that in affairs such as this one could not be too much alone, and went off to make his preparations.

Bonnivet, on his side, did not sleep; and seeing that the time was come to be revenged on the cruel fair one, he went to bed early, had his beard trimmed after the fashion of the Italian's, and his hair cut so that she might not recognise the difference if she touched him. The felt shoes were not forgotten, nor any of the other things which the Italian was accustomed to wear. As he was held in high consideration by the lady's father-in-law, he did not hesitate to go early to the house, being prepared, in case any one perceived him, to go straight to the chamber of the old gentleman, with whom he had some business.

He reached the house at midnight; met several people in it passing to and fro, but no one noticed him, and he made his way into the gallery. He touched the first two doors, and found them shut; the third being open he entered it, and locked it behind him. The chamber was all hung with white, and there was a bed with a drapery of the same colour, of such fine stuff and so excellently wrought with the needle, that nothing could be handsomer. The lady was alone in bed, dressed in the most exquisite night-gear, as he could perceive (himself unseen) through a corner of the curtain, for there was a large wax candle burning in the room. For fear of being recognised, he first put out the light; then he undressed and went to bed to her. The fair one, believing him to be the man she had loved so long, received him with all possible caresses; but he, well knowing that he owed all this to her mistake, took good heed not to say one word to her, his only care being to revenge himself at the cost of her honour, and without being under any obligation to her; but she liked that sweet revenge so well, that she thought she had recompensed him for all his sufferings. This lasted till the clock struck one, when it was time to leave her. Then he asked her, in a very low whisper, if she was as well satisfied with him as he was with her. She, thinking still that he was her lover, replied that she was not only satisfied, but even surprised at the excess of his love, which had kept him an hour without speaking. Upon this he could restrain himself no longer. "Now, madam," he said, laughing outright, "will you refuse me another time, as you have hitherto done?"

The lady, recognising him too late by his voice and his laughter, was overwhelmed with shame and vexation, and called him a thousand times impostor, cheat, traitor, villain! She would have sprung out of bed to look for a knife with which to kill herself for having been so unhappy as to lose her honour for a man whom she did not love, and who, to be revenged upon her, might make known this affair to the whole world. But he held her fast, and vowed so hard that he would love her better than the other, and would faithfully keep her secret, that at last she believed him, and was pacified. He then told her how he had contrived to find himself where he then was, and related to her all the pains he had taken to win her; whereupon she praised his ingenuity, and vowed that she would love him better than the other, who had not been able to keep her secret. She was now convinced, she said, how false were the prejudices that prevailed against the French, who were better men, more persevering and more discreet than the Italians; and from that moment she would cast off the erroneous opinions of her countrypeople, and attach herself heartily to him. Only she entreated him that for some time he would forbear from showing himself at any entertainment or in any place where she might be, unless he were masked; for she knew well she should be so much ashamed, that her countenance would tell tales of her to everybody. Having promised this, he begged her in his turn to receive his friend well when he should come about two o'clock, and afterwards get rid of him by degrees. She made great difficulties about this, and only yielded at last under the strong coercion of her love for Bonnivet, who on taking leave of her behaved so much to her satisfaction that she would gladly have had him stay a little longer.

Having risen and put on his clothes, he went out of the room, and left the door ajar, as he had found it. As it was near two o'clock, he withdrew into a corner near the head of the stairs, lest he should meet the Italian, and soon afterwards saw him pass along the gallery and enter the fair one's chamber. Bonnivet then went home to rest after the fatigues of the night, and remained in bed till nine next morning. The Italian failed not to come to him when he was getting up, and gave him an account of his adventure, which had not turned out quite so agreeably as he had expected; for, said he, "I found the lady out of bed in her dressing-gown, and in a high fever, her pulse beating violently, her face all on fire, and such a great perspiration breaking out upon her, that she begged me to go away for fear she should be obliged to call her women to her. She was so ill, in short, that she had more need to think of death than of love, and to be put in mind of Heaven rather than of Cupid. She was very sorry, she told me, that I had run such a hazard for her sake, since she could not make me any requital in this world, being about, as she hoped, to find herself soon in a better one. I was so shocked at a mischance I so little anticipated, that my fire and my joy were changed to ice and sadness, and I instantly withdrew. At daylight this morning I sent to inquire for her, and have received word that she is extremely ill."

As he delivered this sad report he wept so piteously that one would have thought his soul would have been washed out with his tears. Bonnivet, who was as much disposed to laugh as the other was to weep, consoled him as well as he could, and bade him recollect that things of long duration always seem to have an untoward beginning, and that love had caused this delay only to enhance his future enjoyment. Thereupon the two friends parted. The lady kept her bed for some days, and was no sooner out of it once more than she dismissed her first lover, alleging as her reason the fear of death in which she had been, and the terror of her conscience. She devoted herself wholly to Bonnivet, whose love lasted, as usual, about as long as the bloom and beauty of the flowers.

It strikes me, ladies, that Bonnivet's sly manœuvres were a fair set-off against the hypocrisy of the Milanese lady, who, after playing the prude so long, at last let her lasciviousness be seen.

"You may say what you please of women," said Ennasuite; "but Bonnivet's conduct was anything but that of a man of honour. If a woman loves a man, is that any reason why another should have her by trickery?"

"Set it down for certain," said Geburon, "that when that sort of goods is for sale, they are always carried off by the highest and last bidder. Do not imagine that those who serve ladies take such a world of trouble for their sakes. No, it is for themselves, and for their own pleasure."

"Of that I entertain no manner of doubt," said Longarine; "for, to be frank with you, all the lovers I have had have invariably begun by talking of my interests, and telling me that they loved my life, my welfare, and my honour, and the upshot of it all has no less invariably been their own interest, their own pleasure, and their own vanity. So it is best to dismiss them before they have finished the first part of their sermon; for when you come to the second, you cannot refuse them with so much credit to yourself, since declared vice is a thing to be rejected as a matter of course."

"According to your doctrine, then," said Ennasuite, "one ought to rebuff a man as soon as he opens his mouth, without knowing what he has to say."

"Not so," replied Parlamente. "Every one knows that, at the outset, a woman ought not to let it appear that she understands, still less that she believes, the declaration made to her by a lover; but when he comes to strong oaths, it strikes me that it is more becoming in the lady to leave him in the middle of that fine road than to go with him all the way to the bottom."

"Nay, but are we always to assume that they love us with a criminal passion?" said Nomerfide. "Is it not sinful to think ill of one's neighbour?"

"You may believe this or not, as you please," said Oisille; "but there is so much reason for fearing that such is the case, that the moment you discover the least inkling of it, you cannot be too prompt in getting away from a fire which is too apt to burn up a heart before even it is once perceived."

"That is a very hard law you lay down," replied Hircan. "If women, whom gentleness becomes so well, were all as rigorous as you would have them to be, we men would lay aside meekness and supplication, and have recourse to stratagem and violence."

"The best thing," said Simontault, "is, that every one should follow the bent of his nature, and love or not, as he pleases, but always without dissimulation."

"Would to God," exclaimed Saffredent, "that the observance of this law were as productive of honour as it would be of pleasure!"

But Dagoucin could not refrain from observing, "Those who would rather die than make known their sentiments, could not endure your law."

"Die!" cried Hircan. "The good knight is yet unborn who would die for any such cause. But let us say no more of what is impossible, and see to whom Simontault will give his voice."

"To Longarine," replied the gentleman thus appealed to; "for I observed her just now talking to herself. I suspect she was conning over some good thing, and she is not wont to disguise the truth either against man or woman."

"Since you think me such a friend to the truth," said Longarine, "I will tell you a story, which, though not quite so much to the credit of our sex as I could wish, will, nevertheless, show you that there are women who have as much spirit and as sound wits as men, and are not inferior to them in cunning. If my story is somewhat long, I will endeavour to make you amends by a little gaiety."

NOVEL XV.

A LADY OF THE COURT, SEEING HERSELF NEGLECTED BY HER HUSBAND, WHOSE LOVE WAS BESTOWED ELSEWHERE, RETALIATED UPON HIM.

THERE was at the court of King Francis the First a gentleman whom I could name if I would. He was poor, not having five hundred livres a year; but the king prized him so highly for his great endowments, that he bestowed upon him a wife so wealthy that a great lord might have been satisfied with such a match. As his wife was still very young, the king requested one of the greatest ladies of the court to take her into her household, which she did with great willingness. The gentleman was so well-bred and so good-looking, that he was greatly esteemed by all the court ladies, especially by one of them, whom the king loved, and who was neither so young nor so handsome as his wife. The gentleman loved this lady so passionately, and made so little account of his wife, that he hardly shared her bed one night in the year; and to add to the poor creature's mortification, he never spoke to her, or showed her any token of kindness; a sort of treatment which she found it very hard to bear. Meanwhile he spent her income for his own gratification, and allowed her so small a share of it, that she had not wherewithal to dress as became her quality. The lady with whom she resided often complained of this to the husband. "Your wife," she said, "is handsome, rich, and of a good family, yet you neglect her. Her extreme youth has enabled her hitherto to endure this neglect; but it is to be feared, that when she comes to maturer years, her mirror, and some one who is no friend to you, will so set before her eyes her beauty which you disdain, that resentment will prompt her to do what she would not have dared to think of if you had treated her better." But the gentleman, whose heart was set elsewhere, made light of these judicious remonstrances, and went on in his old ways.

After two or three years, the young wife began to be one of the finest women in France. Her reputation was so great that it was commonly reported at court that she had not her equal. The more sensible she became that she was worthy to be loved, the more poignantly she felt her husband's contemptuous treatment, and but for the efforts of her mistress to console her, she would almost have sunk into hopeless melancholy. After having tried in vain every means to please her husband, she came to the conclusion that it was impossible he should so ill respond to the love she bore him unless he were captivated elsewhere. With this idea in her mind, she set to work so carefully and so shrewdly that she found out where it was he was so occupied every night as to forget his conscience and his wife. When she had thus got certain evidence of the life he led, she fell into such deep despondency that she would wear nothing but black, and shunned all places of amusement. Her mistress perceived this, and omitted nothing by which she could hope to raise her out of that gloomy mood; but all her kind efforts were unavailing. Her husband was made acquainted with her condition, but instead of caring to relieve it, he only laughed at it.

A great lord who was nearly related to the young wife's protectress, and who paid her frequent visits, having one day been informed of the husband's hard-hearted behaviour, was so shocked at it, that he would fain try to console the wife; but he was so charmed with her conversation and manners, and thought her so beautiful, that he had far more desire to make her love him than to talk to her of her husband, except it was to let her know how little cause she had to love such a man. As for the young lady herself, forsaken by him who ought to have loved and cherished her, and wooed by a lord who had everything to recommend him, she thought herself fortunate in having made such a conquest. Though she desired always to preserve her honour, nevertheless she took great pleasure in talking to him, and in seeing that she was loved, a thing whereof she had, so to speak, a famishing need. This tender friendship lasted some time, but at last the king became aware of it, and as he had a great regard for the husband, and would not have any one affront or annoy him, he begged the prince to discontinue his attentions, on pain of incurring the royal displeasure. The prince, who prized the king's good graces above all the ladies in the world, promised to forego his designs, since such was the king's wish, and to go that very evening and bid farewell to the lady.

That evening the husband, being at his window, saw the prince come in and enter his wife's chamber, which was beneath his own. The prince saw him too, but did not turn back for all that. On saying farewell to her whom he was but beginning to love, the only reason he alleged for this change in him was the king's command. After many tears and lamentations, which lasted nearly until one o'clock in the morning, the lady said to him at parting, "I thank God, my lord, for the grace he confers upon me in depriving me of your friendship, since it is so little and so weak that you take it up and lay it down at the commands of men. As for me, I did not consult either mistress, or husband, or myself, whether I should love you or not. Your engaging manners and your good looks won my heart; but since yours is less amorous than timid, you cannot love perfectly, and the friend who is not true and staunch to the uttermost is not the friend for me to love thoroughly, as I had resolved to love you; farewell, then, my lord, you whose timidity does not deserve a love so frank and so sincere as mine."

The prince went away with tears in his eyes, and looking back, he again saw the husband, who had watched him in and out. Next day the prince told him why he had gone to see his wife, and acquainted him with the commands laid upon him by the king, whereat the gentleman was greatly pleased, and gave much thanks to his sovereign. But seeing that his wife was becoming more beautiful every day, and he himself older and less good-looking, he began to change his part, and to assume that which he had long made his wife play; for he sought her more than he had been wont, and took much more notice of her. But the more he sought her the more she shunned him, being very glad to pay him back a part of the distress he had caused her by his indifference. At the same time, not to miss the pleasure which love was beginning to afford her, she cast her eyes on a young gentleman whose person and manners were so engaging, that he was a favourite with all the ladies of the court. By complaining to him of the unkind treatment she had experienced, she inspired him with such pity for her, that he left nothing untried to console her. On her part, to indemnify her for the prince she had lost, she loved this new friend so heartily, that she forgot her past griefs, and thought only of the means of adroitly carrying on her intrigue; and in this she succeeded so well, that her mistress never perceived it, for she took good care never to speak in her presence to her lover. When she had anything to say to him, she went to see certain ladies of the court. Among these was one with whom her husband seemed to be in love.

One dark night after supper she stole away alone, and entered the ladies' room, where she found him whom she loved more than herself. She sat down beside him, and leaning over a table they conversed together, whilst they pretended to be reading a book. Some one whom the husband had set on the watch came and told him whither his wife was gone; and he, like a sensible man as he was, said nothing, but followed her quickly, entered the room, and saw her reading a book. Pretending not to see her, he went straight up to the ladies, who were at the other side of the room; whilst so disconcerted was she at being found by him with a man to whom she had never spoken in his presence, that she scrambled over a table, and ran away as if her husband was pursuing her sword in hand, and went to her mistress, who was just about to retire for the night.

After her mistress was undressed and she had left the room, she met one of her own women coming to tell her that her husband wanted her. She said flatly she would not go to him, for he was so strange and harsh, that she was afraid he would do her some mischief. Nevertheless, she went at last, for fear of worse. Her husband said not a word to her about what had occurred until they were in bed; but then as she could not help crying, he asked her the cause of her tears? She cried, she said, because she was afraid he was angry at having found her reading with a gentleman. The husband replied that he had never forbidden her to speak to anybody; but that he had been surprised at seeing her run away as if she had done something wrong; and that this had made him believe she loved the gentleman. The end of the matter was, that he forbade her thenceforward to speak to any man, either in public or in private, assuring her that otherwise he would kill her without mercy. But to forbid things we like is the surest way to make us desire them more ardently, and it was not long before this poor woman had forgotten her husband's threats and her own promises.

The very same evening, having gone back to sleep with other demoiselles and her attendants, she sent to invite the gentleman to visit her at night. Her husband, whose jealousy kept him awake, and who had heard that the gentleman used to visit his wife at night, wrapped himself up in a cloak, took a valet de chambre with him, and went and knocked at his wife's door. Up she got, and seeing her women all asleep, she went alone in her mantle and slippers to the door, never in the least suspecting who was there. Her inquiry, who was there? was answered in her lover's name, but for her better assurance, she half opened the wicket and said, "If you are the person you say, give me your hand, and

I shall know if you speak truly." The moment she felt her husband's hand, she recognised him, and slamming the wicket, cried out, "Ha, monsieur! it is your hand."

"Yes," cried her husband, in a great passion, "it is the hand that will keep word with you. So fail not to come when I send for you."

With that he went away, and she returned to her chamber more dead than alive. "Get up, my friends," she cried to her women; "get up. You have slept too long for me. I thought to trick you, and I have been tricked myself," and saying this, she fainted away. Her women, thus suddenly roused from their sleep, were astonished at her words, and still more when they saw her lying like a corpse, and they ran hurriedly to and fro in search of means to revive her. When she had recovered her speech, she said to them, "You see before you, my friends, the most wretched creature in the world." Then she related to them her adventure, entreating them to stand by her, for she looked upon herself already as a dead woman. While her women were endeavouring to comfort her, a valet de chambre arrived with a message from her husband, ordering her to come to him instantly. Thereupon she embraced two of her women, and began to cry and shriek, beseeching them not to let her go, for she was sure she should never return. The valet de chambre, however, bade her not be afraid, for he would answer for it with his life that no harm should happen to her. Seeing, then, that resistance was useless, she threw herself into the valet's arms, saying, "Since it must be so, my friend, carry this wretched body to death;" and in fact he carried, rather than led her away, for she was almost in a swoon. The moment she entered her husband's room, she fell on her knees, and said, "Have pity on me, monsieur, I beseech you; and I swear to you before God that I will tell you the whole truth."

"That I am determined you shall," replied the husband in a furious tone, and ordered every one to quit the room. As his wife had always seemed to him very devout, he thought she would not perjure herself if he made her swear on the cross. He therefore sent for a very handsome one he had, and when they were alone he made her swear on that cross that she would speak the truth as to such questions as he should put to her. By this time she had been able to rally her spirits, and having partly recovered from her first terror, she resolved to conceal nothing, but at the same time not to say anything which could compromise her lover. Her husband then put the qustions he deemed necessary, and this was how she replied to them:

"I will not attempt to justify myself, monsieur, or to make little of the love I have entertained for the gentleman who is the cause of your jealousy. Whatever I might say to that effect, you could not and ought not to believe it after what has occurred; but I must tell you what has occasioned this love. Never wife so loved her husband as I loved you; and but for your unkindness I should never have loved any one but you. You know that while I was yet a child, my parents wished to marry me to a man of higher birth than you; but they could never make me consent to it from the moment I had spoken to you. I declared for you in spite of all they could say, and without caring for your poverty. You know in what manner you have treated me hitherto. This has caused me such grief and vexation, that but for the support of the lady with whom you have placed me, I should have sunk under my despair. But at last, seeing myself full-grown, and esteemed fair by every one but you, I began to feel so acutely the wrong you did me, that the love I had for you turned into hatred, and the desire of pleasing you into that of revenging myself. While in this desperate mood, I had opportunity to see a prince, who, more obedient to the king than to love, forsook me at a time when I was beginning to derive consolation from an honourable love. After I had lost the prince, I found one who had no need to be at any pains to woo me, for his good looks, his deportment, and his excellent endowments, are enough to make him an object of interest to all women of sense. At my solicitation, and not at his own, he has loved me with such propriety that he has never asked of me anything inconsistent with my honour. Though the little cause I have to love you might induce me to make light of my wedded faith, yet my love for God and my own honour have hitherto prevented me from doing anything I have need to confess, or which can make me apprehensive of infamy. I do not deny that, under pretence of going to say my prayers, I have retired as often as I could into a *garderobe* to converse with him; for I have never confided the conduct of this affair to any one. Nor yet do I deny, that being in such a private place, and safe from all suspicion, I have kissed him with more hearty good-will than I kiss you; but may God never show me mercy if anything else ever happened in our *tête-à-têtes*, or if he ever asked me for more, or my own heart ever harboured a thought of granting anything besides; for I was so happy, that it seemed to me there could not be in the world a greater pleasure than that which I enjoyed.

"But you, sir, who are the sole cause of my misfortunes, would you desire to be revenged for conduct of which you have so long been setting me an example, with this difference, that what you have done you have done without honour and without conscience? You know, and I know too, that she whom you love does not content herself with what God and reason command. Though the laws of men condemn to infamy women who love any others than their husbands, the law of God, which is infinitely more venerable and more august, condemns men who love any other women than their own wives. If the faults we have both committed be weighed in the balance, you will be found more guilty than I. You are a wise man; you have age and experience enough to know evil, and shun it; but I am young, and have no experience of the force and might of love. You have a wife who loves you, and to whom you are dearer than her own life; and I have a husband who shuns me, hates me, and treats me with such harshness as he would not show to a servant woman. You love a woman in years, lean and lanky, and not so handsome as I am; and I love a gentleman, younger than you, handsomer, and more agreeable. You love the wife of your best friend and the mistress of your sovereign, thus violating friendship and the respect you owe to both; and I love a gentleman who has no other ties than his love for me. Judge now, sir, without partiality, which of us two is the more to be condemned or excused. I do not believe there exists a man of sense and knowledge of the world who would not give his verdict against you, seeing that I am young and ignorant, despised by you and loved by the handsomest and best-bred gentleman in France, and that notwithstanding all that, I love him only because I despair of being loved by you."

Hearing such home truths as these delivered by the lips of

a beautiful woman, with such grace and assurance that it was easy to see she did not think herself deserving of any punishment, the husband was so confounded that he knew not what to reply, except that a man's honour and a woman's were different things. Nevertheless, as she swore that nothing criminal had taken place between her and her lover, it was not his intention to love her less; but he begged that she would offend no more, and that they should both forgive and forget 'the past. She gave a promise to that effect, and the reconciliation being effected, they went to bed together.

Next morning an old demoiselle, who was greatly alarmed for her mistress's life, came to her bedside, and said, " Well, madam, how do you find yourself?" " There is not a better husband in the world than mine," she replied laughing, " for he believed me on my oath." In this way five or six days passed in apparent harmony between the married pair; meanwhile, however, the husband, whose jealousy was not at all allayed, had his wife narrowly watched night and day; but in spite of all this vigilance his spies could not hinder the lady from again entertaining her lover in a dark and very suspicious place. Nevertheless, she managed the matter so secretly, that no one could ever know the truth for certain; only some valet set a story afloat that he had found a gentleman and a lady in a stable which was under the chamber occupied by the mistress of the lady in question. Upon this doubtful evidence the husband's jealousy became so increased that he resolved to have the gallant assassinated; and he assembled for that purpose a great number of relations and friends, who were to despatch him in case they met him. But it happened that one of the principal persons among the confederates was an intimate friend of the man whose death they plotted; and instead of surprising him, he put him fully on his guard; and the gentleman was such a general favourite, and always had such a good escort of friends, that he did not fear his enemy; nor was he ever assailed.

He thought it right, however, to have a conference with the lady under whose protection his fair one resided, and who had never heard a word of the whole affair, for he had never spoken with the young lady in her presence. Going to a church where he knew that she was, he acquainted her with the husband's jealousy, and the design he had formed against his life, and told her, that although he was innocent, he was resolved to go and travel in foreign countries, in order to extinguish the false report that was beginning to gather strength. The princess was greatly astonished at hearing such news, and vowed that the husband did very wrong to suspect so virtuous a woman as his wife, and one in whom she had never seen anything but virtue and propriety. However, considering the husband's influence, and in order to put an end to this scandalous report, she advised him to withdraw for some time, assuring him she would never believe any such idle fancies and suspicions. Furthermore, she advised him to speak to the husband before his departure.

He took her advice, and meeting the husband in a gallery near the king's chamber, he said to him with an assured countenance, and with the respect due to a man of his rank, " I have all my life desired, monsieur, to render you service, and I learn that in return you laid wait, yesterday evening, for my life. I beg you to consider, monsieur, that although you have more power and authority than I, nevertheless I am a gentleman as well as you, and I should be very loth to part with my life for nothing. I entreat you also to consider that you have a virtuous wife, and if any one chooses to say the contrary, I will tell him that he foully lies. For my part, I am not conscious of having done anything that should give you cause for wishing me ill; therefore, if it so please you, I will remain your obedient servant; or if not, I am the king's, and that is enough for me."

The husband replied, that true it was he had suspected him; but he thought him so gallant a man that he would rather be his friend than his enemy; and, taking leave of him, hat in hand, he embraced him as his friend. You may imagine what was said by those who had been commissioned on the preceding evening to kill the gentleman, when they witnessed these demonstrations of esteem and friendship. The lover then set out on his travels; but as he had less money than good looks, his mistress gave him a ring her husband had given her, worth three thousand crowns, which he pawned for fifteen hundred.

Some time after his departure the husband waited on the princess, and begged leave for his wife to pass some months with one of his sisters. The princess was much surprised at this unexpected request, and pressed him so much to tell her the reason of it, that he partially explained it to her. The young lady then having taken her leave of her mistress and the whole court, without shedding tears, or showing the least sign of grief, set out for the place to which her husband chose to send her, under the care of a gentleman who had express orders to watch her carefully, and above all, not to suffer her to speak on the road with the suspected person. Being aware of the nature of the orders given to her escort, she every day gave them alarms, and made game of their vigilance. On the day she began her journey, she fell in with a Cordelier on horseback, and chatted with him from dinner almost till bedtime. When they were within a good league of the inn, she said to him, " Here, father, are two crowns for the consolations you have afforded me ; I have wrapped them in paper as you see, for otherwise I know you would not venture to touch them. Do me the favour to set off at a gallop across the country the moment you quit my side, and take care that you are not seen by the people about me. I say this for your good and for the obligation I am under to you."

Off went the Cordelier accordingly ; and no sooner had he gone, than she said to her attendants, " Good servants you are, forsooth, and very vigilant guards. Properly you fulfil the orders of your master who confided in you. The very person with whom you have been commanded not to suffer me to speak, has been conversing with me the whole day, and you have let him alone. You deserve the stick, and not wages." The gentleman to whose care the fair lady had been entrusted was so vexed at hearing this, that he could not answer her a single word. Taking two men with him, he set spurs to his horse and galloped after the Cordelier, who did his best to escape, seeing himself pursued ; but as they were better mounted they overtook him. The good father, who had no idea why they treated him in that manner, roared for mercy, and in suppliant humility took off his hood and remained bareheaded. They then perceived that he was not the person they had taken him for, and that their mistress had made fools of them ; which she did more cruelly still when they came back from their chase. " You are proper men," she said, " to be entrusted with the care of women. You let them talk without knowing to whom, and then believing anything they choose to tell you, you go and insult God's servants."

After several other pranks as humorous as this, she reached the place of her destination, where her two sisters-in-law and the husband of one of them kept her in great subjection. By this time the husband learned that her ring was pledged for fifteen hundred crowns. To save the honour of his wife and recover the ring, he sent her word to redeem it, and that he would pay the money. Caring nothing for the ring since her lover had the money for it, she wrote to him that her husband constrained her to reclaim it, and lest he should suppose that she loved him less than before, she sent him a diamond which her mistress had given her, and which she prized more than all her other jewels. Her lover cheerfully sent her the merchant's obligation, thinking himself well off to have fifteen hundred crowns and a diamond; but glad above all things at being assured that his mistress loved him still. As long as the husband lived, they remained apart, and could only correspond in writing. Upon the husband's death, the lover, supposing that his mistress still retained the same feelings towards him which she had always professed, lost no time in demanding her hand in marriage; but found that long absence had given him a rival who was preferred to himself. He was so mortified at this, that, shunning all intercourse with ladies, he wooed danger, and died at last, after having distinguished himself as much as ever young man did.

This tale, ladies, in which our sex is not spared, conveys this lesson to husbands: that wives of high spirit suffer themselves to be led astray by resentment and vindictiveness, rather than by the charms of love. The heroine of this novel long resisted that sweet passion, but at last gave way to her despair. A good woman should not do like her, for there is no excuse for a bad action. The more one is exposed to do wrong, the more virtue there is in overcoming one's self and doing well, instead of rendering evil for evil; especially as the ill one thinks to do to another often recoils upon the doer. Happy those women in whom God manifests the virtues of chastity, meekness, and patience.

"It strikes me, Longarine," said Hircan, "that the lady you have been telling us of was inspired by resentment more than by love; for had she loved the gentleman as much as she pretended, she would never have quitted him for another; and therefore she may be called spiteful, vindictive, obstinate, and fickle."

"You talk at your ease on such matters," said Ennasuite; "but you know not what a heart-break it is to love without being loved."

"It is true I have little experience in that way," said Hircan; "for only let a lady show the least coldness towards me, and at once I bid adieu to love and her."

"That is all very well," said Parlamente, "for a man like you, who loves only his own pleasure; but an upright wife ought not to forsake her husband."

"And yet," observed Simontault, "the fair one in question forgot for awhile that she was a woman; for a man could not have revenged himself more signally."

"It is not fair," said Oisille. "to conclude from one instance of a naughty woman, that all others are like her."

"You are all women, however," replied Saffredent; "and however bravely adorned you may be, any one who looked carefully under your petticoats would find that you are so."

"We should do nothing but wrangle all day, if we were to listen to you," said Nomerfide. "But I so long to hear another story, that I beg Longarine to call on some one."

Longarine cast her eyes on Geburon, and said, "If you have a story to tell of some good lady, pray do so now."

"Since you call upon me," replied Geburon, "I will relate to you a thing that happened at Milan."

NOVEL XVI.

A MILANESE LADY TESTED HER LOVER'S COURAGE, AND AFTERWARDS LOVED HIM HEARTILY.

At the time when the Grand-Master of Chaumont was governor of Milan, there was a lady there who passed for one of the most respectable in the city. She was the widow of an Italian count, and resided with her brothers-in-law, not choosing to hear a word about marrying again. Her conduct was so correct and guarded, that she was highly esteemed by all the French and Italians in the duchy. One day, when her brothers and sisters-in-law entertained the Grand-Master of Chaumont, the widow could not help being present, contrary to her custom of never appearing at any festive meeting. The French could not see her without praising her beauty and her grace; one among them especially, whom I will not name. It is enough to inform you that there was not a Frenchman in Italy more worthy to be loved, for he was fully endowed with all the beauties and graces which a gentleman could have. Though he saw the widow dressed in black crape, apart from the young people, and withdrawn into a corner with several old ladies, yet, being one who had never known what it was to fear man or woman, he accosted her, took off his mask, and quitted the dance to converse with her. He passed the whole evening with her and the old ladies her companions, and enjoyed himself more than he could have done with the youngest and sprightliest ladies of the court. So charmed was he with this conversation, that when it was time to retire he hardly believed he had had time to sit down. Though he talked with the widow only upon common topics, suited to the company around her, she failed not to perceive that he was anxious to make her acquaintance, which she was so resolute to prevent, that he could never afterwards meet with her in any company, great or small.

At last, having made inquiries as to her habits of life, and learned that she went often to the churches and religious houses, he set so many people on the watch that she could not go to any of those places so secretly but that he was there before her, and stayed as long as he could see her. He made such good use of his time, and gazed at her with such hearty good-will, that she could not be ignorant of his passion; and to prevent these encounters she resolved to feign illness for some time, and hear mass at home. This was a bitter mortification to the gentleman, for he was thus deprived of his only means of seeing her. At last, when she thought she had baffled his plans, she returned to the churches as before, and Love took care forthwith to make this known to the gentleman, who then resumed his habits of devotion.

Fearing lest she should throw some other obstacle in his way, and that he should not have time to make known to her what he felt, one morning, when she was hearing mass in a little chapel, where she thought herself snugly concealed, he placed himself at the end of the altar, and turning to her at the moment when the priest was elevating the host, said, in a voice of deep feeling, "I swear to you, madam, by Him whom the priest holds in his hands, that you are the sole cause of my death. Though you deprive me of all opportunity to address you, yet you cannot be ignorant of the passion I entertain for you. My haggard eyes and death-like countenance must have sufficiently made known to you my condition." The lady pretended not to understand him, and replied, "God's name ought not to be taken in vain; but the poets say that the gods laugh at the oaths and falsehoods of lovers, wherefore women who prize their honour ought neither to be credulous nor pitiful." So saying, she rose and went home.

Those who have been in the like predicament will readily believe that the gentleman was sorely cast down at receiving such a reply. However, as he did not lack courage, he thought it better to have met with a rebuff than to have missed an opportunity of declaring his love. He persevered for three years, and lost not a moment in which he could solicit her by letters and by other means; but during all that time she never made him any other reply, but shunned him as the wolf shuns the mastiff; and that not by reason of any aversion she felt for him, but because she was afraid of exposing her honour and reputation. The gentleman was so well aware that there lay the knot of the difficulty, that he pushed matters more briskly than ever; till, after a world of trouble, refusals, and sufferings, the lady was touched by his constancy, took pity on him, and granted him what he had so long desired and waited for.

The assignation having been made, and the requisite measures concerted, the gentleman failed not to present himself at the rendezvous, at whatever risk of his life, for the fair widow resided with her relations. But as he was not less cunning than handsome, he managed so adroitly, that he was in the lady's chamber at the moment appointed. He found her alone in a handsome bed; but as he was undressing in eager haste he heard whisperings outside the chamber-door, and the noise of swords clashing against the walls. "We are undone," cried the widow, more dead than alive. "Your life and my honour are in mortal peril. My brothers are coming to kill you. Hide yourself under the bed, I beseech you; for then they will not find you, and I shall have a right to complain of their alarming me without cause."

The gentleman, who was not easily frightened, coolly replied, "What are your brothers that they should make a man of honour afraid? If their whole race was assembled at the door, I am confident they would not stand the fourth lunge of my sword. Remain quietly in bed therefore, and leave me to guard the door."

Then, wrapping his cloak round his left arm, and with his sword in his hand, he opened the door, and saw that the threatening weapons were brandished by two servant maids. "Forgive us, monsieur," they said. "It is by our mistress's orders we do this; but you shall have no more annoyance from us." The gentleman, seeing that his supposed antagonists were women, contented himself with bidding them go to the devil, and slamming the door in their faces. He then jumped into bed to his mistress without delay. Fear had not cooled his ardour, and without wasting time in asking the meaning of the sham alarm, he thought only of satisfying his passion.

Towards daylight he asked his bedfellow why she had so long delayed his happiness, and what was her reason for making her servants behave so oddly? "I had resolved," she said, laughing, "never to love; and I have adhered to that resolution ever since I became a widow. But the first time you spoke to me, I saw so much to admire in you, that I changed my mind, and began from that hour to love you as much as you loved me. It is true that honour, which has always been the ruling principle of my conduct, would not suffer love to make me do anything which might blemish my reputation. But as the stricken deer thinks to change its pain by change of place, so did I go from church to church, hoping to fly from him whom I carried in my heart, the proof of whose perfect love has reconciled honour with love.

But to be thoroughly assured that I gave my heart to a man who was perfectly worthy of it, I ordered my women to do as they have done. I can assure you, if you had been frightened enough to hide under the bed, my intention was to have got up and gone into another room, and never have had anything more to do with you. But as I have found you not only comely and pleasing, but also full of valour and intrepidity to a degree even beyond what fame had reported you; as I have seen that fear could not appal you, nor in the least degree cool the ardour of your passion for me, I have resolved to attach myself to you for the rest of my days; being well assured that I cannot place my life and my honour in better hands than in those of him whom of all men in the world I believe to be the bravest and the best."*

As if human will could be immutable, they mutually promised and vowed a thing which was not in their power—I mean, perpetual affection—which can neither grow up nor abide in the hearts of men, as those ladies know who have learned by experience what is the duration of such engagements. Therefore, ladies, if you are wise, you will be on your guard against us, as the stag would be against the hunter if the animal had reason; for our felicity, our glory, and delight, is to see you captured, and to despoil you of what ought to be dearer to you than life.

"Since when have you turned preacher, Geburon?" said Hircan. "You did not always talk in that fashion."

"It is true," replied Geburon, "that I have all my life long held a quite different language; but as my teeth are bad, and I can no longer chew venison, I warn the poor deer against the hunters, that I may make amends in my old age for the mischiefs I have desired in my youth."

"Thank you, Geburon, for your warning," retorted Nomerfide; "but after all, we doubt that we have much reason to be obliged to you; for you did not speak in that way to the lady you loved so much; therefore, it is a proof that you do not love us, or yet wish that we should love. Yet we believe ourselves to be as prudent and virtuous as those

---

* The hero of this novel is again Admiral de Bonnivet, as we learn from Brantôme.

you so long chased in your young days. But it is a common vanity of the old to believe that they have always been more discreet than those who come after them."

"When the cajolery of one of your wooers," retorted Geburon, "shall have made you acquainted with the nature of men, you will then believe, Nomerfide, that I have told you the truth."

"To me it seems probable," observed Oisille, "that the gentleman whose intrepidity you extol so highly must rather have been possessed by the fury of love, a passion so violent, that it makes the greatest poltroons undertake things which the bravest would think twice before attempting."

"If he had not believed, madam," said Saffredent, "that the Italians are readier with their tongues than with their hands, methinks he must have been frightened."

"Yes," said Oisille, "if he had not had a fire in his heart which burns up fear."

"Since you do not think the courage of this gentleman sufficiently laudable," said Hircan, "I presume you know of some other instance which seems to you more worthy of praise."

"It is true that this gentleman's courage deserves some praise," said Oisille, "but I know an instance of intrepidity that is worthy of higher admiration."

"Pray tell us it, then, madam," said Geburon.

"If you so much extol," said Oisille, "the bravery of a man who displayed it for the defence of his own life and of his mistress's honour, what praise is too great for another, who, without necessity, and from pure valour, behaved in the manner I am about to relate?"

NOVEL XVII.

KING FRANCIS GIVES A SIGNAL PROOF OF HIS COURAGE IN THE CASE OF COUNT GUILLAUME, WHO DESIGNED HIS DEATH.

A GERMAN count named Guillaume, of the House of Saxe, to which that of Savoy is so closely allied that anciently the two made but one, came to Dijon, in Burgundy, and entered the service of King Francis. This count, who was considered one of the finest men in Germany, and also one of the bravest, was so well received by the king, that he not only took him into his service, but placed him near his person, as one of the gentlemen of his chamber. The Seigneur de la Tremouille, Governor of Burgundy, an old knight and a faithful servant of the king, being naturally suspicious and attentive to his master's interests, had always a good number of spies among his enemies to discover their intrigues; and he conducted himself with such wariness that little escaped his notice. One day he received a letter, informing him among other things that Count Guillaume had already received certain sums of money, with promises of more, provided he would have the king put to death in any way in which it could be done. The Seigneur de la Tremouille instantly communicated the intelligence to the king, and made no secret of it to Madame Louise, of Savoy, his mother, who, putting out of consideration that she was related to the German, begged the king to dismiss him forthwith. Instead of doing so, the king begged Madame Louise to say no more about it, declaring it impossible that so gallant a man could be guilty of so villanous an act.

Some time after a second despatch was received, confirmatory of the former one. The governor, burning with zeal for the preservation of his master's life, begged permission of him either to expel the count from the realm, or to take precautionary measures against him; but the king expressly commanded him to make no stir in the matter, doubting not that he should come at the truth by some other means.

One day the king went to the chase, armed with no other weapon than a very choice sword, and took Count Guillaume with him, desiring him to keep close up with him. After having hunted the stag for some time, the king, finding himself alone with Count Guillaume, and far from his suite, turned aside, and rode into the thick of the forest. When they had advanced some way he drew his sword, and said to the count, "What think you? Is not this an excellent sword?" The count, taking it by the point, replied that he did not think he had ever seen a better. "You are right," rejoined the king; "and it strikes me that if a gentleman had conceived the design of killing me, and knew the strength of my arm, the boldness of my heart, and the temper of this good sword, he would think twice of it before he attacked me; nevertheless, I should regard him as a great villain, if, being alone with me, man to man, he durst not attempt to execute what he had dared to undertake."

"The villany of the design would be very great, sire," replied the astounded count; "but not less would be the folly of attempting to put it in execution."

The king sheathed his sword with a laugh, and hearing the sound of the chase, set spurs to the horse, and galloped in the direction from which the sound came.

When he rejoined his suite he said not a word of what had passed, satisfied in his own mind that Count Guillaume, for all his vigour and bravery, was not the man to strike so daring a blow. The count, however, making no doubt that he was suspected, and greatly fearing a discovery, went the next day to Robertet, the secretary of finance, and told him that, on considering the profits and appointments the king had proposed to make him for remaining in his service, he found they would not be sufficient to maintain him for half the year; and that unless his majesty would be pleased to double them, he should be under the necessity of retiring. He concluded by begging that Robertet would ascertain the king's pleasure in the matter, and make him acquainted with it as soon as possible. Robertet said he would lose no time, for he would go that instant to the king: a commission which he undertook the more readily, as he had seen the information obtained by La Tremouille. As soon as the king was awake, Robertet laid his business before him, in presence of Monsieur de la Tremouille and Admiral de Bonnivet, who were not aware of what the king had done the day before.

"You want to dismiss Count Guillaume," said the king, laughing, "and you see he dismisses himself. You may tell him, then, that if he is not satisfied with the terms he accepted when he entered my service, and which many a man of good family would think himself fortunate in having, he may see if he can do better elsewhere. Far from wishing to hinder him, I shall be very glad to have him find as good a position as he deserves."

K

Robertet was as prompt in carrying this reply to the count as he had been in laying the latter's proposals before the king. "That being the case, I must retire from his majesty's service," said the count. Fear made him so eager to be gone, that twenty-four hours sufficed for the rest. He took leave of his majesty as he was sitting down to table, and affected extreme regret at the necessity which compelled him to quit that gracious presence. He also took leave of the king's mother, who let him go with no less gladness than she had welcomed him as a kinsman and friend. The king, seeing his mother and his courtiers surprised at the count's sudden departure, made known to them the alarm he had given the count, adding, that even if he were innocent of what was laid to his charge, he had had a fright sufficient to make him quit a master whose temper he did not yet know.*

I see no reason, ladies, which could have obliged the king thus to expose his person against a man who was reckoned so formidable an adversary, had he not chosen, from mere greatness of soul, to quit the company in which kings find no inferiors to offer them simple combat, in order to put himself upon an equal footing with a man whom he regarded as his enemy, and to prove in person his daring and high courage.

"He was certainly right," said Parlamente; "for the praises of all mankind are not so satisfying to a great heart, as its own experience of the virtues with which God has endowed it."

"The ancients long ago represented," said Geburon, "that one cannot arrive at the temple of Fame without passing through that of Virtue. As I know the two persons of whom you have related this tale, I know perfectly well that the king is one of the most intrepid men in his dominions."

"When Count Guillaume came to France," said Hircan, "I should have been more afraid of his sword than of those of the best four among the Italians who were then at court."

"We all know," said Ennasuite, "that all the praises we

* The fact related in this novel must have occurred in the forest of Argilly, in July, 1521, when Francis I. was at Dijon. The German count in question was Wilhelm von Furstemberg. He is the subject of the thirtieth chapter of Brantôme's *Capitaines Etrangers*.

could bestow on the king would fall far short of his merits, and that the day would be gone before every one should have said all he thinks of him. Therefore, madam, give your voice to some one who may again tell us something to the advantage of men, if any such thing there be."

"I imagine," said Oisille to Hircan, "that as you are so much in the habit of speaking ill of women, you will not find it difficult to tell us something good of your own sex."

"That I can the more easily do," replied Hircan, "as it is not long since I was told a tale of a gentleman whose love, fortitude, and patience were so praiseworthy, that I must not suffer their memory to be lost."

NOVEL XVIII.

A LADY TESTS THE FIDELITY OF A YOUNG STUDENT, HER LOVER, BEFORE GRANTING HIM HER FAVOURS.

THERE was in one of the good towns of France a young seigneur of good family, who was attending the schools, desiring to acquire the knowledge which endows those of quality with honour and virtue. Though he had already made such progress in his studies, that at the age of seventeen or eighteen he was a pattern for other students, Love failed not, nevertheless, to teach him other lessons. To make them more impressive and acceptable, that sly instructor concealed himself under the face and in the eyes of the handsomest lady in the country, who had come to town on business connected with a lawsuit. Before Love employed the charms of this lady to subjugate the young seigneur, he had gained her heart by letting her see the perfections of the gentleman, who for good looks, pleasing manners, good sense, and a winning tongue, was not surpassed by any one. You who know what way this fire makes in a little time, when once it has begun to burn the outworks of a heart, will easily imagine that Love was not long in rendering himself master of two such accomplished subjects, and so filling them with his light, that their thoughts, wishes, and words, were but the flame of that love. The natural timidity of youth made the gallant press his suit with all possible gentleness. But it was not necessary to do violence to the fair one, since love had already vanquished her. Modesty, nevertheless, that inseparable companion of the ladies, obliged her to conceal the sentiments of her heart as long as she could. But at last the citadel of the heart, wherein honour has its dwelling, was so breached, that the poor lady gave her consent to what she had never been loth to. Still, in order to put the patience, fortitude, and passion of her lover to the proof, she surrendered only on one very difficult condition; on his fulfilling which, she assured him. that she would always love him most truly; but if he failed in it, she would do quite the reverse. The condition she proposed was this: she would condescend to talk with him, both being in bed together *en chemise*, but he was to ask nothing of her beyond kisses and sweet words; and he, thinking there was no joy comparable to that which she offered him, accepted the condition without hesitation.

That night the compact was fulfilled. It was in vain she caressed him; he would never break his word, however sharply he felt the promptings of nature. Though he was fully assured that the pains of purgatory were not a whit worse than those he endured, yet his love was so great, and his hopes so strong, that, counting on the perpetual affection it cost him so much to secure, he triumphed by his patience, and got up from beside her just as he laid down. The fair one, more astonished, I rather think, than pleased at such extraordinary forbearance, took it into her head either that his love was not so great as he said, or that he had not found in her all the attractions he had expected; for she made no account at all of the propriety, patience, and religious fidelity of her lover. She resolved, therefore, before she surrendered, to put the love he professed for her once more to the proof. To this end she requested him to gallant a girl she had in her service, one who was very good-looking, and much younger than herself, in order that persons who saw him come so often to her house, might suppose that he came for the sake of the girl and not of herself. The young seigneur, who flattered himself that he had inspired as much love as he harboured in his own bosom, did all that was required of him, and made love to the girl in obedience to her mistress's desire; and the girl, pleased with the addresses of so handsome a youth, who had such a seductive tongue, believed all he said to her, and was in love with him in earnest.

The mistress, seeing that things had come to this pass, and that her lover desisted none the more from pressing her to fulfil her promise, admitted to him that, after having put his love to such severe proofs, it was but just that she should recompense his constancy and submissiveness; accordingly, she promised to meet him an hour after midnight. I need not tell you whether or not the impassioned lover was transported with joy, and was punctual to the assignation. But the fair one, in order to put the force of his passion to a new trial, said to her demoiselle, "I know the love of Seigneur Such-a-one for you, and I know that you are no less in love with him. I take such an interest in your happiness, that I have resolved to contrive means for you both to enjoy a long conversation together in private and at your ease." The demoiselle was in such ecstasy, that she could not dissemble her passion, and in obedience to her mistress's directions, lay down alone on a handsome bed. The mistress then, leaving large candles lighted, the better to display the girl's beauty, and the door open, pretended to go away, but contrived to hide herself near the bed so cunningly, that she could not be discovered. The lover, expecting to find her as she had promised, stole softly into the room at the appointed hour, shut the door, undressed, and got into bed. No sooner had he stretched out his arms to embrace his mistress as he supposed, than the poor girl, who believed him to be all her own, threw her arms round his neck, and spoke to him with such affection, and with such a charming countenance, that there is not a holy hermit in the world but would have forgotten his paternosters for her sake. But when he recognised her form and her face, the love that had made him get so quickly into bed made him jump out of it still more hastily, on finding that his bedfellow was not she who had made him sigh so long. Vexed then alike with the mistress and the maid, "Your folly," he said, "and the malice of her who put you there, cannot make me other than I am. Try to be an honest woman; for you shall not lose your good name through me." So saying, he flung himself out of the room in huge dudgeon, and it was a long time before he again visited his mistress.

Love, however, who is never without hope, suggested to him that the greater his constancy and the more it was made known by such decisive experiments, the longer and more blissful would be his enjoyment. The lady, who had witnessed all, was so delighted and so surprised at the excess and firmness of his love, that she was impatient to see him again, in order to make amends for the sufferings she had inflicted upon him in testing his affection. The moment she saw him she spoke to him so graciously and with such tenderness, that he not only forgot all he had undergone, but even rejoiced at it, seeing that his mistress honoured his constancy, and was convinced of the sincerity of his love. He had no more disappointments to complain of; his services and his love were crowned, and he obtained from the fair one thenceforth all his heart could wish for.

Show me, ladies, if you can, a woman who has evinced the same firmness, patience, and fidelity in love as this gentleman. Those who have been exposed to the like temptations, think those which painters assign to St. Anthony very trivial in comparison. For he who can be chaste and patient in spite of the temptations of beauty, love, opportunity, and the absence of all hindrance, may rely on having virtue enough to overcome all the devils in hell.

"It is a pity," said Oisille, "that the gentleman did not address his love to a lady as virtuous as himself; it would then have been the most decorous and perfect I ever heard of."

"Tell me," said Geburon, "which of this gentleman's two trials do you think was the more difficult?"

"The last, I think," said Parlamente; "for resentment and anger are the most terrible of all temptations."

Longarine said she thought that the first was the most arduous of the two; for in order to keep his promise, he had to be victorious over love and over himself.

"You talk at random," said Simontault; "but we, who know something about the matter, may be allowed to say what we think of it. For my part, I say that he was a fool the first time, and a blockhead the second. It is my belief that in keeping his word to his mistress, he made her suffer as much as himself, or more. She only exacted that promise from him to make herself appear a better conducted woman than she really was; for she could not but know that there is no command, or oath, or anything else in the world, which is capable of stopping the headlong impulses of a violent love. She was very glad to cover her vice under an appearance of virtue, and make believe that she was accessible for nothing beneath a heroic virtue. He was a blockhead the second time to leave her who loved him, and was worth more than the other, especially when he had so good an excuse as the provocation he had received."

"I say quite the contrary," interrupted Dagoucin. "The first time he showed himself firm, patient, and a man of his word; and the second time faithful, and loving to perfection."

"And who knows," said Saffredent, "but he was one of those whom a chapter names *de frigidis et maleficiatis?** But that nothing might be wanting to the glory of this hero, Hircan ought to have acquainted us if he did his duty when he got what he wanted. We should then have been able to judge whether he was so chaste through virtue or through impotence."

"You may be sure," said Hircan, "that if I had been told this, I should not have concealed it any more than the rest. But knowing as I do the man and his temperament, I attribute his conduct to the force of his love, and not at all to impotence or coldness."

"If that is the case," said Saffredent, "he ought to have laughed at his promise. Had the fair one been offended at his doing so, it would not have been very hard to appease her."

"But, perhaps," said Ennasuite, "she would not then have consented."

"That's a fine idea!" cried Saffredent. "Was he not strong enough to force her, since she had given him the opportunity?"

"Holy Mary!" exclaimed Nomerfide, "how you talk!

---

* This is an allusion to the penalties pronounced by several councils, and repeated in the Capitularies and the Decretals of Pope Boniface VIII. against those who were supposed guilty of having by magical practices deprived a bridegroom of the power of consummating his nuptials.

Is that the way to win the good graces of a lady who is believed to be chaste and modest?"

"It seems to me," replied Saffredent, "that one cannot do more honour to a woman of whom one desires to have that sort of thing than to take it by force, for there is not the pettiest demoiselle of them all but dearly loves to be long wooed and entreated. There are some who can only be won by dint of presents; others are so stupid that they are hardly pregnable on any side. With these latter one must think of nothing but how to hit upon the means of having them. But when one has to do with a dame so wary that one cannot deceive her, and so good that she is not to be come at either by presents or by fair words, is it not allowable to try all possible means of success? Whenever you hear that a man has forced a woman you may be sure that she had left him no other means to accomplish his ends; and you ought not to think the worse of a man who has risked his life to satisfy his love."

"I have seen in my time," said Geburon, laughing, "places besieged and taken by storm, because there was no means of bringing the governors to terms either by money or threats; for they say that a fortress which treats is half taken."

"One would think," said Ennasuite, "that love is built only upon these follies. There have been many who have loved constantly with other intentions."

"If you know one such instance," said Hircan, "tell it us."

"I know one," said Ennasuite, "which I will willingly relate."

NOVEL XIX.

TWO LOVERS, IN DESPAIR AT BEING HINDERED FROM MARRYING, TURN MONK AND NUN.

IN the time of the Marquis of Mantua, who had married the sister of the Duke of Ferrara, there was in the service of the duchess a demoiselle named Pauline, so much loved by a gentleman who was in the service of the marquis, that every one was surprised at the excess of his passion; for, being poor, but a handsome man, and, moreover, in great favour with the marquis, it was thought that he ought to attach himself to a lady who had wealth enough for them both: but he regarded Pauline as the greatest of all treasures, which he hoped to make his own by marriage. The marchioness, who loved Pauline, and wished that she should make a wealthier match, dissuaded her from this one as much as she could, and often hindered the lovers from seeing each other, telling them that if they married they would be the poorest and most miserable couple in Italy. But the gentleman could not admit the validity of this argument. Pauline, on her part, dissembled her love as much as she could; but she only thought of it the more for all that. Their courtship was long, and they hoped their fortune would mend in time.

While they were awaiting this happy change, war broke out, and the gentleman was made prisoner, along with a Frenchman who was as much in love in his own country as the other was in Italy. Being fellows in misfortune, they began reciprocally to communicate their secrets. The Frenchman told his companion that his heart was captive, without saying to whom; but as they were both in the service of the Marquis of Mantua, the Frenchman knew that his comrade loved Pauline, and, having his interest at heart, advised him to abandon that connexion. This the Italian vowed it was impossible for him to do, and added that, unless the Marquis of Mantua, in recompense for his imprisonment and his good services, bestowed his mistress upon him at his return, he would turn Cordelier, and never serve any other master than God. The Frenchman, who saw in him no signs of religion, with the exception of his devotion to Pauline, could not believe that he spoke in earnest. At the end of nine months the Frenchman was set at liberty, and exerted himself to such effect that he procured that of his comrade also, who immediately on his liberation renewed his importunities to the marquis and the marchioness for their sanction to his marriage with Pauline. It was in vain they represented to him the poverty to which they would both be reduced; the relations on both sides, who would not consent to the match, forbade him to speak any more to Pauline, in hopes that absence and impossibility would cure him of his headstrong passion: but all this was unavailing to change his feelings. Seeing himself forced to submit, he asked leave of the marquis and marchioness to bid farewell to Pauline, after which he would see her no more, and his request was forthwith granted.

"Since heaven and earth are against us," said he to Pauline when they met, "and we are not only forbidden to marry, but even to see each other, the marquis and marchioness, our master and mistress, who exact such a cruel kind of obedience of us, may boast of having with one word smitten two hearts, whose bodies can henceforth only languish to death. By so unfeeling a mandate they plainly show that they have never known love or pity. I know well that their purpose is to see us both prosperously established in wealthy marriages; but they know not that people are truly rich only when they are content. However, they have so wronged and incensed me, that it is impossible I should remain in their service. I have no doubt, that if I had never talked of marrying you, they would not have carried their scruples so far as to forbid our speaking to each other; but as for me, I can assure you, that having long loved you so honestly and truly, I shall continue to love you all my life. And forasmuch as seeing you I could not endure the monstrous hardship of not being allowed to speak to you, and not seeing you, my heart, which could not remain void, would be filled with a despair which might end fatally for me, I have for a long time resolved to retreat into the cloister. Not but that I well know one may work out his salvation in any condition of life; but I believe that in these retreats one has more leisure to meditate on the greatness of the Divine goodness, which will have pity, I trust, on the faults of my youth, and dispose my heart to love the things of heaven as much as I have loved those of earth. If God gives me the grace to be able to obtain his, my continual occupation will be to pray for you. I entreat you, by the faithful and constant love we have borne to one another, to remember me in your prayers, and to beseech the Lord to give me as much constancy when I cease to see you, as he gave me gladness in beholding you. As I have hoped all my life to have from you through marriage what honour and conscience allow, and have contented myself with that hope, now that I lose it, and can never be treated by you as a husband, I entreat, that in bidding me farewell, you will treat me as a brother, and let me kiss you."

Poor Pauline, who had manifested rigour enough towards him, seeing the extremity of his grief and the reasonableness of his request, which was so moderate under such circumstances, could only reply by throwing herself in tears on his neck. So overcome was she, that speech, sense, and motion failed her, and she fainted in his arms, whilst love, sorrow, and pity produced the same effect on him. One of Pauline's companions, who saw them fall, called for help, and they were recovered by force of remedies. Pauline, who wished to hide her affection, was ashamed when she was aware how vehemently she had suffered it to display itself; however, she found a good excuse in the commiseration she had felt for the gentleman. That heart-broken lover, unable to utter the words, "Farewell for ever!" hurried away to his chamber, fell like a corpse on his bed, and passed the night in such bitter lamentations, that his servants supposed he had lost all his relations and friends, and all he was worth in the world. Next morning he commended himself to our Lord, and after dividing the little he possessed among his domestics, only retaining a very small sum of money for his immediate use, he forbade his servants to follow him, and wended his way alone to the convent of the Observance, to ask for the monastic habit, with the determination of wearing none other as long as he lived. The warden, who had known him formerly, thought at first that he was joking, or that he himself was dreaming; indeed, there was not a man in all the country who had less the look of a Cordelier, or was better gifted with the graces and endowments which one could desire to see in a gentleman. But after having heard him, and seen him shed floods of tears, the source of which was unknown to him, the warden kindly received him as a guest, and soon afterwards, seeing his perseverance, he gave him the robe of the order, which the poor gentleman received with great devotion.

The marquis and marchioness were made acquainted with this event, and were so much surprised at it that they could hardly believe it. Pauline, to show that she was without passion, did her best to dissemble her regret for her lover, and succeeded so well that everybody said she had forgotten him, whilst all the time she would fain have fled to some hermitage, to shun all commerce with the world. But one day, when she went to hear mass at the Observance with her mistress, when the priest, the deacon, and the sub-deacon issued from the vestry to go to the high altar, her lover, who had not yet completed the year of his noviciate, served as acolyte, and led the procession, carrying in both hands the two *canettes* covered with silk-cloth, and walking with downcast eyes. Pauline, seeing him in that garb, which augmented rather than diminished his good looks, was so surprised and confused, that, to conceal the real cause of her heightened colour, she began to cough. At that sound, which he recognised better than the bells of his monastery, the poor lover durst not turn his head; but as he passed before her, he could not hinder his eyes from taking the direction to which they had been so long used. Whilst gazing sadly on his mistress, the fire he had thought almost extinct blazed up so fiercely within him, that, making an effort beyond his strength to conceal it, he fell full length on the floor. His fear lest the cause of this accident should be known prompted him to say that the floor of the church, which was broken at that spot, had thrown him down. Pauline perceived from this circumstance that he had not changed his heart along with his habit; and believing that, as it was now so long since he had retired from the world, every one imagined she had forgotten him, she resolved to put into execution her long-meditated design of following her lover's example.

Having now been more than fourteen months privily making all necessary arrangements previous to her taking the veil, she one morning asked leave of the marchioness to go to hear mass at the convent of St. Claire. Her mistress granted this request without knowing why it was preferred. Calling at the Franciscan monastery on her way, Pauline begged the warden to let her see her lover, whom she called her relation. She saw him in private, in a chapel, and said to him: "If I could with honour have retired to the cloister as soon as you, I should have been there long ago. But now that by my patience I have prevented the remarks of those who put a bad construction upon everything rather than a good one, I am resolved to renounce the world, and adopt the order, habit, and life which you have chosen. If you fare well, I shall have my part; and if you fare ill, I do not wish to be exempt. I desire to go to paradise by the same road as you, being assured that the Being who is supremely perfect, and alone worthy to be called Love, has drawn us to his service by means of an innocent and reasonable affection, which He will convert entirely to himself through His Holy Spirit. Let us both forget this perishing body, which is of the old Adam, to receive and put on that of Jesus Christ who is our spirit."

The cowled lover wept with joy to hear her express such a holy desire, and did his utmost to confirm it. "Since I can never hope for more than the satisfaction of seeing you," he said, "I esteem it a great blessing that I am in a place where I may always have opportunity to see you. Our conversations will be such that we shall both be the better for them, loving as we shall do with one love, one heart, one mind, led by the goodness of God, whom I pray to hold us in His good hands, in which no one perishes." So saying, and weeping with love and joy, he kissed her hands; but she stooped her face as low as her hand, and they exchanged the kiss of love in true charity.

From the Franciscan monastery Pauline went straight to the convent of St. Claire, where she was received and veiled. Once there, she sent word to her mistress, who, hardly crediting such strange news, went to see her next day, and did all she could to dissuade her from her purpose. The only reply she received from Pauline was, that she ought to be satisfied with having deprived her of a husband of flesh, the only man in the world she had ever loved, without seeking likewise to separate her from Him who is immortal and invisible, which neither she nor all the creatures on earth could do. The marchioness, seeing her so strong in her pious resolution, kissed her, and left her in her convent with extreme regret.

These two persons lived afterwards such holy and devout lives, that it cannot be doubted that He whose law is charity, said to them at the end of their course, as to Mary Magdalen, "Your sins are forgiven, since you have loved so much," and removed them in peace to the blessed abode, where the recompense infinitely surpasses all human merits.

You cannot but own, ladies, that the man's love was the greater of the two; but it was so well repaid, that I would all those who love were so richly recompensed.

"In that case there would be more fools than ever," said Hircan.

"Do you call it folly," said Oisille, "to love virtuously in youth, and then to centre all our love in God?"

"If despite and despair are laudable," replied Hircan, laughing, "then I must say that Pauline and her lover are worthy of high praise."

"Yet God has many ways of attracting us to Him," said Geburon; "and though their beginnings seem bad, their end is, nevertheless, very good."

"I believe," said Parlamente, "that no one ever perfectly loved God who did not perfectly love some of his creatures in this world."

"What do you call loving perfectly?" said Saffredent. "Do you believe that those enamoured cataleptics who worship ladies at a hundred paces' distance, without daring to speak out, love perfectly?"

"I call perfect lovers," replied Parlamente, "those who seek in what they love some perfection, be it goodness, beauty, or charming demeanour; who aim always at virtue, and whose hearts are so noble and so spotless that they would rather lose their lives than devote them to low things forbidden by honour and conscience; for the soul which is created only to return to its sovereign good, so long as it is imprisoned in the body, does but long to arrive at that high destination. But because the senses, which can give it views thereof, are obscured and carnal since the sin of our first parents, they can only present to it those visible objects which approach nearest to perfection. In that direction the soul rushes forth, and thinks to find in outward beauty, in visible graces, and in moral virtues, the supreme beauty, grace, and virtue. But after having sought and proved them, and not found what it loves, the soul lets them go, and passes on its way, like the child who loves apples, pears, dolls, and other trivial things the handsomest it can see, and thinks that to amass little pebbles is to be wealthy; but as it grows up it loves living dolls, and amasses things necessary to human life. After a longer experience has shown it that there is neither perfection nor felicity in the things of this earth, it seeks the true felicity, and Him who is its source and principle. Still, if God did not open the eyes of its faith, it would be in danger of passing from ignorance to infidel philosophy; for it is faith alone that demonstrates and makes the soul receive that good which the carnal and animal man cannot know."

"Do you not see," said Longarine, "that even the uncultivated ground which produces only trees and useless herbs, is, nevertheless, an object of desire, in the hope that when it is well cultivated and sown it will produce good grain? In like manner the heart of man, which is conscious only of visible things, will never arrive at the condition of loving God but through the seed of the Word; for that heart is a sterile, cold, and corrupted soil."

"Thence it comes," said Saffredent, "that most doctors are not spiritual, because they never love anything but good wine and ugly sluts of chambermaids, without making trial of what it is to love honourable ladies."

"If I could speak Latin well," said Simontault, "I would quote St. John to you, who says: 'He who loves not his brother whom he sees, how shall he love God whom he doth not see?' In loving visible things, one comes to love things invisible."

"Tell us where is the man so perfect as you describe, *et laudabimus eum*," said Ennasuite.

"There are such men," replied Dagoucin; "men who love so strongly and so perfectly, that they would rather die than entertain desires contrary to the honour and conscience of their mistresses, and who yet would not have either them or others be aware of their sentiments."

"These men are like the chameleon, who lives on air," observed Saffredent. "There is no man in the world but is very glad to have it known that he loves, and delighted to know that he is loved. Also, I am convinced, that there is no fever of affection so strong but passes off as soon as one knows the contrary. For my part, I have seen palpable miracles in that way."

"I beg, then," said Ennasuite, "that you will take my place, and tell us a story of some one who has been restored from death to life, by having discovered in his mistress the reverse of what he desired."

"I am so much afraid," said Saffredent, "of displeasing the ladies, whose most humble servant I have always been, and always shall be, that without an express command I should not have dared to speak of their imperfections. But, in token of obedience, I will speak the truth."

NOVEL XX.

A GENTLEMAN FINDS HIS CRUEL FAIR ONE IN THE ARMS OF HER GROOM, AND IS CURED AT ONCE OF HIS LOVE.

There was a gentleman in Dauphiné named the Seigneur De Riant, of the household of King Francis I., and one of the best-looking and best-bred men of his day. He paid his court for a long time to a widow, whom he loved and respected so much, that, for fear of losing her good graces, he durst not ask of her that which he longed for with the utmost passion. As he was conscious of being a handsome man and well worthy of being loved, he firmly believed what she often swore to him—namely, that she loved him above all men in the world; and that if she were constrained to do anything for any one, it would be for him alone, who was the most accomplished gentleman she had ever known. She begged he would content himself with this, and not attempt to exceed the limits of decorous friendship, assuring him, that upon the least symptom of his craving anything more, she should be lost to him for ever.

The poor gentleman not only contented himself with these fine words, but even deemed himself happy in having won the heart of a person he believed to be so virtuous. It would be an endless affair to give you a circumstantial detail of his love, of the long intercourse he had with her, and of the journeys he made to see her. Enough to say, that this poor martyr to a fire so pleasing, that the more one is burned by it the more one likes to be burned, daily sought the means of aggravating his martyrdom. One day he was seized with a desire to travel post to see her whom he loved better than himself, and whom he prized above all the women in the world. On arriving at her house he asked where she was. They told him she had just come back from vespers, and was gone to take a turn in the warren to finish her devotions. He dismounts, goes straight to the warren, and meets her woman, who tells him that she is gone to walk alone in the great alley. Upon this he began to hope more than ever for some good fortune, and continued to search for her as softly as possible, desiring above all things to steal upon her when she was alone. But on coming to a charming pleached arbour, in his impatience to behold his adored, he darted into it abruptly, and what did he see then but the lady stretched on the grass, in the arms of a groom, as ugly, nasty, and disreputable, as De Riant was all the reverse. I will not pretend to describe his indignation at so unexpected a spectacle; I will only say it was so great, that in an instant it extinguished his long-cherished flame. "Much good may it do you, madam," said he, as full of resentment as he had been of love. "I am now cured and delivered of the continual anguish which your fancied virtue had caused me;" and without another word he turned on his heel and went back faster than he had come. The poor woman had not a word to say for herself, and could only put her hands over her face, that as she could not cover her shame she might at least cover her eyes, and not see him who saw her but too plainly, notwithstanding her long dissimulation.

So, ladies, unless you choose to love perfectly, never think of dissembling with a proper man, and giving him displeasure for sake of your own glory; for hypocrisy is paid as it deserves, and God favours those who love frankly.*

"It must be confessed," said Oisille, "that you have kept something good in reserve for us to the end of the day. If we were not pledged to tell the truth, I could not believe that a woman of such station could have forgotten herself so much as to quit so handsome a gentleman for a nasty groom."

"If you knew, madam," replied Hircan, "the difference there is between a gentleman who has all his life worn harness and followed the army, and a servant who has led a sedentary life and been well fed, you would excuse this poor widow."

"Say what you will," rejoined Oisille, "I doubt that you would admit any excuse for her."

"I have heard," said Simontault, "that there are women

* This is a very old story, though told by the Queen of Navarre with name and date, as one of her own time. It occurs in the introduction to the Arabian Nights, in the eighteenth canto of the Orlando Furioso, and in the novels of Morlini, the first edition of which was printed at Naples in 1520. La Fontaine has put it at the beginning of his tale of Joconde.

L

who are very glad to have apostles to preach up their virtue and their chastity; they treat them with the most gracious kindness and familiarity, and assure them that they would grant them what they sue for, did conscience and honour permit it. When the poor dupes are in company they talk of these excellent ladies, and swear they would put their hands in the fire if they are not women of virtue, relying on the proof they think they have personally obtained for their assertion. But the ladies thus praised by these simple gentlemen show themselves in their real colours to those who are like themselves, and choose for the objects on whom they bestow their favours men who have not the boldness to tell tales, and of so abject a condition, that even, were they to blab, they would not be believed."

"I have heard the same thing said before by extravagantly jealous folk," said Longarine. "But surely this is what may be called painting a chimera; for though such a thing may have happened to one wretched woman, is it thence to be inferred that all women do the same thing?"

"The more we talk on this subject," said Parlamente, "the more we shall be maligned. We had better go hear vespers, that we may not keep the monks waiting for us as we did yesterday." This proposal was unanimously agreed to.

"If any one," said Oisille, as they were walking back to the monastery, "gives thanks to God for having told the truth to day, Saffredent ought to implore his pardon for having told such a villanous tale against the ladies."

"I give you my oath," said Saffredent, "that although I have only spoken upon hearsay, what I have told you is, nevertheless, the strict truth. But if I chose to tell you what I could relate of women from my own knowledge, you would make more signs of the cross than they do in consecrating a church."

"Since you have so bad an opinion of women," said Parlamente, "they ought to banish you from their society."

"There are some who have so well practised what you advise," he replied, "that if I could say worse of them, and do worse to them all, to excite them to avenge me on her who does me so much injustice, I should not be slow to do so."

While he was speaking, Parlamente put on her half-mask and went with the rest into the church, where they found that although the bell had been rung for vespers there were no monks to say them. The fathers had been apprised of the agreeable manner in which the company spent their time in the meadow, and being fonder of pleasure than of their prayers, they had gone and crouched down there in a ditch behind a very thick hedge, and had listened to the tales with so much attention that they had not heard the vesper-bell. The consequence was, that they came running in with such haste that they were quite out of breath when they should have begun vespers. After service, some of the company inquiring of them why they had come in so late and chanted so badly, they confessed the cause; and for the future they were allowed to listen behind the hedge, and to sit at their ease. The supper was a merry one; and during it were uttered such things as any of the company had forgotten to deliver in the meadow. This filled up the rest of the evening, until Oisille begged them to retire that they might prepare for the morrow, saying that an hour before midnight was better than three after it. Thereupon they sought their respective chambers, and so ended the second day.

THIRD DAY.

EARLY as it was next morning when the company assembled in the refectory, they found Madame Oisille already there. She had been meditating for half an hour on what she was to read to them; and so intent were they upon listening to her that they did not hear the bell, and a monk had to come and tell them that high mass was about to begin. After hearing mass and dining soberly, in order to have their memories more clear, they all retired to their chambers to review their several repertories of tales previously to the next meeting in the meadow. Those who had some droll story to tell were already so merry, that one could not look in their faces without being prepared beforehand for a hearty laugh. When all were seated, they asked Saffredent to whom he addressed his call. "The fault I committed yesterday," he said, "being as you say so great, and knowing not how to repair it, I call on Parlamente. Her excellent sense will enable her to praise the ladies in such a manner as will make you forget the truth I have told you."

"I do not undertake to repair your faults," replied Parlamente; "but I will take good care not to imitate them. To this end, without departing from the truth we have pledged ourselves to speak, I will show you that there are ladies who in their love have had no other end in view than virtue and honour. As the lady of whom I have to speak is of a good family, I will change nothing in her story but the names. You will see, ladies, from what I am going to narrate, that love can make no change in a chaste and virtuous heart."

NOVEL XXI.

VIRTUOUS LOVE OF A YOUNG LADY OF QUALITY AND A BASTARD OF AN ILLUSTRIOUS HOUSE—HINDRANCE OF THEIR MARRIAGE BY A QUEEN—SAGE REPLY OF THE DEMOISELLE TO THE QUEEN—HER SUBSEQUENT MARRIAGE.

THERE was a queen in France who had in her household several young ladies of good birth, and among the rest, one named Rolandine, who was her near relation. But the queen being displeased with this young lady's father, punished the innocent for the guilty, and behaved not very well to Rolandine. Though this young lady was neither a great beauty nor the reverse, such was the propriety of her demeanour and the sweetness of her disposition, that many great lords sought her in marriage, but obtained no reply, for Rolandine's father was so fond of his money that he neglected the establishment of his daughter. On the other hand, she was so little in favour of her mistress, that she was not wooed by those who wished to ingratiate themselves with the queen. Thus, through the negligence of her father and the disdain of her mistress, this poor young lady remained long unmarried. At last she took this sorely to heart, not so much from eagerness to be married, as from shame at not being so. Her grief reached such a pitch that she forsook the pomp and mundane pursuits of the court to occupy herself only with prayer and some little handiworks. In this tranquil manner she passed her youth, leading the most blameless and devout of lives.

When she was approaching her thirtieth year, she became acquainted with a gentleman, a bastard of an illustrious house, and one of the best-bred men of his day, but ill endowed by fortune, and of so little comeliness that no one but herself would have readily chosen him for a lover. As this poor gentleman had remained solitary like herself, and as the unfortunate naturally seek each other's society, he one day accosted Rolandine. There being a strong similitude between them in point of temperament and fortune, they poured their griefs into each other's ears, and that was the beginning of a very intimate friendship between them. Seeing that they both laboured under the same misfortune, they everywhere sought each other out for mutual consolation, and thus they became more and more attached to each other to an extraordinary degree. Those who had known Rolandine so coy that she would hardly speak to any one, were shocked to see her every moment with the bastard, and told her gouvernante that she ought not to permit such long conversations. The gouvernante spoke to Rolandine on the subject, telling her that it was taken amiss that she should be on such familiar terms with a man who was neither rich enough to marry her, nor good-looking enough to be loved. Rolandine, who had hitherto been reproved for her austerity, rather than for her mundane ways, replied, "You see, mother, that I cannot have a husband of my own quality. I have hitherto always attached myself to the young and good-looking; but as I am afraid of falling into the pit into which I have seen so many fall, I now attach myself to this gentleman, who, as you know, is so correct and so virtuous that he never talks to me but of seemly things. What harm, then, do I do to you, and to those who make a talk about it, consoling my sorrows by means of an innocent converse?"

The poor woman, who loved her mistress more than herself, made answer, "I see plainly, mademoiselle, that you are right, and that your father and your mistress do not treat you as you deserve. But since this acquaintance gives rise to remarks which are not to the advantage of your honour, you ought to break it off, though the man were your own brother."

"I will do so, since such is your advice," replied Rolandine, weeping, "but it is very hard to have no consolation in the world."

The bastard came to see her as usual, but, with tears in her eyes, she related to him in detail all that her gouvernante had said to her, and begged him not to visit her any more until this tattle should have subsided; and he complied with her entreaty. Both of them having lost their consolation through this separation, they began to feel an uneasiness such as neither had ever before experienced. Her whole time was spent in prayer, fasting, and journeying; for the sentiment of love, so totally new to her, caused her such agitation that she did not know a moment's rest. The bastard was not in a much better plight; but as he had made up his mind to love her and try to obtain her for a wife, and saw that it would be a very glorious thing for him to succeed in the attempt, his only thought was how he should press his suit, and how he should secure the gouvernante in his interest. To this end he represented to her the deplorable condition of her mistress, who was wilfully deprived of all consolation. The good woman thanked him with tears for the interest he took in her mistress's welfare, and cast about with him for means to enable him to have an interview with her. It was arranged between them that Rolandine should pretend to be troubled with a headache, which made all noise insupportable to her; and that when her companions left her in her chamber, the bastard and she might remain alone, and converse together without restraint. The bastard, delighted with the expedient, gave himself up entirely to the guidance of the gouvernante, and in this way he was enabled to talk with his mistress whenever he pleased.

But this pleasure was not of long duration; for the queen, who disliked Rolandine, asked what she was doing in her chamber. Some one replied that she had a headache; but somebody else, either disliking her absence or wishing to cause her annoyance, said that the pleasure she took in conversing with the bastard would be sure to cure her headache. The queen, who regarded as mortal sins in Rolandine what would have been venial sins in others, sent for her, and forbade her ever to speak to the bastard, except in her own chamber or hall. Rolandine professed obedience, and replied, that had she known that the bastard, or any one else, was displeasing to her majesty, she would never have spoken to him. At the same time she was inwardly resolved to find out some other expedient, of which the queen should know nothing. As she fasted on Wednesdays, Fridays, and Saturdays, and did not quit her chamber, she took care to be visited on those days by the bastard, whom she was beginning to love greatly, and had time to talk with him in presence of her gouvernante whilst the others were at supper. The less time they had at their disposal, the more fervid and impassioned was their language; for they stole the time for mutual conversation, as the thief steals something precious. But there is no secret which is not found out at last. A varlet, having seen the bastard come in one day, mentioned it in a place where it failed not to be repeated, till it reached the ears of the queen, who put herself into such a towering passion, that the bastard never afterwards durst enter the chamber of the demoiselles. He often pretended to go a journey, in order to have opportunity to see the object of his affections, and every evening he used to return to the chapel of the château, dressed sometimes as a Cordelier, sometimes as a Jacobin, and always so well disguised that no one knew him except Rolandine and her gouvernante, who failed not at once to accost the good father.

The bastard, feeling assured that Rolandine loved him, did not scruple to say to her one day, "You see, mademoiselle, to what I expose myself for your service, and how the queen has forbidden you to speak to me. You see, too, that nothing is further from your father's thoughts than disposing of you in marriage. He has refused so many good offers, that I know no one far or near who can have you. I know that I am poor, and that you could not marry a gentleman who was not richer than myself; but if to have a great deal of love were to be rich, I should think myself the most opulent man in the world. God has given you great wealth, and the expectation of still greater. If I were so happy as to be chosen by you for your husband, I would be all my life your spouse, your friend, and your servant. If you marry one who is your own equal—and such a one, I think, will not easily be found—he will insist on being the master, and will have more regard to your wealth than to your person, to beauty than to virtue; he will enjoy your wealth, and will not treat you as you deserve. My longing to enjoy this contentment, and my fear that you will have none with another, oblige me to entreat that you will make me happy, and yourself the best-satisfied and best-treated wife in the world."

Rolandine, hearing from her lover's lips the declaration she had made up her mind to address to him, replied with a glad face, "I rejoice that you have anticipated me, and have said to me what I have long resolved to say to you. Ever since I have known you, now two years, not a moment has passed in which I have not thought over all the arguments that could be adduced in your favour and against you; but at last, having resolved to engage in matrimony, it is time that I should make a beginning, and choose the man with whom I think I can pass my life with most quiet and satisfaction. I have had as suitors men of good figure, wealthy and of high birth; but you are the only one with whom it seems to me that my heart and mind can best agree. I know that in marrying you I do not offend God, but that, on the contrary, I do what he commands. As for my father, he has so much neglected the duty of establishing me, and has rejected so many opportunities, that the law empowers me to marry without his having a right to disinherit me; but even should I have nothing but what belongs to myself, I shall esteem myself the happiest woman in the world in having such a husband as you. As for the queen my mistress, I need make no scruple of disobeying her to obey God, since she has not scrupled to frustrate all the advantages that offered themselves to me during my youth. But to prove to you that my love for you is founded on honour and virtue, I require your promise, that in case I consent to the marriage you propose, you will not ask to consummate it until after the death of my father, or until I shall have found means to obtain his consent."

The bastard having promised this with alacrity, they gave each other a ring in pledge of marriage, and exchanged kisses in the church before God, whom they called to witness their mutual promise; and never afterwards was there anything between them of a more intimate nature than kisses. This slight satisfaction quite contented these two perfect lovers, who were a long time without seeing each other, or ever giving way to mutual suspicion. There was hardly a place where honour was to be acquired to which the bastard did not repair, being assured that he could never be poor, since God had bestowed on him a rich wife; and she during his absence so faithfully preserved that perfect affection for him, that she made no account of any other man. There were some who sought her in marriage, and had for answer, that having been so long unmarried, she was resolved to remain so for ever. This reply obtained such publicity that it reached the ears of the queen, who asked her the reason of such language. Rolandine replied that it was dictated by obedience; that she well knew her majesty had never chosen to marry her when very advantageous matches had offered; and that age and patience had taught her to be content with her present condition. Whenever marriage was mentioned to her, she always replied to the same effect.

The war being ended, and the bastard having returned to court, she did not speak to him before others, but always in the church under pretext of confession, for the queen had forbidden both of them, on pain of their lives, ever to converse except in public. But virtuous love, which fears no prohibitions, was more ingenious in suggesting to them means and opportunity to meet and converse than their enemies in hindering them. There was no monastic habit which the bastard did not successively assume; and by that means their intercourse was always agreeably maintained, until the king went to one of his country seats near Tours, which was so situated that the ladies could not go on foot to any other church than that of the château, which had such an exposed confessional, that the confessor would have easily been recognised. But as often as one opportunity failed them, love furnished them with another. At that very time there came to the court a lady nearly related to the bastard. She and her son were lodged in the king's residence; and the young prince had a projecting chamber, detached as it were from the king's apartments, and so placed, that from his window one could see and speak to Rolandine, their windows being exactly at the angle of the main building and the wing. The chamber which was over the king's hall was that of Rolandine and the other ladies of honour. Rolandine having frequently seen the young prince at the window, sent word of the fact by her gouvernante to the bastard. The latter having reconnoitred the ground, pretended to take great pleasure in reading the book of the

Knights of the Round Table, which was one of those belonging to the prince; and towards dinner-hour he used to beg a valet de chambre to let him in, and leave him shut up in the chamber to finish reading his book. The valet, knowing him to be his master's relation, and a gentleman to be trusted, let him read as much as he pleased. Rolandine, on her part, used to come to her window, and in order to be free to remain there the longer, she pretended to have a sore leg; and she took her meals so early that she had no need to go to the table of the ladies of honour. She also bethought her of working at a crimson silk coverlet, which she hung at the window where she was very glad to be left alone to converse with her husband, who spoke in such a manner that no one could overhear them. When she saw any one coming she coughed, and made signs to the bastard to retire. Those who had orders to watch them were persuaded that there was no love between them, for she never quitted a chamber in which he certainly could not see her, the entrée being forbidden him.

The mother of the young prince being one day in her son's chamber, placed herself at the window where lay the big book. Presently one of Rolandine's companions in office, who was at the window of their chamber, saluted the lady. The latter asked her how Rolandine was. The other replied that she should see her if she pleased, and made her come to the window in her nightcap. After some conversation about Rolandine's illness, both parties retired. The lady, casting her eyes on the big book of the Round Table, said to the valet de chambre who had charge of it, "I am astonished that young people give up their time to reading such follies." The valet de chambre replied that he was still more surprised that persons of ripe years, and who passed for sensible people, were more attached to them than the young; and thereupon he told her, as a curious fact, how the bastard, her relation, spent four or five hours every day in reading that book. The lady at once guessed the reason, and ordered the valet de chambre to conceal himself, and watch narrowly what the bastard did. The valet de chambre executed his commission, and found that, instead of reading, the bastard planted himself at the window, and that Rolandine came and talked with him. He even overheard many expressions of their love, which they thought they had so well concealed. Next day, the valet having told his mistress what he had seen and heard, she sent for her cousin, the bastard, and after some sharp remonstrances, forbade him ever more to place himself at that window. In the evening she spoke to Rolandine, and threatened she would inform the queen if she persisted in that foolish attachment. Rolandine, without losing her presence of mind, replied, that whatever the lady might have been told, she had not spoken to the bastard since she had been prohibited from doing so by her mistress, as her companions and her servants could witness. As for the window of which the lady spoke, she had never talked there with the bastard.

The lover now fearing lest his intrigue should be exposed, withdrew from the danger, and absented himself for a long time from court, but not without writing to Rolandine, which he managed to do with such address, that, in spite of all the queen could do, Rolandine heard from him twice a week. In the first instance he employed a monk to convey his letters; but this means failing, he sent a little page, dressed sometimes in one colour, sometimes in another. The page used to post himself at the places through which the ladies passed, and, mingling with the other servants, found means always to deliver his letters to Rolandine. The queen going into the country, one of those persons whom she had charged to be on the watch regarding this affair recognised the page, and ran after him; but the page, who was a cunning lad, darted into the house of a poor woman, who was boiling her pot, and instantly thrust his letters into the fire. The gentleman who pursued him having caught and stripped him naked, searched him all over, but, finding nothing, let him go. When the page was gone, the good woman asked the gentleman why he had searched the poor boy in that manner. He replied, that it was because he believed the boy had letters about him. "You were not likely to find them," she said; "he had hidden them too well." "Where, pray?" inquired the gentleman, who now made sure of having them. He was quite confounded when he heard that they were burnt, and saw that the page had been too clever for him. However, he went at once, and told the queen what he had ascertained.

The bastard not being able to employ the page any more, sent in his stead an old domestic, who, without caring for the threats of death which he well knew the queen had proclaimed against all who should meddle in this affair, undertook to convey the letters to Rolandine. Having entered the château, he stationed himself at a door which was at the foot of a great staircase used by all the ladies; but a valet, who had formerly known him, recognised him at once, and denounced him to the queen's maître d'hôtel, who gave orders for his instant arrest. The wary servant, seeing that he was watched, turned to the wall, under a certain pretence, tore his letters into the smallest possible pieces, and threw them behind the door. Immediately afterwards he was arrested and searched, but nothing being found on him, he was interrogated upon oath as to whether he had not carried letters. Nothing was left untried in the way of promises or threats to make him confess the truth, but, in spite of all they could do, they could never get anything out of him. This unsatisfactory result was reported to the queen; but some one having thought of looking behind the door, found there the fragments of the letters. The king's confessor was sent for; and having arranged all the pieces on a table, he read the whole of the letter, in which the secret marriage was plainly revealed, for the bastard called Rolandine his wife. The queen, who was not of a humour to conceal her neighbour's fault, made a great noise about the matter; and insisted on every means being employed to make the man confess the truth respecting the letter, the identity of which he could not deny; but say to him or show him what they would, there was no possibility of making him avow anything. Those who had been commissioned in this matter took him to the edge of the river, and put him into a sack, telling him that he lied to God and the queen, contrary to the proved truth. Choosing rather to die than to betray his master, he asked for a confessor, and after having set his conscience right, he said to them, "I pray you, Sir, to tell the bastard my master, that I commend to him my wife and my children, and that I die with a good heart for his service. Do with me what you please, and be assured that you will never extract anything from me to my master's disadvantage." Then, to frighten him more, they threw him into the water, shut up as he was in the sack, and shouted to him that his life should be saved if he would speak the truth; but seeing that he made no reply, they took him out of the water, and reported his firm behaviour to the queen. "Neither the king nor myself," said her majesty, "is so fortunate in servants as the bastard, who has not wherewithal to reward them." She did all she could to engage the worthy fellow in her service, but he would never quit his master, until the latter permitted him to enter the service of the queen, in which he lived happy and contented.

Having discovered the secret marriage by means of the intercepted letter, the queen sent for Rolandine, and with great violence of manner called her several times wretch instead of cousin, upbraiding her with the dishonour she had done to her house, and to her who was her mistress, in having thus married without her consent. Rolandine, who was long aware of the little kindness the queen entertained for her, fully returned that feeling. As there was no love between them, fear no longer availed; and as Rolandine saw plainly that a reprimand so publicly given was prompted less by regard for her than by the wish to put her to shame, and that the queen was more pleased in mortifying her than grieved to find her in fault, she replied with an air as calm and composed as that of the queen was agitated and passionate, "If you did not know your own heart, madam, I would set before you the bad feeling you have long entertained towards my father and me; but you know it so well, that you will not be surprised to hear that it is not a secret for anybody. For my part, madam, I have seen and felt it to my cost. If you had been as kind to me as to those who are not so nearly related to you, I should now be married in a manner that would do honour both to you and to me; but you have forsaken me, and not shown me the least mark of favour, so that I have missed all the good offers I have had through my father's negligence and the little account you have made of me. This unkind treatment threw me into such despair, that if my health had been strong enough to endure the austerities of a convent, I would gladly have entered one to escape from the continual vexations which your harshness caused me. In the midst of this despondency I became acquainted with one who would be of as good a house as myself, if the love of two persons was as much esteemed as the matrimonial ring; for you know that his father would take precedence of mine. He has long loved and cheered me; but you, madam, who have never forgiven me the least fault, or praised any good act I may have done, though you knew by experience that it was not my wont to talk of love and mundane vanities, and that I lived a more religious life than any other of your servants, you have not hesitated from the first to take offence at my speaking to a gentleman as unfortunate as myself, and in whose friendship I sought nothing else than consolation of mind. When I saw that I was entirely deprived of this, my despair was so great that I resolved to seek my repose with as much solicitude as you took to deprive me of it. From that very hour we interchanged promises of marriage which were sealed with a ring. It seems to me, then, madam, that you wrong me in calling me wicked. The great and perfect friendship which subsists between the bastard and myself would have given me occasion to do wrong if I had been so disposed, yet we have never gone further than kissing, it being my conviction that God would do me the grace to obtain my father's consent before the consummation of our marriage. I have done nothing against God or against my conscience. I have waited till the age of thirty to see what you and my father would do for me; and my youth has been passed in such chastity and virtue that no one in the world can justly cast the least reproach upon me in that respect. Finding myself on the decline, and without the hope of obtaining a husband of my own rank, reason determined me to take one according to my taste, not for the lust of the eyes, for, as you know, he whom I have chosen is not comely; nor yet for that of the flesh, since there has been no consummation; nor for the pride and ambition of this life, for he is poor, and of little preferment; but I have had regard purely and simply to the virtue and good qualities he possesses, as to which all the world is constrained to do him justice, and to the great love he has for me, which affords me the hope of enjoying quiet and contentment with him.

After having maturely considered the good and the evil which might result to me, I took the course which appeared to me the best, and finally resolved, after two years' examination, to end my life with him; and this I so fully resolved, that no torments which could be inflicted upon me, nor death itself, could make me change my purpose. So, madam, I beseech you to excuse in me what is highly excusable, as you very well know, and leave me to enjoy the peace and quiet I expect to find with him."

The queen, unable to make any reasonable reply to language so resolute and so true, could only renew her passionate chiding and abuse, and, bursting into tears, "Wretch," she said, "instead of humbling yourself, and testifying repentance for the fault you have committed, you speak with audacity, and, instead of blushing, you do not so much as shed one tear; thereby giving plain proof of your obstinacy and hardness of heart. But if the king and your father do as I would have them, they will put you in a place where you will be constrained to hold other language."

"Since you accuse me, madam, of speaking with audacity," replied Rolandine, "I am resolved to say no more, unless you are pleased to permit me to speak." The queen having given her permission, she continued: "It is not for me, madam, to speak to you with audacity. As you are my mistress, and the greatest princess in Christendom, I must always entertain for you the respect which is your due; and it has never been my intention to depart from it. But as I have no advocate but the truth, and as it is known to myself alone, I am obliged to speak it boldly, in the hope that if I have the good fortune to make you thoroughly cognisant of it, you will not believe me to be such as you have been pleased to call me. I am not afraid that any mortal creature should know in what manner I have conducted myself in the affair which is laid to my charge, for I know that I have not done anything contrary either to God or to my honour. This, madam, is what makes me speak without fear, being well assured that He who sees my heart is with me; and with such a judge on my side, I should be wrong to fear those who are subject to His judgment. Wherefore should I weep, madam, since honour and conscience do not upbraid me? As to repentance, madam, I am so far from repenting of what I have done, that were it to be done again, I would do it. It is you, madam, who have great reason to weep, both for the wrong you have done me in the past, and for that which you now do me in censuring me publicly for a fault of which you are more guilty than I. If I had offended God, the king, you, my kindred, and my conscience, I ought to testify my repentance by my tears; but I ought not to weep for having done an act that is good, just, and holy, which would never have been spoken of but with honour, if you, madam, had not prematurely divulged it, and given it an air of culpability; thereby plainly showing that you are more bent on dishonouring me than on preserving the honour of your house and your kindred. But since it is your pleasure, madam, to act thus, it is not for me to gainsay you. Innocent as I am, I shall feel no less pleasure in submitting to the punishment you may choose to inflict upon me, than you in imposing it. You and my father, madam, have but to say what you desire that I should suffer, and you shall be promptly obeyed. I reckon upon it, madam, that he will not be backward in this; and I shall be very glad if he will share your sentiments, and if, after having agreed with you in the negligence he has shown in providing for my welfare, he imitates your activity now that the question is how to do me harm. But I have another Father in heaven, who, I hope, will give me patience enough to endure the evils I see you are preparing for me; and it is in Him alone I put my whole trust."

The queen, bursting with rage, gave orders that Rolandine should be taken out of her sight, and shut up alone in a chamber where she should not be allowed to speak to any one. Nevertheless, her gouvernante was left with her, and through her it was that Rolandine made known her present condition to the bastard, asking his advice at the same time as to what she should do. The bastard, believing that the services he had rendered to the king would be counted for something, repaired at once to the court. He found the king at the chase, told him the truth of the matter, reminded him of his poverty, and besought his majesty to appease the queen and permit the consummation of the marriage. The king made no other reply than to say, "Do you assure me that you have married her?"

"Yes, sire," replied the bastard, "by words and by presents only; but if your majesty pleases, the ceremony shall be completed."

The king looked down, and without saying another word returned to the château. On arriving there, he called for the captain of his guards, and ordered him to arrest the bastard. However, one of the friends of the latter, who guessed the king's intention, sent him warning to get out of the way and retire to one of his houses which was not far off, promising, that if the king should send in search of him, as he expected would be the case, he should have prompt notice, so that he might quit the kingdom; and that should matters be more favourable, he would send him word to return. The bastard took his friend's advice, and made such good speed that the captain of the guards did not find him.

Meanwhile, the king and queen having conferred together as to what should be done with the poor lady who had the honour to be their relation, it was decided, at the queen's suggestion, that she should be sent back to her father, who should be made acquainted with the truth of the matter. Before she went away, several ecclesiastics and people of sage counsel went to see her, and represented to her that, being engaged only by word of mouth, the marriage could easily be dissolved, provided both parties were willing, and that it was the king's pleasure she should do so, for the honour of the house to which she belonged; but she replied, that she was ready to obey the king in all things, provided conscience was not implicated; but what God had joined men could not put asunder. She besought them not to ask of her a thing so unreasonable. "If the love and the good-will which are founded only on the fear of God," she added, "are a true and solid bond of marriage, then am I so closely bound that neither steel, nor fire, nor water can loose me. Death alone can do so, and to it alone will I surrender my ring and my oath; so, gentlemen, I beg you will say no more to me on the subject." She had so much steadfastness, that she would rather die and keep her word, than live after having broken it.

This resolute reply was reported to the king, who, seeing

that it was impossible to detach her from her husband, gave orders that she should be taken away to her father's; and thither she was carried with such little ceremony or regard to her quality, that none who saw how she was treated could restrain their tears. She had transgressed, indeed; but her punishment was so great and her fortitude so singular, that they made her fault seem a virtue. Her father, on hearing this disagreeable news, would not see his daughter, but sent her away to a castle situated in a forest, and which he had formerly built for a reason well worthy to be narrated. There she was for a long time a prisoner, and every day she was told, by her father's orders, that if she would renounce her husband he would treat her as his daughter, and set her at liberty. But nothing could shake her constancy. One would have thought she made pleasant pastime of her sufferings, to see how cheerfully she bore them for the sake of him she loved.

What shall I say here of men? The bastard, who was under such obligations to her, fled to Germany, where he had many friends, and showed by his inconstancy that he had attached himself to Rolandine through avarice and ambition, rather than through real love; for he became so enamoured of a German lady, that he forgot to write to her who was suffering so much for his sake. However cruel fortune was towards them, she yet left it always in their power to write to each other; but this sole comfort was lost through the bastard's inconstancy and negligence; whereat Rolandine was distressed beyond measure. The few letters he did write were so cold and so different from those she had formerly received from him, that she felt assured some new amour had deprived her of her husband's heart, and done what vexations and persecutions had been incapable of effecting. But her love for him was too great to allow of her taking any decisive step on mere conjectures. In order, therefore, to know the truth, she found means to send a trusty person, not to carry any letters or messages to him, but to observe him, and make careful inquiries. This envoy, on his return, informed her that the bastard was deeply in love with a German lady, and that it was said she was very rich, and that he wished to marry her. So extreme was poor Rolandine's affliction on learning this news, that she fell into a dangerous illness.

Those who were aware of its cause told her, on the part of her father, that since the bastard's inconstant and dastardly behaviour were known, she had a perfect right to abandon him; and they tried hard to persuade her to do so. But it was in vain they tormented her; she remained unchanged to the end, displaying alike the greatness of her love and of her virtue. In proportion as the bastard's love diminished, Rolandine's augmented, the latter gaining as it were all that the former lost. Feeling that in her bosom alone was lodged all the love that had formerly dwelt in two, she resolved to cherish it until the death of the one or the other.

The divine goodness, which is perfect charity and true love, took pity on her sorrows, and had so much regard for her patience, that the bastard died soon after in the midst of his wooing of another woman. The news being brought her by persons who had been present at his burial, she sent to her father, begging he would be so good as to allow her to say a few words to him. Her father, who had never spoken to her during the whole time of her captivity, went to her forthwith. After having heard her plead her justification at very great length, instead of condemning and thinking of killing her, as he had often threatened, he embraced her, and said, with swimming eyes, "You are more just than I, my daughter; for if you have committed a fault, I am the principal cause of it. But since it has pleased God that things should happen thus, I will try to make amends for the past." Accordingly, he took her home, and treated her as his eldest daughter.

A gentleman who bore the name and the arms of the family at last sought her in marriage. This gentleman, who was very prudent and virtuous, often saw Rolandine, and conceived so much esteem for her, that he praised her for what others blamed, persuaded as he was that she acted only upon virtuous principles. The chevalier being liked both by the father and the daughter, the marriage was forthwith concluded. It is true that a brother she had, and who was the father's sole heir, would never give her a portion of the family wealth, under pretext that she had been wanting in obedience to her father; after whose death he treated her so cruelly, that she and her husband, who was a younger son, found it a hard matter to subsist. But God provided a remedy, for the brother, who wished to retain all, died, leaving behind him both his own wealth and that of his sister, which he unjustly retained. By this means Rolandine and her husband were raised to great affluence. They lived honourably, according to their quality, were grateful for the favours bestowed on them by Providence, had much love for one another, and, after they had brought up two sons, with whom it pleased God to bless their marriage, Rolandine joyfully yielded up her soul to him in whom she had always put her whole trust.*

Ladies, let the men who regard us as inconstancy's very self show us a husband like the wife of whom I have been telling you, one who had the same goodness, fidelity, and constancy. I am sure they will find the task so very hard, that I will acquit them of it altogether, rather than put them to such infinite pain. As for you, ladies, I beg that, for the maintenance of your dignity, you will either not love at all, or love as perfectly as this demoiselle. Do not say that she exposed her honour, since by her firmness she has been the means of so augmenting ours.

"It is true, Oisille," said Parlamente, "that your heroine was a woman of a very lofty spirit, and the more commendable for her steadfastness, as she had to do with an unfaithful husband, who wished to quit her for another."

"That, I think," said Longarine, "must have been the hardest thing for her to bear; for there is no burden so heavy which the love of two persons who are truly united may not bear with ease and comfort; but when one of the two deserts his duty, and leaves the whole burden to the other, the weight becomes insupportable."

* The Bibliophiles Français have clearly enough identified the persons in this story. The Queen of France is the celebrated Anne of Bretagne, wife of Charles VIII. and of Louis XII. Rolandine is Anne de Rohan, third child and eldest daughter of Jean II., Viscount of Rohan, Count of Porhoet, Leon, and La Garnache. She married in 1517 Pierre de Rohan, Baron of Frontenay, by whom she had two sons. The bastard appears to have been Jean, Bastard of Angoulême, legitimised in 1458 by Charles VII.; and the lady, the mother of the young prince, who forbade the bastard to continue his interviews with Rolandine at the window, and who must, therefore, have had a certain right to command him, was probably Louise of Savoy.

"You ought then to have pity on us," said Geburon, "since we have to bear the whole weight of love, and you will not so much as help with a finger-end to ease the burden."

"The burdens of the man and of the woman are often different," observed Parlamente. "The wife's love, founded on piety and virtue, is so just and reasonable, that he who is untrue to the duties of such a friendship ought to be regarded as a dastard, and wicked in the sight of God and man. But as men love only with a view to pleasure, women, who in their ignorance are always the dupes of wicked men, often engage themselves too deeply in a commerce of tenderness; but when God makes known to them the criminal intentions of those whom they supposed to entertain none but good ones, they may break off with honour, and without damage to their reputation, for the shortest follies are always the best."

"That is a mere whim of your own," said Hircan, "to assert that virtuous women may honourably cease to love men, whilst the latter may not in like manner cease to love women; as if the heart of the one sex was different from that of the other. For my part, I am persuaded that, in spite of diversity in faces and dresses, the inclinations of both are the same; the only difference is, that the more hidden guilt is the worse."

"I am very well aware," said Parlamente, with some anger, "that in your opinion the least guilty women are those whose guilt is known."

"Let us change the subject," interrupted Simontault, "and dismiss that of the heart of man and of woman by saying that the best of them is good for nothing. Let us see to whom Parlamente will give her voice."

"To Geburon," she said.

"Since I have begun with mentioning the Cordeliers," said he, "I must not forget the monks of St. Benedict, and cannot forbear relating what happened in my time to two of these good fathers; at the same time, let not what I am going to tell you of a wicked monk hinder you from having a good opinion of those that deserve it. But as the Psalmist says that *all men are liars*, and that *there is none that worketh righteousness, no not one*, it seems to me that one cannot fail to esteem a man such as he is. In fact, if there is good in him, it is to be attributed, not to the creature, but to Him who is the principle and the source of all good. Most people deceive themselves in giving too much to the creature, or in too much esteeming themselves. And that you may not suppose it impossible to find extreme concupiscence under an extreme austerity, I will relate to you a fact which happened in the time of King Francis I."

NOVEL XXII.

A HYPOCRITICAL PRIOR TRIES EVERY MEANS TO SEDUCE A NUN, BUT AT LAST HIS VILLANY IS DISCOVERED.

There was at St. Martin-des-Champs, at Paris, a prior, whose name I will not mention, because of the friendship I once bore him. He led so austere a life until the age of fifty, and the fame of his sanctity was so strong throughout the kingdom, that there was no prince or princess who did not receive him with veneration when he paid them a visit. No monastic reform was effected in which he had not part; and he received the name of the "Father of true monasticism." He was elected visitor of the celebrated society of the Ladies of Fontevrault, who were in so much awe of him, that when he came to any of their convents the nuns trembled with fear, and treated him just as they might have treated the king, hoping thereby to soften his rigour towards them. At first, he did not wish that such deference should be paid him; but as he approached his fifty-fifth year, he at last came to like the honours he had refused in the beginning; and coming by degrees to regard himself as the public property of the religious societies, he was more careful to preserve his health than he had been. Though he was bound by the rules of his order never to eat meat, he granted himself a dispensation in that respect, a thing he would never do for any one else, alleging as his reason, that the whole burden of the brethren's spiritual interests rested upon him. Accordingly, he pampered himself, and to such good purpose, that from being a very lean monk he became a very fat one.

With the change in his manner of living a change took place in his heart also, and he began to look at faces on which he had before made it matter of conscience to cast his eyes casually. By dint of looking at beauties, rendered more desirable by their veils, he began to lust after them. In order to satisfy his unholy passion he changed from a shepherd into a wolf; and if he found an Agnes in any of the convents under his jurisdiction, he failed not to corrupt her. After he had long led this wicked life, Divine goodness taking pity on the poor misused sheep, was pleased to unmask the villain, as you shall hear.

He had gone one day to visit a convent near Paris named Gif, and while he was confessing the nuns there came before him one named Sister Marie Herouet, whose sweet and pleasing voice indicated that her face and heart were not less so. The mere sound inspired the good father with a passion exceeding all he had ever felt for other nuns. In speaking to her he stooped down to look at her, and seeing her mouth so rosy and charming, he could not help lifting up her veil to satisfy himself if her eyes corresponded to the beauty of her lips. He found what he sought, and noted it so well that his heart became filled with a most vehement ardour; he lost his appetite for food and drink, and even all countenance, in spite of his efforts to dissemble. On his return to his priory there was no rest for him. He passed his days and nights in extreme disquietude, his mind continually occupied in devising means to gratify his passion, and make of this nun what he had made of so many others. As he had observed that she possessed steadiness of character and quickness of perception, the thing appeared to him hard to accomplish. Conscious, moreover, that he was ugly and old-looking, he resolved not to attempt to win her by soft words, but extort from her by fear what he could not hope to obtain for love.

With this intention, he returned a few days after to th convent of Gif, and displayed more austerity there than ever he had done before, angrily rating all the nuns. One did not wear her veil low enough; another carried her head too high; another did not make obeisance properly like a nun. So severe was he with regard to all these trifles, that he seemed as terrible as the picture of God on the day of judgment. Being gouty, he was much fatigued in visiting all the parts of the convent, and it was about the hour of vespers (an hour assigned by himself) that he reached the dormitory. The abbess told him it was time to say vespers. "Have them said, mother," replied the prior, "for I am so tired that I will remain here, not to repose, but to speak to Sister Marie about a scandalous thing I hear of her; for I am told that she babbles like a worldling." The prioress, who was aunt to Sister Marie's mother, begged that he would chapter her soundly, and left her in the hands of the prior, quite alone, except that a young monk was with him.

Left alone with Sister Marie, he began by lifting up her veil, and bidding her look in his face. Sister Marie replied, that her rule forbade her to look at men. "That is well said, my daughter," said the prior, "but you are not to believe that monks are men."

For fear, then, of being guilty of disobedience, Sister Marie looked at him, and thought him so ugly, that it seemed to her more a penance than a sin to look at him. The reverend father, after talking of the love he bore her, wanted to put his hand on her breasts. She repulsed him as she ought; and the reverend father, vexed at so untoward a beginning, exclaimed in great anger, "What business has a nun to know that she has breasts?"

"I know that I have," replied Sister Marie; "and I am very certain that neither you nor any one else shall ever touch them. I am neither young enough nor ignorant enough not to know what is a sin and what is not so."

Seeing, then, that he could not compass his designs in that way, he had recourse to another expedient, and said, "I must declare my infirmity to you, my daughter; I have a malady which all the physicians deem incurable, unless I delight myself with a woman whom I passionately love. I would not for my life commit a mortal sin; but even should it come to that, I know that simple fornication is not to be compared to the sin of homicide. So, if you love my life, you will hinder me from dying, and save your own conscience."

She asked him what sort of diversion it was that he contemplated; to which he replied, that she might rest her conscience on his, and he assured her that he would do nothing which would leave any weight on either. To let her judge by the preliminaries what sort of pastime it was he asked of her, he embraced her and tried to throw her on a bed. Making no doubt then of his wicked intention, she cried out, and defended herself so well that he could only touch her clothes. Seeing, then, that all his devices and efforts were fruitless, like—I will not say a madman, but like a man without conscience or reason, he put his hand under her robe, and scratched all that came under his nails with such fury, that the poor girl, shrieking with all her might, fell in a faint. The abbess, hearing her cries, ran to the dormitory, reproaching herself for having left her relation alone with the reverend father. She stood for a moment at the door to listen, but, hearing her niece's voice, she pushed open the door, which was held by the young monk. When she entered the dormitory, the prior, pointing to her niece, said, " You did wrong, mother, not to acquaint me with Sister Marie's constitution ; for, not knowing her weakness, I made her stand before me, and while I was reprimanding her, she fainted away, as you see."

Vinegar and other remedies being applied, Sister Marie recovered from her faint ; and the prior, fearing lest she should tell her aunt the cause of it, found means to whisper in her ear, " I command you, my daughter, on pain of disobedience and eternal damnation, never to speak of what I have done to you. It was my great love for you that made me do it; but since I see that you will not respond to my passion, I will never mention it to you while I live. I may, however, assure you for the last time, that if you will love me I will have you chosen abbess of one of the best abbeys in this kingdom."

She replied that she would rather die in perpetual imprisonment than ever have any other friend than Him who had died for her on the cross; deeming herself happier in suffering all ills with Him, than in enjoying without Him all the pleasures the world can afford. She warned him once for all not to speak to her any more in that manner, if he did not wish her to complain of it to the abbess; but if he desisted, she would say nothing of what was past. Before this bad shepherd withdrew, in order to appear quite different from what he was in reality, and to have the pleasure of again gazing on her he loved, he turned to the abbess and said, "I beg, mother, that you will make all your daughters sing a *Salvo Regina* in honour of the Virgin, in whom I rest my hope." The *Salve Regina* was sung; and all the while the fox did nothing but weep, not with devotion, but with regret at having so ill succeeded. The nuns, who attributed his emotion to the love he felt for the Virgin Mary, regarded him as a saint; but Sister Marie, who knew his hypocrisy, prayed to God in her heart to confound a villain who had such contempt for virginity.

The hypocrite returned to St. Martin's, carrying with him the criminal fire which consumed him day and night, and occupied his mind only in trying to find means for accomplishing his unrighteous end. Being afraid of the abbess, whose virtue he was aware of, he thought he could not do better than remove her from that convent. With that view, he went to Madame de Vendôme, who was then residing at La Fère, where she had built and endowed a convent of the order of St. Benedict, named Mont d'Olivet. In his professed character of a sovereign reformer, he represented to her that the abbess of Mont d'Olivet was not capable of governing such a community. The good lady begged him to name one who should be worthy to fill that office. This was just what he wanted, and he at once recommended her to take the abbess of Gif, whom he depicted to her as the abbess of the greatest capacity in France. Madame de Vendôme sent for her forthwith, and gave her the government of her convent of Mont d'Olivet; whilst the prior, who commanded the suffrages of all the communities, had one who was devoted to him elected abbess of Gif.

This being done, he went to the convent to try once more if by prayers or promises he could prevail over Sister Marie He succeeded no better than the first time, and returning in despair to St. Martin's, he there contrived more villany. As much with a view to accomplish his original purpose as to be revenged on the uncomplying nun, and for fear the affair should obtain publicity, he had the relics stolen from the convent of Gif by night, accused the confessor of the convent, an aged and worthy monk, of having committed the theft, and imprisoned him at St. Martin's. Whilst he kept him there he suborned two witnesses, who deposed that they had seen the confessor and Sister Marie committing an infamous and indecent act in a garden; and this he wanted to make the old monk confess. The good man, who knew all the prior's tricks, begged him to assemble the chapter, and said he would state truly all he knew in presence of the monks. This demand he took care not to grant, fearing lest the confessor's justification should condemn himself; but finding the latter so invincibly steadfast, he treated him so ill that some say he died in prison; others say that the prior forced him to unfrock and quit the realm. Be it as it may, he was never seen afterwards.

The prior, having, as he thought, such a great hold on Sister Marie, went to Gif, where the abbess his creature never disputed a word that fell from his lips. He began by exercising his authority as visitor, and summoned all the nuns one by one, that he might hear them in chamber in form of confession and visitation. Sister Marie, who had lost her good aunt, having at last appeared in her turn, he began by saying to her, "You know, Sister Marie, of what a crime you are accused; and consequently you know that the great chastity you affect has availed you nothing, for it is very well known that you are anything but chaste."

"Produce my accuser," replied Sister Marie, undauntedly, "and you will see how he will maintain such a statement in my presence."

"The confessor himself has been convicted of the fact, and that must be proof enough for you," returned the prior.

"I believe him to be such a good man," said Sister Marie, "that he is incapable of confessing such a falsehood. But even should he have done so, set him before me and I will prove the contrary."

The prior, seeing she was not daunted, said, "I am your father, and as such I wish to be tender with your honour; I leave the matter between you and your conscience, and will believe what you shall tell me. I conjure you then, on pain of mortal sin, to tell me the truth. Were you a virgin when you entered this house?"

"My age at that time, father, is warrant for my virginity. I was then but five years old."

"And since then, my daughter, have you not lost that fair flower?"

She swore she had not, and that she had never undergone any temptation except from him.

"I cannot believe it," the hypocrite replied; "it remains to be proved."

"What proof do you require?"

"That which I exact from other nuns. As I am the visitor of souls, so am I also of bodies. Your abbesses and prioresses have all passed through my hands, and you must not scruple to let me examine your virginity. Lay yourself on that bed, and turn the front of your robe over your face."

"You have told me so much of your criminal love for me," replied Sister Marie, indignantly, "that I have reason to believe your intention is not so much to examine my virginity as to despoil me of it. So be assured I will never consent."

"You are excommunicated," returned the prior, "to refuse obedience; and unless you do as I bid you, I will dishonour you in full chapter, and will state all I know of you and the confessor."

Sister Marie, without suffering herself to be dismayed, replied that He who knew the hearts of His servants would be her stay. "And since you carry your malevolence so far," she said, "I would rather be the victim of your cruelty than the accomplice of your criminal desires; because I know that God is a just judge."

In a rage that may be more easily imagined than described, the prior hurried off to assemble the chapter. Summoning Sister Marie before him, he made her kneel, and thus addressed her: "It is with extreme grief, Sister Marie, that I see how the wholesome remonstrances which I have addressed to you on so capital a fault have been of no avail, and I am compelled with regret to impose a penance upon you contrary to my custom. I have examined your confessor touching certain crimes of which he was accused, and he has confessed to me that he has abused you, and that in a place where two witnesses depose to having seen you. Instead, then, of the honourable post of mistress of the novices in which I had placed you, I ordain that you be the lowest of all, and also that you eat your diet of bread and water on the ground in the presence of all the sisters, until you shall have merited pardon by your repentance."

Sister Marie, having been warned beforehand, by one of her companions who knew her whole affair, that if she made any reply which was displeasing to the prior he would put her *in pace*, that is, immure her for ever in a cell, heard her sentence without saying a word, raising her eyes to heaven, and praying that He who had given her the grace to resist sin, would give her the patience necessary to endure her sufferings. This was not all. The venerable prior further prohibited her speaking for three years to her mother or her relations, or writing any letter excepting in community.

After this the wretch went away and returned no more. The poor girl remained a long time in the condition prescribed by her sentence; but her mother, who had a more tender affection for her than for her other children, was surprised at not hearing from her, and said to one of her sons that she believed her daughter was dead, and that the nuns concealed her death in order the longer to enjoy the annual payment made for her maintenance. She begged him to inquire into the matter and see his sister if it were possible. The brother went at once to the convent, was answered with the usual excuses, and was told that for three years his sister had not quitted her bed. The young man would not be put off with that reply, and swore that unless she were shown to him he would scale the walls and break into the convent. This threat so alarmed the nuns that they brought his sister to the grating; but the abbess followed her so closely, that she could not speak to her brother without being heard by the good mother. But Sister Marie, having her wits about her, had taken the precaution beforehand to write down all the facts I have related, together with the details of a thousand other stratagems which the prior had employed to seduce her, and which, for the sake of brevity, I omit.

I must not, however, forget to mention that, whilst her aunt was abbess, the prior, fancying that it was on account of his ugliness he was repulsed, caused Sister Marie to be tempted by a young and handsome monk, hoping that, if she yielded to the latter for love, he himself might afterwards have his will of her through fear. But the young monk having accosted her in a garden, with words and gestures so infamous that I should be ashamed to repeat them, the poor girl ran to the abbess, who was talking with the prior, and cried to her, "Mother, they are demons, and not monks, who come to visit us." Upon this the prior, afraid of being discovered, said to the abbess, with a laugh, "Certainly, mother, Sister

Marie is right." He then took her hand, and said, in presence of the abbess, "I had heard that Sister Marie spoke very well, and with such facility as led people to believe that she was mundane. For this reason I have done violence to my nature, and have spoken to her as worldlings speak to women, so far as I know that language from books; for in point of personal experience I am as ignorant as I was the day I was born. And as I attributed her virtue to my age and ugliness, I ordered my young monk to speak to her in the same tone. She has made, as you see, a sage and virtuous resistance. I am pleased with her for it, and esteem her so highly, that henceforth I desire that she be the first after you, and the mistress of the novices, in order that her virtue may be fortified more and more." The venerable prior did many feats of the same sort during the three years he was in love with the nun, who, as I have said, gave her brother a written narrative of her sad adventures through the grating.

The brother carried the paper to his mother, who hurried distractedly to Paris, where she found the Queen of Navarre, only sister to the king, and laid this piteous tale before her, saying, "Put no more trust, madam, in these hypocrites. I thought I had placed my daughter on the outskirts of heaven, or at least on the way to it; but I find I have placed her in hell, and in the hands of people worse than all the devils there; for the devils tempt us only so far as we are ourselves consenting parties, but these wretches try to prevail over us by violence when they cannot do so by love." The Queen of Navarre was greatly perplexed. She had implicit confidence in the prior of St. Martin's, and had committed to his charge the abbesses of Montivilliers and of Caen, her sisters-in-law. On the other hand, the crime appeared to her so black and horrible, that she longed to avenge the poor innocent girl, and communicated the matter to the king's chancellor, who was then legate in France.* The legate made the prior appear before him, and all that the latter could allege in excuse for himself was that he was seventy years of age. He appealed to the Queen of Navarre, beseeching, by all the pleasures she would ever wish to do him, and as the sole recompense of his past services, that she would have the

* Antoine Duprat, cardinal-legate, chancellor of France, was appointed legate in 1530, and died 1535. The events related in this novel must have occurred between those years.

goodness to put a stop to these proceedings, assuring her
he would avow that Sister Marie Herouet was a pearl of
honour and chastity. The queen was so astounded at this
speech, that, not knowing how to reply to it, she turned her
back upon him, and left him there. The poor monk, overwhelmed with confusion, retired to his monastery, where he
never more would let himself be seen by anybody, and died
a year afterwards. Sister Marie Herouet, esteemed as the
virtues God had given her deserved, was taken from the
abbey of Gif, where she had suffered so much, and was
made by the king abbess of the abbey of Giy, near Montargis. She reformed the abbey which his majesty had
given her, and lived like a saint, animated by the spirit of
God, whom she praised all her life long for the repose He
had procured her, and the dignity with which He had invested her.*

There, ladies, is a story which well confirms what St. Paul
says to the Corinthians, that God makes use of weak things
to confound the strong, and of those who seem useless in
men's eyes to overthrow the glory and splendour of those who,
thinking themselves something, are yet in reality nothing.
There is no good in any man but what God puts into him
by His grace; and there is no temptation out of which one
does not come victorious, when God grants us aid. You
see this by the confession of a monk, who was believed to be
a good man, and by the elevation of a girl whom he wished
to exhibit as criminal and wicked. In this we see the truth
of our Lord's saying, that "He that exalteth himself shall
be humbled, and he that humbleth himself shall be exalted."

"How many worthy people this monk deceived!" said
Oisille; "for I have seen how they trusted in him more than
in God."

"I should not have been one of those he deceived," said
Nomerfide, "for I have such a horror of the very sight of a
monk that I could not even confess to them, believing them
to be worse than all other men, and never to frequent any
house without leaving in it some shame or dissension."

* The prior who figures in this novel was Etienne Gentil, who became prior in 1508, and died in 1536. The abbey of St. Martin-des-Champs stood on the site now occupied by the Conservatoire des Arts et Métiers. The church and the refectory are still standing.

"There are some good men amongst them," said Oisille "and the wickedness of an individual ought not to be imputed to the whole body; but the best are those who least frequent secular houses and women."

"That is very well said," observed Ennasuite, "for the less one sees and knows them the better one esteems them; for upon more experience one comes to know their real nature."

"Let us leave the monastery where it is," said Nomerfide, "and see to whom Geburon will give his voice."

"To Madame Oisille," replied Geburon, "in order that she may tell us something in honour of the regular clergy."

"We have pledged ourselves so strongly to speak the truth," replied Oisille, "that I could not undertake that task. Besides, your tale reminded me of a piteous one, which I must relate to you, as I come from the neighbourhood of the country where the thing occurred in my own time. I choose this story of recent date, ladies, in order that the hypocrisy of those who believe themselves more religious than others may not so beguile you as to make your faith quit the right path, and induce you to hope for salvation in any other than Him who will have no companion in the work of our creation and redemption. He alone is almighty to save us in eternity, and to comfort us in this life, and deliver us out of all our afflictions. You know that Satan often assumes the appearance of an angel of light, in order that the eye, deceived by the semblance of sanctity and devotion, may attach itself to the things it ought to shun."

NOVEL XXIII.

A CORDELIER IS THE CAUSE OF THREE MURDERS, THAT OF HUSBAND, WIFE, AND CHILD.

THERE was in Perigord a gentleman whose devotion to St. Francis was such that he imagined all those who wore that saint's habit were, as a matter of course, as holy as the sainted founder of their order. In honour of that good saint he fitted up a suite of apartments in his house to lodge the Franciscan monks, by whose advice he regulated all his affairs, even to the smallest household matters, thinking that he could not but walk safely when he followed such good guides. It happened that the wife of this gentleman, a handsome lady, and as virtuous as she was handsome, was delivered of a fine boy; for which her husband, who already loved her much, now regarded her with redoubled affection. The better to entertain his wife, the gentleman sent for one of his brothers-in-law; and a Cordelier, whose name I shall conceal for the honour of the order, arrived also. The gentleman was very glad to see his spiritual father, for whom he had no secrets; and after a long conversation between the lady, her brother, and the monk, they all sat down to supper. During the repast, the gentleman, looking wistfully at his lovely wife, said aloud to the good father, "Is it true, father, that it is a mortal sin to be with one's wife during the month of her confinement?"

The Cordelier, who was anything but what he seemed, replied, "Certainly, sir, I think it is one of the greatest sins that can be committed in marriage. I need only refer you to the example of the blessed Virgin, who would not enter the Temple till the day after her purification, though she had no need of that ceremony. This alone should teach you the indispensable necessity of abstaining from this little pleasure, since the good Virgin Mary, in order to obey the law, abstained from going to the Temple in which was her whole consolation. Besides, the physicians say that there is reason to fear for the children that might be begotten under such circumstances."

The gentleman, who had expected that the monk would give him permission to lie with his wife, was much annoyed at a reply so contrary to his hope; however, he let the matter drop. The reverend father having drunk a little more than was reasonable during the conversation, cast his eyes on the lady, and concluded within himself that if he was her husband, he would lie with her without asking any one's advice. As the fire kindles little by little, and at last waxes so strong and fierce that it burns down the house, so the poor monk felt himself possessed with such vehement concupiscence, that he resolved all at once to satisfy the desire he had cherished in secret for three years. After the supper-things had been taken away, he took the gentleman by the hand, led him to the side of the bed, and said to him, in the presence of his wife, " Knowing, sir, as I do, the affection that subsists between you and mademoiselle, I compassionate the feelings with which your great youth inspires you both. Therefore I will impart to you a secret of our holy theology. You must know, then, that the law which is so rigorous on account of the abuses committed by indiscreet husbands, is not so strict with regard to husbands so prudent and moderate as you. Hence, sir, after having stated before others what is the severity of the law, I must tell you in private what is its mildness. Know, then, that there are women and women, as there are men and men. Before all things, then, it is necessary that mademoiselle, who has been delivered these three weeks, should tell you if her flux of blood has quite ceased."

The demoiselle replied very positively that it had.

" That being the case, my son," resumed the Cordelier, " I permit you to lie with her without scruple, on these two conditions: first, that you mention it to no one, and that you come to her secretly; secondly, that you do not come to her until two hours after midnight, in order not to disturb your wife's digestion."

The gentleman promised to observe both these conditions, and confirmed his promise by so strong an oath that the monk, who knew him to be more of a fool than a liar, did not doubt that he would keep his word. After a pretty long conversation he bade them good night, gave them plenty of benedictions, and retired to his chamber. As he was leaving the room he took the gentleman by the hand, and said, " Certes, sir, it is time for you to retire also, and leave mademoiselle to repose." The gentleman obeyed, and withdrew, telling his wife in the good father's presence to leave the door open.

On reaching his chamber the good monk thought of anything but sleeping. As soon as he found that the house was all still, that is to say, about the hour when he was wont to go to matins, he went straight to the chamber where the gentleman was expected. He found the door open, and having entered, he began by putting out the candle, and then got into bed to the lady as fast as he could. "My dear, this is not what you promised the good father," said the demoiselle, who mistook him for her husband; "you said you would not come here until two o'clock." The Cordelier, who was more intent on action than on contemplation, and was afraid, too, of being recognised if he spoke, made no reply, but proceeded at once to gratify the criminal passion which had long poisoned his heart; whereat the demoiselle was much astonished. The hour when the husband was to come being at hand, the Cordelier got out of bed and returned to his chamber; but as love had before hindered him from sleeping, so now the fear that always follows crime allowed him no repose. He got up, went to the porter, and said, "My friend, monsieur has commanded me to go back at once to our convent, where I am to put up prayers for him. So pray let me have my beast, and open the door for me without letting any one know, for this business requires secrecy." The porter, knowing that to obey the Cordelier was to serve his master, opened the gate and let him out.

At that moment the gentleman awoke, and seeing that it was near the time when he was to go to his wife, he wrapped his dressing-gown about him, and went to his wife's bed, whither he might have gone in accordance with God's law without asking leave of any one. His wife being ignorant of what had occurred, and finding her husband beside her, and hearing his voice, said to him, in surprise, "What, sir! is this the promise you made the good Cordelier, that you would be cautious of your health and mine? Not content with having come hither before the time, you now come again. Do think better of it, I entreat you."

Confounded at being addressed in this manner, and unable to conceal his vexation, the husband replied, "What is this you say? It is three weeks since I have been in bed with you, and you accuse me of coming to you too often. If you continue to talk to me in that strain, you will make me believe that my company is distasteful to you, and constrain me to do what I have never yet done, that is, to seek elsewhere the lawful pleasure you refuse me."

The lady, who thought he was joking, replied, "Do not

deceive yourself, sir, in thinking to deceive me. Though you did not speak to me the first time you came, I knew very well that you were there."

The gentleman then perceived that they had both been duped, and solemnly vowed that he had not been there before; and the wife, in an agony of grief, begged he would find out at once who it could be that had deceived her, since the only persons who had slept in the house were her brother and the Cordelier. The husband's suspicions falling immediately on the latter, he ran to his chamber, and found it empty. To make sure whether or not he had fled, he called the porter, and asked if he knew what had become of the Cordelier. The porter told him what had passed, and the poor gentleman, convinced of the monk's villany, went back to his wife, and said, "Be assured, my dear, that person who lay with you and performed such feats was no other than our father confessor."

The lady, to whom honour had always been most precious, was so horror-stricken, that, forgetting all humanity and the natural gentleness of her sex, she entreated her husband on her knees to revenge her for such a cruel outrage; whereupon he mounted his horse, and rode off in pursuit of the Cordelier. The wife, left alone in her bed, without any one to counsel her, and without any consolation except her newborn babe, pondered over the hideous adventure which had befallen her, and making no account of her ignorance, regarded herself as guilty, and as the most miserable woman in the world. And then, having never learned anything from the Cordelier but confidence in good works, satisfaction for sins by austerity of life, fasting, and discipline, and being wholly ignorant of the grace given by our good God through the merits of His Son, the remission of sins through His blood, the reconciliation of the Father with us through His death, and the life given to sinners by His sole goodness and mercy, she was so bewildered between her horror at the enormity of the deed and her love for her husband and the honour of her line, that she thought death far happier than such a life as hers. Thus rendered desperate by her grief, she lost not only the hope which every Christian ought to have in God, but common sense too, and the recollection of her own nature. Not knowing, then, either God or herself, but, on the contrary, full of rage and madness, she undid one of the cords of her bed, and strangled herself with her own hands. In the agony of that painful death, amidst the last violent efforts of nature, the unfortunate woman pressed her foot upon her infant's face, and its innocence could not secure it from a death as piteous as its mother's.

Roused by a great cry uttered by the expiring lady, a woman who slept in her room got up, and lighted a candle. Seeing her mistress hanging dead by the bedcord, and her infant smothered at her feet, the horrified servant went to the bedroom of the deceased's brother, and took him to see that sad spectacle. The brother, as deeply afflicted as a man would naturally be who tenderly loved his sister, asked the servant who had perpetrated such a crime? She could not tell at all; the only thing she could say was, that no one had entered the room but her master, who had quitted it but a moment ago. The brother, hurrying instantly to his brother-in-law's chamber, and not finding him there, was firmly persuaded that he had done the deed. Mounting his horse without more delay, or waiting for fuller information, he rode after his brother-in-law, and met him as he was returning from his ineffectual pursuit of the Cordelier. "Defend yourself, base villain!" cried the brother-in-law; "I trust that God will revenge me with this sword on the greatest miscreant on earth." The husband would have expostulated; but the brother-in-law pressed him so hard, that all he could do was to defend himself, without knowing what was the cause of the quarrel. They dealt each other so many wounds, that they were compelled, by loss of blood and weakness, to dismount and rest a little. While they were taking breath, the husband said, "Let me at least know, brother, why the friendship we have always had for one another has been changed into such rancorous hatred?"

"Let me know why you have put my sister to death, one of the best women that ever lived," replied the brother; "and why, under pretext of going to sleep with her, you have hung her with the bedcord?"

More dead than alive on hearing these words, the poor husband faltered out, "Is it possible, brother, that you found your sister in the state you say?" Being assured that this was the exact truth. "Pray, brother, listen to me," he continued, "and you shall know why I left the house." And then he related the adventure of the Cordelier. The astonished brother now bitterly repented the precipitation with which he had acted, and earnestly implored forgiveness. "If I have wronged you," said the husband, "you are avenged; for I am wounded beyond hope of recovery." The brother-in-law set him on his horse as well as he could, and led him back to his own house, where he died the next day, and the survivor confessed before all his relations and friends that he was the cause of his death.

For the satisfaction of justice, the brother-in-law was advised to go and solicit his pardon of King Francis I. To this end, after having honourably interred the father, mother, and child, he set out one Good Friday, to solicit his pardon at court; and he obtained it through the favour of François Olivier, chancellor of Alençon, afterwards, in consideration of his great endowments, chosen by the king to be chancellor of France.

I am persuaded, ladies, that after this story, which is the very truth, there is not one of you but will think twice before giving reception to such guests. Let it at least teach you, that the more hidden the venom, the more dangerous it is.

"Surely," said Hircan, "this husband was a great fool to bring such a gallant to sup by the side of such a handsome and virtuous woman."

"I have seen the time," said Geburon, "when there was not a house in our country in which there was not a chamber for the good fathers; but at present people know them so well, that they are more feared than adventurers."

"It seems to me," said Parlamente, "that a woman in bed ought never to let monk or priest into her room except to administer to her the sacraments of the church; and for my part, when I summon any of them to my bedside, it may be taken for a sure sign that I am very far gone."

"If everybody was as austere as you," said Ennasuite, "the poor clergy would no longer be free to see women when and where they pleased, and that would be worse to them than excommunication."

"Have no fear on their account," said Saffredent; "these worthies will never want for women."

"Is not this too bad?" exclaimed Simontault. "It is they who unite us with our wives in the bonds of wedlock, and they have the wickedness to try to disunite us, and make us break the oath they have imposed upon us."

"It is a pity," said Oisille, "that they who have the administration of the sacraments make light of them in this manner. They ought to be burned alive."

"You would do better to honour them than to blame them," replied Saffredent, "and to flatter instead of abusing them, for it is they who have the power to burn and dishonour others; therefore, let them alone; and let us see, whom does Oisille call on?"

"On Dagoucin," she replied; "for I see he is so pensive, that it strikes me he must have something good at the tip of his tongue."

"Since I cannot and dare not say what I think," said Dagoucin, "at least I will speak of a man to whom cruelty was prejudicial and afterwards advantageous. Although love has such a good opinion of its own strength and potency that it likes to show itself quite naked, and finds it extremely irksome, nay, insupportable to go cloaked, yet those who in obedience to its dictates make too great haste to disclose themselves, often suffer for it, as happened to a gentleman of Castile, whose story I shall relate to you."

NOVEL XXIV.

INGENIOUS DEVICE OF A CASTILIAN IN ORDER TO MAKE A DECLARATION OF LOVE TO A QUEEN, AND WHAT CAME OF IT.

THERE was at the court of a king and queen of Castile, whose names history does not mention, a gentleman of such good birth and comely person, that his equal there was not in all Spain. Every one held his endowments in admiration, but still more his eccentricity; for it had never been perceived that he loved or courted any lady, though there were many at the court who might have fired ice itself; but there was not one who could kindle the heart of Elisor, for so this gentleman was named. The queen, who was a woman of great virtue, but a woman nevertheless, and not more exempt than the rest of her sex from that flame which is the more violent the more it is compressed—the queen, I say, surprised that this gentleman did not attach himself to any of her ladies, asked him one day if it was true that he was as indifferent as he appeared? He replied, that if she saw his heart as she saw his face, she would not have asked him that question. Eager to know what he meant, she pressed him so hard, that he confessed he loved a lady whom he believed to be the most virtuous in all Christendom. She did all she could by entreaties and commands to make him say who the lady was, but all to no purpose; till at last she pretended to be most deeply incensed against him, and swore that she would never speak to him again if he did not name the lady he loved so passionately. To escape from her importunities, he was forced to say, that he would rather die than do what she required of him; but at last, finding that he was about to be deprived of the honour of seeing her, and to be cast out of her favour for not declaring a truth in itself so seemly that no one could take it in bad part, he said to her, trembling with emotion, "I cannot and dare not, madam, name the person; but I will show her to you the first time we go to the chase; and I am sure that you will say as well as I, that she is the most beautiful and most accomplished lady in the world."

After this reply, the queen went to the chase sooner than she would otherwise have done. Elisor had notice of this, and prepared to wait on her majesty as usual. He had got made for himself a great steel mirror in the shape of a corslet, and this he placed on his chest, concealed beneath a mantle of black frieze, all bordered with purl and gold. He rode a black horse, very richly caparisoned. His harness was all gilded and enamelled black in the Moorish fashion, and his black silk hat had a buckle adorned with precious stones, and having in the centre, for a device, a Love concealed by Force. His sword, poniard, and the devices upon them, corresponded to the rest; in short, he was admirably accoutred; and he was such a good horseman, that all who saw him neglected the pleasures of the chase to see the paces and the leaps which Elisor made his horse perform. After escorting the queen to the place where the toils were spread, he alighted and went to aid her majesty to dismount. At the moment she held out her arms, he opened his cloak, which covered his new cuirass, and said, " Be pleased, madam, to look here ;" and without awaiting her reply he set her gently on the ground.

When the chase was ended, the queen returned to the palace without speaking to Elisor. After supper she called him to her, and told him he was the greatest liar she had ever seen, for he had promised to show her at the chase the lady of his love, and yet he had done no such thing; but for her part, she was resolved for the future to make no account of him. Elisor, fearing that the queen had not understood what he had said to her, replied that he had kept his word, and that he had shown her not only the woman, but also that thing in all the world which he loved best. Affecting ignorance of his meaning, she declared she was not aware that he had shown her any of her ladies. "That is true," replied Elisor; "but what did I show you when you dismounted from your horse ?"

"Nothing," said the queen, "but a mirror you had on your chest."

" And what did you see in the mirror ?"

" Nothing but myself."

" Consequently, madam, I have kept my word and obeyed you. Never did anything enter my heart but that which you saw when you looked at my chest. She who was there pictured is the only one whom I love, revere, and adore, not as a woman merely, but as an earthly divinity, on whom my life and death depend. The only favour I ask of you, madam, is, that the perfect passion, which has been life to me whilst concealed, may not be my death now that I have declared it. If I am worthy that you should regard me and receive me as your most impassioned servant, suffer me at least to live, as I have hitherto done, upon the blissful consciousness that I have dared to give my heart to a being so perfect and so worthy of all honour, that I must be content to love her, though I can never hope to be loved in return. If the knowledge you now possess of my intense love does not render me more agreeable to your eyes than heretofore, at least do not deprive me of life, which for me consists in the bliss of seeing you as usual. I now receive from you no other favour than that which is absolutely necessary for my existence. If I have less you will have a servant the less, and will lose the best and most affectionate one you have ever had or ever will have."

The queen, whether it was that she might appear other than she really was, or that she might put his love for her to a longer proof, or that she loved another whom she would not forsake for him, or, lastly, that she was glad to have this lover in reserve in case her heart should become vacant through any fault which might possibly be committed by him whom she loved already, said to him, in a tone which expressed neither anger nor satisfaction, "I will not ask you, Elisor, although I know not the power of love, how you can have been so presumptuous and so extravagant as to love me; for I know that the heart of man is so little at his own command, that one cannot love or hate as one chooses. But since you have so well concealed your feelings, I desire to know how long you have entertained them?"

Elisor, looking in her beautiful face, and hearing her inquire about his malady, was not without hopes that she would afford him some relief; but, on the other hand, seeing the self-command and the gravity with which she questioned him, he feared he had to do with a judge who was about to pronounce sentence against him. Notwithstanding this fluctuation between hope and fear, he protested that he had loved her since her early youth; but that it was only within the last seven years he had been conscious of his pain, or rather of a malady so agreeable that he would rather die than be cured.

"Since you have been constant for seven years," said the queen, "I must be no more precipitate in believing you than you have been in declaring your love to me. Therefore, if you speak the truth, I wish to convince myself of it in a manner that shall leave no room for doubt; and if I am satisfied with the result of the trial, I will believe you to be such towards me as you swear that you are; and then, when I find you to be indeed what you say, you shall find me to be what you wish."

Elisor besought her to put him to any proof she pleased, there being nothing so hard that would not appear to him very easy, in the hope that he might be happy enough to convince her of the perfect love he bore her. He only waited, he said, to be honoured with her commands.

"If you love me, Elisor, as much as you say," replied the queen, "I am sure that nothing will seem hard to you to obtain my good graces; so I command you, by the desire you have of possessing them, and the fear of losing them, that to-morrow, without seeing me more, you quit the court and go to a place where for seven years you shall hear nothing of me, nor I of you. You know well that you love me, since you have had seven years' experience of the fact. When I shall have a similar seven years' experience, I shall believe what all your protestations would fail to assure me of."

This cruel command made Elisor believe at first that her intention was to get rid of him; but, upon second thoughts, he accepted the condition, hoping that the proof would do more for him than all the words he could utter. "If I have lived seven years without any hope," he said, "under the painful necessity of dissembling my love, now that it is known to you, and that I have some gleam of hope, I shall pass the other seven years with patience and calmness. But, madam, since in obeying the command you impose upon me, I am deprived of all the joy I have ever had in the world, what hope do you give me that, at the end of seven years, you will own me for your faithful servant?"

Drawing a ring off her finger, "Let us cut this ring in two," said the queen; "I will keep one half and you the other, in order that I may recognise you by that token in case length of time makes me forget your face."

Elisor took the ring, divided it in two, gave the queen one half, and kept the other. Then, taking leave of her, more dead than those who have already given up the ghost, he went home to give orders for his departure. Sending his whole retinue to the country, he went away with only one attendant to a place so lonely and sequestered, that none of his relations and friends had any tidings of him for seven years. How he lived during that time, and what sorrow absence made him endure, are things beyond my telling; but those who love can be at no loss to conceive them.

Precisely at the end of seven years, and at the moment when the queen was going to mass, a hermit with a long beard came to her, kissed her hand, and presented to her a petition, which she did not peruse at once, though her custom was to receive all the petitions that were presented to her, however poor were the people who referred them. When mass was half said, she opened the petition, and found enclosed in it the half of the ring she had given to Elisor. This was an agreeable surprise for her, and before she read the paper she ordered her almoner to bring her straightway the hermit who had presented the petition. The almoner sought for him in all directions, but all he could learn was, that he had been seen to mount and ride away, but no one could tell which way he had gone. While awaiting the return of her almoner, the queen read the petition, which turned out to be a letter, composed in the best possible manner, and but for the desire I feel to make it intelligible to you, I should never have ventured to translate it; for I must beg you to understand, ladies, that the Castilian is better adapted than the French tongue to express the emotions of love. The letter was as follows:

"Time, a mighty teacher, gave me perfectly to know the nature of love. Time was afterwards assigned me, that the incredulous one might see by my protracted woe what love could not convince her of. Time hath shown me on what foundation my heart built its great love. That foundation was your beauty, which concealed great cruelty. Time teaches me that beauty is nothing, and that cruelty is the cause of my weal. Exiled by the beauty whose regards I so yearned for, I have come to be more conscious of your extreme unkindness. I obey your cruel order, however, and am perfectly content to do so; for time has had such pity on me that I have wished to return to this place to bid you, not a good day, but a last farewell. Time has shown me love just as it is, poor and naked; and I have no sense of it except regret. But time has likewise shown me the true love, which I have known only in that solitude where for seven years I have been doomed to mourn in silence. Through time I have come to know the love that dwells on high, at sight of which the other love vanishes, and I have given myself wholly to the one, and weaned my affections from the other. To that better love I devote my heart and my body, to do suit and service to it and not to you. When I served you, you esteemed me nothing. I now give you back entirely the love you put into my heart, having no need either of it or of you. I take my leave of cruelty, pain, torment, scorn, hatred, and the burning fire with which you are filled, no less than you are adorned with beauty. I cannot better bid farewell to all woes and pains and intolerable distresses, and to the hell of the amorous woman, than in bidding farewell to you, madam, without the least prospect that wherever you or I may be we shall ever look upon each other more."

This letter was not read without tears and incredible surprise and regret. Indeed, the queen could not but feel so keenly the loss of a servant who loved her so perfectly, that not all her treasures, nor even her crown, could hinder her from being the poorest and most miserable princess in the world, since she had lost that which no wealth could replace. After hearing mass, she returned to her chamber, where she gave utterance to the lamentations her cruelty had merited. There was no mountain, rock, or forest to which she did not send in quest of the hermit; but he who had taken him out of her hands hindered him from falling into them again, and removed him to Paradise before she could discover his retreat in this world.

This example shows that no one can tell what can do him harm only and no good. Still less, ladies, should you carry distrust and incredulity so far as to lose your lovers, through desiring to put them to too severe a proof.

"All my life long, Dagoucin," said Geburon, "I have heard the lady in question spoken of as the most virtuous woman in the world; but now I regard her as the most cruel that ever lived."

"It seems to me, however," said Parlamente, "that she did him no such great wrong, if he loved her as much as he said, in exacting from him seven years of trial. Men are so accustomed to lie on these occasions, that one cannot take too many precautions before trusting them—if they are ever to be trusted."

"The ladies of our day," said Hircan, "are wiser than those of times past; for in seven days' trial they are as sure with regard to a lover as the others were in seven years."

"Yet are there those in company," said Longarine, "who have been wooed for seven years without ever being won."

"That is true," said Simontault; "but with your leave

they ought to be classed with the ladies of bygone times, for in the modern class they would not be received."

"After all," said Oisille, "Elisor was greatly indebted to the queen, since she was the cause of his giving his heart entirely to God."

"It was great luck for him," said Saffredent, "to find God in his way, for crossed as he was I wonder he did not give himself to the devil."

"When your lady ill-used you," inquired Ennasuite, "did you give yourself to such a master?"

"Thousands of times; but the devil would never take me, seeing that the tortures of hell were less than those she made me suffer, and that there is no devil more insupportable than a woman who is passionately loved and will not love in return."

"If I was in your place and entertained such sentiments," said Parlamente, "I would never love a woman."

"Such has always been my unfortunate propensity," replied Saffredent, "that when I cannot command I think myself very happy in being able to serve. But tell me, pray, in conscience, now, do you applaud this princess for such excessive rigour?"

"Yes," said Oisille, "for I believe she did not choose either to love or be loved."

"That being the case," said Simontault, "why give him hopes after seven years should have passed?"

"You are right," said Longarine; "and I think that ladies who do not choose to love should cut the matter short at once, and hold out no hopes to their suitors."

"Perhaps," said Nomerfide, "she loved another who was not so worthy as Elisor, and preferred the worse man to the better."

"It is my belief," said Saffredent, "that she was glad to keep him in play, that she might have him ready to her hand whenever she cast off the lover she then preferred to him."

"I see plainly," said Oisille, "that as long as the conversation runs upon this topic, those who do not like to be treated harshly will say everything bad they can of us; so be pleased, Dagoucin, to give your voice to some one."

"I give it to Longarine," said he, "being assured that she

will tell us something novel, and speak the very truth without sparing either men or women."

"Since you have such a good opinion of my sincerity," said Longarine, "I will relate an anecdote of a great prince who surpassed in endowments all the princes of his time. Permit me also to remark, that falsehood and dissimulation are things which should be least of all used, unless in a case of extreme necessity. They are a very ugly and disgraceful vice, especially in princes and great lords, whom truth becomes still more than other men. But there is no prince in the world, however glorious or rich he may be, who does not acknowledge the empire of love, and submit to its tyranny. Indeed, that arrogant god disdains all that is common, and delights only in working miracles every day, such as weakening the strong, strengthening the weak, making fools of the wise, and knowing persons of the ignorant, favouring the passions, destroying reason, and, in a word, turning everything topsy-turvy. As princes are not exempt from it, no more so are they from the necessity in which they are put by the desire of amorous servitude. Thence it comes that they are forced to use falsehood, hypocrisy, and feigning, which, according to Maître Jean de Meun, are means for vanquishing enemies. Though conduct of this nature is laudable in a prince, though it be censurable in all other men, I will recount to you the device employed by a young prince who tricked those who are used to trick all the world."

NOVEL XXV.

CUNNING CONTRIVANCE OF A YOUNG PRINCE TO ENJOY THE WIFE OF AN ADVOCATE OF PARIS.

THERE was in Paris an advocate more esteemed than any nine others in his profession; and as his knowledge and ability made him sought by all clients, he became the richest of all the men of the gown. Now, seeing that he had no children by his first wife, he thought he should have some by a second; for though he was old, he had, nevertheless, the heart and the hope of a young man. He made choice of a

Parisian of eighteen or nineteen, very handsome in face and complexion, and handsomer still in figure and plumpness. He loved her and treated her as well as possible; but he had no children by her any more than by his first wife; which the fair one at last took sorely to heart. As youth cannot carry the burden of care very far, the advocate's young wife resolved to seek elsewhere the pleasure she did not find at home, and used to go to balls and feasts; but this she did, nevertheless, with such outward propriety and so much caution, that her husband could not take offence, for she was always with those ladies in whom he had most confidence.

One day, when she was at a wedding entertainment, there happened to be present a young prince, who told me the story, and forbade me to name him. All I can tell you is, that there never was, and never will be, I think, a prince in France of finer person and demeanour. The eyes and the countenance of the advocate's lady inspired the prince with love. He spoke to her so well and with such grace, that she took pleasure in his discourse, and ingenuously owned to him that she had long had in her heart the love for which he craved, and begged he would spare himself the pains of trying to persuade her to a thing to which love had already made her consent at mere sight. The frankness of love having bestowed on the prince what was well worth the pains of being won by time, he failed not to thank the god who favoured him; and he plied his opportunity so well, that they agreed there and then upon the means of seeing each other in less crowded company. The time and the place being assigned, the prince appeared punctually, but in disguise, that he might not compromise the honour of the fair one. As he did not wish to be known by the rogues and thieves who roam by night, he had himself escorted by some trusty gentlemen, from whom he separated on entering the street where the lady resided, saying to them, "If you hear no noise within a quarter of an hour, go away, and return about three or four o'clock." The quarter of an hour having expired, and no noise having been heard, the gentlemen withdrew.

The prince went straight to the advocate's house, and found the door open as he had been promised, but on going up the staircase he met the advocate with a candle in his hand, who saw him first. Love, however, which gives wit and boldness in proportion to the crossings and thwartings it occasions, prompted the prince to go up at once to the advocate and say to him, "You know, master advocate, the confidence which I and all my house repose in you, and that I regard you as one of my best and most faithful servants. I am come to see you privately, as well to recommend my affairs to you as to beg you will give me something to drink, for I am very thirsty, and not let anybody know that I have been here. When I quit you I shall have to go to another place where I should not like to be known."

The poor man, delighted with the honour the prince did him by this familiar visit, begged him to enter his room, and told his wife to prepare a collation of the best fruits and the most exquisite confections she could find; which she did right gladly, with all possible daintiness. Though she was in kerchief and mantle, and appeared to more than usual advantage in that négligé, the prince affected not to look at her, but talked continually about his business to her husband, who had always had the management of it. Whilst the wife knelt before the prince to present him some confections, and the husband was going to the buffet to fetch him something to drink, she found time to tell him not to fail, on departing, to enter a *garderobe* on the right, where she would soon join him. When he had drunk, he thanked the advocate, who wished by all means to accompany him; but this the prince would not allow, assuring him he was going to a place where he had no need of company. Then turning to the wife he said, "I will not deprive you of your good husband, who is one of my old servants. You are so happy in having him that you have reason to thank God. You must serve and obey him well; and if you did otherwise you would be very ungrateful." So saying, he went out, shut the door after him, that he might not be followed to the staircase, and entered the *garderobe*, where the fair one joined him as soon as her husband was asleep. She took him into a cabinet as elegant as could be, but in truth there was nothing in it handsomer than he and she; and I doubt not that she kept word with him as to all she had promised. He left her at the hour he had told his people, and found them at the place where he had desired them to wait for him.

As the intrigue was of long duration, the prince chose a

shorter way to go to the advocate's; this was to pass through a monastery. He managed matters so well with the prior, that every night the porter opened the door for him towards midnight, and did the same when he returned. The advocate's house not being far from the monastery, he took no one with him. Notwithstanding the prince led the life I have described, still he loved and feared God, so true it is that man is a whimsical mixture of good and evil, and a perpetual contradiction. On his way to the advocate's he only passed through the monastery, but on his return he never failed to remain a long time at prayer in the church. The monks seeing him on his knees as they went to matins, or returned from them, believed he was the most pious of men.

The prince had a sister who was much in the habit of frequenting that convent. As she loved her brother above all men, she used to commend him to the prayers of all the good people she knew. One day when she was thus speaking for him with great earnestness to the prior of this monastery, the good father replied, " Why, madam, what is this you ask of me? You name the very man above all others to whose prayers I most desire to be myself commended; for if he is not pious and righteous, I never expect to see one that is so." Thereupon he quoted the text which says that " Blessed is he who can do evil, and doeth it not." The sister, who longed to know what proof the prior had of her brother's sanctity, questioned him so earnestly that he said to her, as if he was revealing a secret of the confessional, " Is it not a marvellous and goodly thing to see a young and handsome prince abandoning pleasures and repose to come frequently to our matins? He does not come like a prince who seeks to be honoured of men, but quite alone like a simple monk, and he goes and hides himself in one of our chapels. This devotion so confounds my brethren and myself, that we do not think ourselves worthy to be called men of religion in comparison with him?"

The sister did not know what to think of this; for though her brother was very mundane, she knew, nevertheless, that he had a good conscience, that he believed in God and loved him much; but she could never have imagined that he would make a practice of going to church at that hour. As soon as she saw him, she told him what a good opinion the monks had of him. He could not help laughing, and in such a manner, that she, who knew him as she did her own heart, readily guessed that there was something concealed under this pretended devotion. She teazed him so much that at last he told her the whole truth as you have heard from me, and as she did me the honour to relate it to me.*

* Francis I. is the young prince who figures in this novel. The same story has been told of him, with additional circumstances, by some historians and others. It is thus related by a physician named Louis Guyon, sieur de la Nauche, who flourished at the end of the 16th century. " Francis I. was enamoured of a lady of great beauty and great grace, the wife of an advocate of Paris, whom I will not name, for he has left children in high estate, and who are persons of good repute. The lady would never comply with the king's desires, but on the contrary repulsed him with many rude words, which hurt him sore. Knowing this, some courtiers and royal pimps told the king he might take her authoritatively and by the power of his royalty. One of them actually went and said this to the lady, who reported it to her husband. The advocate saw plainly that they must quit the realm, and that, moreover, they should find it very hard to escape, unless they obeyed. Finally the husband allowed his wife to comply with the king's desire; and that he might be no hindrance, he pretended to have business in the country for eight or ten days. Meanwhile he remained concealed in Paris, frequenting the brothels, trying to catch the pox to give to his wife, that the king might take it from her. He quickly got what he sought, infected his wife, and she the king, who gave it to several other women with whom he conversed; and he never could be thoroughly cured, for all the rest of his life he was unhealthy, sad, peevish, and inaccessible." (*Diverses Leçons de Louis Guyon, sieur de la Nauche.* Lyon, 1610, t. 11, p. 109.) Brantôme also speaks of the malady contracted by the king through his gallantries, and says that it shortened his life; but he does not mention any woman in particular, or allude to the story of the advocate's wife. " Many have thought that she was no other than 'La belle Féronnière,' so called because she was married to an advocate of the Le Féron family, many members of which were distinguished in the bar of Paris."

" We must, then," say the Bibliophiles Français (though for our own part we cannot see the force of the inference, based as it is upon nothing more absolute than a *many have thought*), "we must then number among apocryphal anecdotes the last and vilest part of the adventure of the advocate of Paris. What is true, Margaret has made known to us; modern historians, even those who have shown themselves most unfavourable to Francis I., have not reproduced the fact stated by Louis Guyon. M. Genin, editor of Margaret's letters, has even published the postscript of a letter of Cardinal d'Armagnac, which proves that at least a year before his death the king was in perfect health. (See *Lettres de Marguerite d'Angoulême,* &c., 1841, 8vo.

You see by this, ladies, that there are no advocates so crafty, or monks so shrewd, but that they may be tricked in case of need, when one loves well. Since, then, love teaches how to trick the tricksters, how much reason have we to fear it, we who are poor simple creatures?

"Though I guess pretty well," said Geburon, "who is the hero of this tale, I cannot help saying that he is to be praised for having kept the secret; for there are few great lords who give themselves any concern either about the honour of women or public scandal, provided they have their pleasure. Frequently, even, they act in such a manner as to make people believe more than the truth."

"It would be well," said Oisille, "if all young lords followed this example, for often the scandal is worse than the sin."

"You may well believe," said Nomerfide, "that the prayers he offered up in church were very sincere and very acceptable to God."

"That is not a question for you to decide," said Parlamente; "for, perhaps, his repentance was such on his return from his assignation, that his sin was forgiven."

"It is very difficult," said Hircan, "to repent of a thing that gives such pleasure. For my part, I have often confessed, but hardly repented it."

"If one does not repent, it were better not to confess," observed Oisille.

"Sin displeases me, madam," rejoined Hircan; "I am vexed at offending God; but pleasure pleases me."

"You would be very glad, you and others like you," remarked Parlamente, "that there were neither God nor law but what agreed with your own inclination."

"I confess," said Hircan, "I should be glad if my pleasures were as pleasing to God as they are to me. In that case, I would often give matter for rejoicing."

"You will not make a new God, however," said Geburon;

p. 473.) Thus is annihilated the ignoble accusation of a shameful disease which should have hastened the death of Francis I."

In Grammont's Memoirs it is related that the Duke of York, afterwards James II., was the victim of the same sort of revenge on the part of a jealous husband as that attributed to the advocate of Paris There is nothing new under the sun.

"and so the best thing we can do is to obey the one we have. But let us leave these disputes to theologians, and see to whom Longarine will give her voice."

"To Saffredent," said Longarine, "on condition that he tells us the finest tale he can recollect, and that he is not so intent on speaking ill of women as not to do them justice when he can say anthing to their advantage."

"With all my heart," said Saffredent. "I recollect, quite *à propos*, a story of a loose woman and a staid one; so you may choose whichever example of the two you prefer. You will see from this story that love makes bad acts be done by persons of bad heart; it also makes people of worth do things deserving of praise; for love is good in itself, but the depravity of the individual often makes it take a new title, such as lascivious, light, cruel, or vile. You will see, nevertheless, from the tale I am about to tell, that love does not change the heart, but makes it appear such as it is: wanton in the wanton, sober in the sober.

NOVEL XXVI.

BY THE ADVICE AND SISTERLY AFFECTION OF A VIRTUOUS LADY THE LORD OF AVANNES WAS WEANED FROM HIS DISSOLUTE AMOURS WITH A LADY OF PAMPELUNA.

In the time of king Louis XII., there was a young lord named Monsieur d'Avannes, son of Monsieur d'Albret, the brother of John, king of Navarre, with whom d'Avannes usually resided. This young lord was so handsome, and had such an engaging demeanour at the age of fifteen, that he seemed to be made only to be beloved and admired; and so he was by all who saw him, and above all, by a lady who lived in Pampeluna, in Navarre, and was married to a very wealthy man, with whom she lived happily. Though she was but three-and-twenty, yet as her husband was nearly fifty, she dressed so modestly that she had more the appearance of a widow than of a married woman. She was never seen at weddings or festivities but with her husband, whose worth she prized so highly, that she preferred it to the good looks of all other men. The husband, on his side, knew her to be so discreet, and had so much confidence in her, that he entrusted all the affairs of the house to her prudence.

This rich man and his wife were one day invited to the wedding of one of their female relations. D'Avannes was present to do honour to the bridal, and also because he was fond of dancing, in which he acquitted himself better than any man of his day. When dinner was over and the ball began, the rich man begged D'Avannes to dance. The latter asked with whom he would have him dance: whereupon the rich man, taking his wife by the hand, presented her to D'Avannes, and said, "If there was a handsomer lady in the room, monsieur, or one so much at my disposal, I would present her to you as I do this one, begging you, monsieur, to do me the honour to dance with her." The prince gladly complied; and he was still so young, that he took more pleasure in dancing and skipping than in gazing on ladies' charms. It was not so with his partner, who paid more attention to the handsome figure and good looks of her cavalier than to the dance; but she took care not to let this appear.

Supper time being come, M. d'Avannes took leave of the company and retired to the château. The rich man escorted him thither, mounted on his mule, and said to him on the way, "Monsieur, you have to-day done so much honour to my relations and myself, that I should be ungrateful if I did not make you every offering in my power. I know, monsieur, that lords like you, who have strict and close-handed fathers, have often more need of money than we, who, with our small retinue and good management, do nothing but amass. God, who has given me everything that could be desired in a wife, has thought fit to leave me still something to wish for in this world, since I am deprived of the joy which fathers derive from children. I know, monsieur, that it does not belong to me to adopt you; but if you please to regard me as your servant, and confide your little affairs to me, as far as a hundred thousand crowns may go, you shall never want for aid in your need."

M. d'Avannes was very glad of this offer, for he had just such a father as the other had mentioned; and after thanking his generous friend, he called him his father by alliance. Thenceforth the rich man was so fondly attached to M.

d'Avannes, that he failed not to ask him every morning and evening if he wanted anything; and he made no secret of this to his wife, who was much pleased with it. M. d'Avannes never afterwards wanted anything he could desire. He often went to see his father by alliance, and eat with him; and when he did not find him at home, the wife gave him whatever he asked for, and spoke to him so sagely, exhorting him to virtue, that he feared and loved her above all women in the world. For her part, having the fear of God and honour before her eyes, she contented herself with seeing and speaking to him, which is enough for a virtuous love; nor did she ever give him any indication from which he could conjecture that she entertained for him any other than a sisterly and Christian regard. About the age of seventeen, M. d'Avannes began to attach himself more to the ladies than he had been used to do; and though he would more gladly have loved his own good lady than any other, the fear of losing her friendship hindered him from speaking, and made him fix his choice elsewhere.

He addressed himself to a lady near Pampeluna, who had a house in the town, and had married a young man whose ruling passion was horses, dogs, and hawks. For her sake he gave a thousand entertainments, such as tournaments, games, races, wrestling-matches, masquerades, balls, &c.; but as the husband was of a jealous temper, and the lady's father and mother knew her to be fair and frolicsome, and were afraid of her tripping, they watched her so closely that all M. d'Avannes could do was to whisper a word or two in her ear at a ball, although he well knew, and this made the matter still more provoking, that nothing but time and place was wanting for the consummation of their mutual inclinations. He went to his good father, told him he had a mind to visit Notre Dame de Montferrat, and begged he would receive his whole retinue into his house, for it was his wish to go alone. This request was instantly granted; but as love is a great prophet, and as the wife was under the influence of that power, she guessed the truth at once, and could not help saying to M. d'Avannes, "The Notre Dame you adore, monsieur, is not outside the walls of this town. Take care of your health, I beseech you." M. d'Avannes, who, as I have already said, feared and loved her, blushed so much at these words, that he tacitly betrayed the truth, and went away.

After buying two handsome Spanish horses, he dressed himself as a groom, and disguised himself so well that no one could have known him. The husband of the wanton lady, being fond of horses above all things, saw the two belonging to M. d'Avannes, and immediately offered to buy them. The bargain being concluded, he took particular notice of the groom, and seeing that he managed the horses very well, asked if he would enter his service. M. d'Avannes at once agreed to do so, and said he was a poor groom, who could do nothing but take care of horses, but this he could do so well that his master would be satisfied with him. The gentleman gave him the charge of all his horses, and when he reached home told his wife that he was going to the château, and that he begged her to look after his groom and his horses. As much to please her husband as because she had no other recreation, the lady went to see the horses, and noticed the new groom, who seemed to her a good-looking man; but she did not recognise him. Seeing this, he made his obeisance to her in the Spanish fashion, took her hand and kissed it, and in so doing pressed it so strongly that she knew him, for he had often done the same thing in dancing with her. From that moment she thought of nothing but how she might contrive to speak with him in private; and this she did that very evening. She was invited to an entertainment to which her husband was to have taken her; but she feigned indisposition, and would not go. Her husband, not wishing to disappoint his friends, begged her, since she would not accompany him, to look after his dogs and his horses, and see that they wanted for nothing. This commission was most agreeable to her; but the better to play her part, she replied that, since he would not employ her in higher things, she would prove to him, by her care for the least, how much she desired to please him.

No sooner was her husband gone than she went to the stable, where she found that something was not as it should be. To set matters right, she gave so many orders to the men that she was left alone with the head groom, and, for fear of any one coming upon them, she told him to go into the garden and wait for her in a little corner at the end of an alley, which he did with such haste that he had not time even to thank her. Having given her orders in the stables, she went to see the dogs, and busied herself so much about them, that it seemed as though from being mistress she had become servant. All this being done, she went back to her chamber, and complained so much of fatigue that she had to go to bed. All her women withdrew except one, in whom she specially confided; and this one she sent to the garden with orders to bring her the man she should find at the end of the alley. The chambermaid found the head-groom, brought him straightway to her mistress, and then mounted guard outside, to give warning should the husband return. M. d'Avannes, finding himself alone with his fair one, stripped off his groom's dress, his false nose and false beard, and not as a timorous groom, but in his own proper character, boldly stepped into bed to her without asking leave, and was received as the handsomest man of his time by the most wanton woman in the country. There he remained until the return of the husband, when he resumed his mask, and quitted the place he so cunningly usurped.

The husband, on entering his court-yard, found that his wife had carefully executed his orders, and thanked her for it. "I have only done my duty, my dear," she said. "It is true, that if one had not an eye on the varlets, you have not a dog but would be mangy, or a horse but would be out of condition; but as I know their laziness and your wishes, you shall be better served than ever you have been." The husband, who thought he had got the best groom in the world, asked her what she thought of him. "I assure you, monsieur," said she, "that he knows his business as well as any man you could find. Still he requires to be kept to his work, for he is the sleepiest varlet I ever saw." The wedded pair were on better terms with each other than they had ever been, and the husband became quite cured of his jealousy, because his wife was now as attached to her household concerns as she had previously been fond of feasts, dances, and company. Formerly she used always to spend four hours at her toilette; but now she dressed very simply. Her husband, and those who did not know that a worse devil had driven out a lesser, extolled her for so happy a change. Meanwhile this virtuous-seeming hypocrite led such a licentious life, that reason, conscience, order, or moderation had no longer any place in her. M. d'Avannes, being young and of a delicate constitution, could not long sustain all this; but became so pale and thin that he had no need of a mask to conceal his identity. His extravagant love for this woman had so infatuated him, that he imagined he had strength to accomplish devoirs for which that of Hercules would not have been sufficient. Having fallen ill at last, and being teased by the lady, who was not so fond of him sick as sound, he asked for his discharge, which the husband granted with regret, making him promise to return as soon as he was recovered.

M. d'Avannes had no need of a horse for his departure, for he had only the length of a street to travel. He went at once to his good father's, and found there only his wife whose virtuous love for him had not at all decreased through absence. When she saw him so pale and thin, she could not help saying to him, "I do not know, monsieur, what is the present state of your conscience; but I do not perceive that your pilgrimage has increased your plumpness. I am very much mistaken if your travels by night have not fatigued you more than those by day. If you had made the journey to Jerusalem on foot, you would have come back more sunburnt, but not so lean and weak. Recollect this ride, and pay no more devotions to such images, which, instead of resuscitating the dead, bring the living to death. I should say more to you, but I see that if you have sinned, you have been so punished that it would be cruel to add to your distress."

M. d'Avannes, more ashamed than penitent, replied, "I have heard, madam, that repentance follows close upon the fault. This I experience, to my cost; and I pray you, madam, to excuse my youth, which is punished by the experience of the mischief it would not be warned against."

The lady changed the conversation, and made him lie down in a fine bed, where he remained for a fortnight, taking nothing but restoratives; and the husband and the wife were so assiduous in their attentions, that one or other was always with him. Though he had committed the folly you have heard against the feelings and the advice of the excellent lady, she nevertheless continued to love him as before, in the hope that when this great fire of youth had passed away, he would reform and come to love rightly, and then he would be all her own.

During the fortnight he remained in her house, she talked so much and so well to inspire him with a love of virtue, that he began to hate vice, and to be disgusted with his fault.

Gazing one day on the virtuous lady, who appeared to him much handsomer than the wanton, and knowing her excellent qualities better than he had ever done, he banished all fear, and thus addressed her, "I see no better means, madam, of becoming as good as you would have me to be, than to turn my whole heart to the love of virtue. Pray tell me, madam, I beseech you, would you not have the goodness to give me all the aid in your power to that end?"

The lady, delighted to see him come to the point to which she wished to lead him, replied, "I promise you, monsieur, that if you love virtue as much as becomes a lord of your rank, I will spare nothing to render you all the services of which I may be capable."

"Remember your promise, madam," returned d'Avannes; "and consider that God, whom the Christian knows only by faith, has deigned to assume flesh like that of the sinner, in order that attracting our flesh to the love of His humanity, He might also attract our spirits to the love of His divinity, thus employing visible things to make us love the invisible. As this virtue which I wish to love all my life long has nothing visible about it except the outward effects it produces, it is necessary that it should assume some body, in order to make itself known to men. It has assumed that body, madam, in putting on yours, the most perfect it could have found. I own, therefore, that you are not only virtuous, but actually virtue itself; and I, who see that virtue shine beneath the veil of the most beautiful body that ever existed, wish to serve and honour it all my life, and to renounce for ever the love that is criminal and vain."

The lady, though no less delighted than surprised to hear him speak thus, was able completely to conceal her feelings, and said, "I will not take upon me, monsieur, to reply to your theology; but as I am much more disposed to fear the evil than to believe the good, I beg you will not address me in a language which gives you so poor an opinion of those who are weak enough to believe it. I know very well that I am a woman like any other, and a woman that has so many defects that virtue would do something greater in transforming me into itself than in transforming itself into me, unless it wished to remain unknown to the world. No one would think of recognising it under such a garb as mine. Howbeit, with all my faults, my lord, I still love you as much as a woman can and ought who fears God and cherishes honour; but this love shall not be declared to you until your heart is capable of the patience which a virtuous love requires. When that time comes, monsieur, I know what I shall have to tell you. Meanwhile, be assured that your welfare, your person, and your honour are dearer to me than to yourself."

Trembling, and with tears in his eyes, M. d'Avannes begged to be allowed to take a kiss as a pledge of her word, but she refused, saying that she did not choose to violate the custom of the country for him. Presently the husband arrived. "I am so much indebted, father," said D'Avannes, "to you and your wife, that I entreat you always to regard me as your son." The good man willingly expressed his assent. "Let me kiss you, then, in assurance of that affection," continued D'Avannes. This was done. "If I were not afraid," he said next, "of contravening the law, I would request the same favour of my mother, your wife." The husband desired his wife to kiss him, which she did without testifying either repugnance or alacrity; whilst the fire which the previous conversation had already kindled in the heart of M. d'Avannes grew hotter at this kiss so ardently longed for, and before so peremptorily denied him.

After this M. d'Avannes went back to the king, his brother, and told all sorts of stories about his journey to Montferrat. To his great vexation he learned that his brother was going to Oly and Taffares, and fearing that the journey would be a long one, he resolved to try before his departure if the lady were not better disposed towards him than she appeared. To this end he went to lodge in town, and took, in the street in which she lived, a dilapidated old wooden house, to which he set fire about midnight. The whole town was in great alarm; the rich man was roused by the noise, and calling out from the window to know where the fire was, he was told that it was at the house of M. d'Avannes. Hurrying thither with all his domestics, he found the young lord in the street in his shirt. Such was his pity for him that, taking him in his arms, and covering him with his own robe, he hastened home with him, and said to his wife, "Here is a prisoner, my dear, whom I commit to your custody. Treat him like myself."

He was no sooner gone than M. d'Avannes, who would have been glad to be treated as her husband, jumped into the bed, hoping that the opportunity and the place would inspire the chaste lady with more humane sentiments; but he was quite disappointed, for as he got in at one side she got out at the other, carrying away her *chamarre*, which she put on; and seating herself at the bedside, she said, "What! monsieur, did you imagine that opportunity could change a virtuous heart? Know that as gold becomes purer in the fire, so a chaste heart grows stronger amid temptations. Often it grows stronger among them than elsewhere, and becomes more cold the more it is attacked by its opposite. Be assured, then, that if I had entertained any other sentiments than those I have avowed, I should not have lacked means, and that I neglect them only because I do not choose to use them. If you would have me continue to love you, banish not only the desire but the thought that, do what you may, you can ever bring me to be other than what I am."

Her women now coming in, she ordered them to prepare a collation of all sorts of confections; but D'Avannes could neither eat nor drink, so great was his vexation at having missed his blow, and exposed himself, as he feared, by that demonstration of his desires, to lose the position of familiarity in which he had been with her. The husband having taken measures for extinguishing the fire, returned, and prevailed on M. d'Avannes to pass the night in his house; but he passed it in such a manner that his eyes were more occupied in weeping than in sleeping. He went and bade them adieu at the bedside very early in the morning, and plainly perceived, in kissing the lady, that she felt more pity than anger for his fault. This was a fresh brand to the fire of his love. After dinner he set out for Taffares with the king; but before his departure he went twice more to take a final farewell of his good father and his wife, who, since her husband's first command, no longer made any scruple to kiss M. d'Avannes as her son.

There is no doubt that the more virtue did violence to the poor lady's eyes and countenance, constraining them to hide the fire that was in her heart, the more it augmented and became insupportable. Unable, then, any longer to endure the conflict between love and honour, which yet she had resolved should never be manifested, and having no longer the pleasure and consolation of seeing and conversing with him for whom she lived, she fell into a continuous fever, caused by a melancholy humour which she was forced to conceal, and which rendered the extremities of her body quite cold, though the inside burned continually. The physicians, a class of men on whose hands hangs not the health of men, began to despair on account of an obstruction of the spleen, which rendered her melancholy, and they advised the husband to warn his wife to think of her conscience, saying that she was in the hands of God; as if people in good health were not there also. The husband, who was excessively fond of his wife, was so overwhelmed at this news, that he wrote, for his own consolation, to M. d'Avannes, begging he would take the trouble to come and see them, in the hope that his presence would be a comfort to the patient. M. d'Avannes, on receipt of the letter, instantly started off post-haste, and on entering the house, he found the domestics of both sexes as full of grief for their mistress as she deserved. Shocked at what he saw, he remained at the door as if paralysed, until his good father came and embraced him with tears, and without being able to utter a word, led him to the sick woman's chamber. Turning her languid eyes full upon him, she held out her hand, and drew him towards her with all the little strength left her.

"The moment is come, my lord," she said, embracing him, "when all dissimulation must cease, and I must declare to you the truth I have had so much difficulty in concealing; it is, that if you have had much love for me, I have had no less for you. But my pain is greater than yours, because I have been compelled to hide it. Conscience and honour have never allowed me to declare to you the sentiments of my heart, for fear of augmenting in you a passion which I wished to diminish. But know, my lord, that the *no* which I have said to you so often, and which it has cost me so much pain to pronounce, is the cause of my death. I die with satisfaction, since, by God's grace, notwithstanding the excess of my love, I have nothing to reproach myself with in regard to piety and honour. I say the excess of my love, for a less

fire than mine has destroyed greater and stronger edifices.
I die happy, since before quitting this world, I can declare
my affection, which corresponds to yours, save only that the
honour of men and that of women are not the same thing.
I pray you, my lord, henceforth not to be afraid to address
yourself to the greatest and most virtuous ladies you can;
for it is hearts of that character which have the strongest
passions, and which control them most wisely; and your
grace, good looks, and good breeding will always enable you
to gather the fruits of your love. I will not ask you to pray
to God for me, for I know that the gate of Paradise is not
shut against true lovers, and that love is a fire which punishes
lovers so well in this life, that they are exempted from the
sharp torment of Purgatory. And now farewell, my lord; I
commend to you your good father, my husband. Tell him
truly, I beg you, what you know of me, in order that he may
know how much I have loved God and him. And come no
more before my eyes, for henceforth I wish to employ my
mind only in putting myself in a condition to receive the
promises made to me by God before the foundation of the
world."

So saying, she embraced him with all the strength of her
weak arms. M. d'Avannes, on whom compassion produced
the same effect as pain and sickness in the lady, retired without
being able to say a word, and threw himself upon a bed
which was in the room, where he fainted several times. The
lady then called her husband, and after many becoming demonstrations,
she recommended M. d'Avannes to him, assuring
him that next to himself that was the person she had
loved best in the world. Having kissed her husband she bade
him farewell, and then the holy sacrament of the altar was
brought her after extreme unction, which she received with
joy, and an entire assurance of her salvation. Finding at
last that her sight was leaving her, and that her strength
was failing, she began to repeat aloud her *In manus*, hearing
which, M. d'Avannes sat up in the bed, and saw her render up
with a gentle sigh her glorious soul to Him from whom it
came. When he saw that she was dead, he threw himself
upon the body, which he had never approached without
trembling while she lived, and embraced it so, that it was
with difficulty he was forced away from it. The husband,

who had never supposed he loved her so much, was surprised, and said, "It is too much, my lord." And thereupon they withdrew.

After they had long deplored, the one his wife, the other his mistress, M. d'Avannes recounted his love to the husband, and told him that until her death the deceased had never shown him any other signs than those of rigid reserve. This increased the husband's admiration for his departed wife, and still more his grief for her loss, and all his life afterwards he rendered service to M. d'Avannes. The latter, who was then but eighteen, returned to the court, and it was a long time before he would speak to any of the ladies there, or even see them; and for more than two years he wore mourning.

You see, ladies, what a difference there is between a chaste woman and a wanton. Their love, too, produced very different effects; for the one died a glorious death, and the other lived but too long after the loss of her reputation and her honour. As much as the death of the saint is precious before God, so is that of the sinner the reverse.

"Truly, Saffredent," said Oisille, "anything finer than the story you have just narrated one could not wish to hear; and if the rest of the company knew the persons as I do, they would think it still finer, for I never saw a handsomer gentleman, or one of better deportment, than M. d'Avannes."

"Must it not be owned," replied Saffredent, "that this was a chaste and good woman, since, in order to appear more virtuous than she was in reality, and to hide the love which reason and nature willed that she should have for so perfect a gentleman, she let herself die for want of giving herself the pleasure she desired without owning it."

"If she had felt that desire," said Parlamente, "she would not have lacked either place or opportunity to reveal it; but she had so much virtue that reason always controlled her desire."

"You may paint her portrait as you please," said Hircan; "but I know that a greater devil always drives out a less, and that the pride of the ladies seeks rather carnal pleasure than the fear and love of God. They are perpetual enigmas, and they are such clever dissemblers, that it is impossible to know what is in their hearts. If the world had not annexed infamy to the loss of their honour, it would be universally found that nature has made them with the same inclinations and the same affections as ourselves. Not daring to take the pleasure they long for, they have changed that vice into another which they think more decorous, I mean a cruelty quite as much pretended as real, by which they think to gain immortal renown; and through the petty vanity of resisting the vice of nature's law (if nature is vicious), they resemble not only the brutes in cruelty and inhumanity, but even the devils, whose pride and craft they borrow."

"It is a pity you have a good woman for your wife," said Nomerfide, "since, not content with despising the virtue of other women, you would fain have it believed that they are all vicious."

"I am very glad," replied Hircan, "to have a wife who gives no ground for scandal; a thing which I would not do either; but as for chastity of heart, I believe that she and I are children of Adam and Eve: so, if we examine ourselves well, we have no business to cover our nakedness with leaves, but rather to confess our weakness."

"I know well," said Parlamente, "that we all have need of the grace of God, being as we are by nature disposed to sin; but it must be owned, nevertheless, that our temptations are not similar to yours: and if we sin through pride, no one suffers for it, and neither our body nor our hands receive any stain. But your pleasure consists in dishonouring women, and your glory in killing men in war; which are two things absolutely opposed to the law of God."

"I admit what you say," remarked Geburon; "but when God says that *whoever looks upon a woman to lust after her hath already committed adultery in his heart*, and that *whoever hateth his neighbour is a homicide*, do you suppose he does not also mean to speak of women?"

"God, who knoweth the heart, will decide," said Longarine. "Meanwhile, it is always a good thing that men should have no power to accuse us, for God's goodness is so great that He will not judge us without an accuser. Not judge us, did I say? The frailty of our hearts is so well known to Him, that He will give us credit for not having proceeded to overt acts."

"Pray let us drop this dispute," said Saffredent. "We are here to tell tales, not to preach sermons. I therefore give my voice to Ennasuite, and beg that she will not forget to make us laugh."

"I shall not fail to do so," replied Ennasuite. "On my way hither I was told a story of two servants of a princess, which seemed to me so droll, and made me laugh so much, that I forgot the dismal tale I had prepared for to-day, and which I will postpone until to-morrow, my countenance being now too merry to make it pass well with you."

NOVEL XXVII.

A SECRETARY HAD THE IMPUDENCE TO SOLICIT THE FAVOURS OF HIS HOST'S WIFE, AND HAD ONLY THE SHAME FOR HIS PAINS.

THERE was at Amboise a man who served a princess in the capacity of chamberlain, and who, being an obliging, civil person, gladly entertained people who came to him, especially his own comrades. Not long ago, one of his mistress's secretaries came to lodge with him, and remained ten or twelve days. This secretary was so ugly, that he was more like a king of the cannibals than a Christian. Though his host treated him as a friend and a brother, yet he behaved to him like a man who had—I will not say forgotten all decency, but who had never had a feeling of it in his heart: this was, to solicit in the way of lawless love his companion's wife, who not only had nothing engaging in her, but looked the very antidote of criminal pleasure, and as good and virtuous a woman as any in Amboise. On becoming aware of the man's bad intentions, the woman thought it better to expose his turpitude than to suppress and conceal it by a prompt and decisive refusal; she therefore pretended to listen to his suit. He, thinking that he had made a conquest, pressed her incessantly, without considering that she was fifty, that she was not handsome, and that she had the reputation of a good woman who loved her husband. One day among others, when the husband was at home, and they were in a lower room, she pretended that the only thing requisite was to find a safe place for a tête-à-tête, where they might entertain each other as he wished. He proposed that they should go up to the garret. She rose at once, and begged him to go first, promising to follow him. He, laughing and grinning like an amorous monkey, went up-stairs and posted himself in the garret. Whilst he was waiting for what he had so hotly desired, he listened with all his ears for his fair one's footsteps; but, instead of them, he heard her voice crying out, "Wait a bit, master secretary, till I go and ask my husband if it is his pleasure that I should go to you." Imagine how the man looked in tears who had cut such an ugly figure when laughing. He hurried down stairs with tears in his eyes, and begged her for God's sake to say nothing, and not set her husband against him. "I am certain," she replied, "that you are too much his friend to wish to say anything which might not be repeated to him; so I am going to speak to him about this matter." And so she did, in spite of all he could do to prevent her. He ran away, and was as much ashamed as the husband was glad to hear of the trick his wife had played him. So satisfied was the good man with his wife's virtue, that he gave himself no concern about his companion's villany, thinking him sufficiently punished in having the shame he had intended for him recoil upon his own head.

This tale teaches us, ladies, that honest folk ought never to attach themselves to those who have neither conscience, heart, nor wit enough to know God, honour, and true love.

"Though your tale be short," said Oisille, "it is as amusing as any I have heard, and to the honour of a worthy woman."

"It is no great thing to boast of," said Simontault, "for an honest woman to refuse a man so ugly as you represent this secretary to have been. Had he been handsome and well-bred, her conduct would then have been some evidence of virtue. As I think I know the man, if it was my turn to tell a story, I think I could give you one about him not less droll than this."

"Well, do so," said Ennasuite.

"Courtiers, and inhabitants of great cities," he continued, "have such a good opinion of their own capacity, that they regard others as very small folk in comparison with themselves. Though craft and cunning are of all countries and all conditions, yet as those who think themselves the shrewdest do so only through vanity, they are only the more laughed at when they happen to make some mistake, as I shall instance to you in an affair of recent occurrence."

NOVEL XXVIII.

A SECRETARY, THINKING TO DUPE A CERTAIN PERSON, WAS HIMSELF DUPED.

When King Francis I. was at Paris with his sister the Queen of Navarre, that princess had a secretary named Jean, who was not one of those who let anything worth having be lost for want of picking it up. There was neither president nor counsellor with whom he was not acquainted, merchant nor rich man whose house he did not frequent. At the same time there also arrived in Paris a merchant of Bayonne, named Bernard du Ha, who, having business in hand, and being in need of protection, addressed himself to the *lieutenant criminel*, who was of his country. The Queen of Navarre's secretary used also to go frequently to see the same person, as a good servant of his master and mistress. One holiday, when he went to the house, he found neither the lieutenant nor his lady at home; but there was Bernard du Ha, playing a viol or some other instrument for the servant-women of the house, and teaching them to dance the branles of Gascony. When the secretary saw this, he wanted to make Bernard believe that he was doing wrong, and that if the lieutenant and his lady knew of it they would be very angry. Having talked to him in so alarming a manner that the other begged him not to tell what he had seen, he said, "What will you give me not to say a word about it?" Bernard du Ha, who was not so frightened as he made believe, perceiving that the secretary wanted to dupe him, promised to give him a pasty of the best Basque ham he had ever eaten. The secretary was highly pleased, and begged that he might have the pasty on the following Sunday after dinner, which the other promised.

Counting on this promise, the secretary went to see a lady of Paris whom he passionately desired to marry, and said to her, "On Sunday, madam, I will come and sup with you, if you please; but do not trouble yourself about anything but good bread and good wine, for I have so gulled a stupid fellow of Bayonne, that he will be at the cost of the rest: I will bring you the best Basque ham that ever was tasted in Paris." The lady, taking his word for it, invited two or three of her fair neighbours, and assured them she would treat them to something they had never tasted before. Sunday being come, the secretary went in quest of the merchant, and found him at the Pont au Change. Saluting him very politely, he said, "To the devil with you for having given me such trouble to find you."

"Many a one has taken more trouble than you," replied Bernard du Ha, "and has not been so well rewarded in the end." So saying, he produced the pasty, which he had under his cloak, and which was big enough to set before a small army. The secretary was so pleased, that although he had an enormous ugly mouth, he squeezed it up so small that one would have thought he could not bite the ham. Hastily clutching the pasty, he turned his back upon the merchant without inviting him to partake of the treat, and carried it to his mistress, who was very curious to know if the eatables of Guienne were as good as those of Paris. Supper-time being come, the company began to fall to at the soup with much vigour. "Leave those insipid things," said the secretary, "and let us taste this whet for wine." So saying, he opened the pasty, and set about cutting the ham, but it was so hard that he could not stick the knife into it. After trying again and again, he found that he was hoaxed, and that instead of a ham he had been given a wooden shoe, such as is worn in Gascony, with a stick thrust into the end of it, and the whole smeared with suet and powdered with rust of iron and spices, which gave out a very pleasant odour. The secretary was greatly ashamed both of having been duped by the person he thought to dupe, and having deluded his mistress, contrary to his intentions; to say nothing of his sore disappointment at having to content himself with soup for supper. The ladies, who were as vexed as himself, would have accused him as the author of the trick if they had not seen by his face that he was anything but pleased with its success.

After making a light supper, the secretary retired in great dudgeon, and seeing that Bernard du Ha had not kept his word, he did not think himself bound by his own. Accordingly he went to the *lieutenant criminel*, intending to say everything bad he could of the merchant; but the latter had been beforehand with him, and had already related the adventure to the lieutenant, who laughed in the secretary's face, and told him that he had learned to his cost what it was to play tricks on Gascons. And so all he got was the shame of having been the dupe of his own cunning.

The same thing happens to many, who, wishing to deceive, find themselves deceived. Therefore it is best to do to others only as we would be done by.

"I assure you," said Geburon, "that I have often witnessed such occurrences; and those who pass for village boobies often overreach persons who think themselves very clever; for there is no greater ninny than a man who thinks himself cunning, nor any one wiser than he who knows that he is not so."

"He who knows his own incapacity, knows something, after all," said Parlamente.

"For fear time should fail us, I give my voice to Nomerfide," said Simontault. "I am sure she will not delay us long by her rhetoric."

"You shall have from me the satisfaction you desire," said Nomerfide. "I am not surprised, ladies, if love inspires princes and well-educated persons with the art of extricating themselves from danger. In fact, they are brought up in intercourse with so many persons of knowledge, that it would be very surprising if they were ignorant of anything. But address in love appears with much greater lustre when those who display it are persons of less intelligence. I shall, then, relate to you a piece of cleverness exhibited by a priest through the prompting of love alone; for he was so ignorant in all other things, that he could hardly say mass."

NOVEL XXIX.

A VILLAGER, WHOSE WIFE INTRIGUED WITH THE PARISH PRIEST, SUFFERED HIMSELF TO BE EASILY DECEIVED.

THERE was at Carrelles, a village in the county of Maine, a rich husbandman, who in his old age married a handsome young wife, by whom he had no children; but she consoled herself for this disappointment with several friends. When gentlemen and persons of mark failed her, she reverted to her last resource, which was the church, and chose for the accomplice of her sin him who could absolve her—that is to say, her priest, who paid frequent visits to his sheep. The dull old husband suspected nothing; but as he was a rough and sturdy old fellow, she played her game as secretly as she could, being afraid that her husband would kill her if he came to know of it.

One day, when the husband was gone into the fields, and his wife did not expect him back for some time, she sent for master parson to confess her; but during the time they were making good cheer together, the husband arrived so suddenly, that the priest had not time to steal off. Intending then to hide, he went by the wife's directions up into a loft, and covered the trap-hole in the floor by which he had got in with a winnowing basket. Meanwhile the wife, who was afraid her husband might suspect something, regaled him well at dinner, and plied him so well with wine, that the good man, having taken a little drop too much, and being fatigued with walking, fell asleep in a chair by the fireside. The priest, who found it dull work waiting in the loft, on ceasing to hear any noise in the room below, leaned over the trap-hole, and stretching out his neck as far as he could, saw that the good man was asleep. But while making his observations he inadvertently leaned with so much weight on the winnowing basket, that down fell basket, priest and all, by the side of the good man, and woke him up with the noise. But the priest was on his legs before the other had opened his eyes, and said, "There's your winnowing basket, gossip, and I'm much obliged to you;" and so saying, he walked off.

The poor husbandman, quite bewildered, asked his wife what was the matter? "It is your winnowing basket, my dear," she replied, "which the priest had borrowed and has now returned."

"It is a very clumsy way of returning what one has borrowed," said the good man, grumbling, "for I thought the house was falling."

In this way the priest saved himself at the expense of the husbandman, who objected to nothing but the abrupt manner in which his reverence had returned his winnowing basket. The master he served, ladies, saved him for that time, in order to possess and torment him longer.

"Do not imagine that simple folk are more exempt from craft than we are," said Geburon; "far from it, they have a great deal more. Look at thieves, murderers, sorcerers, false coiners, and other people of that sort, whose wits are always at work; they are all simple folk."

"I am not surprised that they have more craft than others," said Parlamente, "but I am surprised that, having their wits directed to so many other things, they can think of love. Is it not strange that so fine a passion can enter such vulgar hearts?"

"You know, madam, what Maître Jean de Meun says:

> *Aussi bien sont amourettes*
> *Sous bureau que sous brunettes.*

Besides, the love of which the tale speaks is not that which makes one wear harness. The poor, who have not wealth and honours like us, have in compensation more of the commodities of nature. Their viands are not so delicate as ours, but good appetite makes amends for that deficiency, and they fare better on coarse bread than we on dainties. Their beds are not so handsome or so well made as ours, but their sleep is sounder. Their ladies are neither painted nor decked out like ours whom we idolise, but they receive pleasure from them much oftener than we, without fearing any other tongues than those of the beasts and birds that see them. In a word, they lack what we have, and have abundance of what we have not."

"Pray let us have done with this peasant and his wife,"

said Nomerfide, "and finish the day before vespers. It is for Hircan to do so."

"I will finish it, then, with a very dismal tale," said Hircan. "Though I do not willingly speak ill of ladies, knowing as I do that men are malicious enough to deduce from the fault of one conclusions disparaging to all the rest, yet the singularity of the adventure overcomes my fear, and the exposure of ignorance will perhaps make others wiser."

NOVEL XXX.

NOTABLE EXAMPLE OF HUMAN FRAILTY IN A LADY WHO, TO CONCEAL AN EVIL, COMMITS A STILL GREATER ONE.

In the time of Louis XII., the legate at Avignon being then a lord of the house of Amboise, nephew to the Legate of France, whose name was George, there was a lady in Languedoc who had an income of more than four thousand ducats. Her name I will not mention, for sake of her relations. She was still very young when her husband died, leaving her but one son; and whether from regret for her husband, or love of her son, she resolved never to marry again. To avoid all occasion for doing so, she frequented only the society of the devout, thinking that opportunity makes sin, and not knowing that sin forges opportunity. She gave herself up wholly to the divine service, shunning all parties of pleasure and everything worldly, insomuch that she made it a matter of conscience to be present at a wedding, or to hear the organ played in church. When her son was seven years old, she chose a man of holy life as his preceptor, to bring him up in piety and sanctity. But when he was between fourteen and fifteen, nature, who is a very mysterious schoolmaster, finding him well grown and idle, taught him a very different lesson from any he had learned from his preceptor; for under that new instruction he began to look upon and desire such things as seemed to him fair, and among others a demoiselle who slept in his mother's room. No one had the least suspicion of this, for he was regarded as a child, and nothing was ever heard in the house but goodly discourse.

The young gallant having begun secretly to solicit this girl, she went and told her mistress. The mother loved her son so much, that she believed this to be a story told to get him into disgrace; but the girl repeated her complaints so often, that her mistress at last said she would find out the truth of the matter: if it was as the girl stated, she would punish her son severely, but if not, the accuser should pay the penalty. In order, then, to come at the truth, she ordered the demoiselle to make an appointment with the young gentleman that he should come to her at midnight, to the bed in which she lay alone near the door in his mother's chamber. The demoiselle obeyed her orders, and that night the mother lay down in the demoiselle's bed, resolving that if her son came thither she would chastise him in such a manner that he should never lie with a woman without remembering it. Such were her angry thoughts when her son actually entered the bed in which she lay; but unable still to bring herself to believe that he had any unchaste intention, she waited for some plainer evidence of his bad purpose before she would speak to him. But she waited so long, and nature is so frail, that her anger ended in an abominable pleasure, and she forgot that she was a mother. As water retained by force is more impetuous when let loose, so was it with this unfortunate woman, who made her whole pride consist in the violence she did her body. When she began to descend the first step from her chastity she found herself at once at the bottom, and became pregnant that night by him whom she wished to hinder from getting others with child.

No sooner was the sin committed than she was seized with the most poignant remorse, and her repentance lasted as long as her life. So keen was her anguish on rising from beside her son, who never discovered his mistake, that entering a closet, and calling to mind the firm resolution she had formed, and which she had so badly executed, she passed the whole night alone in an agony of tears. But instead of humbling herself, and owning that of ourselves alone, and 'without the aid of God, we can do nothing but sin, she thought by her own efforts and by her tears to repair the past and prevent future mischief, always imputing her sin to the occasion, and not to wickedness, for which there is no remedy but the grace of God. As if there was but one sort of sin which could bring damnation, she applied her whole mind to avoid that one; but pride, which the sense of extreme sinfulness should destroy, was too strongly rooted in her heart, and grew in such a manner, that, to avoid one evil, she committed many others.

Early next morning she sent for her son's governor, and said to him, "My son is coming to maturity, and it is time that he should be removed from the house. One of my relations, who is beyond the mountains with the Grand Master of Chaumont, will be glad to have him. Take him away, then, forthwith; and to spare me the pain of parting, do not let him come to bid me farewell." Without more ado she gave him money for the journey, and he set out the next day with his pupil, who was very glad of it; and having had what he wanted of his mistress, desired nothing better than to go to the wars. The lady was long plunged in extreme grief, and but for the fear of God she could have wished that the unhappy fruit of her womb should perish. To conceal her fault she pretended to be ill; and having a bastard brother in whom she confided above all men, and to whom she had made large donations, she sent for him, informed him of the misfortune that had happened to her, but not of her son's share in it, and begged him to save her honour by his help; which he did. Some days before she expected to be confined he advised her to try change of air, and remove to his house, where she would be more likely to recover than at home. She went thither with hardly any attendants, and found there a midwife, who had been sent for as if to attend her brother's wife, and who, without knowing the lying-in-woman, delivered her by night of a fine little girl. The gentleman put the infant out to nurse as his own; and the lady, after a month's stay, returned home, where she lived more austerely than ever.

Her son being grown up, and Italy being at peace, he sent to beg his mother's permission to return to her. But as she was afraid of relapsing into the same crime, she put him off from time to time as well as she could; but he pressed her so much, that at last she gave him leave to come home, having no plausible reason to allege for persisting longer in her refusal. She sent him word, however, not to appear before her until he was married; to choose a wife whom he loved passionately; and not to let his choice be determined by wealth, for if he chose a comely wife that was enough.

During this time the daughter, who had been left with the bastard brother, having grown up into a very handsome girl, her guardian thought of removing her to some place where she should not be known. He consulted the mother on the subject, and it was her wish that she should be given to the Queen of Navarre, named Catherine. The girl was so handsome and well-bred at the age of thirteen, that the Queen of Navarre had a great regard for her, and wished much to marry her well; but the girl being poor, many lovers presented themselves, but no husband. The unknown father, returning from Italy, visited the court of the Queen of Navarre, and no sooner saw his daughter than he fell in love with her. As he had his mother's permission to marry any woman he liked, he only asked was she of noble lineage, and being told that she was, he demanded her in marriage of the Queen of Navarre, who very gladly bestowed her upon him, knowing well that the cavalier was as wealthy as he was well-bred and handsome.

The marriage having been consummated, the gentleman wrote to his mother, saying she could no longer close her doors against him, since he brought with him a wife as handsome and as perfect as she could wish for. His mother made inquiries as to the wife he had taken, and found that it was their own daughter, which caused her such excessive affliction, that she was near dying suddenly, seeing that the means she employed to put a stop to the course of her misfortune only served to make it greater. Finding no remedy for what had occurred, she went to the Legate of Avignon, confessed the enormity of her crime, and asked his advice. The legate, to satisfy her conscience, summoned several theologians, to whom he submitted the affair without naming the person concerned. The decision of this council of conscience was, that the lady was never to reveal the secret to her children, who had not sinned, inasmuch as they had known nothing; but that, as for herself, she was to do penance all her life. So the poor lady returned home, where soon after arrived her son and her daughter-in-law, who loved each other so much, that never was there a fonder couple, or one more like each other, she being his daughter, sister and wife; and he her father, brother, and husband. Their love continued unabated to the last, whilst their profoundly penitent mother never saw them caress but she withdrew to weep.*

* This novel is founded on a popular tradition, traces of which are found in several places in France. Millin, in his *Antiquités Nationales*, speaking of the collegial church of Ecouis, says: "There was found in the middle of the nave, in the cross aisle, a white marble slab, on which was inscribed this epitaph:

> 'Ci-gît l'enfant, ci-gît le père,
> Ci-gît la sœur, ci-gît le frère,
> Ci-gît la femme et le mari,
> Et ne sont que deux corps ici.'"

[Here lies the child, here lies the father, here lies the sister, here lies the brother, here lie the wife and the husband, and there are but two bodies here.]

"The tradition is, that a son of Madame d'Ecouis had by his mother, without knowing her or being recognised by her, a daughter named Cécile. He afterwards married in Lorraine that same Cécile, she being then with the Duchess of Bar. Thus Cécile was her husband's daughter and sister. They were interred in the same grave at Ecouis, in 1512." Millin says that the same story is told (but with modifications) in other churches of France; for instance, in that of Alincourt, a village between Amiens and Abbeville, is seen the following epitaph:

> "Ci-gît le fils, ci-gît la mère,
> Ci-gît la fille avec le père,
> Ci-gît la sœur, ci-gît le frère,
> Ci-gît la femme et le mari,
> Et ne sont que trois corps ici."

[Here lies the son, here lies the mother, here lies the daughter with the father, here lies the sister, here lies the brother, here lie the wife and the husband, and there are only three bodies here.]

Gaspard Meturas, who has inserted this epitaph in his *Hortus Epitaphiorum Selectorum*, 1648, says that it is found in a church of Clermont, in Auvergne, and adds: "The key to it consists in saying that the mother engendered her husband by lying with (*en épousant*) her own father; for it thence follows that he was her son, her brother, and her husband, even legitimately, the marriage having been effected with a righteous ignorance on both sides.

Dunlop, in his History of Fiction, says that the thirty-fifth novel of the second part of Bandello "is the same story with the plot of the Mysterious Mother of Horace Walpole, and the thirtieth tale of the Queen of Navarre. The first part of this story had already been told in the twenty-third novel of Massuccio. The second part, which relates to the marriage only, occurs in Bandello and the Queen of Navarre. It is not likely, however, that the French or Italian novelists

There, ladies, is what happens to those of your sex who think to vanquish, by their own strength, love and nature with all the faculties which God has given them. Better were it to own their weakness, avoid exposure to temptation, and say to God, like David, "Lord I suffer force: answer for me."

"It is impossible to imagine a stranger case," said Oisille. "Methinks there is no man or woman who ought not to humble himself and fear God, seeing how the hope of doing a good thing was so productive of mischief."

"Be assured," said Parlamente, "that the first step man takes in self-confidence, removes him so far from the confidence he ought to have in God."

"Man is wise," said Geburon, "when he recognises no greater enemy than himself, and distrusts his own will and counsel, however good and holy they may seem in his eyes."

"For no apparent prospect of good to come of it, however great," said Longarine, "should a woman expose herself to

borrowed from one another. The tales of Bandello were first published in 1554, and as the Queen of Navarre died in 1549, it is improbable that she had an opportunity of seeing them. On the other hand, the work of the queen was not printed till 1558, nine years after her death, so it is not likely that any part of it was copied by Bandello, whose tales had been edited some years before. It may therefore be presumed that some current traditions furnished both with the horrible incident they report. Indeed Bandello declares, in the introduction to the tale, that it happened in Navarre, and was told to him by a lady of that country. In Luther's Colloquia Mensalia, under the article Auricular Confession, it is said to have occurred at Erfurt, in Germany. It is also related in the eleventh volume of Byshop's Blossoms, and in L'Inceste Innocent, a novel by Desfontaines, published in 1638. Julio de Medrano, an old Spanish writer of the sixteenth century, says that he heard a similar story when he was in the Bourbonnais, where the inhabitants showed him the house in which the pardes had lived, and repeated to him this epitaph, which was inscribed on their tomb" (that in four lines quoted above). "Mr. Walpole disclaims having had any knowledge of the tale of the Queen of Navarre or Bandello when he wrote his drama. Its plot, he says, was suggested by a story he had heard when very young, of a lady who, under uncommon agonies of mind, waited on Archbishop Tillotson, revealed her crime, and besought his counsel in what manner she should act, as the fruit of her horrible artifice had lately been married to her son, neither party being aware of the relation that subsisted between them. The prelate charged her never to let her son or daughter know what had passed. For herself, he bade her almost despair."

share the same bed with a man, however nearly related to her. Fire and tow are no safe neighbours."

"Assuredly," said Ennasuite, "this woman was a conceited fool, who thought herself such a saint that she could not sin, as some would have simple folks believe of them, which is a gross and pernicious error."

"Is it possible," exclaimed Oisille, "that there are people so foolish as to believe anything of the sort?"

"They do still more," said Longarine; "they say that it is necessary to habituate oneself to chastity; and to try their strength, they talk with the handsomest women and those they love best, and by kissing and touching them make trial of themselves as to whether or not they are in a condition of complete mortification of the flesh. When they find that this pleasure moves them, they fall back on solitude, fasting, and discipline; and when they have so subdued the flesh that neither conversation nor kissing causes them any emotion, the fools try the temptation of lying together and embracing without any voluptuous desire. But, for one who resists, a thousand succumb. Thence have ensued so many mischiefs, that the Archbishop of Milan, where this religious practice was introduced, was compelled to separate the sexes, and put the women into the women's convent, and the men into that of the men."

"Was there ever a more extravagant folly?" said Geburon. "A man wants to make himself sinless, and seeks with avidity provocations to sin."

"Some there are," said Saffredent, "who do quite the reverse; they shun temptation as much as possible, and yet concupiscence clings to them everywhere. The good Saint Jerome, after having soundly flogged and hid himself in the desert, confessed that he had been unable to overcome the fire of lust that burned in his marrow. The sovereign remedy, then, is to commend oneself to God; for, unless He upholds us by His power, His virtue, and His goodness, we not only fall, but take pleasure in falling."

"You do not see what I do," said Hircan; "which is, that whilst we were telling our stories the monks who were behind that hedge did not hear the vesper-bell; but no sooner did they hear us talk of God than away they went, and now they are ringing the second bell."

"We shall do well to follow them," said Oisille, "and praise God for his grace in enabling us to pass this day so happily."

Upon this the whole company rose and went to the church, where they devoutly heard vespers. At supper they talked over the conversation of the day, and many things which had occurred in the time, each citing what he thought most worthy of recollection. After a cheerful evening, they retired to their beds, in the hope of resuming next day a pastime which was so agreeable to them. Thus ended the third day.

FOURTH DAY.

MADAME OISILLE rose earlier than the rest, according to her good custom, and meditated on Holy Writ whilst awaiting the gradual assemblage of the company. The laziest excused themselves with the words of Scripture, "I have a wife and I cannot come so soon." Thus it was, that when Hircan and his wife made their appearance, Madame Oisille had already begun her reading; but she knew how to pick out the passages in which those are censured who neglect the hearing of the Word. She not only read the text, but she made them such good and holy exhortations, that it was impossible for them to take offence at them. When these devotional exercises were ended, Parlamente said to her, "I was vexed when I came in at having been lazy, but I now congratulate myself on my laziness, since it has made you speak so well. I derive a double advantage from it—repose of body, and satisfaction of mind."

"For penance, then, let us go to mass," said Oisille, "to pray to our Lord for the will and the strength to do His commands; and then let Him command what he pleases."

As she said these words they entered the church, and after having heard mass with much devotion, they sat down to table, where Hircan did not fail to banter his wife for her laziness. After dinner every one retired to study his part, and at the appointed hour they all repaired punctually to the usual rendezvous. Oisille asked Hircan who should begin the day. "If my wife had not been the first speaker yesterday," he said, "I would give my voice for her; for though I have always believed that she loved me better than any man in the world, she has shown me to-day that she loves me a great deal better than God and his Word, since she has preferred my company to your reading. Since, then, I cannot give my voice to the most discreet of the women, I will give it to the most discreet of the men—I mean Geburon, whom I entreat not to spare the monks."

"It is not necessary to make the entreaty," replied Geburon. "I hold them too well in mind to forget them. It is not long since I heard a story told by Monsieur de Saint Vincent, then the emperor's ambassador, which is too good to be lost."

NOVEL XXXI.

A MONASTERY OF CORDELIERS WAS BURNED AND THE MONKS IN IT, IN PERPETUAL MEMORY OF THE CRUELTY OF ONE OF THEM WHO WAS IN LOVE WITH A LADY.

THERE was in the dominions of the Emperor Maximilian of Austria a monastery of Cordeliers, held in high esteem, near which was the house of a gentleman. He was so infatuated with these Cordeliers that there was nothing he did not give them, in order to have part in the benefit of their fastings and prayers. Among others, there was in this monastery a tall, handsome young Cordelier, whom the gentleman had taken for his confessor, and who was as absolute in the house as the master himself. The Cordelier, struck by the exceeding beauty and propriety of the gentleman's wife, became so enamoured of her, that he could neither eat nor drink, and lost all natural reason. Resolved to execute his design, he went all alone one day to the gentleman's house. Finding no one at home, the monk asked the lady whither her husband was gone? She replied that he was gone to one of his estates, where he was to remain two or three days; but that if he wanted him she would send an express to bring him back. The Cordelier told her that was not necessary, and began to go to and fro about the house, as if he had some affair of consequence in his head.

As soon as the monk had left the lady's room, she said to

one of her women (there were but two of them), "Run after the father, and learn what he wants; for I know by his looks that he is not pleased." The girl, finding him in the courtyard, asked him if he wanted anything? He said he did, and drawing her into a corner, he plunged into her bosom a poniard he carried in his sleeve. He had hardly done the deed when one of the gentleman's men, who had gone to receive the rent of a farm, entered the yard on horseback. As soon as he had dismounted, he saluted the Cordelier, who embraced him, and buried the poniard in his back, after which he closed the gates of the château.

The lady, seeing that her servant did not return, and surprised at her remaining so long with the Cordelier, said to the other woman, "Go see why your companion does not come back." The servant went, and no sooner came in sight of the Cordelier than he called her aside, and served her as he had done the other. Knowing that he was then alone in the house, he went to the lady, and told her that he had long loved her, and that it was time she should obey him. She, who could never have suspected him of anything of the kind, replied, "I believe, father, that if I were so unhappily inclined, you would be the first to condemn me and cast a stone at me."

"Come out into the yard," said the monk, "and you will see what I have done."

The poor woman did so, and seeing her two women and her man lying dead on the ground, was so horrified, that she remained motionless and speechless as a statue. The villain, who did not want to have her for an hour only, did not think fit to offer her violence then, and said to her, "Have no fear, mademoiselle; you are in the hands of that man in all the world who loves you most." So saying, he took off his robe, beneath which he had a smaller one, which he presented to the demoiselle, threatening, if she did not put it on, that he would treat her as he had done the others. The demoiselle, more dead than alive, made a show of obeying him, as well to save her life as to gain time, in hopes that her husband would return. She took off her head-dress by the Cordelier's order as slowly as she could; and when she had done so, the monk, without regard to the beauty of her hair, cut it off in haste, made her strip to her shift and put on the small robe, and then, resuming his own, set off with all the speed he could make along with the little Cordelier he had so long coveted.

God, who has pity on the wronged innocent, was touched by the tears of this poor lady, and so ordered things that her husband, having despatched his business sooner than he expected, took that very road to return home by which the Cordelier was carrying off his wife. The monk, descrying the husband from a distance, said to the lady, "Here comes your husband. I know that if you look at him he will try to get you out of my hands; so walk before me, and do not turn your head in his direction, for if you make him the least sign, I shall have plunged my poniard in your breast sooner than he will have delivered you." Presently the gentleman came up, and asked him whence he came? "From your house, monsieur," replied the Cordelier. "I left mademoiselle quite well, and she is expecting you." The gentleman rode on without perceiving his wife; but the valet who accompanied him, and who had always been in the habit of conversing with the Cordelier's companion, named Friar John, called to his mistress, thinking that she was that person. The poor woman, who durst not turn her head towards her husband, made no reply to the valet; and the latter crossed the road, that he might see the face of this pretended Brother John. The poor lady, without saying anything, made a sign to him with her eyes, which were full of tears. The valet then rode up to his master, and said, "In conscience, monsieur, Friar John is very like mademoiselle your wife. I had a look at him as I crossed the road. It is certainly not the usual Friar John; at least, I can tell you, that if it is, he weeps abundantly, and that he gave me a very sorrowful glance of his eye."

The gentleman told him he was dreaming, and made light of what he said. The valet, however, still persisting in it that there was something wrong, asked leave to ride back and see to it, and begged his master to wait for him. The gentleman let him go, and waited to see what would be the upshot. But the Cordelier, hearing the valet coming after him with shouts to Friar John, and making no doubt that the lady had been recognised, turned upon the valet with a great iron-bound staff, gave him such a blow on the side that

he knocked him off his horse, and springing instantly upon
him with the poniard, speedily despatched him. The gentleman, who from a distance had seen his valet fall, and supposed
that this had happened by some accident, spurred towards
him at once to help him. As soon as he was within reach,
the Cordelier struck him a blow of the same staff with
which he had struck the valet, unhorsed and fell upon him;
but the gentleman, being very strong, threw his arms round
the Cordelier, and hugged him so roughly, that he not only
prevented his doing him any more mischief, but made him
drop the poniard. The wife caught it up at once and gave it
to her husband. At the same time she seized him by his
hood and held him with all her might, whilst her husband
stabbed him several times with the poniard. The Cordelier,
being unable to do anything else, begged for quarter, and
confessed the crime he had committed. The gentleman
granted him his life, and begged his wife to go for his people,
and a cart to carry the prisoner away, which she did, throwing off her Cordelier's robe, and hurrying home in her shift
and her cropped hair. The gentleman's retainers all hastened
to help him to bring home the wolf he had captured; and the
culprit was afterwards sent by the gentleman to Flanders to
be tried by the emperor's officers.

He not only confessed the crime for which he was tried,
but also avowed a fact, which was afterwards verified on the
spot by special commissioners sent for that purpose, which
was, that several other ladies and handsome girls had been
taken to that convent in the same manner as this Cordelier
had attempted to carry off the lady of whom we are speaking;
and if he did not succeed, this was owing to nothing else
than the goodness of God, who always takes upon Him the
defence of those who trust in Him. The girls and the other
stolen spoil found in the monastery were removed, and the
monks were burned with the monastery, in perpetual memorial of a crime so horrible. We see from this that there is
nothing more cruel than love when its principle is vice, as
there is nothing more humane or more laudable when it
dwells in a virtuous heart.*

* Notwithstanding what is said in the prologue to the fourth day
respecting the recent origin of this tale, it is found in several writers of

I am very sorry, ladies, that truth does not furnish us with so many tales to the advantage of the Cordeliers as contrariwise. I like this order, and should be very glad to know some story in which I could praise them. But we are so pledged to speak the truth, that I cannot conceal it after the report of persons so worthy of belief; though, at the same time, I assure you that if the Cordeliers of the present day did anything worthy of memory which was to their honour, I would do justice to it with more alacrity than I have told the truth in the story I have just related to you.

"In good faith, Geburon," said Oisille, "that sort of love might well be called cruelty."

"I am surprised," said Simontault, "that he did not ravish the lady at once when he saw her in her shift, and in a place where he was master."

"He was not picksome but gluttonous," said Saffredent. "As he intended to have his fill of her every day, he had no mind to amuse himself with nibbling at her."

"That is not it," said Parlamente. "A ruffian is always timorous. The fear of being surprised and losing his prey made him carry off his lamb, as the wolf carries off a sheep, to devour it at his ease."

"I cannot believe he loved her," said Dagoucin, "nor can I conceive that so exalted a passion as love should enter so cowardly and villanous a heart."

"Be it as it may," said Oisille, "he was well punished for it. I pray God that all who do the like deeds may suffer the like penalties. But to whom do you give your voice?"

"To you, madam," said Geburon, "for I know you will not fail to tell us a good tale."

"If new things are good," replied Oisille, "I will tell you one which cannot be bad, since the event happened in my time, and I have it from an eye-witness. You are, doubtless, not ignorant that death being the end of all our woes, it

earlier date. It is identical, for instance, with a fabliau by Rutebeuf, entitled *Frère Denise* (See *Fabliaux de Legrand d'Aussy*), iv. 383, and has some resemblance to No. LX. of the *Cent Nouvelles Nouvelles*. The Queen of Navarre's tale has been copied by Henry Stephens, in his Apology for Herodotus, by L'Etoile, in his journal of the reign of Henri III., anno 1577, and by Malespini, in his *Ducento Novelle*, No. LXXV.

may, consequently, be called the beginning of our felicity and our repose. Thus man's greatest misery is to wish for death and not be able to obtain it. The greatest ill which can befal a criminal is not to be put to death, but to be made to suffer so much that he longs for death, while his sufferings, though continual, are of such a nature as not to be capable of abridging his life. It was in this way that a gentleman treated his wife, as you shall hear."

NOVEL XXXII.

A HUSBAND SURPRISES HIS WIFE IN FLAGRANTE DELICTO, AND SUBJECTS HER TO A PUNISHMENT MORE TERRIBLE THAN DEATH ITSELF.

King Charles VIII. sent to Germany a gentleman named Bernage, Lord of Sivray, near Amboise. This gentleman, travelling day and night, arrived very late one evening at the house of a gentleman, where he asked for a night's lodging, and obtained it but with difficulty. The owner of the house, nevertheless, learning in whose service he was, came to him and begged he would excuse the incivility of his servants, stating that certain of his wife's relations, who meant him mischief, obliged him to keep his doors thus closed. Bernage told him on what business he was travelling, and his host expressing his readiness to render the king his master all possible services, received his ambassador into his house, and lodged and treated him honourably. Supper-time being come, he showed him into a richly-tapestried hall, where, entering from behind the hangings, there appeared the most beautiful woman that ever was seen; but her hair was cropped close, and she was dressed in black garments of German cut. After the gentleman had washed with Bernage, water was set before this lady, who washed also, and took her seat at the end of the table without speaking to any one, or any one to her. Bernage often looked at her, and thought her one of the handsomest women he had ever seen, except that her face was very pale, and her air extremely sad. After she had eaten a little, she asked for drink, which was given to her by a domestic in a very singular vessel. This was a death's head, the holes of which were stopped with silver; and out of this vessel she drank two or three times. After she had supped and washed, she made a reverence to the master of the house, and retired again behind the tapestry without speaking to any one.

Bernage was so surprised at this extraordinary spectacle that he became quite sombre and pensive. His host perceived this, and said to him, "You are surprised, I see, at what you have beheld at table. Now, the courteous demeanour I have marked in you does not permit me to make a secret of the matter to you, but to explain it, in order that you may not suppose me capable of acting so cruelly without great reason. That lady whom you have seen is my wife, whom I loved more than man ever loved woman. I risked everything to marry her, and I brought her hither in spite of her relations. She, too, evinced so much love for me, that I would have hazarded a thousand lives to obtain her. We lived long in such concord and pleasure that I esteemed myself the happiest gentleman in Christendom; but honour having obliged me to make a journey, she forgot hers and the love she had for me, and conceived a passion for a young gentleman I had brought up in this house. I was near discovering the fact on my return home, but I loved her so ardently that I could not bring myself to doubt her. At last, however, experience opened my eyes, and I saw what I feared more than death. The love I had felt for her changed into fury and despair. Feigning one day to go into the country, I hid myself in the chamber which she at present occupies. Soon after my pretended departure, she retired to it, and sent for the young gentleman. I saw him enter the room and take liberties with her which should have been reserved for me alone. When I saw him about to enter the bed with her, I issued from my hiding-place, seized him in her arms, and slew him. But as my wife's crime seemed to me so great that it would not have been a sufficient punishment for it had I killed her as I had killed her gallant, I imposed upon her one which I believe is more insupportable than death; which was, to shut her up in the chamber in which she used to enjoy her stolen pleasures. I have hung there in a press all the bones of her gallant as one hangs up something precious in a cabinet; and that she may not forget them at her meals, I have her served, as she sits opposite to me at table, with the skull of that ingrate instead of a cup, in order that she may see living him whom she has made her mortal enemy by her crime, and dead, for her sake, him whose love she preferred to mine. In this way, when she dines and when she sups, she sees the two things which must afflict her most, namely, the living enemy and the dead friend; and all this through her guilt. In other respects, I treat her as I do myself, except that her hair is cropped; for the hair is an ornament no more appropriate to the adulteress than the veil to a harlot; therefore, her cropped head denotes that she has lost honour and chastity. If you please to take the trouble to see her, I will take you into her room."

Bernage willingly accepted the offer, and going down stairs with his host, found the lady seated alone by an excellent fire in a very handsome chamber. The gentleman drew back a curtain which concealed a great press, and there he saw all the bones of a man suspended. Bernage had a great wish to speak to the lady, but durst not for fear of the husband, until the latter, guessing his thoughts, said to him, "If you like to say anything to her, you will see how she expresses herself."

"Your patience, madam," said Bernage, turning to her, "is equal to your torture; I regard you as the most unhappy woman in the world."

The lady, with eyes filled with tears, and with incomparable grace and humility, replied, "I confess, sir, that my fault is so great, that all the ills which the master of this house, whom I am not worthy to call husband, could inflict upon me, are nothing in comparison to the grief I feel for having offended him." So saying, she wept profusely.

The gentleman took Bernage by the arm and led him away. Next morning he continued his journey upon the king's service; but on taking leave of the gentleman he could not help saying to him, "The esteem I entertain for you, sir, and the courtesies you have shown me in your house, oblige me to tell you, that, in my opinion, considering the great repentance of your poor wife, you ought to forgive her; the more so as you are young and have no children. It would be a pity that a house like yours should fall, and that those who perhaps do not love you should become inheritors of your substance."

The gentleman, who had resolved never to forgive his wife, pondered long over what Bernage had said to him, and at last, owning that he had spoken the truth, promised that if she persevered in her present humility, he would forgive her after some time. Bernage, on his return to the court, related the whole story to the king, who directed inquiries to be made into the matter, and found that it was all just as Bernage had reported. The description he gave of the lady's beauty so pleased the king, that he sent his painter, Jean de Paris, to take her portrait exactly as she was, which he did with the husband's consent. After she had undergone a long penance, and always with the same humility, the gentleman, who longed much for children, took pity on his wife, reinstated her, and had by her several fine children.

If all those wives who have done the same sort of thing had to drink out of similar vessels, I am greatly afraid, ladies, that many a gilt cup would be turned into a death's head. God keep us from the like, for, if His goodness does not restrain, there is not one of us but may do worse; but if we trust in Him, He will guard those who own that they cannot guard themselves. Those who rely on their own strength run great risk of being tempted, and of being constrained by experience to acknowledge their infirmity. I can assure you that there are many who have stumbled through pride in this way, whilst others, who were reputed less discreet, have been saved through their humility. The old proverb says truly, What God keeps is well kept.

"I look upon the punishment inflicted in this case as quite reasonable," said Parlamente; "for, as the offence was worse than death, so also ought the penalty to be."

"I am not of your opinion," said Ennasuite. "I would rather see the bones of all my lovers hung up in my cabinet all my life long than die for them. There is no misdeed that cannot be repaired, but from death there is no return."

"How can infamy be repaired?" asked Longarine. "Do what she may, you know that a woman cannot retrieve her honour after a crime of this nature."

"I should like to know," returned Ennasuite, "if the

Magdalen is not now in more honour among men than her sister who was a virgin?"

"I admit," replied Longarine, "that we praise her for her love for Jesus Christ, and for her great penitence; nevertheless, the name of sinner clings to her always."

"Much I care what name men give me," said Ennasuite; "only let me have God's pardon and my husband's too, there is no reason why I should wish to die."

"If this lady loved her husband as she ought," said Dagoucin, "I am surprised she did not die of grief at looking upon the bones of him whom her crime had brought to death."

"Why, Dagoucin," said Simontault, "have you yet to learn that women know neither love nor regret?"

"Yes," he replied, "for I have never ventured to prove their love for fear of finding it less than I should have wished."

"You live, then, on faith and hope," said Nomerfide, "as the plover lives on wind. You are easily kept."

"I content myself with the love I feel in my own heart," he replied, "and with the hope that there is the same in the hearts of ladies. But if I was quite sure that that love corresponded to my hope, I should feel a pleasure so extreme, that I could not sustain it and live."

"Keep yourself safe from the plague," said Geburon, "for as for the other malady, I warrant you against it. But let us see to whom Madame Oisille will give her voice."

"I give it," she said, "to Simontault, who I know will spare no one."

"That is as much as to say that I am rather given to evil speaking," said he. "I shall nevertheless let you see that people who have been regarded in that same light have yet spoken the truth. I believe, ladies, you are not so simple as to put faith in everything a person tells you, however sanctified an air he may assume, unless the proof is clear beyond doubt. Many an abuse is committed under the guise of a miracle. Therefore I intend to relate to you a story not less honourable to a religious prince than shameful to a wicked minister of the church."

NOVEL XXXIII.

INCEST OF A PRIEST WHO GOT HIS SISTER WITH CHILD UNDER THE CLOAK OF SANCTITY, AND HOW IT WAS PUNISHED.

THE Count Charles d'Angoulême, father of Francis I., and a prince of great piety, being one day at Coignac, some one told him that in a village named Cherves there was a maiden who lived with such austerity that it was a marvel, yet she was with child, and did not even make any secret of it, but assured everybody that she had never known man, and that she knew not how it had happened to her, unless it was the work of the Holy Ghost. The people readily gave credit to this delusion, and looked upon the girl as a second Virgin Mary, the more so as she had been known to be so well-behaved from her childhood, and never to have shown the least sign of a disposition to mundane vanities. She not only fasted at the seasons appointed by the church, but also made several voluntary fasts every week, and never stirred from the church as long as there was any service going on in it. The common people made so much account of this manner of life, that every one flocked to see her as though she were a living miracle, and fortunate was he who could touch her gown. The priest of the parish was her brother, a man in years, of an austere life, and a reputed saint. So rigorously did he treat his sister, that he had her shut up in a house, whereat the people were greatly displeased, and the affair made so much noise, that it came, as I have already said, to the ears of Count Charles, who seeing the delusion into which everybody had fallen, resolved to put an end to it.

To this end, he sent a referendary and an almoner, both of them worthy men, to ascertain the truth. They went to the spot, inquired into the fact as carefully as possible, and applied to the priest, who was so vexed at the affair, that he begged them to be present at the verification he hoped to make of it. Next morning the priest celebrated mass, his sister, who was very big, being present on her knees. After it was over, he took the *corpus Domini*, and said to his sister in presence of the whole congregation,

"Wretch that thou art, here is He who suffered death for thee, in whose presence I ask thee if thou art a virgin as thou hast always assured me." She replied boldly and fearlessly that she was so. "How, then, is it possible that thou art pregnant, yet still a virgin?" "All I can say," she replied, "is, that it is the grace of the Holy Ghost, who does in me whatever he pleases; but also I cannot deny the grace which God has done me in preserving me a virgin. Never have I had even a thought of marrying."

Her brother then said to her, "I give thee here the precious body of Jesus Christ, which thou wilt take to thy damnation if thou dost not speak the truth; whereof will be witnesses these gentlemen, who are here present on the part of my lord the count."

The girl, who was about thirteen years of age, then made oath as follows: "I take the body of Our Lord here present to my condemnation before you, sirs, and you my brother, if ever man has touched me any more than you." So saying, she received the body of Our Lord.

The referendary and the almoner went away quite confounded, not being able to believe that any one would lie after such an oath, and they made their report to the count, whom they tried to bring to entertain the same belief as themselves. But he being a wise man, after much thought, made them repeat the very words of the oath; and having well weighed them, he said, "She told you that *never man touched her any more than her brother*. I am persuaded that it was her brother who got her with child, and that she seeks to conceal his incest by prevarication. We, who believe that Jesus Christ is come, must not expect another. Return then to the place, and put the priest in prison; I am sure he will confess the truth."

They executed their orders, but unwillingly, and not without remonstrating against the necessity of putting such a scandal upon a good man. The priest was no sooner committed to prison than he confessed his crime, and owned that he had instructed his sister to speak as she had done, in order to conceal the intercourse between them, and this not only to baffle inquiry by so slight a device, but also to secure to themselves universal esteem and veneration by this false statement. Being asked how he could carry his wickedness

to such an excess as to make his sister swear upon Our
Lord's body, he replied, that his audacity had not reached
that length, and that he had used an ordinary wafer, which
was neither consecrated nor blessed.

All this having been reported to the Count d'Angoulême,
he sent the affair before the courts of justice. Execution was
delayed until the sister was delivered of a fine boy. After
her delivery the brother and sister were burned, to the great
astonishment of all the people, who had beheld a monster so
horrible under such a garb of holiness, and so detestable a
crime under the appearances of a life so laudable and regenerate.

The good Count d'Angoulême's faith, ladies, was proof
against outward signs and miracles. He knew that we have
but one Saviour, who when he said *consummatum est*,
showed thereby that we are not to expect a successor for
our salvation.

"Truly," said Oisille, "that was a monstrous piece of
effrontery covered with unparalleled hypocrisy. It is the
height of impiety to cover so enormous a crime with the
mantle of God and religion."

"I have heard," said Hircan, "that those who commit
acts of cruelty and tyranny under pretence of having the
king's commission, are doubly punished, the reason being
that they make the king's name a cover for their injustice.
Likewise, it is seen, that although hypocrites prosper for
some time under the cloak of godliness, God no sooner unmasks them, than they appear such as they are; and then
their nakedness, their filth, and their infamy are the more
horrible the more august and sacred was the wrapper with
which they concealed them."

"There is nothing more agreeable," said Nomerfide, "than
to speak frankly and as the heart feels."

"It serves to make one fat," replied Longarine, "and I
imagine you decide from your own case."

"Let me tell you," returned Nomerfide, "I remark that
fools live longer than the wise, unless some one kills them;
for which I know but one reason, namely, that fools do not
dissemble their passions. If they are angry they strike; if
they are merry they laugh; but those who deem themselves

wise hide their defects with so much care that their hearts are all poisoned with them."

"I believe that is true," said Geburon, "and that hypocrisy, whether as regards God, men, or nature, is the cause of all the evil that befals us."

"It would be a fine thing," said Parlamente, "if faith so filled our hearts with Him who is all virtue and all joy, that we should show them to every one without disguise."

"That will be when there is no longer any flesh on our bones," observed Hircan.

"Yet," remarked Oisille, "the spirit of God, which is mightier than death, can change our hearts without changing our bodies."

"You speak, madam," said Saffredent, "of a gift which God hardly makes to men."

"He does make it," rejoined Oisille, "to those who have faith. But as this is a matter above the comprehension of flesh, let us see to whom Simontault gives his voice."

"To Nomerfide," he said. "As she has a merry heart, I do not think her words will be sad."

"Since you have a mind to laugh," said Nomerfide, "I must serve you after your own way, and give you matter for laughter. I wish to show you that fear and ignorance are equally mischievous, and that one often sins only for want of knowing things. With this view I will relate to you what happened to two poor Cordeliers of Niort, who, for not understanding the language of a butcher, had like to die of fright."

NOVEL XXXIV.

TWO OVER-INQUISITIVE CORDELIERS HAD A GREAT FRIGHT WHICH HAD LIKE TO COST THEM THEIR LIVES.

BETWEEN Niort and Fors there is a village named Grip, which belongs to the Lord of Fors. Two Cordeliers of Niort arrived late one night at this village, and took up their quarters with a butcher. As their bedroom was separated from their host's only by an ill-jointed boarded partition, they had a mind to listen to what passed between the husband and wife, and they clapped their ears to the partition close to the head of the host's bed. As the butcher had no suspicion of his guests, he talked to his wife about his business, and said, "My dear, I must be up betimes to-morrow, and see about our Cordeliers. One of them is very fat; we will kill him and salt him forthwith, and we shall make a good thing of him."

Though the butcher talked of his pigs, which he called Cordeliers, the two poor friars, hearing this, set it all down to their own account, and awaited daylight with great terror. One of them was very fat, the other very lean; and the fat one set about confessing himself to his companion, alleging that a butcher, having lost the love and fear of God, would make no more of slaughtering them than an ox or any other beast. As they were shut up in their chamber, from which there was no issue but through their host's, they gave themselves up for dead men, and earnestly commended their souls to God. The young man, who was not so overcome by fear as the elder, said to him, that since they could not get out at the door, they must try to escape through the window; at the worst they could only be killed in the attempt, and death one way or the other was the same thing in the end. The fat friar consented to the expedient. The young one opened the window, and, as it was not very high, dropped lightly to the ground, and ran away as fast and as far as he could, without waiting for his companion, who was not so lucky, for, being very bulky, he fell so heavily that he hurt one leg severely, and was unable to rise from the ground. Deserted by his companion and unable to follow him, he looked about for some place where he might hide, and saw nothing but a pigsty, into which he dragged himself the best way he could. When he opened the door, two big porkers which were inside rushed out and left the place free to the Cordelier, who shut himself in, hoping that he might hear people passing by, to whom he would call and obtain help.

As soon as daylight appeared the butcher got ready his big knives, and told his wife to come and help him to kill the two pigs. Going to the sty, he opened the little door, and cried out, "Come, turn out here, my Cordelier. I'll have your chitterlings for my dinner to day." The Cordelier, who could not stand on his leg, crawled out on his hands and knees, roaring for mercy. If he was in a great fright, the butcher and his wife were no less so. The first idea that came into their heads was that St. Francis was angry with them because they had called pigs Cordeliers; and under that notion they fell on their knees before the poor friar, begging pardon of St. Francis and his order. On the one side was the Cordelier bawling for mercy to the butcher, on the other side, the butcher making the same appeal to the Cordelier. At last the Cordelier, finding that the butcher had no intention of hurting him, told him why he had hid himself in that place. Fear then gave place to laughter, except on the part of the poor friar, whose leg pained him so much that he had no inclination to laugh. The butcher, to console him in some degree, took him back to the house and had his hurt carefully attended to. As for his companion, who had forsaken him in distress, he ran all night, and arrived in the morning at the house of the Lord of Fors, where he made loud complaints of the butcher, who, he supposed, had by that time killed his companion, since the latter had not followed him. The Lord of Fors sent immediately to Grip to see how matters stood, and his messengers brought back matter for laughter, which he failed not to communicate to his mistress, the Duchess d'Angoulême, mother of Francis I.

It is not good, ladies, to listen to secrets when one is not invited, and to have a curiosity to hear what others say.

"Did not I tell you," exclaimed Simontault, "that Nomerfide would not make us cry, but laugh? Every one of us, I think, has done so very heartily."

"Whence comes it," said Oisille, "that one is always more disposed to laugh at a piece of nonsense than at a good thing?"

"Because," replied Hircan, "the nonsense is more agreeable to us, being more conformable to our own nature, which of itself is never wise. Thus every one is fond of his like: fools love folly, and wise men wisdom. I am sure, however, that neither fools nor wise could help laughing at this story?"

"There are some," said Geburon, "who are so engrossed

with the love of wisdom that nothing you could say to them would make them laugh. Their joy and their satisfaction are so moderate, that no accident is capable of altering them."

"Who are these persons?" inquired Hircan.

"The philosophers of past times," replied Geburon, "who hardly felt either mirth or sadness; at least they showed no manifestation of either, so possessed were they with the belief that there is virtue in vanquishing oneself."

"I am as much convinced as they that it is good to vanquish a vicious passion," said Saffredent, "but to vanquish a natural passion, which has no evil tendency, seems to me a useless victory."

"Nevertheless, that was regarded as a great virtue," remarked Geburon.

"But then," returned Saffredent, "it is not said that all the ancients were sages; and I would not swear that there was not in them more of the appearance of sense and virtue than of the reality."

"You see, however," said Geburon, "that they condemn everything that is bad, and even that Diogenes trampled on Plato's coverlet, because he thought it too rich and curious; and to show that he despised and wished to trample under foot Plato's vainglory and avarice, 'I trample,' said he, 'on the pride of Plato.'"

"You do not tell all," replied Saffredent; "you forget that Plato at once retorted upon him, 'Thou tramplest on it, indeed, but with still more pride.' In fact, it was only through a certain arrogance that Diogenes despised elegance.

"In truth," said Parlamente, "it is impossible to overcome ourselves by ourselves; nor can one think to do so without prodigious pride, the vice of all others the most to be feared, since it rears itself upon the ruins of all the rest."

"Did I not read to you this morning," said Oisille, "that those who believed themselves wiser than others, and who came by the light of reason to know a God, the creator of all things, for having been vain thereof, and not having attributed this glory to Him to whom it belonged, and for having imagined that they had acquired this knowledge by their own labours, became more ignorant and less reasonable—I will not say than other men, but than the very brutes? In fact, their minds having run astray, they ascribed to themselves what belongs to God alone, and manifested their errors by the disorders of their lives, forgetting their very sex, and abusing it, as St. Paul says in his Epistle to the Romans."

"There is not one of us," said Parlamente, "but recognises, on reading that epistle, that outward sins are the fruits of inward unbelief, the more dangerous to eradicate the more it is covered by virtue and miracles."

"We men," said Hircan, "are nearer to salvation than women, for as they do not hide their fruits they easily know their roots. But you women, who dare not produce yours, and who do so many acts that are fair in appearance, hardly know the root of pride, that grows under so goodly a covering."

"I own," said Longarine, "that if God's word does not show us by faith the leprosy of unbelief that is hidden in our hearts, God does us a great grace when He suffers us to commit a visible fault, which manifests our hidden disposition. Blessed are they whom faith has so humbled that they have no need of outward acts to make them conscious of the weakness and corruption of their natures."

"Do let us consider, I beseech you," said Simontault, "what a course our conversation has taken. From an instance of extreme folly we have come to philosophy and theology. Let us leave these matters to those who are more competent to discuss them, and ask Nomerfide to whom she gives her voice."

"To Hircan," she replied, "but on condition that he will be tender of the honour of the ladies."

"The condition fits me very aptly," said Hircan, "for the story I have to tell you is the very one to fulfil it. You shall see from it, nevertheless, that the inclination of men and of women is naturally vicious, unless it be kept right by the goodness of Him to whom we ought to impute all the victories we achieve over ourselves. And to abate the airs you give yourselves when any story is told which does you honour, I will tell you one which is strictly true."

NOVEL XXXV.

CONTRIVANCE OF A SENSIBLE HUSBAND TO CURE HIS WIFE OF HER PASSION FOR A CORDELIER.

There was at Pampelune a lady who was reputed fair and virtuous, and at the same time the most devout and chaste in the country. She loved her husband much, and was so obsequious to him that he had entire confidence in her. She was wholly occupied with God's service, and never missed a single sermon, and omitted nothing by which she could hope to persuade her husband and her children to be as devout as herself, who was but thirty years old, an age at which women commonly resign the pretensions of beauties for those of new she-sages.

On the first day of Lent this lady went to church to receive the ashes which are a memorial of death. A Cordelier, whose austerity of life had gained him the reputation of a saint, and who, in spite of his austerity and his macerations, was neither so meagre nor so pale but that he was one of the handsomest men in the world, was to preach the sermon. The lady listened to him with great devotion, and gazed no less intently on the preacher. Her ears and her eyes lost nothing that was presented to them, and both alike found wherewithal to be gratified. The preacher's words penetrated to her heart through her ears; and the charms of his countenance passing through her eyes, insinuated themselves so deeply into her mind, that she felt as it were in an ecstasy. The sermon being ended, the Cordelier celebrated mass, at which the lady was present, and she took the ashes from his hand, which was as white and shapely as that of any lady. The devotee paid much more attention to the monk's hand than to the ashes he gave her, persuading herself that this spiritual love could not hurt her conscience, whatever pleasure she received from it. She failed not to go every day to the sermon, and to take her husband with her; and both so highly admired the preacher, that at table and elsewhere they talked of nothing but him.

This fire, for all its spirituality, at last became so carnal, that the heart of this poor lady, which was first kindled by it, consumed all the rest. Slow as she had been to feel the flame, she was equally prompt to take fire, and she felt the pleasure of her passion before she was aware that passion had possession of her. Love, which had rendered himself master of the lady, no longer encountered any resistance on her part; but the mischief was, that the physician who might have relieved her pain was not aware of her malady. Banishing, therefore, all fear, and the shame she ought to have felt in exposing her wild fantasy to so sober-minded a man, and her incontinence to one so saintly and virtuous, she resolved to acquaint him in writing of the love she cherished for him; which she did as modestly as she could, and gave her letter to a little page, with instructions as to what he was to do, especially enjoining him to take good care that her husband did not see him go to the Cordeliers.

The page, taking the shortest road, passed through a street where his master happened, by the merest chance, to be sitting in a shop. The gentleman seeing him pass, stepped forward to see which way he was going; and the page perceiving this, hid himself with some trepidation. His master saw this, followed him, and seizing him by the arm, asked him whither he was going. His embarrassed and unmeaning replies, and his manifest fright, aroused the suspicions of the gentleman, who threatened to beat him if he did not tell the truth. "Oh, sir," said the little page, "if I tell you, my mistress will kill me." The gentleman no longer doubted that his wife was making a bargain without him, encouraged the page, and assured him that nothing should befal him if he spoke the truth—on the contrary, he should be well rewarded; but if he told a lie, he should be imprisoned for life. Thus urged by fear and hope, the page acquainted him with the real fact, and showed him the letter his mistress had written to the preacher, whereat the husband was the more shocked, as he had been all his life assured of the fidelity of his wife, in whom he had never seen a fault.

Being a wise man, however, he dissembled his anger, and further to try his wife, he answered her letter in the preacher's name, thanking her for her gracious inclination, and assuring her that it was fully reciprocated. The page, after being sworn by his master to manage the affair discreetly, carried this letter to his mistress, who was so transported with joy, that her husband perceived it by the change in her countenance; for instead of her fastings in Lent having emaciated her, she looked handsomer and fresher than ever. It was now Mid-Lent, but the lady, without concerning herself about the Lord's Passion or the Holy Week, wrote as usual to the preacher, the theme being always her amorous rage. When he turned his eyes in her direction, or spoke of the love of God, she always imagined that he addressed himself covertly to her, and so far as her eyes could explain what was passing in her heart, she did not suffer them to be idle.

The husband, who regularly replied to her in the name of the Cordelier, wrote to her after Easter, begging she would contrive to give him a meeting in private; and she, impatiently longing for an opportunity to do so, advised her husband to go see some land they had near Pampelune. He said he would do so, and went and concealed himself in the house of one of his friends; whereupon the lady wrote to the Cordelier that her husband was in the country, and that he might come and see her.

The gentleman, wishing to prove his wife's heart thoroughly, went and begged the preacher to lend him his robe. The Cordelier, who was a good man, replied that his rule forbade him to do so, and that for no consideration would he lend his robe to go masking in. The gentleman assured him it was not for any idle diversion he wanted it, but for an important matter, and one necessary to his salvation; whereupon the Cordelier, who knew him to be a worthy, pious man, lent him the robe. The gentleman then procured a false beard and a false nose, put cork in his shoes to make himself as tall as the monk, put on the robe, which covered the greater part of his face, so that his eyes were barely seen, and, in a word, dressed himself up so that he might easily be mistaken for the preacher. Thus disguised, he stole by night into his wife's chamber, where she was expecting him in great devotion. The poor creature did not wait for him to come to her, but ran to embrace him like a woman out of her senses. Keeping his head down to avoid being recognised, he began to make the sign of the cross, pretending to shun her, and crying, "Temptation! temptation!"

"Alas! you are right, father," said she, "for there is no more violent temptation than that which proceeds from love.

You have promised to afford me relief, and I pray you to have pity on me now that we have time and opportunity."

So saying she made great efforts to embrace him, while he kept dodging her in all directions, still making great signs of the cross, and crying, "Temptation! temptation!" But when he found that she was pressing him too closely, he drew a stout stick from under his robe, and thrashed her so soundly that he put an end to the temptation. This done, he left the house without being known, and immediately returned his borrowed robe, assuring the owner that he had used it to great advantage. Next day he returned home as if from a journey, and found his wife in bed. Pretending not to know the nature of her malady, he asked her what ailed her. She replied that she was troubled with a kind of catarrh, and that she could neither move hand nor foot. The husband, who had a great mind to laugh, pretended to be very sorry, and by way of cheering her, said that he had invited the pious preacher to supper. "Oh, my dear!" said she, "don't think of inviting such people, for they bring ill-luck wherever they go."

"Why, my love," replied the husband, "you know how much you have said to me in praise of this good father. For my part, I believe if there is a holy man on earth, it is he."

"They are all very well at church and in the pulpit," she rejoined; "but in private houses they are antichrists. Don't let me see him, my dear, I entreat you, for, ill as I am, it would be the death of me."

"Well, you shall not see him, since you do not choose to do so; but I cannot help having him to supper."

"Do as you please," said she; "only, for mercy's sake, let me not set eyes on him, for I cannot endure such folk."

After entertaining the Cordelier at supper, the husband said to him, "I look upon you, father, as a man so beloved by God, that I am sure he will grant any prayer of yours. I entreat you, then, to have pity on my poor wife. She has been possessed these eighteen days by an evil spirit, so that she wants to bite and scratch everybody, and neither cross nor holy water does she care for one bit; but I believe firmly, that if you put your hand on her, the devil will go away. From my heart, I beseech you to do so."

"All things are possible to him who believes, my son,"

replied the good father. "Are you not well assured that God never refuses his grace to those who ask for it with faith?"

"I am assured of this, father."

"Be assured also, my son, that He is able and willing, and that He is not less mighty than munificent. Let us strengthen ourselves in faith to resist this roaring lion, and snatch from him his prey, which God has made His own by the blood of his Son Jesus Christ."

Thereupon the gentleman conducted the excellent man into the room where his wife was resting on a couch. Believing that it was he who had beaten her, she was roused to a prodigious degree of fury at the sight of him, but her husband's presence made her hang down her head and hold her tongue. "As long as I am present," said the husband to the good father, "the devil does not torment; but as soon as I leave her, you will sprinkle her with holy water, and then you will see how violently the evil spirit works her." So saying, the husband left him alone with his wife, and stopped outside the door to see what would ensue.

When she found herself alone with the Cordelier, she began to scream at him like a mad woman, "Villain! cheat! monster! murderer!" The Cordelier, believing in good faith that she was possessed, wanted to take hold of her head, in order to pray over it; but she scratched and bit him so fiercely that he was obliged to stand further off, throwing plenty of holy water over her, and saying many good prayers. The husband, seeing it was time to put an end to the farce, entered the room again, and thanked the Cordelier for the pains he had taken. The moment he appeared there was an end to the wife's termagant behaviour, and she meekly kissed the cross for fear of her husband. The pious Cordelier, who had seen her in such a fury, believed firmly that our Lord had expelled the devil at his prayer, and went away praising God for this miracle. The husband, seeing his wife so well cured of her folly, would never tell her what he had done, contenting himself with having brought her back to the right way by his prudence, and having put her into such a frame of mind that she mortally hated what she had so unwisely loved, and was filled with detestation for her own infatuation. Thenceforth she was weaned from all superstition, and devoted herself to her husband and her family in a very different way from what she had done before.

Here you may see, ladies, the good sense of the husband, and the weakness of one who was regarded as a woman of strict propriety. If you attend well to this example, I am persuaded that, instead of relying on your own strength, you will learn to turn to Him on whom your honour depends.

"I am very glad," said Parlamente, "that you are become the ladies' preacher; you would be so with better right if you would address the same sermons to all those you hold discourse with."

"Whenever you please to hear me," he replied, "I assure you I will speak the same language to you."

"That is to say," observed Simontault, "that when you are not by he will talk to a different purpose."

"He will do as he pleases," said Parlamente; "but, for my own satisfaction, I would have him always speak thus. The example he has adduced will at least be of service to those women who think that spiritual love is not dangerous; but to me it seems that it is more so than any other."

"I cannot think, however," remarked Oisille, "that one should scorn to love a man who is virtuous and fears God; for, in my opinion, one cannot but be the better for it."

"I pray you to believe, madam," rejoined Parlamente, "that nothing can be more simple-willed and easy to deceive than a woman who has never loved; for love is a passion which takes possession of the heart before one is aware of it. Besides, this passion is so pleasing, that provided one can wrap oneself up in virtue as in a cloak, it will be scarcely known before some mischief will come of it."

"What mischief can come of loving a good man?" said Oisille.

"There are plenty, madam," replied Parlamente, "who pass for good men as far as ladies are concerned; but there are few who are so truly good before God that one may love them without any risk to honour or conscience. I do not believe that there is one such man living. Those who are of a different opinion, and trust in it, become its dupes. They begin this sort of tender intimacy with God, and often end it with the devil. I have seen many a one who, under colour of talking about divine things, began an intimacy which at last they wished to break off but could not, so fast were they held by the fine cloak with which it was covered. A vicious love perishes and has no long abode in a good heart; but decorous love has bonds of silk so fine and delicate that one is caught in them before one perceives them."

"According to your views, then," said Ennasuite, "no woman ought ever to love a man. Your law is too violent; it will not last."

"I know that," replied Parlamente; "but for all that it is desirable that every woman should be content with her own husband, as I am with mine."

Ennasuite, taking these words personally, changed colour, and said, "You ought to think every one the same at heart as yourself, unless you set yourself up for being more perfect than the rest of your sex."

"To avoid dispute," said Parlamente, "let us see to whom Hircan will give his voice."

"I give it to Ennasuite," said he, "in order to make up matters between her and my wife."

"Since it is my turn to speak," said Ennasuite, "I will spare neither man nor woman, so as to make both sides even. You find it hard to overcome yourselves and admit the probity and virtue of men. This obliges me to relate a story of the same nature as the preceding one."

NOVEL XXXVI.

A PRESIDENT OF GRENOBLE, BECOMING AWARE OF HIS WIFE'S IRREGULARITIES, TOOK HIS MEASURES SO WISELY, THAT HE REVENGED HIMSELF WITHOUT ANY PUBLIC EXPOSURE OF HIS DISHONOUR.

There was at Grenoble a president whose name I shall not mention. It is enough to say that he was not a Frenchman, that he had a very handsome wife, and that they lived very happily together. The husband, however, being old, the lady thought fit to love a young clerk named Nicolas. When the husband went in the morning to the Palace of Justice, the clerk used to step into the bedchamber and take his place. An old domestic of the president's, who had been in his service for thirty years, discovered this, and as a faithful servant, could not help revealing it to his master. The president, who was a prudent man, would not believe the fact without inquiry, and told the servant that he wanted to create dissension between him and his wife; adding, that if the fact was as he stated, he could easily give him ocular proof of it; and if he failed to do so, then he, the president, would believe that the servant had trumped up this lying tale to make mischief between husband and wife. The valet assured him that he should see what he had told him.

One morning when the president had gone to the palace, and the clerk had stolen into the bedroom as usual, the valet sent one of his fellow-servants to apprise the president, while he himself remained on the watch before the bedroom door, to see if Nicolas came out. The president, on seeing the messenger beckon to him, immediately quitted the court on pretence of sudden illness, and hurried home, where he found his old servant standing sentry at the bedroom door, and was assured by him that Nicolas was inside, having gone in not long before. "Remain at the door," said the president. "There is no other way to get in or out of the room as thou knowest, except a little closet, of which I always keep the key."

The president enters the room, and finds his wife and the clerk in bed together. Nicolas, who did not expect such a visit, threw himself in his shirt at his master's feet and implored pardon, whilst the lady fell a crying. "Though what you have done," said the president to her, "is as bad as it can be, I do not choose to have the credit of my house blasted for you, and the daughters I have had by you made the sufferers. I command you, then, to cease your crying, and see what I am going to do. As for you, Nicolas," said he to the clerk, "hide yourself in my cabinet, and make no noise." Nicolas having done as he ordered, he opened the door, and calling in the old servant, said to him, "Didst thou not assure me thou wouldst show me my clerk in bed with my wife? I came hither on the strength of thy word, and thought to kill my wife I have found nothing, though

I have searched everywhere. Search thyself, under the beds and in all directions."

The valet, having searched and found nothing, said to his master, " The devil must have flown away with him; for I saw him go in, and he did not come out by the door; however, I see he is not here."

" Thou art a very bad servant," said his master, " to want to put such division between my wife and me. Begone, I discharge thee, and for the services thou has rendered me, I will pay thee what I owe thee and more; but get thee gone quickly, and beware how thou art found in this city after twenty-four hours are past."

The president paid him his wages, and five or six years over; and as he had reason to be satisfied with his fidelity, he resolved within himself to reward him still more. When the valet had gone away, with tears in his eyes, the president called the clerk out of the cabinet, and after having given him and his wife such a lecture as they deserved, he forbade them both to give the least hint of the matter to any one. His wife he ordered to dress more elegantly than she had been used to do, and to let herself be seen at all parties and entertainments. As to the clerk, he ordered him to make better cheer than before; but that as soon as he should whisper in his ear the words " Go away," he should take good care not to remain three hours longer in the city.

For a fortnight the president did nothing but feast his friends and neighbours, contrary to his previous custom, and after the repast he gave a ball to the ladies. One day, seeing that his wife did not dance, he ordered the clerk to dance with her. The clerk, thinking he had forgotten the past, danced gaily with the lady; but when the ball was over, the president, feigning to have some order to give him about household matters, whispered in his ear, " Begone, and never come back." Sore loth was Nicolas to leave the lady-president, but very glad to get off safe and sound. After the president had fully impressed all his relations and friends, and all the inhabitants of Grenoble, with the belief that he was very fond of his wife, he went one fine day in the month of May into his garden to gather a salad. I do not know what herbs it was composed of; but I know that his wife did not live twenty-four hours after eating of it, whereat he appeared greatly afflicted, and played the disconsolate widower so well, that no one ever suspected him of having killed her. In this way he revenged himself and saved the honour of his house.*

I do not pretend, ladies, to laud the president's conscience; but my design is to exhibit the levity of a woman, and the great patience and prudence of a man. Do not be offended, ladies, I beseech you, with the truth, which sometimes tells against you as well as against the men; for women, too, have their vices as well as their virtues.

"If all those who have intrigued with their valets were compelled to eat such salads," said Parlamente, "I know those who would not be so fond of their gardens as they are, but would pluck up all the herbs in them, to avoid those which save the honour of children at the expense of a wanton mother's life."

Hircan, who guessed for whom she meant this, replied with

---

* In a manuscript French dictionary of the Beauties and Curiosities of Dauphiné, there is an article which says that "in the Rue des Clercs, at Grenoble, was formerly to be seen over the hall door of the house of Nicholas Prunier de Saint André, president of the Parliament of Grenoble, a stone escutcheon, supported by an angel, and bearing a lion de gueule on a field or. These arms were those of the Carles family, which became extinct in the seventeenth century. The angel that supported the escutcheon held the forefinger of one hand to his mouth in a mysterious manner, as if to enjoin secrecy. Geoffroy Carles, sole president of the Parliament of Grenoble in 1505, put it up over that house, which belonged to him. He, indeed, had long dissembled before he found an opportunity to be revenged for the infidelity of his wife, by causing her to be drowned by the mule she rode at the passage of a torrent. He had purposely ordered that the mule should be left several days without drink. This occurrence, which appeared in print in several places, was made the subject of one of the novels of that time, in which, however, the names of the persons concerned are not given. Geoffroy was so learned in the Latin tongue and in the humanities, that Queen Anne of Bretagne, wife of Louis XII., selected him to teach that tongue and the belles lettres to her daughter Renée, who was afterwards Duchess of Ferrara. This same Geoffroy Carles was made knight of arms and of laws by Louis XII. in 1509." This is probably the person meant by the Queen of Navarre, though she gives a different account of the manner in which he put his wife to death. The story, however, appears to be older than the times of Geoffroy Carles, since it is related of a president of Provence in the *Cent Nouvelles Nouvelles* (No. 47), which were composed between the years 1456 and 1461, and first printed in Paris in 1486.

great warmth, "A woman of honour should never suspect another of things she would not do herself."

"To know is not to suspect," rejoined Parlamente. "However, this poor woman paid the penalty which many deserve. Moreover, I think that the president, being bent on avenging himself, could not set about it with more prudence and discretion."

"Nor with more malice," Longarine subjoined. "It was a cold-blooded and cruel vengeance, which plainly showed that he respected neither God nor his conscience."

"What would you have had him do then," said Hircan "to revenge the most intolerable outrage a wife can ever offer to her husband?"

"I would have had him kill her," she answered, "in the first transports of his indignation. The doctors say that such a sin is more pardonable, because a man is not master of such emotions; and consequently, the sin he commits in that state may be forgiven."

"Yes," said Geburon, "but his daughters and his descendants would have been disgraced for ever."

"He ought not to have poisoned her," said Longarine, "for since his first great wrath was past, she might have lived with him like an honest woman, and nothing would ever have been said about the matter."

"Do you suppose," said Saffredent, "that he was appeased, though he pretended to be so? For my part, I'm persuaded that the day he mixed his salad his wrath was as hot as on the very first day. There are people whose first emotions never subside until they have accomplished the dictates of their passion."

"It is well to ponder one's words," said Parlamente, "when one has to do with people so dangerous as you. What I said is to be understood of an anger so violent, that it suddenly engrosses the senses, and hinders reason from acting."

"I take it in that very sense," replied Saffredent, "and I say, that of two men who commit a fault, he who is very amorous is more pardonable than the other who is not so; for when one loves well, reason is not easily mistress. If we would speak truly, we must own there is not one of us but has some time or other experienced that furious madness, and yet hopes for grace. Let us say then, that true love is a ladder by which to ascend to the perfect love which we owe to God. No one can ascend to it but through the afflictions and calamities of this world, and through the love of his neighbour, to whom he ought to wish as much good as to himself. This is the true bond of perfection; for as St. John says, 'How can you love God whom you do not see, unless you love your neighbour whom you do see?'"

"There is no fine text in Scripture which you may not warp to your own purposes," said Oisille. "Beware of doing like the spider, which extracts a poison from every good viand; for I warn you, that it is dangerous to quote Scripture out of place, and without necessity."

"Do you mean to say, then," returned Saffredent, "that when we talk to your unbelieving sex, and call God to our aid, we take His name in vain? If there is sin in this, it all lies at your door, since your unbelief constrains us to use all the oaths we can think of; and even so we cannot kindle your icy hearts."

"A plain proof," said Longarine, "that you all lie; for if you spoke the truth, it is so potent that it would persuade us. All that is to be feared is lest the daughters of Eve too easily believe in the serpent."

"I see plainly how it is," said Saffredent; "the women are invincible. So I give up the game to see on whom Ennasuite will call."

"On Dagoucin," she said, "who, I think, will not be disposed to speak against the ladies."

"Would to God," said he, "that they were as favourable to me as I am disposed to speak so of them. To show you that I have endeavoured to do honour to the virtuous of their sex by the pains I have taken to learn their good actions, I will relate one of these to you. I will not say, ladies, that the patience of the gentleman of Pampeluna and of the president of Grenoble was not great, but I maintain that their vindictiveness was no less so. In praising a virtuous man, we must not so much exalt a single virtue, as to make it serve as a cloak and cover for so great a vice. A woman who has done a virtuous action for the love of virtue itself is truly laudable. An instance of this I will give you in the story I am about to tell you of a young married lady, whose good deed had for motive only the honour of God and the salvation of her husband"

NOVEL XXXVII.

JUDICIOUS PROCEEDINGS OF A WIFE TO WITHDRAW HER HUSBAND FROM A LOW INTRIGUE WITH WHICH HE WAS INFATUATED.

There was a lady of the house of Loue who was so good and virtuous, that she was loved and esteemed by all her neighbours. Her husband with good reason confided to her all his affairs, which she managed so discreetly, that in a short while their house became under her hands one of the richest and best furnished in Anjou and Touraine. She lived long with her husband, and had several fine children by him; but as there is no enduring felicity here below, hers began to be crossed. Her husband, not feeling satisfied with a life of such perfect ease, had a mind to try if trouble would increase his enjoyment. His wife was no sooner asleep, than he used to get up from beside her, and not return till daylight. The lady took this conduct so much to heart, that falling into a profound melancholy, which yet she tried to conceal, she neglected the affairs of her house, her person, and her family, thinking she had lost the fruit of her labours in losing her husband's love, to preserve which there were no pains she would not willingly have sustained. But as she saw he was lost to her, she became so negligent of everything else, that the consequences were soon seen in the mischief that ensued. On the one hand, the husband spent without order or measure; on the other hand, the wife no longer attending to the affairs of the house, they soon became so involved, that the timber began to be felled, and the lands to be mortgaged. One of her relations who knew her secret grief, remonstrated with her on the fault she committed, and told her, that if she did not regard the fortunes of the family for her husband's sake, she ought at least to consider her poor children. This argument struck her; she rallied her spirits, and resolved to try by every means to regain her husband's love.

Next night, perceiving that he rose from beside her, she also got up, put on her night-wrapper, had her bed made, and sat down to read for hours until his return. When he entered the room, she went up and kissed him, and presented a basin and water to him to wash his hands. Her husband, astonished at this extraordinary behaviour, told her that he had only been to the privy, and that he had no need to wash. She replied, that although it was no great matter, still it was decent to wash one's hands when one came from so nasty a place, thereby wishing to make him know and hate his wicked way of life. As this did not produce any amendment in him, she continued the same course of proceeding for a year, but still without success.

This being the case, one night, when she was waiting for her husband, who stayed away longer than usual, she took it into her head to go after him. She did so, and looking for him in chamber after chamber, she at last found him in a back lumber-room in bed with the ugliest and dirtiest servant wench about the house. To teach him to quit so handsome and so cleanly a wife for so ugly and frousy a servant, she took some straw and set it on fire in the middle of the room. But seeing that the smoke would as soon smother her husband as awake him, she pulled him by the arm, crying out "Fire! fire!" If the husband was ashamed and confounded at being found by so worthy a wife with such a swinish bedfellow, it was not without great reason. "For more than a year, sir," said his wife, "have I been endeavouring by gentleness and patience to withdraw you from such a wicked life, and make you comprehend that, while washing the outside, you ought to make the inside clean also; but when I saw that all my efforts were useless, I bethought me of employing the element which is to put an end to all things. If this does not correct you, sir, I know not if I shall be able another time to withdraw you from the danger as I have done now. I pray you to consider that there is no greater despair than that of slighted love, and that if I had not had God before my eyes, I could not have been patient so long."

The husband, glad to be let off so cheaply, promised that for the future he would never give her cause for sorrow. The wife gladly believed him, and with his consent turned away the servant who offended her. They lived so happily afterwards, that even past faults were for them a source of increased satisfaction, in consequence of the good that had resulted from them.

If God gives you such husbands, ladies, do not despair, I entreat you, before you have tried all means to reclaim them. There are four-and-twenty hours in the day, and there is not a moment in which a man may not change his mind. A wife ought to esteem herself happier in having regained her husband by her patience, than if fortune and her relations had given her one more faultless.*

"There," said Oisille, "is an example for all married women to follow."

"Follow it who will," said Parlamente; "but for my part it would be impossible for me to be so patient. Although, in every condition in which one is placed, patience is a fine virtue, it seems to me, nevertheless, that in matrimonial matters it at last produces enmity. The reason is, that suffering from one's mate, one is constrained to keep aloof from the offender as much as possible. From this alienation springs contempt for the faithless one, and this contempt gradually diminishes love; for one loves a thing only in proportion as one esteems it."

"But it is to be feared," said Ennasuite, "that the impatient wife would meet with a furious husband, who, instead of patience, would cause her sorrow."

"And what worse could a husband do than we have just heard?" said Parlamente.

"What could he do?" rejoined Ennasuite. "Beat his wife soundly, make her sleep on the little bed, and put her he loves into the best bed."†

"I believe," said Parlamente, "it would be less painful to a right-minded woman to be beaten in a fit of passion than to be depised by a husband who was not worthy of her. After the rupture of wedded affection, the husband could do nothing which could be more painful to the wife. Accordingly, the tale states that the lady took pains to bring back the

---

* The subject of this novel is the same as that of the story of the Dame de Langalier, related by the Seigneur de Latour-Landry to his daughters, in the book he wrote for their instruction. (See Leroux de Lincy, *Femmes Célèbres de l'Ancienne France*, i. 356.)

† In France, formerly, it was customary to have in all well-furnished bedrooms two beds, a principal one, and another much smaller for the confidential servant, who always slept in his master's room. See Novel XXXIX.

truant only for the sake of her children—a fact I can readily believe."

"Do you think it a great proof of patience in a woman," said Nomerfide, "to kindle a fire on the floor of a room in which her husband is sleeping?"

"Yes," said Longarine, "for when she saw the smoke she woke him up; and that was perhaps the greatest fault she committed, for the ashes of such husbands would be good to make lye withal."

"You are cruel, Longarine," said Oisille. "Yet that is not the way in which you lived with your husband."

"No," replied Longarine, "for, thank God, he never gave me cause; on the contrary, I must regret him as long as I live, instead of complaining of him."

"And if he had treated you otherwise," said Nomerfide, "what would you have done?"

"I loved him so much," replied Longarine, "that I believe I should have killed him, and myself afterwards. After having thus avenged myself, I should have found more pleasure in dying than in living with a faithless man."

"So far as I can see," observed Hircan, "you love your husbands only for your own sakes. If they commit the least fault on Saturday, they lose their whole week's labour. Do you want to be mistresses, then? For my part, I am willing to have it so, if other husbands will consent to it."

"It is reasonable that the man should rule us," said Parlamente; "but it is not reasonable that he should forsake and ill use us."

"God has so wisely ordained, both for the man and for the woman," said Oisille, "that I believe marriage, provided it be not abused, is one of the best and happiest conditions in life. I am persuaded that all present are as much impressed with that opinion as myself, or even more so, however they may affect to think otherwise. As the man esteems himself wiser than the woman, the fault will be more severely punished if it comes from him. But enough of this. Let us know on whom Dagoucin will call."

"On Longarine," was the reply.

"You give me great pleasure," said Longarine; "for I have a story which is worthy to follow yours. Since we are upon the praise of virtuous patience in ladies, I will tell you of one whose conduct was still more laudable than hers of whom you have just heard, and was the more commendable as she was a city lady, a class who are usually less trained to virtue than others."

NOVEL XXXVIII.

MEMORABLE CHARITY OF A LADY OF TOURS WITH REGARD TO HER FAITHLESS HUSBAND.

THERE was at Tours a handsome and discreet bourgeoise, who, for her virtues, was not only loved but feared by her husband. However, as husbands are frail, and often grow tired of always eating good bread, hers fell in love with one of his métayères.* He used frequently to go from Tours to visit his métairie, always remained there two or three days, and always came back so jaded and out of sorts, that his poor wife had trouble enough to set him up again. But no sooner was he himself once more, than back he would go to his métairie, where pleasure made him forget all his ailments. His wife, who loved his life and health above all things, seeing him always come back in such a bad plight, went to the métairie, where she found the young woman whom her husband loved, and said to her, not angrily, but in the gentlest manner possible, that she knew her husband often visited her, but was sorry she treated him so badly as invariably to send him home ill. The poor woman, constrained by respect for her mistress and by the force of truth, had not courage to deny the fact, and besought pardon. The Tourangeaude† desired to see the room and the bed in which her husband slept. The room struck her as so cold and dirty, that she was struck with pity, and sent straightway for a good bed, fine blankets, sheets, and counterpane after her husband's taste. She had the room made clean and neat, and hung with tapestry, gave the woman a handsome service

* *Métayère.* It was usual in France, before the Revolution, for the owner of a farm to supply the tenant with seed, &c., and to receive a proportion of the crop in lieu of rent. A farm managed on this principle was called a *métairie*, and the farmer a *métayer*, feminine, *métayère*.
† Woman of Touraine.

of plate, a pipe of good wine, sweetmeats, and confections, and begged her for the future not to send her husband back to her in so broken-down a condition.

It was not long before the husband went to see the métayère as usual; and great was his surprise to find the sorry room become so neat, but still greater was it when she gave him a silver cup to drink out of. He asked her where it came from, and the poor woman told him with tears that it was his wife who, pitying his poor entertainment, had thus furnished the house, enjoining her to be careful of his health. Struck by the great goodness of his wife, who thus returned so much good for so much evil, the gentleman reproached himself for ingratitude as great as his wife's generosity. He gave his métayère money, begged her thenceforth to live like an honest woman, and went back to his wife. He confessed the whole truth to her, and told her that her gentleness and goodness had withdrawn him from a bad course, from which it was impossible he should ever have escaped by any other means; and forgetting the past, they lived thenceforth together in great peace and concord.*

There are very few husbands, ladies, whom the wife does not win in the long run by patience and love, unless they are harder than the rocks which yet the weak and soft water pierces in time.

"Why, this woman had neither heart, nor gall, nor liver!" exclaimed Parlamente.

"What would you have?" said Longarine; "she did as God commands, rendering good for evil."

"I fancy," said Hircan, "that she was in love with some

---

* This tale is related by the author of the *Ménagier de Paris*, i. 237, ed. 1847, published by the Société des Bibliophiles Français. It is the 72nd of Morlini, and is in the manuscript copy of the *Varii Succedi* of Orologi, mentioned by Borromo. The French and Italian tales agree in the most minute circumstances, even in the name of the place where the lady resided. Erasmus also relates this tale in one of his colloquies, entitled Uxor Μεμψαγαμος sive Conjugium; and it occurs in Albion's England, a poem by William Warner, who was a celebrated writer in the reign of Queen Elizabeth: those stanzas which contain the incident have been extracted from that poetical epitome of English history, and published in Percy's Relics under the title of the Patient Countess.

Cordelier, who ordered her as a penance to have her husband so well treated in the country, in order that while he was there she might have leisure to treat himself well in town."

"In this you plainly show the wickedness of your own heart," said Oisille, "judging so ill of a good deed. I believe, on the contrary, that she was so penetrated by the love of God, that she cared for nothing but her husband's welfare."

"It strikes me," said Simontault, "that he had more reason to return to his wife during the time he was in such bad case at the métairie than when he was made so comfortable there."

"I see," said Saffredent, "that you are not of the same way of thinking as a rich man of Paris, who, when he lay with his wife, could not lay aside the least of his mufflings without catching cold; but when he went to see the servant girl in the cellar, without cap or shoes, in the depth of winter, he never was a bit the worse for it. Yet his wife was very handsome, and the servant very ugly."

"Have you not heard," said Geburon, "that God always helps madmen, lovers, and drunkards? Perhaps the Tourangeau was all three."

"Do you mean thence to infer," said Parlamente, "that God does nothing for the chaste, the wise, and the sober?"

"Those who can help themselves," replied Geburon, "have no need of aid. He who said, that He came for the sick and not for the hale, came by the law of His mercy to aid our infirmities, and cancelled the decrees of His rigorous justice; and he who thinks himself wise is a fool in the sight of God. But to end the sermon, whom do you call upon, Longarine?"

"On Saffredent," she said.

"Then I will prove to you by an example," said he, "that God does not favour lovers. Though it has been already said, ladies, that vice is common to women and to men, yet a woman will invent a cunning artifice more promptly and more adroitly than a man. Here is an example of the fact."

NOVEL XXXIX.

SECRET FOR DRIVING AWAY THE HOBGOBLIN.

A LORD of Grignaux, gentleman of honour to Anne, Duchess of Brittany and Queen of France, returning home after an absence of more than two years, found his wife at another estate he had, not far from that in which he usually resided. He asked the reason of this, and was told that the house was haunted by a spirit which made such a disturbance that no one could live in it. Monsieur de Grignaux, who was not a man to give credit to these fancies, replied that if it was the devil himself he should not fear him, and took his wife home with him to their usual abode. At night he had plenty of torches lighted, the better to see this spirit; but, after watching a long time without seeing or hearing anything, he at last fell asleep. No sooner had he done so than he was awakened by a sound box on the ears, after which he heard a voice crying " Brenigne, Brenigne," which was the name of his deceased grandmother. He called to a woman who slept in the chamber to light a candle, for he had had all the torches put out, but she durst not rise. At the same time, Monsieur de Grignaux felt his bed-clothes pulled off, and heard a great noise of tables, trestles, and stools tumbled about the room with a din that lasted until day. But he never believed that it was a spirit; he was not so frightened as vexed at losing his night's rest.

On the following night, being resolved to catch Master Goblin, he had no sooner lain down, than he pretended to snore with all his might, keeping his open hand over his face. While thus awaiting the arrival of the spirit, he heard something approach, and began to snore louder than ever. The spirit, which by this time had become familiar, gave him a great thump, whereupon Monsieur de Grignaux seized its hand, crying out " Wife, I have caught the spirit." His wife rose instantly, lighted a candle, and behold you, it turned out that the spirit was the girl who slept in their chamber. She threw herself at their feet, begging to be forgiven, and promised to tell them the truth, which was, that the love she long entertained for a domestic had made her play this trick in order to drive the master and mistress out of the house, and that they two who had charge of it might make good cheer, which they failed not to do when they were alone. Mousieur de Grignaux, who was not a man to be trifled with, had them both beaten in a manner they never forgot, and then turned them both out of doors. In this way he got rid of the spirits who had haunted his house for two years.

Love, ladies, works wonders. It makes women lose all fear, and torment men to arrive at their ends. Condemning the wickedness of the servant, we must equally applaud the good sense of the master, who knew that the departed spirit does not return.

"Decidedly," said Geburon, "the valet and the wench were not then favoured by love. I agree with you, however, that the master had need of much good sense."

"The girl, however," said Ennasuite, "lived for a long while to her heart's content, by means of her stratagem."

"That is a very wretched content," said Oisille, "which begins with sin, and ends with shame and punishment."

"That is true," rejoined Ennasuite; "but there are many persons who suffer whilst living righteously, and who have not the wit to give themselves in the course of their lives as much pleasure as the pair in question."

"I firmly believe," replied Oisille, "that there is no perfect pleasure unless the conscience is at rest."

"The Italian maintains," said Simontault, "that the greater the sin the greater the pleasure."

"One must be a perfect devil to entertain such a thought," said Oisille; "but let us drop the subject, and see to whom Saffredent will give his voice."

"No one remains to speak but Parlamente," said Saffredent; "but though there were a hundred others, she should have my voice, as a person from whom we are sure to learn something."

"Since I am to finish the day," said Parlamente, "and promised yesterday to tell you why Rolandine's father had the castle built in which he kept her so long a prisoner, I will now fulfil my word."

NOVEL XL.

THE COUNT DE JOSSEBELIN HAS HIS BROTHER-IN-LAW PUT TO DEATH, NOT KNOWING THE RELATIONSHIP.

The Count de Jossebelin, father of Rolandine, had several sisters. Some made wealthy marriages, others became nuns, and one, who was incomparably handsomer than the rest, remained in his house unmarried. The brother was so fond of this sister, that he preferred neither his wife nor his children to her; and though she had many eligible offers of marriage, they were all rejected, from his fear of losing her, and being obliged to pay down money. Consequently she remained a great part of her life unmarried, living with strict propriety in her brother's house. There was a young and handsome gentleman who had been reared in the house, and who as he grew in age grew also in personal and mental endowments, to that degree that he completely governed his master. When the latter had any message to send his sister, he always made this young gentleman the bearer of it; and as this took place morning and evening, it led to such a familiarity as presently ripened into love. The young gentleman durst not for his life offend his master; the demoiselle was not without scruples of honour; and so they had no other fruition of their love than in conversing together, until the brother had said again and again to the lover, that he wished he was of as good family as his sister, for he had never seen a man he would rather have for a brother-in-law. This was repeated so often, that after consulting together the lovers came to the conclusion that if they married secretly they should easily be forgiven. Love, which makes people readily believe what they desire, persuaded them that no bad consequences would ensue for them; and with that hope they married, unknown to any one except a priest and some women.

After having for some years enjoyed the pleasure which two handsome persons who passionately love each other can reciprocally bestow, fortune, jealous of their happiness, roused up an enemy against them, who, observing the demoiselle, became aware of her secret delights, being yet ignorant of her marriage. This person went and told the brother that the gentleman in whom he had such confidence visited his sister too often, and at hours when a man ought never to enter her chamber. At first he could not believe this, such was his trust in his sister and the gentleman. But, as he loved his house's honour, he caused them to be observed so closely, and set so many people on the watch, that the poor innocent couple were at last surprised.

One evening, word being brought the brother that the gentleman was with his sister, he went straightway to her chamber, and found them in bed together. Choking with rage and unable to speak, he drew his sword, and ran after the gentleman to kill him; but the latter being very nimble, evaded him; and, as he could not escape by the door, he jumped out of a window that looked upon the garden. The poor lady threw herself in her shift on her knees before her brother, crying, "Spare my husband's life, monsieur, for I have married him, and if he has offended you, let me alone suffer the punishment, for he has done nothing but at my solicitation."

"Were he a thousand times your husband," replied the incensed brother, "I will punish him as a domestic who has deceived me." So saying, he went to the window, and called out to his people to kill him, which was forthwith done before his eyes and those of his sister.

At this sad spectacle, which her prayers and supplications had been unable to prevent, the poor wife was like one distracted. "Brother," she said, "I have neither father nor mother, and I am of an age to marry as I choose. I chose a man whom you told me repeatedly that you would have liked me to marry. And because I did so, as by law I had a right to do without your interference, you put to death the man you loved best in the world. Since my prayers have not availed to save him, I conjure you by all the affection you have ever had for me to make me the companion of his death as I have been of all his fortunes. Thereby you will glut your cruel and unjust wrath, and give repose to the body and soul of a wife who will not and cannot live without her husband."

Though the brother was beside himself with passion, he had so much pity on his sister, that, without saying yes or no, he left her and withdrew. After having carefully investigated the matter, and ascertained that the murdered man had been wedded to his sister, he would have been glad if the deed had not been done. Being afraid, however, that his sister, to revenge it, would appeal to justice, he had a castle built in the midst of a forest, and there he confined her, with orders that no one should be admitted to speak to her.

Some time after, to satisfy his conscience, he tried to conciliate her, and caused her to be sounded upon the subject of marriage; but she sent him word that he had given her such a bad dinner she had no mind to be regaled with the same dish for supper; that she hoped to live in such wise that he should never have the pleasure of killing a second husband of hers; and that after dealing so villanously with the man he loved best in the world, she could not imagine that he would pardon another. She added, that notwithstanding her weakness and impotence, she trusted that He who was a just judge, and would not suffer wrong to go unpunished, would do her the grace to avenge her, and let her finish her days in her hermitage in meditating on the love and charity of her God. And this she did. She lived in that place with so much patience and austerity, that after her death every one visited her remains as those of a saint. From the moment of her death her brother's house began to fall into decay, so that of six sons not one remained to continue it. They all died miserably; and in the end Rolandine, his daughter, remained sole heiress of all, as you have been told in another tale, and succeeded to her aunt's prison.*

I wish, ladies, that you may profit by this example, and that none of you may think of marrying for your own pleasure, without the consent of those to whom you owe obedience. Marriage is an affair of such long duration, that

---

* Josselin, a little town of Le Morbihan, was included in the domains of the Viscount of Rohan, whose name the Queen of Navarre disguises by calling him Count of *Jossebelin*. Jean II., Viscount of Rohan, had one uterine sister, named Catherine, and several half sisters. Catherine de Rohan, who is said by the authors of *Histoire Généalogique de la Maison de France*, iv. 57, to have died unmarried, is the heroine of this novel, and the murder of the Count of Keradreux, for which the Viscount of Rohan was imprisoned, is no doubt the one of which the Queen of Navarre speaks.

one cannot engage in it with too much deliberation; and deliberate ever so well and so sagely, yet one is sure to find in it at least as much pain as pleasure.

"Were there no God or law to teach maidens discretion," said Oisille, "the example might suffice to make them have more respect for their relations than to marry without their knowledge."

"Nevertheless, madam," replied Nomerfide, "when one has one good day in the year, one is not wholly unfortunate. She had the pleasure of seeing and conversing for a long time with him whom she loved better than herself. Besides, she enjoyed it through marriage without scruple of conscience. I regard this satisfaction as so great, that, to my thinking, it fairly counterbalanced the grief that subsequently befel her."

"You mean to say, then," said Saffredent, "that the pleasure of bedding with a husband is more to a woman than the pain of seeing him killed before her eyes."

"No such thing," said Nomerfide; "were I to say so, I should speak contrary to my own experience of women. What I mean is, that an unaccustomed pleasure like that of marrying the man one loves best must be greater than the pain of losing him by death, which is an ordinary occurrence."

"That may be true of natural death," said Geburon; "but the one in question was too cruel. I think it very strange that this lord, who was neither her father nor her husband, but only her brother, should have dared to commit such a cruel deed, seeing even that his sister was of an age at which the laws allow girls to marry as they think fit."

"For my part, I see nothing strange in that," said Hircan. "He did not kill his sister whom he loved so fondly, and over whom he had no jurisdiction; but he dealt as he deserved with the young gentleman, whom he had brought up as his son and loved as his brother. He had advanced and enriched him in his service, and then, by way of gratitude, the young gentleman married his sister, which he ought not to have done."

"Again," resumed Nomerfide, "it was no common and ordinary pleasure for a lady of such high family to marry a gentleman domestic. Thus, if the death was a surprise, the pleasure also was novel, and the greater as it was contrary to the opinion of all the wise, and was helped by the satisfaction of a heart filled with love, and by repose of soul, seeing that God was not offended. As to the death you call cruel, it seems to me that death being necessary, the quicker it is the better; for do we not know that death is a passage which must inevitably be crossed? I regard as fortunate those who do not linger long in the outskirts of death, and who by good luck, which alone deserves that name, pass at one bound into everlasting felicity."

"What do you call the outskirts of death?" said Simontault.

"Sorrows, afflictions, long maladies," replied Nomerfide. "Those who have to sustain such extreme pangs of body or of mind that they come to despise death and complain of its too tardy approach, are in the outskirts of death, and they will tell you how the inns are named in which they have sighed more than reposed. The lady in question could not help losing her husband by death; but her brother's anger saved her from the pain of seeing him for a long time an invalid or ill-tempered, and she could deem herself happy in converting to the service of God the satisfaction and joy she had with her husband."

"Do you count for nothing the shame she underwent and the tedium of her prison?" said Longarine.

"I am persuaded," replied Nomerfide, "that when one loves well, and with a love founded on God's command, one makes no account of shame, except so far as it lessens love; for the glory of loving well knows no shame. As for her prison, as her heart was wholly devoted to God and her husband, I imagine she hardly felt the loss of her liberty; for where one cannot see what one loves, the greatest blessing one can have is to think of it incessantly. A prison is never narrow when the imagination can range in it as it will."

"Nothing can be truer than what Nomerfide alleges," said Simontault; "but the madman who effected this separation ought to have deemed himself a very wretch, offending as he did God, love, and honour."

"I am astonished," said Geburon, "that there is so much diversity in the nature of women's love; and I see plainly that those who have the most love have the most virtue;

but those who have the least love are the virtuous in false seeming."

"It is true," said Parlamente, "that a heart that is virtuous towards God and man loves with more passion than a vicious heart, because the former is not afraid that the real nature of its sentiments should be apparent."

"I have always understood," said Simontault, "that men are not blamable for paying court to women; for God has put into the heart of man love and the boldness to sue, and into that of woman fear and the chastity to refuse. If a man has been punished for having used the power implanted in him, he has been treated with injustice."

"But was it not a monstrous inconsistency in this brother," said Longarine, "to have persisted so long in praising this young gentleman to his sister? It seems to me that it would be a great folly, not to say cruelty, in a man who had charge of a fountain to praise its water to one who gazed on it, parched with thirst, and then to kill him for offering to drink of it."

"The fire of his encomiums on the young man," said Parlamente, "unquestionably kindled the fire of love in the lady's heart; and he was wrong to put out with his sword a fire he himself had lighted by his sweet words."

"I am surprised," said Saffredent, "that it should be taken amiss that a simple gentleman, by dint of courtship alone, and not through any false pretences, should come to marry a lady of so illustrious a house, since the philosophers maintain that the least of men is worthier than the greatest and most virtuous of women."

"The reason is," said Dagoucin, "that in order to preserve the public tranquillity, regard is only had to the degree of the families, the age of the persons, and the laws, men's love and virtue being counted as nothing, in order not to confound the monarchy. Thence it comes that in the marriages which take place between equals, and in accordance with the judgment of men and of the relations, the persons are often so different in heart, temperament, and disposition, that instead of entering into an engagement which leads to salvation, they throw themselves into the confines of hell."

"Instances have also been seen," said Geburon, "of persons who have married for love, with hearts, dispositions, and temperaments mutually conformable, without concerning themselves about difference of birth, and who have nevertheless repented of what they have done. In fact, a great but indiscreet love often changes into jealousy and fury."

"To me it seems," said Parlamente, "that neither the one course nor the other is commendable, and that those persons who submit to the will of God, regard neither glory, nor avarice, nor voluptuousness. They alone are to be commended, who, actuated by virtuous love, sanctioned by the consent of their relations, desire to live in the married state as God and nature ordain. Though there is no condition without its troubles, I have yet seen these latter run their course without repenting that they had entered upon it. The present company is not so unhappy as not to number in it married persons of this class."

Thereupon Hircan, Geburon, Simontault, and Saffredent vowed that they had all married in that very spirit, and that accordingly they had never repented of the act. Whether that was true or not, the ladies whom it concerned were nevertheless so pleased with the declaration, that, being of opinion they could hear nothing better than it, they rose to go and give thanks for it to God, and found that the monks were ready for the vesper service. Their devotions ended, they supped, but not without reverting to the subject of marriage, every one recounting his own experience whilst wooing his wife. But as they interrupted each other, it was not possible to make a full record of their several stories; which was a pity, for they were not less agreeable than those they had recounted in the meadow. This conversation was so interesting, that bedtime arrived before they were aware of it. Madame Oisille was the first to perceive that it was time to retire, and her example was followed by the rest. All went to bed in the gayest humour, and I do not think the married couples slept more than the others, but spent a part of the night in talking over their affections in times past, and giving each other evidences of its present existence. Thus the night passed agreeably away.

FIFTH DAY.

When day dawned, Madame Oisille prepared for them a spiritual breakfast of such good savour, that it fortified their minds and bodies alike; and the company were so attentive to it, that it seemed they had never heard a sermon to more advantage. The second bell for mass having rung, they went to meditate on the good things they had heard. After mass they took a little walk while waiting for dinner, anticipating as agreeable a day as the preceding one. Saffredent said that he was so charmed with the good cheer they made and the recreation they enjoyed, that he could wish it might be a month yet before the bridge was finished; but as it was no comfort to the abbot to live along with so many respectable people, into whose presence he durst not bring his usual female pilgrims, he urged the workmen to make all possible speed. When the company had rested awhile after dinner, they returned to their usual pastime, and every one being seated, they asked Parlamente who should begin. "It strikes me," she said, "that Saffredent would do so very well, for his face does not seem to me adapted to make us cry."

"Nay, ladies, you will be very cruel," he replied, "if you bestow no pity upon a Cordelier whose story I am going to relate to you. You will say, perhaps, as has been already remarked of other incidents of this kind, that they are things which have happened to ladies, and would not have been attempted but for the facility of their execution; but that is not the case: on the contrary, you shall see from the example I am about to adduce, that the Cordeliers are so blind in their lust, that they know neither fear nor prudence."

NOVEL XLI.

STRANGE AND NOVEL PENANCE IMPOSED BY A CORDELIER CONFESSOR ON A YOUNG LADY.

In the year when Margaret of Austria came to Cambrai on the part of the emperor her nephew to negotiate the peace between him and the Most Christian King, who sent on his part Louise of Savoy his mother, there was in the suite of Margaret of Austria the Countess of Aiguemont, who passed in that assembly for the most beautiful of the Flemish ladies. After the conference the Countess of Aiguemont returned home, and the season of Advent being come, she sent to a monastery of Cordeliers, requiring a preacher, a good man, fit to preach to and confess the countess and her household. The warden, who received great benefits from the house of Aiguemont, and from that of Fiennes, to which the countess belonged, sent the best preacher in the society, and the one who was regarded as the most upright man. He performed his duty very well in preaching the Advent sermons, and the countess was perfectly satisfied with him.

On Christmas night, when the countess intended to receive her Creator, she sent for her confessor, and after having well and duly confessed in a chapel carefully closed that the confession might be more secret, she gave place to her lady of honour, who, having made her confession, next sent her daughter. After the young penitent had told all she knew, the good confessor knew something of her secrets, which prompted him to impose upon her an extraordinary penance, and he was bold enough to say to her, " Your sins, my daughter, are so great, that I order you, for penance, to wear my cord on your bare flesh."

The demoiselle, who had no wish to disobey him, replied, " Give it me, father, and I will not fail to wear it."

"No, daughter," replied the holy man, "it would not be meet for you to fasten it on. That must be done by these very hands from which you are to receive absolution, and afterwards you will be absolved from all your sins."

The demoiselle began to cry, and said she would do no such thing. " What!" exclaimed the confessor, " are you a heretic, to refuse the penances which God and our holy Mother Church have ordained?"

"I make of confession the use which the Church has commanded," replied the demoiselle. " I am quite willing to receive absolution, and to do penance; but I will not have you put your hands to it; for in that case, I refuse to submit to your penance."

" That being the case," said the confessor, " I cannot give you absolution."

The demoiselle withdrew, sorely troubled in conscience, for she was so young that she was afraid she had transgressed by the refusal she had given to the reverend father. After mass was over, and the Countess of Aiguemont had taken the communion, her lady of honour, intending to do the same, asked her daughter if she was ready. The girl replied, with tears, that she had not yet confessed. "Then, what have you been doing so long with the preacher?" inquired her mother.

"Nothing," replied the daughter; "for, as I would not submit to the penance he ordered me, he would not grant me absolution."

Thereupon the mother questioned her so shrewdly, that she learned the nature of the extraordinary penance which the monk wished to impose upon her daughter. She made her confess to another, and afterwards they both communicated.

As soon as the countess returned from church, the lady of honour complained to her of the preacher, to the countess's great surprise, for she had a very good opinion of him. All her anger, however, did not hinder her from laughing at the oddity of the penance; but neither did her laughter hinder her from having the good father chastised. He was handsomely thrashed in the kitchen, and so compelled, by dint of blows, to confess the truth; after which, he was sent away, bound hand and foot, to his warden, with a request that another time he would commission better men to preach the Word of God.

Consider, ladies, if the monks do not scruple to display their wickedness in so illustrious a house, what are they not capable of doing in the poor places to which they commonly go to make their gatherings, and where they have such full opportunities that it is a miracle if they quit them without scandal? This obliges me to entreat, ladies, that you will change your scorn into compassion, and consider that the power which can blind the Cordeliers does not spare the ladies, when he finds them a fair mark for his shafts.

"Assuredly, this was a wicked Cordelier," said Oisille. "A monk, a priest, and a preacher, to be guilty, on Christmas-day, of such an infamy, and that in the house of God, and under the sacred veil of confession! This was carrying impiety and villany to the very climax."

"Why," said Hircan, "to hear you talk, one would think the Cordeliers should be angels, or more chaste than other men; but they are quite the reverse, as you must know from many an example. As for this one, it appears to me that he was very excusable, finding himself, as he did, shut up alone with a handsome girl."

"Nay," said Oisille, "but it was Christmas night."

"The very thing that makes him the more excusable," said Simontault, "for, being in Joseph's place, beside a beautiful virgin, he had a mind to try and beget a baby, in order to play the mystery of the Nativity to the life."

"Truly," said Parlamente, "if he had thought of Joseph and the Virgin Mary, he would not have harboured such a wicked purpose. At any rate, he was an audacious villain to make such a criminal attempt upon no encouragement."

"The manner in which the countess had him castigated," said Oisille, "might serve, methinks, as a warning to others like him."

"I do not know if she did well," said Nomerfide, "thus to scandalise her neighbour, and if it would not have been better to remonstrate with him on his fault in private and gently, than thus to divulge it."

"That I think would have been better," said Geburon, "for we are commanded to reprove our neighbour in secret, before we speak of his offence, not only to the Church, but to any person whatever. When a man is deprived of all motives on the side of honour, it is very hard for him to reform; and the reason is, that shame keeps as many from sin as does conscience."

"I think," said Parlamente, "that every one should practise the precepts of the Gospel, and it is very scandalous that those who preach them should do the reverse; therefore, we need have no fear of scandalising those who scandalise others. On the contrary, it appears to me meritorious to make them known for what they are, so that we may be on our guard against their wiles with regard to the fair sex, who are not always wary and prudent. But to whom does Hircan give his voice?"

"Since you ask me," he replied, "I give it to you, to whom no sensible man could refuse it."

"Well then," rejoined Parlamente, "I will tell you a story to which I can testify of my own knowledge. I have always heard that the weaker the vessel in which virtue abides, and the more violently it is assaulted by a powerful and formidable antagonist, the more worthy is it of praise, and the more conspicuously is its nature displayed. That the strong defends himself against the strong is no matter for wonder; but to see the weak beat the strong is a thing to be extolled by all the world. Knowing the persons of whom I mean to speak, methinks it would be wronging the truth I have seen hid under so mean a garb that no one made any account of it, if I did not speak of her by whom were done the honourable actions of which I am about to tell you."

NOVEL XLII.

CHASTE PERSEVERANCE OF A MAIDEN, WHO RESISTED THE OBSTINATE PURSUIT OF ONE OF THE GREATEST LORDS IN FRANCE.—AGREEABLE ISSUE OF THE AFFAIR FOR THE DEMOISELLE.

In one of the best towns of Touraine lived a lord of great and illustrious family, who had been brought up from his youth in the province. All I need say of the perfections, beauty, grace, and great qualities of this young prince is, that in his time he never had his equal. At the age of fifteen, he took more pleasure in hunting and hawking than in beholding fair ladies. Being one day in a church, he cast his eyes on a young girl who, during her childhood, had been brought up in the château in which he resided. After the death of her mother, her father had withdrawn thence, and gone to reside with his brother in Poitou. This daughter of his, whose name was Françoise, had a bastard sister, whom her father was very fond of, and had married to this young prince's butler, who maintained her on as handsome a footing as any of her family. The father died, and left to Françoise for her portion all he possessed about the good town in question, whither she went to reside after his death; but as she was unmarried and only sixteen, she would not keep house, but went to board with her sister.

The young prince was much struck with this girl, who was very handsome for a light brunette, and of a grace beyond her rank; for she had the air of a young lady of quality, or of a princess, rather than of a bourgeoise. He gazed upon her for a long while; and as he had never loved, he felt in his heart a pleasure that was new to him. On returning to his chamber, he made inquiries about the girl he had seen at church, and recollected that formerly, when she was very young, she used often to play in the château with his sister, whom he put in mind of her. His sister sent for her, gave her a very good reception, and begged her to come often to see her, which she did whenever there was any entertainment or assembly. The young prince was very glad to see her, and so glad that he chose to be deeply in love with her. Knowing that she was of low birth, he thought he should easily obtain of her what he sought; and, as he had no opportunity to speak with her, he sent a gentleman of his chamber to her, with orders to acquaint her with his intentions, and settle matters with her. The girl, who was good and pious, replied that she did not believe that so handsome a prince as his master would care to look upon a plain girl like herself, especially as there were such handsome ones in the château that he had no need to look elsewhere; and that she doubted not he had said all this to her out of his own head and without orders from his master.

As obstacles make desire more violent, the prince now became more hotly intent on his purpose than ever, and wrote to her, begging her to believe everything the gentleman should say to her on his part. She could read and write very well, and she read the letter from beginning to end; but for no entreaties the gentleman could make would she ever reply to it, saying that a person of her humble birth should never take the liberty to write to so great a prince; but that she begged he would not take her for such a fool as to imagine that he esteemed her enough to love her as much as he said. Moreover, he was mistaken if he fancied that because she was of obscure birth, he might do as he pleased with her, and that to convince him of the contrary, she felt obliged to declare to him that, bourgeoise as she was, there was no princess whose heart was more upright than hers. There were no treasures in the world she esteemed so much as honour and conscience. And the only favour she begged of him was, that he would not hinder her from preserving that treasure all her life long, and that he might take it for certain that she would never change her mind though it were to cost her her life.

The young prince did not find this answer to his liking. Nevertheless, he loved her but the more for it, and failed not to lay siege to her when she went to mass; and during the whole service he had no eyes but to gaze on that image to which he addressed his devotions. But when she perceived this, she changed her place and went to another chapel, not that she disliked to see him, for she would not have been a reasonable creature if she had not taken pleasure in looking on him; but she was afraid of being seen by him, not thinking highly enough of herself to deserve being loved with a view to marriage, and being too high-minded to be able to accommodate herself to a dishonourable love. When she saw that in whatever part of the church she placed herself, the prince had mass said quite near it, she went no more to that church, but to the most distant one she could find. Moreover, when the prince's sister often sent for her, she always excused herself on the plea of indisposition.

The prince, seeing he could not have access to her, had recourse to his butler, and promised him a large reward if he served him in this affair. The butler, both to please his master and for the hope of lucre, promised to do so cheerfully. He made it a practice to relate daily to the prince all she said and did, and assured him, among other things, that she avoided as much as possible all opportunities of seeing him. The prince's violent desire for an interview with her, set him upon devising another expedient. As he was already beginning to be a very good horseman, he bethought him of going to ride his great horses in a large open place of the town, exactly opposite to the house of the butler, in which Françoise resided. One day, after many courses and leaps, which she could see from her chamber window, he let himself fall off his horse into a great puddle. Though he was not hurt, he took care to make great moans, and asked if there was no house into which he might go and change his clothes. Every one offered him his own; but some one having remarked that the butler's was the nearest and the best, it was chosen in preference to any of the others. He was shown into a well-furnished chamber, and as his clothes were all muddy, he stripped to his shirt and went to bed. Every one except his gentleman having gone away to fetch other clothes for the prince, he sent for his host and hostess, and asked them where was Françoise? They had a good deal of trouble to find her, for as soon as she had seen the prince come in, she had gone and hid herself in the remotest corner of the house. Her sister found her at last, and begged her not to be afraid to come and see so polite and worthy a prince.

"What! sister," said Françoise, "you, whom I regard as my mother, would you persuade me to speak to a young prince of whose intentions I cannot be ignorant, as you well know?"

But her sister used so many arguments, and promised so earnestly not to leave her alone, that Françoise went with her, with a countenance so pale and dejected, that she was an object rather to inspire pity than love. When the young prince saw her at his bedside, he took her cold and trembling hand, and said, "Why, Françoise, do you think me such a dangerous and cruel man that I eat the women I look at? Why do you so much fear a man who desires only your honour and advantage? You know that I have everywhere sought in vain for opportunities to see and speak to you. To grieve me the more, you have shunned the places where I had been used to see you at mass, and thereby you have deprived me of the satisfaction of my eyes and my tongue. But all this has availed you nothing. I have done what you have seen in order to come hither, and have run the risk of breaking my neck in order to have the pleasure of speaking to you without restraint. I entreat you then, Françoise, since it would be hard for me to have taken all this pains to no purpose, that as I have so much love for you, you will have a little for me."

After waiting a long while for her reply, and seeing she had tears in her eyes, and durst not look up, he drew her towards him and almost succeeded in kissing her. "No, my lord, no," she then said, "what you ask cannot be. Though I am but a worm in comparison with you, honour is so dear to me that I would rather die than wound it in the least degree for any pleasure in the world; and my fear, lest those who have seen you come in conceive a false opinion of me, makes me tremble as you see. Since you are pleased to do me the honour to address me, you will also pardon the liberty I take in replying to you as honour prescribes. I am not, my lord, so foolish or so blind as not to see and know the advantages with which God has endowed you, and to believe that she who shall possess the heart and person of such a prince will be the happiest woman in the world. But what good does that do me? That happiness is not for me or for any woman of my rank; and I should be a downright simpleton if I even entertained the desire. What reason can I believe you have for addressing yourself to me, but that the ladies of your house, whom you love, and who have so much grace and beauty, are so virtuous that you dare not ask of them what the lowness of my condition makes you easily expect of me? I am sure that if you had of such as me what you desire, that weakness would supply you with matter to entertain your mistresses for two good hours; but I beg you to believe, my lord, that I am not disposed to afford you that pleasure. I was brought up in a house in which I learned what it is to love. My father and mother were among your good servants. Since then it has not pleased God that I should be born a princess to marry you, or in a rank sufficiently high to be your friend, I entreat you not to think of reducing me to the rank of the unfortunates of my sex, since there is no one who esteems you more than I, or more earnestly desires that you may be one of the happiest princes in Christendom. If you want women of my station for your diversion, you will find plenty in this town incomparably handsomer than myself, and who will spare you the trouble of soliciting them so much. Attach yourself, then, if you please, to those who will gladly let you buy their honour, and harass no longer a poor girl who loves you better than herself; for if God were this day to require your life or mine, it would be a happiness to me to sacrifice mine in order to save yours. If I shun your person, it is not for want of love, but rather because I too well love your conscience and mine, and because my honour is more precious to me than my life. I ask you, my lord, if you please, to continue to honour me with your

good-will, and I will pray to God all my life for your health
and prosperity. It is true that the honour you do me will
give me a better opinion of myself among persons of my own
station; for after having seen you, where is the man of my
own condition whom I would deign to regard? Thus my
heart will be free and under no obligation, except that which
I shall ever acknowledge, to pray to God for you, which is all
I can do for you while I live."

Contrary as this reply was to the prince's desires, nevertheless he could not help esteeming her as she deserved. He
did all he could to make her believe he would never love any
one but herself; but she had so much sense that he never
could bring her to entertain so unreasonable a notion.
Though, during the course of this conversation, it was often
intimated to the prince that fresh clothes had been brought
him, he was so glad to remain where he was that he sent back
word he was asleep. But at last, supper-time being come,
and not daring to absent himself from respect for his mother,
who was one of the most correct ladies in the world, he went
away, more impressed than ever with the excellence of Françoise. He often talked of her to the gentleman who slept
in his chamber. That person, imagining that money would
be more effectual than love, advised him to present a considerable sum to the girl in consideration of the favour he
solicited. As the young prince's mother was his treasurer,
and his pocket money was not much, he borrowed, and out
of his own funds and those of his friends he made up a sum
of five hundred crowns, which he sent to Françoise by his
gentleman, commissioning him to beg that she would change
her mind.

"Tell your master," she said, when the gentleman offered
her the present, "that my heart is so noble and generous,
that were it my humour to do what he desires, his good looks
and his pleasing qualities would have already made a conquest of me; but since these are incapable of making me
take the slightest step at variance with honour, all the money
in the world could not do it. You will take back his money
to him, if you please, for I prefer honest poverty to all the
wealth he could bestow upon me."

Baffled by this downright refusal, the gentleman was
tempted to think that a little violence might succeed, and he

dropped threatening hints of her master's influence and power. "Make a bugbear of the prince," she said, laughing in his face, "to those who do not know him; but I, who know him to be wise and virtuous, can never believe that you say this by his order; and I am persuaded that he will disavow it all if you repeat it to him. But even were it true that you had his authority for what you say, I tell you that neither torments nor death could ever shake my resolution, for, as I have said before, since love has not changed my heart, no earthly good or evil can ever effect what that has failed to accomplish."

It was with indescribable vexation that the gentleman, who had undertaken to humanise her, carried back this answer to his master, whom he urged to carry his point by all possible means, representing to him that it would be shameful for him to have undertaken such a conquest and not achieve it. The young prince, who wished to employ only fair means, and who was afraid, besides, of his mother's anger if the story got abroad and reached her ears, durst not take any further step, until at last the gentleman suggested to him an expedient, which seemed to him so good, that he felt already as if the fair one was his own. To this end he spoke to the butler, who, being ready to serve his master on any terms, consented to everything required of him. It was arranged, then, that the butler should invite his wife and his sister-in-law to go see their vintage at a house he had near the forest; he did so, and they agreed to the proposal. The appointed day being come, he gave notice to the prince, who was to go to the same place, accompanied only by his gentleman. But it pleased God that his mother was that day adorning a most beautiful cabinet, and had all her children to help her; so that the proper time passed by before the prince could get away. This was no fault of the butler's, who had fully performed his part; for he made his wife counterfeit illness, and when he was on horseback with his sister-in-law on the croup, she came and told him that she could not go. But the hour having passed by and no prince appearing, "I believe," said he to his sister-in-law, "we may as well go back to town."

"Who hinders us?" said Françoise.

"I was waiting for the prince, who had promised to come," said the butler.

His sister, clearly discerning his wicked purpose, replied, "Wait no longer for him, brother; for I know that he will not come to-day."

He acquiesced, and took her home again. On arriving there she let him know her dissatisfaction, and told him plainly that he was the devil's valet, and did more than he was commanded; for she was very sure that it was his work and the gentleman's, not the prince's; that they both liked better to flatter his weaknesses, and gain money, than to do their duty as good servants; but that since she knew this she would no longer remain in his house. Thereupon she sent for her brother to take her away to his own country, and immediately quitted her sister's house.

The butler having missed his blow, went to the château to know why the prince had not come, and met him on the way, mounted on his mule, with no other attendant than his confidential gentleman.

"Well," said the prince, the moment he saw him, "is she still there?"

The butler told him what had happened, and the prince was greatly vexed at having missed the rendezvous, which he regarded as his last hope. However, he took such pains to meet Françoise, that at last he fell in with her in a company from which she could not escape, and upbraided her strongly for her cruelty to him, and for quitting her brother-in-law's house. Françoise told him she had never known a more dangerous man, and that he, the prince, was under great obligations to him, since he employed in his service not only his body and his substance, but also his soul and his conscience. The prince could not help feeling that there was no hope for him; he therefore resolved to press her no more, and he continued all his life to entertain a great esteem for her. One of his domestics, charmed by her virtue, wished to marry her; but she could never bring herself to consent without the approbation and command of the prince, on whom she had set her whole affection. She had him spoken to on the subject; he consented to the marriage, and it took place. She lived all her life in good repute, and the prince did her much kindness.*

---

* The young lord spoken of in this novel is evidently Francis I.; and the town of Touraine is Amboise, where Louise of Savoy resided with her children.

What shall we say, ladies? Are we so low-spirited as to make our servants our masters? She whose story I have related to you was not to be overcome either by love or by importunity. Let us imitate her example and be victorious over ourselves. Nothing is more praiseworthy than to subdue one's passions.

"I see but one thing to regret in this case," said Oisille, "which is, that actions so virtuous did not take place in the time of the historians. Those who have so lauded Lucretia would have left her story to relate the virtues of this heroine. They seem to me so great, that I could hardly believe them had we not sworn to speak the truth."

"Her virtue does not seem to me so great as you make it out to be," said Hircan. "You must have seen plenty of squeamish invalids, who left good and wholesome food for what was bad and unwholesome. Perhaps this girl loved some one else, for whose sake she despised persons of the first order."

To that Parlamente replied, that the life and end of this girl showed that "she had never loved but him whom she loved above her life, but not above her honour."

"Put that out of your head," said Saffredent, "and learn what was the origin of that phrase *honour*, which prudes make such a fuss about. Perhaps those who talk so much about it do not know what it means. In the time when men were not over crafty—the golden age, if you will—love was so frank, simple, and strong, that no one knew what it was to dissemble, and he who loved most was the most esteemed. But malignity, avarice, and sin, having taken possession of men's hearts, drove out from them God and love, and put there, instead of them, self-love, hypocrisy, and feigning. The ladies seeing that they had not the virtue of true and genuine love, and that hypocrisy was very odious amongst mankind, gave it the name of honour. Those, then, who could not compass that true love, said that they were forbidden by honour. This practice they have erected into so cruel a law, that even those of their sex who love perfectly, dissemble, and think that this virtue is a vice; but such of them as have good sense and sound judgment never fall into this error. They know the difference between darkness and light; and know that genuine love consists in manifesting chastity of heart, which lives upon love alone, and does not pride itself on dissimulation, which is a vice."

"Yet it is said," observed Dagoucin, "that the most secret love is the most commendable."

"Secret," replied Simontault, "for those who might misjudge it, but clear and avowed at least for the two persons concerned."

"So I understand it," said Dagoucin. "Nevertheless, it were better it were unknown by one of the two, than known to a third. I believe that the subject of the tale loved the more strongly that she did not declare her love."

"Be this as it may," said Longarine, "virtue is to be esteemed; and the highest virtue is to overcome one's own heart. When I consider the means and opportunities she had, I maintain that she was entitled to be called a heroine."

"Since you make self-mortification the measure of virtue," said Saffredent, "the prince deserved more praise than she did. To be convinced of this, one has only to consider his passion for her, his power, his opportunities, and the means he might have employed, yet would not, that he might not violate the rule of perfect affection, which makes the indigent equal to the prince, but contented himself with employing the means which fair dealing permits."

"There is many a one who would not have done that," said Hircan.

"He is the more to be esteemed," replied Longarine, "because he overcame the evil disposition common to men. Blessed, unquestionably, is he who has it in his power to do evil, yet does it not."

"You put me in mind," said Geburon, "of a woman who was more afraid of offending men than God, her honour, and love."

"Pray tell us the story," said Parlamente.

"There are people," he continued, "who own no God, or who, if they believe there is one, think Him so remote, that He can neither see nor know the bad acts they commit; or if He does, they suppose Him to be so careless and indifferent to what is done here below, that He will not punish them. Of this way of thinking was a lady, whose name I shall conceal for the honour of her race, and call her Jambicque. She used often to say that to care only for God was all very well, but the main point with her was to preserve her honour before men. But you will see, ladies, that her prudence and her hypocrisy did not save her. Her secret was revealed, as you shall find from her story, in which I will state nothing but what is true, except the names of the persons and the places, which I will change."

NOVEL XLIII.

HYPOCRISY OF A COURT LADY DISCOVERED BY THE DÉNOUEMENT OF HER AMOURS, WHICH SHE WISHED TO CONCEAL.

A PRINCESS of great eminence lived in a very handsome château, and had with her a lady named Jambicque, of a haughty and audacious spirit, who was, nevertheless, such a favourite with her mistress, that she did nothing but by her advice, believing her to be the most discreet and virtuous lady of her time. This Jambicque used to inveigh loudly against illicit love; and if ever she saw that any gentleman was enamoured with one of her companions, she used to reprimand the pair with great bitterness, and tell a very bad tale of them to her mistress, so that she was much more feared than loved. As for her, she never spoke to a man except aloud, and with so much haughtiness, that she was universally regarded as an inveterate foe to love; but, in her heart, she was quite otherwise. In fact, there was a gentleman in her mistress's service with whom she was as much in love as a woman could be; but so dear to her was her good name, and the reputation she had made herself, that she entirely dissembled her passion.

After suffering for a year, without choosing to solace herself, like other women, by means of her eyes and her tongue, her heart became so inflamed, that she was driven to seek the ultimate remedy; and she made up her mind that it was better to satisfy her desire, provided none but God knew her heart, than to confide it to one who might betray her secret. Having come to this resolution, one day when she was in her mistress's chamber, and was looking out on a terrace, she saw the gentleman she loved so much walking there. After gazing on him until darkness concealed him from her sight, she called her little page, and, pointing out the gentleman to him, "Do you see," she said, "that gentleman in a crimson satin doublet, and a robe trimmed with lynx fur? Go and tell him that a friend of his wishes to see him, and is waiting for him in the gallery in the garden."

Whilst the page was doing his errand, she went out the back way, and went to the gallery, after putting on her mask and pulling down her hood. When the gentleman entered the gallery, she first fastened both the doors, so that no one should come in upon them, and then, embracing him with all her might, she said in a low whisper, "This long time, my friend, the love I have for you has made me long for place and time to speak with you; but my fear for my honour has been so great that I have been constrained, in spite of myself, to conceal my passion. But at last love has prevailed over fear; and as your honour is known to me, I declare that if you will promise to love me, and never to speak of it to any one, or inquire whom I am, I will be all my life your faithful and loving friend; and I assure you I will never love any but you; but I would rather die than tell you who I am."

The gentleman promised all she asked, and thereby encouraged her to treat him in the same way—that is to say, refuse him nothing. It was in winter, about five or six o'clock in the evening, when of course he could not see much. But if his eyes were of little service to him on the occasion, his hands were not so. Touching her clothes he found they were of velvet, a costly stuff in those times, and not worn every day, except by ladies of high family. As far as the hand could judge, all beneath was neat and in the best condition. Accordingly he tried to regale her to the best of his ability; she too performed her part equally well, and the gentleman easily perceived she was married.

When she was about to return to the place whence she came, the gentleman said to her, "Highly do I prize the favour you have conferred on me without my deserving it; but that will be still more precious to me which you will grant at my entreaty. Enchanted as I am by your gracious favour, I beg you will tell me if I am to expect a continuance of it, and in what manner I am to act; for, not knowing you, how am I to address you elsewhere to solicit the renewal of my happiness?"

"Give yourself no concern about that," replied the fair one, "but rely upon it that every evening after my mistress has supped, I shall be sure to send for you, if you are on the terrace where you were just now. But, above all things, do not forget what you have promised. When I simply send word that you are wanted, you will understand that I await you in the gallery; but if you hear speak of going to meat, you may either retire or come to our mistress's apartment. Above all, I beg you never to attempt to know who I am, unless you wish to break our friendship."

The lady and the gentleman then went their several ways. Their intrigue lasted a long while without his ever being able to know who she was, though he had a marvellous longing to satisfy his curiosity on the point. He wearied his imagination in vain to guess who she might be, and could not conceive that there was a woman in the world who did not choose to be seen and loved. As he had heard some stupid preacher say that no one who had seen the face of the devil would ever love him, he imagined that she might possibly be some evil spirit. To clear up his doubts, he resolved to know who she was who received him so graciously. The next time, therefore, that she sent for him, he took some chalk, and in the act of embracing her, marked her shoulder without her perceiving it. As soon as she had left him, he hastened to the princess's chamber, and stationed himself at the door to observe the shoulders of the ladies who entered. It was not long before he saw that same Jambicque advance to the door, with such an air of lofty disdain, that he durst not think of scrutinising her like the others, feeling assured that she could not be the person he sought. But when her back was turned, he could not help seeing the mark of the chalk, though such was his astonishment he could hardly believe his own eyes. However, after having well considered her figure, which corresponded precisely to that he was in the habit of touching in the dark, he was convinced that it was she herself; and he was very glad to see that a woman who had never been suspected of having a gallant, and was renowned for having refused so many worthy gentlemen, had at last fixed upon him alone.

Love, who never remains in one mood, could not suffer him long to enjoy that satisfaction. The gentleman conceived such a good opinion of his own powers of pleasing, and flattered himself with such fair hopes, that he resolved to make his love known to her, imagining that when he had done so, he should have reason to love her still more passionately. One day, when the princess was walking in the garden, the Lady Jambicque turned into an alley by herself. The gentleman, seeing her alone, went to converse with her, and feigning not to have seen her elsewhere, said to her, "I have long loved you, mademoiselle, but durst not tell you so, for fear of offending you. This constraint is so irksome to me that I must speak or die; for I do not believe that any one can love you as I do."

Here the Lady Jambicque cut him short, and looking sternly upon him, "Have you ever heard," she said, "that I had a lover? I trow not; and I am amazed at your presumption in daring to address such language to a lady of my character. You have seen enough of me here to be aware that I shall never love any one but my husband. Beware, then, how you venture again to speak to me in any such way."

Astonished at such profound hypocrisy, the gentleman could not help laughing. "You have not always been so rigid, madam," he said. "What is the use of dissembling with me? Is it not better we should love perfectly than imperfectly?"

"I neither love you perfectly nor imperfectly," replied Jambicque, "but regard you just as I do my mistress's other servants. But if you continue to speak to me in this manner, I am very likely to hate you in such sort, that you will repent of having given me provocation."

The gentleman, pushing his point, rejoined, "Where are the caresses, mademoiselle, which you bestow upon me when I cannot see you? Why deprive me of them now that day reveals your exquisite beauty to me?"

"You are out of your senses," exclaimed Jambicque, making a great sign of the cross, "or you are the greatest liar in the world; for I don't believe I ever bestowed on you more or less caresses than I do this moment. What is it you mean, pray?"

The poor gentleman, thinking to force her from her subterfuges, named the place where he had met her, and told her of the mark he had put upon her with chalk in order to recognise her. Her exasperation was then so excessive, that instead of confessing, she told him he was the most wicked of men to have invented such an infamous lie against her, but that she would try to make him repent it. Knowing what influence she had with her mistress, he tried to appease her, but all in vain. She rushed from him in fury, and went to where her mistress was walking, who quitted the company with her to converse with Jambicque, whom she loved as herself. The princess, seeing her so agitated, asked her what was the matter? Jambicque concealed nothing, but told her all the gentleman had said, putting it in so artful a manner and so much to the poor gentleman's disadvantage, that his mistress that very evening sent him orders to go home instantly, without saying a word to any one, and to remain there until further orders. He obeyed for fear of worse. As long as Jambicque was with the princess he remained in exile, and never heard from Jambicque, who had warned him truly that he should lose her if ever he tried to know her.*

You may see, ladies, how she, who preferred the world's respect to her conscience, lost both the one and the other; for everybody now knows what she wished to conceal from her lover; and through her desire to avoid being mocked by one alone, she has now become an object of derision to all the world. It cannot be said in her excuse that hers was an ingenuous love, the simplicity of which claims every one's pity; for what makes her doubly deserving of condemnation is that her design was to cover the wickedness of her heart with the mantle of glory and honour, and pass before God

---

* Brantôme (*Dames Galantes*, Discours ii.) gives a detailed analysis of this novel in a very lively style, and says of the too-talkative gallant, "Those who knew the temper of this gentleman will hold him excused, for he was neither cold nor discreet enough to play that game, and mask himself with that discretion. According to what I have heard from my mother, who was in the Queen of Navarre's service and knew some secrets of her novels, and was herself one of the confabulators (*devisantes*), it was my late uncle La Chastaigneraye, who was brusque, hasty, and rather volatile." This Seigneur de La Chastaigneraye is the same who fought the famous duel with the Sire de Jarnac, in which he was killed with a sword-pass known by the name of *coup de Jarnac*. Brantôme says that the lady was a *grande dame*, but he does not name her

and man for what she was not. But He who will not give His glory to another was pleased to unmask her, and make her appear doubly infamous.

"Truly," said Oisille, "this woman was wholly inexcusable; for who can say a word for her, since God, honour, and love are her accusers?"

"Who?" exclaimed Hircan, "why, pleasure and folly, two great advocates for the ladies."

"If we had no other advocates," said Parlamente, "our cause would be ill defended. Those who let pleasure get the better of them, ought no longer to call themselves women, but men; for the honour of that sex is not sullied but exalted by lust and concupiscence. A man who revenges himself on his enemy, and kills him for giving him the lie, passes for a brave man, and is so, indeed. It is the same thing when a man loves a dozen women besides his own wife. But the honour of women has a different foundation—that is to say, gentleness, patience, and chastity."

"You speak of the wise among them," rejoined Hircan.

"I do not choose to know any others," said Parlamente.

"If there were no foolish ones," said Nomerfide, "those who would fain be believed by everybody would prove to have been often liars."

"Pray, Nomerfide," said Geburon, "let me give you my voice, in order that you may tell us a tale to that purpose."

"Since virtue constrains me, and you make it my turn, I will tell you what I know to that effect. I have not heard any one here present fail to speak to the disadvantage of the Cordeliers, and in pity for them I propose to say some good of them in the tale you are about to hear."

NOVEL XLIV.

A CORDELIER RECEIVED A DOUBLE ALMS FOR TELLING THE PLAIN TRUTH.

A Cordelier came to the house of Sedan to ask Madame de Sedan, who was of the house of Coucy, for a pig she used to give them every year as alms. Monseigneur de Sedan, who was a wise and facetious man, made the good father eat at his table, and to put him on his mettle, he said to him among other things, "You do well, good father, to make your gatherings whilst you are not known, for I am greatly afraid that if once your hypocrisy is discovered, you will no longer have the bread of poor children earned by the sweat of their fathers." The Cordelier was not abashed by this remark, but replied, "My lord, our order is so well founded that it will endure as long as the world, for our foundation will never fail so long as there are men and women on earth." Monseigneur de Sedan being curious to know what was this foundation he spoke of, pressed him strongly to tell. After many attempts to excuse himself, the Cordelier said, "Know, my lord, that we are founded on the folly of women; and as long as there is a foolish woman in the world, we shall not die of hunger."

Madame de Sedan, who was very choleric, hearing this speech, flew into such a passion, that if her husband had not been there, she would have had the Cordelier roughly handled; and she swore very decidedly he should never have the pig she had promised; but Monseigneur de Sedan, seeing he had not disguised the truth, swore he should have two, and had them sent to his monastery.

Thus it was, ladies, that the Cordelier being sure that ladies' offerings could not fail him, contrived to have the favour and the alms of men for speaking the plain truth. Had he been a flatterer and dissembler, he would have been more pleasing to the ladies, but not so profitable to himself and his brethren.

The novel was not ended without making the company laugh, especially those of them who knew the lord and lady of Sedan. "The Cordeliers then," said Hircan, "ought never to preach with a view to make women wise, since their folly serves them so well."

"They do not preach to them to be wise," said Parlamente, "but only to believe themselves so; for those women who are wholly mundane and foolish, give them no great alms; but those who by reason of frequenting their monasteries, and carrying paternosters marked with a death's head, and wearing their hoods lower than others, think themselves the wisest, are those who may well be called foolish; for they rest their salvation on the confidence they have in those unrighteous men whom, in consideration of a little seeming, they esteem demigods."

"But who can help believing them," said Ennasuite, "seeing that they are ordained by our prelates to preach the Gospel, and reprove us for our sins?"

"Those can," replied Parlamente, "who have known their hypocrisy, and who know the difference between God's doctrine and the devil's."

"Jesus!" exclaimed Ennasuite, "can you suppose that those people would dare to preach a bad doctrine?"

"Suppose?" returned Parlamente, "nay, I am sure there is nothing they believe less than the Gospel; I mean the bad ones among them, for I know many good men who preach the Scriptures purely and simply, and live likewise without scandal, without ambition or covetousness, and in chastity that is neither feigned nor constrained. But the streets are not so full of such men as of their opposites; and the good tree is known by its fruits."

"In good faith, I thought," said Ennasuite, "that we were bound under pain of mortal sin to believe all they tell us from the pulpit of truth, when they speak only of what is in Holy Writ, or adduce the expositions of holy doctors divinely inspired."

"For my part," said Parlamente, "I cannot ignore the fact that there have been among them men of very bad faith; for I know well that one of them, a doctor in theology and a principal of their order, wanted to persuade several of his brethren that the Gospel was no more worthy of belief than Cæsar's Commentaries, or other histories written by authentic doctors; and from the hour I heard that I would never believe a preacher's word, unless I found it conformable to God's, which is the true touchstone for distinguishing true words and false."

"Be assured," said Oisille, "that they who often read it in humility will never be deceived by human fictions or inventions; for whoso has a mind filled with truth cannot receive a lie."

"Yet it seems to me that a simple person is more easily deceived than another," observed Simontault.

"Yes," said Longarine, "if you esteem silliness to be simplicity."

"I say," returned Simontault, "that a good, gentle, simple woman is more easily beguiled than one who is cunning and crafty."

"I suppose you know some one who is too full of such goodness," said Nomerfide; "if so, tell us about her."

"Since you have so well guessed, I will not disappoint you," replied Simontault; "but you must promise me not to weep. Those who say, ladies, that your craftiness exceeds that of men, would find it hard to produce such an example as that I am now about to relate to you, wherein I intend to set forth the great craft of a husband, and the simplicity and good-nature of his wife."

[The preceding novel and epilogue, which are found in all the MSS., are wanting in the edition of 1585. Claude Gouget has substituted the following for them in that of 1559.]

HOW TWO LOVERS CLEVERLY CONSUMMATED THEIR AMOURS, THE ISSUE OF WHICH WAS HAPPY.

THERE were in Paris two citizens, one of them a lawyer, the other a silk-mercer, who had always been great friends, and on the most familiar terms. The lawyer had a son named Jacques, a young man very presentable in good society, who often visited his father's friend, the mercer; but it was for sake of a handsome daughter the latter had, named Françoise, to whom Jacques paid his court so well, that he became assured she loved him no less than he loved her. Whilst matters stood thus, an army was sent into Provence to oppose the descent which Charles of Austria was about to make in that quarter; and Jacques was forced to join that army, being called out in his order. He had hardly arrived in the camp when he received news of his father's death. This was a double grief to him: on the one hand, from the loss of his father; on the other hand, from the obstacles he plainly foresaw he should encounter on his return to seeing his mistress as often as he had hoped. Time allayed the first of these griefs, but made him feel the other more acutely. As death is in the course of nature, and it is usual for parents to die before their children, the grief that is felt for their loss gradually subsides. But it is quite otherwise with love; for instead of bringing us death, it brings us life, by giving us children who render us immortal, so to speak; and this it is, principally, which renders our desires the more ardent.

Jacques being then returned to Paris, thought of nothing but how to renew his intimacy with the mercer, in order to traffic in the choicest of his wares under pretext of pure friendship. As Françoise had beauty and sprightliness, and had long been marriageable, she had had several suitors during the absence of Jacques; but whether it was that her father was stingy, or that, having but that one child, he wished to establish her well, he had not made much account of any of these suitors. As people do not wait now-a-days before talking scandal until they have just grounds for it, especially where the honour of our sex is concerned, this set people talking ill of Françoise. Her father not choosing to do like many others, who, instead of reproving the faults of their wives and children, seem, on the contrary, to incite them thereto, did not shut his ears or his eyes to the popular opinion, but watched his daughter so closely, that even those who sought her with no other intention than marriage saw her but rarely, and then only in her mother's presence. It need not be asked whether or not such vigilance was irksome to Jacques, who could not conceive that they should treat her so rigorously without some important reason to him unknown. This conjecture distressed him, and distracted his feelings between love and jealousy.

Resolved at all cost to know what might be this mysterious reason, he proposed to ascertain in the first place if she still retained the same tender sentiments towards him; and he went about so assiduously that at last he found means one morning at mass to place himself near her, when he perceived from her manner that she was as glad to see him as he her. As he knew that the mother was not so strict as the father, he sometimes took the liberty, when he met them on their way to church, to accost them familiarly and with ordinary politeness; and this as if he had met them by mere chance, the whole being with a view to prepare matters for the design he meditated.

By-and-by, when the year of mourning for his father was nearly expired, he resolved, when changing his garments, to put himself on a good footing, and do honour to his ancestors. He spoke of his intention to his mother, who approved of it, and longed the more ardently to see him well married, as she had but two children, himself and a daughter, who was already settled in life. Like an honourable lady as she was, she encouraged her son to virtue by setting before him the example of a great number of young men of his own age, who were making way by themselves, or who at least showed that they were worthy of the parents from whom they derived their being. As the only question now was where they should make their purchases, the good lady said to her son, "It is my opinion, Jacques, that we cannot do better than go to Daddy Pierre's (this was the father of Françoise). He is one of our friends, and would not cheat us."

This was tickling her son where he itched; however, he stood out, and said, "We will go and deal where we are best served, and cheapest. However, as Daddy Pierre was the intimate friend of my late father, I shall be very glad to give him the first call before we go elsewhere."

One morning, accordingly, the mother and son went to see the Sire Pierre, who received them very well, as you know that merchants can do when they scent profit. They had quantities of silk unfolded for their inspection, and chose what suited them; but they could not agree upon the price, for Jacques haggled on purpose, because his mistress's mother did not make her appearance. At last they left the place without making any purchase, and went to look elsewhere; but Jacques could see nothing he liked in any house but his mistress's, and they returned thither some time afterwards. Françoise's mother was there, and gave them the best possible reception. After the little ceremonies were gone through which are practised in such shops, the mercer's wife putting a higher price on her goods than her husband had done, "You are very hard, madam," said Jacques; "but I see how it is. Father is dead, and our friends don't know us now." So saying, he pretended to wipe his eyes, as if the thought of his father had drawn tears from them; but this was only a device to help things forward. His mother, who took the matter up in perfect good faith, said thereupon, in a dolorous tone, "Since the death of my poor good man, we are visited no more than if we had never been known. Little do people care for poor widows."

Hereupon there ensued new demonstrations of friendship, and mutual promises to visit more frequently than ever. Some other merchants now came in, and were taken by the mercer himself into the back shop. The young man took advantage of this favourable moment to say to his mother, "Madame was formerly in the habit of visiting, on Saints' days, the holy places in our neighbourhood, especially the convents. If she would take the trouble sometimes to look in upon us in passing, and take her wine, she would do us much honour and pleasure."

The mercer's wife, who suspected nothing, replied that for more than a fortnight past she had intended to go into their quarter; that she would probably do so on Sunday, if the weather was fine, and would not fail to call and see the lady. The conclusion of this affair was followed by that of the bargain for the silks; for it was no time to stand out for a trifle, and risk losing such a fine opportunity.

Things being in this position, and Jacques considering that he could not bring his project to bear without assistance, he resolved to confide the secret of it to a trusty friend. The two took such good measures together, that nothing remained but to put them in execution. Sunday being come, the mercer's wife and her daughter failed not, on their return from their devotions, to call upon the widow, whom they found chatting with one of her female neighbours in a gallery in the garden, whilst her daughter was walking about the alleys with her brother and his friend, whose name was Olivier. On seeing his mistress, Jacques so commanded his face, that not the least change was visible in it, and he went to welcome the mother and daughter with a gay and unembarrassed air. As elderly people usually seek each other's society, the three old ladies seated themselves on a bench with their backs turned to the garden, into which the two lovers gradually moved off, and joined the other two who were walking there. After a little exchange of compliments, all four renewed their promenade, in the course of which Jacques recounted his piteous case to Françoise so movingly, that she could neither grant nor refuse what her lover sued for. It needed no more to make him aware that she was smitten.

I must tell you, that during this ambulatory conversation, in order to prevent suspicion, they frequently passed to and fro before the bench on which the good women were seated, taking care always to talk of trivial and indifferent matters, and now and then romping in the garden. After the old ladies had been accustomed to the noise for half an hour, Jacques made a sign to Olivier, who played his part with the other girl so well, that she did not notice the two lovers going into an orchard full of cherries, and inclosed with thick hedges of roses and very tall gooseberry-bushes. They pretended to go into a corner of the orchard to pluck almonds, but it was to pluck prunes. There Jacques, instead of giving his mistress a green gown, gave her a red one, for the colour flushed into her cheeks to find herself surprised before she was aware. They had so quickly gathered their prunes, because they were ripe, that Olivier could not have believed it, but that the girl drooped her head, and looked so ashamed. This betokened the truth to him, for before she walked with her head erect, without any fear that the vein in her eye, which ought to be red, should be seen to have the azure hue. Perceiving her confusion, Jacques recalled her to her usual deportment by suitable remonstrances.

The lovers took two or three more turns about the garden, but not without much crying and sobbing on the part of the fair one. "Alas!" she exclaimed, "was it for this you loved me? If I could have thought it, my God! What shall I do? I am undone for ever. What account will you make of me henceforth, at least if you are one of those who love only for pleasure? Oh, that I had died before committing such a fault!" Then followed another violent burst of tears. But Jacques exerted himself so much to console her, and made such promises, confirmed by so many oaths, that before they had taken three more turns about the garden, Jacques made another sign to his friend, and they entered the orchard again by another path. In spite of all she could do, she could not help receiving more pleasure from this second green gown than from the first. In short, she liked it so well that they resolved then and there to seek means for meeting oftener and more commodiously until such time as her father should be more favourably inclined.

A young woman, a neighbour of the mercer's, distantly related to Jacques, and a good friend to Françoise, was of great help to them in bringing the good man to reason. I am informed that they continued their intrigue without discovery or scandal until the consummation of their marriage. Françoise, who was an only child, proved to be very rich for the daughter of a shopkeeper. It is true that Jacques had to wait for the greater part of his wife's fortune until the death of the father, who was so close-fisted and distrustful that what he held in one hand he imagined the other stole from him.

There, ladies, you have an example of a tender connexion well begun, well continued, and better ended: for although it is usual with men to despise a woman or a girl as soon as she has given you what you sue to her for with most eagerness, yet this young man, loving well and in good faith, and having found in his mistress what every husband desires to find in his bride; knowing, moreover, that the girl was of good family, and correct in all but the fault into which he himself had led her, would not commit adultery elsewhere, or trouble the peace of another household: conduct for which I deem him highly commendable.

"They were both very blamable, however," said Oisille; "nor was the friend even excusable for having ministered to the crime, or at least acquiesced in such a rape."

"Do you call it a rape when both parties are willing?" said Saffredent. "Are there any better marriages than those which are thus brought about by furtive amours? It has passed into a proverb that marriages are made in heaven; but this applies neither to forced marriages nor to those which are made for money, and which are regarded as well and duly approved as soon as the father and mother have given their consent."

"You may say what you please," replied Oisille, "but parental authority must be obeyed, and if there be no father or mother, the will of the other relations must be respected. Otherwise, if every one was free to marry according to fancy, how many cornuted marriages would there not be? Can any one imagine that a young man and a girl from twelve to fifteen years of age know what is good for them? Any one who should carefully examine, would find that there are as many unhappy marriages among those made for love as those made by constraint. Young people who do not know what they want take the first they meet without inquiry; and then, when they come gradually to know the mistake they have committed, this knowledge leads them into still greater errors. Those, on the contrary, who have not been married voluntarily, have entered into that engagement by the advice and at the solicitation of persons who have seen more and possess more judgment than themselves: so that when they come to experience the good they did not know, they enjoy it much better, and embrace it with much more affection."

"Ay, madam," said Hircan, "but you forget that the girl was of ripe years and marriageable, and that she knew the injustice of her father, who let her virginity grow musty for fear of rubbing the rust off his crown-pieces. Do you not know that nature is a frisky jade? She loved, she was loved, she found what she wanted ready to her hand, and she might call to mind the old proverb: 'She that will not when she may, when she will she shall have nay.' All these considerations, added to the promptitude of the assailant, left her no time to defend herself. It has been remarked, too, that immediately afterwards a great change was noticed in her countenance. This change was the result of her dissatisfaction at having had so little time to judge whether the thing was good or bad: accordingly, she did not require very long coaxing to prevail on her to make a second trial."

"For my part," said Longarine, "I should not think her excusable but for the good faith of the young man, who, acting like an honest man, did not forsake her, but took her such as he had made her; for which I think him the more deserving of praise, as youth in these days is very corrupt. I do not pretend for all that to excuse his first fault, which virtually amounted to rape with regard to the daughter, and subornation with regard to the mother."

"Not at all, not at all," interrupted Dagoucin; "there was neither rape nor subornation, but all happened voluntarily, both on the part of the mothers, who did not prevent it, though they were duped, and on that of the girl, who liked it well, and never complained."

"All this," said Parlamente, "was only the consequence of the good-nature and simplicity of the mercer's wife, who in good faith led her daughter to the butchery without knowing it."

"Why not say to the wedding?" said Simontault, "since this simplicity was not less advantageous to the girl than it was prejudicial to a wife who was too easily the dupe of her husband."

"Since you know the story," said Nomerfide, "tell it us."

"With all my heart," replied Simontault, "on condition you promise me not to weep. Those who say, ladies, that you have more craft than men, would find it hard to produce an example like that of which I am going to speak. I purpose to exhibit to you not only the great craft of a husband, but also the extreme simplicity and good-nature of his wife."

NOVEL XLV.

A HUSBAND, GIVING THE INNOCENTS TO HIS SERVANT GIRL, PLAYS UPON HIS WIFE'S SIMPLICITY.

There was at Tours a shrewd, cunning fellow, who was upholsterer to the late Duke of Orleans, son of King Francis I. Though this upholsterer had become deaf in consequence of a severe illness, he nevertheless retained the full use of his wits, and was so well endowed in that respect, that there was not a man in his trade more cunning than himself. As for other matters, you shall see from what I am about to relate to you how he contrived to acquit himself. He had married a good and honourable woman, with whom he lived very peaceably. He was greatly afraid of displeasing her, and she also studied to obey him in all things. But for all the great affection the husband had for his wife, he was so charitable, that he often gave his female neighbours what belonged to her; but this he always did as secretly as possible. They had a good stout wench as a servant, of whom the upholsterer fell in love. Fearing, however, lest his wife should perceive it, he affected often to scold her, saying she was the laziest creature he had ever seen; but that he did not wonder at it since her mistress never beat her.

One day, when they were talking of giving the Innocents,* the upholsterer said to his wife, "It would be a great charity to give them to that lazy jade of yours, but it would not do for her to receive them from your hand, for it is too weak, and your heart is too tender. If I were to put my own hand to the job, we should be better served by her than we are." The poor woman, suspecting nothing, begged that he

---

* The learned Gregory, in his treatise on the Boy Bishop, preserved in his posthumous works, observes that "it hath been a custom, and yet is elsewhere, to whip up the children upon Innocents' Day morning, that the memorie of Herod's murder of the Innocents might stick the closer, and in a moderate proportion to act over the crueltie again in kinde." This custom is mentioned by Haspinian, De Orig. Festor. Christianor. fol. 160: "Hujus lanienæ truculentissimæ ut pueri Christianorum recordentur, et simul discant odium, persecutionem, crucem, exilium, egestatemque statim cum nato Christo incipere, virgis cædi solent in aurora hujus diei adhuc in lectulis jacentes a parentibus suis." That which was at first a serious parody of the martyrdom of Bethlehem, afterwards degenerated into a jocular usage, and persons past the age of childhood, young women especially, were made to play the part of the Innocents. It is related that a Seigneur du Rivau, taking leave of some ladies to join a hunting-party at a considerable distance, heard one of them whisper to another, "We shall sleep at our ease, and pass the Innocents without receiving them." This put Du Rivau on his mettle. He kept his appointment, galloped back twenty leagues by night, arrived at the lady's house at dawn on Innocents' Day, surprised her in bed, and used the privilege of the season. "Vous savez," says the author of the *Escraignes* (*Veillées*) *Dijonnaises*, "que l'on a à Dijon cette peute coutume de fouetter les filles le jour des Innocens, la quelle est entretenue par les braves amoureux, pour avoir occasion de donner quelque chose aux estrennes à leurs amoureuses." Clement Marot has the following epigram on this subject:

> "Très chère sœur, si je savois où couche
> Votre personne au jour des Innocents,
> De bon matin j'irois en votre couche
> Veoir ce gent corps que j'aime entre cinq cents.
> Adonc ma main (veu l'ardeur que je sens)
> Ne se pourroit bonnement contenter
> De vous toucher, tenir, taster, tenter:
> Et si quelqu'un survenoit d'aventure,
> Semblant ferois de vous innocenter,
> Seroit-ce pas honneste couverture?"

would perform the operation, confessing that she had neither the heart nor the strength to do it. The husband willingly undertook the commission, and as if he intended to flog the wench soundly, he bought the finest rods he could procure; and to show that he had no mind to spare her, he steeped them in pickle, so that the poor woman felt more compassion for her servant than suspicion of her husband.

Innocents' Day being come, the upholsterer rose betimes, went to the upper room, where the servant lay alone, and gave her the Innocents in a very different manner from that he had talked of to his wife. The servant fell a-crying, but her tears were of no avail. For fear, however, that his wife should come up, he began to whip the bedpost at such a rate that he made the rods fly in pieces, and then he carried them broken as they were to his wife. "I think, my dear," said he, showing them to her, "that your servant will not soon forget the Innocents."

The upholsterer having gone out of doors, the servant went and threw herself at her mistress's feet, and complained that her husband had behaved to her in the most shameful way that ever a servant was treated. The good woman imagining that she spoke of the flogging she had received, interrupted her, and said, "My husband has done well, and just as I have been begging him to do this month and more. If he has made you smart I am very glad of it. You may lay it all to me. He has not given you half as much as he ought."

When the girl perceived that her mistress approved of such an act, she concluded that it was not such a great sin as she had supposed, seeing that a woman who was considered so virtuous was the cause of it; and so she never ventured to complain of it again. The upholsterer, seeing that his wife was as glad to be deceived as he was to deceive her, resolved frequently to give her the same satisfaction, and gained the servant's consent so well, that she cried no more for getting the Innocents. He continued the same course for a long time without his wife's knowing anything of the matter, until winter came, and there was a great fall of snow. As he had given his servant the Innocents in the garden on the green grass, he took a fancy to give them to her also on the snow; and one morning before any one was awake, he took her out into the garden in her shift, to make the crucifix on the snow. They romped and pelted each other, and among the sport that of the Innocents was not forgotten. One of the neighbours meanwhile had gone to her window to see what sort of weather it was. The window looked right over the upholsterer's garden, and the woman saw the game of the Innocents that was going on there, and was so shocked that she resolved to inform her good gossip, that she might no longer be the dupe of such a wicked husband and vicious servant. After the upholsterer had finished his fine game, he looked round to see if he had been noticed by any one, and to his great vexation he saw his neighbour at her window. But as he knew how to give all sorts of colours to his tapestry, so he thought he should be able to put such a colour on this fact that his neighbour would be no less deceived than his wife. No sooner had he got to bed again than he made his wife get up in her shift, and took her to the very spot where he had been toying with the servant. He frolicked awhile with her at snowball throwing, as he had done with the servant; next he gave her the Innocents as he had done to the other; and then they went back to bed.

The next time the upholsterer's wife went to mass, her neighbour and good friend failed not to meet her there, and entreated her with very great earnestness, but without saying more, to discharge her servant, who was a good-for-nothing, dangerous creature. The upholsterer's wife said she would do no such thing, unless the other told her why she thought the wench so good-for-nothing and dangerous. The neighbour, thus pressed, stated at last that she had seen her one morning in the garden with her husband.

"It was I, gossip dearie," replied the good woman, laughing.

"What!" cried the neighbour. "Stripped to your shift in the garden at four o'clock in the morning!"

"Yes, gossip," said the upholsterer's wife. "In good sooth, it was myself."

"They pelted each other with snow," continued the neighbour, "and he played with her teaties and all that sort of thing as familiarly as you please."

"Yes, gossip, it was myself."

"But, gossip," rejoined the neighbour, "I saw them do upon the snow a thing that seems to me neither decent nor proper."

"That may be, gossip dearie," replied the upholsterer's wife; "but as I told you before and tell you again, it was myself and no one else that did all this; for my good husband and I divert ourselves in that way together. Don't be shocked, pray. You know that we are bound to please our husbands."

The end of the matter was that the neighbour went home much more disposed to wish that she had such a husband, than to pity her good friend. When the upholsterer came home, his wife repeated to him the whole conversation she had had with her neighbour. "It is well for you, my dear," he replied, "that you are a good and sensible woman; for but for that, we should have been separated long ago. But I trust that by God's grace we shall love each other in time to come as much as we have in the past, and that to His glory, and to our own comfort and satisfaction."

"Amen, my dear," said the good woman. "I hope too that you will never find me fail to do my part towards maintaining the good understanding between us."*

One must be very incredulous, ladies, if, after hearing so true a story, one were of opinion that there was as much wickedness in you as in men; though, to say the truth, without wronging any one, one cannot help coming to the conclusion with regard to the man and woman in question, that neither the one nor the other was good for anything.

"This man was prodigiously wicked," said Parlamente; "for on the one hand he deceived his wife, and on the other his servant."

---

* Dunlop thinks that this novel was probably taken from the fabliau of some Trouveur, who had obtained it from the East, as it corresponds with the story of the Shopkeeper's Wife in Nakshebi's Persian Tales, known by the name of Tooti Nameh, or Tales of a Parrot. The Queen of Navarre's version of the story has been imitated by Lafontaine, under the title of La Servante Justifiée. He was particularly struck by the exceedingly comic reiteration of the phrase, "It was I, gossip," in the dialogue between the simple-witted wife and her neighbour, and says in his opening lines:

"Pour cette fois, la Reine de Navarre
D'un c'ETOIT MOI naïf autant que rare,
Entretiendra dans ces vers le lecteur."

"You cannot have rightly understood the story," said Hircan; "for it states that he satisfied them both in one morning: a great feat, considering the contrariety of their interests."

"In that respect, he was doubly a knave," replied Parlamente, "to satisfy the simplicity of the one by a lie, and the malice of the other by an act of vice. But I am quite aware that such as these will always be pardoned when they have such judges as you."

"I assure you, however," rejoined Hircan, "that I will never undertake anything so great or so difficult, for provided I satisfy you, my day will not have been ill employed."

"If mutual love does not content the heart," returned Parlamente, "all the rest cannot do so."

"That is true," said Simontault. "I am persuaded there is no greater pain than to love, and not to be loved."

"In order to be loved," said Parlamente, "one should turn to those who love; but very often those women who will not love are the most loved, and those men love most who are the least loved."

"That reminds me," said Oisille, "of a tale which I had not intended to introduce among good ones."

"Pray tell it us," said Simontault.

"I will do so with pleasure," replied Oisille.

NOVEL XLVI.

A SANCTIMONIOUS CORDELIER ATTEMPTS TO DEBAUCH THE WIFE OF A JUDGE, AND ACTUALLY RAVISHES A YOUNG LADY, WHOSE MOTHER HAD FOOLISHLY AUTHORISED HIM TO CHASTISE HER FOR LYING TOO LATE IN BED.

In the town of Angoulême, where Count Charles, father of King Francis, often resided, there was a Cordelier named De Vale, who was esteemed a learned man and a great preacher. One Advent he preached in the town before the count, and was so much admired that those who knew him eagerly invited him to dinner. Among these was the Judge of Exempts of the county, who had married a handsome and virtuous wife, of whom the Cordelier was dying for love, though he had not the boldness to tell her so; she, however, perceived it, and held him and his passion in disdain. One day he observed her going up to the garret all alone, and thinking to surprise her, he went up after her; but on hearing his steps she turned round, and asked whither he was going. "I am coming after you," he replied. "I have a secret to tell you."

"Don't come after me, good father," said the judge's wife, "for I do not choose to talk with such as you in secret, and if you come another step higher you shall repent of it."

The friar, seeing her alone, took no heed of her words, and ran up; but she being a woman of spirit, as soon as he was at the top gave him a kick in the belly, saying, "Down, down, sir," and sent him rolling from the top to the bottom. The poor friar was so much ashamed of his discomfiture that he forgot his hurt, and ran out of the town as fast as he could, for he was sure she would not conceal the matter from her husband. No more she did, nor from the count and countess, so that the Cordelier durst not appear again in their presence.

To complete his wickedness, he went away to the house of a lady who loved the Cordeliers above all other folk; and after he had preached a sermon or two before her, he cast eyes upon her daughter, who was very handsome; and because she did not rise in the morning to go and hear his sermon, he often scolded her before her mother, who used to say, "I wish to God, father, she had tasted a little of the discipline which you and your pious brethren administer to each other." The good father vowed he would give her some of it if she continued to be so lazy, and the mother begged he would do so. A day or two after the good father entered the lady's room, and not seeing her daughter, asked where she was. "She fears you so little, that she is still in bed," replied the lady.

"Assuredly it is a very bad habit in young people to be so lazy," replied the friar. "Few people make much account of the sin of laziness; but for my part I esteem it one of the most dangerous of all, both for the body and the soul; wherefore you should chastise her well for it; or, if you will leave

the business to me, I warrant I will cure her of lying in bed
at an hour when she should be at her devotions."

The poor lady, believing that he was a good man, begged
he would be pleased to correct her daughter, which he proceeded to do forthwith. Going up a little wooden staircase
he found the girl all alone in bed, fast asleep, and sleeping
as she was, he ravished her. The poor girl, waking up, knew
not whether it was a man or a devil, and began to scream as
loud as she could, and cry for help to her mother, who called
out from the foot of the stairs, "Do not spare her, sir; give
it her again, and chastise the naughty hussey." When the
Cordelier had accomplished his wicked purpose he went down
to the lady, and said to her with his face all on fire, "I think,
madam, your daughter will not forget the discipline I have
given her."

After thanking him heartily the mother went up to her
daughter, who was making such lamentation as a virtuous
woman well might who had been the victim of such a crime;
and when she had learned the truth she sent everywhere to
look for the Cordelier, but he was already far away, and never
afterwards was he found in the realm of France.

You see, ladies, what comes of giving such commissions to
persons who are not fit to be trusted with them. The cor-
rection of men belongs to men, and of women to women; for
in correcting men, women would be as pitiful as men would
be cruel in correcting women.

"Jesus! madam," said Parlamente, "what a wicked villain
of a Cordelier!"

"Say, rather," said Hircan, "what a silly fool of a mother,
who, cajoled by hypocrisy, allowed so much familiarity to one
of a class of men who ought never to be seen but in church."

"Truly," said Parlamente, "I own she was one of the
silliest mothers that ever was; and if she had been as wise
as the judge's wife, she would rather have made him go down
the stairs than up them. But your half-angel devil is the
most dangerous of all, and knows so well how to transform
himself into an angel of light, that one makes it matter of
conscience to suspect him for what he is; and it seems to me
that the person who is not suspicious deserves praise."

"Nevertheless," said Oisille, "one ought to suspect the evil that is to be avoided; especially so should those who have charge of others; for it is better to suspect mischief where it does not exist, than to fall through foolishly believing in the harmlessness of that which does exist. I have never seen a woman deceived for being slow to believe the word of men, but many a one for having too readily put faith in lies. Therefore I say that the mischief which may happen cannot be too much suspected by those who have charge of men, women, towns, and states; for, in spite of the best watch, wickedness and treachery greatly prevail, and the shepherd who is not vigilant will always suffer from the wiles of the wolf."

"Nevertheless," said Dagoucin, "a suspicious person cannot maintain a perfect friendship, and many friends have been parted by a suspicion."

"Supposing that you know a case in point," said Oisille, "I call upon you to relate it."

"I know one so true that you will take pleasure in hearing it," replied Dagoucin. "I will tell you what is most sure to break friendship, ladies, and that is, when the very confidence of the friendship begins to give occasion for suspicion; for, as trusting a friend is the greatest honour one can do him, so doubting him is the greatest dishonour, for it shows that he is thought other than one would have him be, which is the cause of breaking many friendships and turning friends into enemies, as you will see by the tale I am about to relate to you."

[This novel is wanting in the edition of 1558, and the following is substituted for it in that of 1559.]

A CORDELIER'S SERMONS ON THE SUBJECT OF HUSBANDS
BEATING THEIR WIVES.

In Angoulême, where Count Charles, father of King Francis I., often made his residence, there was a Cordelier named De Valles, a man of knowledge, and so esteemed as a preacher, that he was selected to preach the Advent sermons before the count, a fact which still further enhanced his reputation. It happened during Advent, that a young scatterbrain of the town, who had married a young and very pretty woman, continued to run after other women right and left, just as dissolutely as though he were unmarried. The young wife, discovering this, could not conceal her resentment, and was often paid for it sooner and otherwise than she would have liked. All this did not hinder her from continuing her lamentations, and sometimes even from proceeding to abuse and railing, by which conduct she so exasperated her husband that he beat her black and blue, and then she made more noise than ever. The neighbours' wives, who knew the cause of their quarrels, could not keep silence, but cried out publicly in the streets, "Fie for shame! To the devil with such husbands!"

By good luck the Cordelier de Valles was passing that way. Having heard the noise, and learned the cause of it, he resolved to touch upon it next day in his sermon; and so he did, bringing in the subject of marriage, and the affection which ought to accompany it. He pronounced a eulogy on the wedded state, strongly censured those who violated its duties, and instituted a comparison between conjugal and parental love. Among other things, he said that a husband was more to be condemned for beating his wife than for beating his father or mother; "For," said he, " if you beat your father or mother, you will be sent for penance to Rome; but if you beat your wife, she and her female neighbours will send you to all the devils, that is to say, to hell. Now just see the difference there is between these two penances. One usually comes back from Rome; but from hell there is no returning. *Nulla est redemptio.*"

Subsequently he was informed that the women took advantage of what he had said, and that their husbands could no longer be masters: and this mischief he desired to remedy, as he had that under which the women had laboured. To this end, in another sermon he compared women to devils, and said that the two were man's greatest enemies and perpetual persecutors, which he could not get rid of, especially women. " In fact," said he, " the devils fly when they are shown the cross, and women do quite the contrary, for it is that which tames them, makes them go and come, and is the cause of their putting their husbands into no end of passions. Would you know, my good people," said he to the husbands, " the way this is to be remedied ? Here it is. When you see that your wives torment you incessantly, as is their wont, take the handle of the cross, and thrash them well with it. You will not have done this above three or four times before you will find yourselves the better for it, and will see that as the devil is driven away by the cross, so you will drive your wives away, and make them hold their tongues, by virtue of the handle of the same cross, provided it be not attached."

There, ladies, is a sample of the sermons of the venerable Cordelier de Valles, of whose life I will tell you no more, and for good reason. I will only say that for all he put a good face on the matter, for I knew the man, he was much more for the women than the men.

"He gave a very bad proof of that in this last sermon of his," said Parlamente, "since he instructed the men to maltreat them."

"You do not discern his cunning," said Hircan. "As you have not much experience of war, you cannot be acquainted with the stratagems that are necessary in it, one of the greatest of which is to create division in the enemy's camp; for then he is more easily beaten. Just so Master Monk knew that aversion and anger between husband and wife often occasion a loose rein to be given to female honour. As virtue is the guard of that honour, it finds itself under the fangs of the wolf before it is aware that it is gone astray."

"Be that as it may," said Parlamente, "I could never love a man who had sown discord between my husband and me to the extent of coming to blows; for with beating there is an end to love. Yet they can be so very demure, as I have heard, when they want to cajole some woman or another, and talk in so engaging a manner, that I am sure there would be more danger in listening to them in secret than in publicly receiving blows from a husband who in other respects was a good one."

"In truth," said Dagoucin, "they have made themselves so notorious that one has good cause to fear them, though, in my opinion, it is a laudable thing not to be suspicious."

"One ought, however, to suspect the evil that may be avoided," said Oisille, "and it is better to fear an imaginary ill than to fall into a real one for want of belief. For my part, I have never known a woman to have been beguiled for having been slow to believe men; but I have known many a one who has been beguiled for too easily believing their falsehoods. Consequently I maintain that those who have charge of men, women, towns, and states, can never too much fear and suspect the evil that may happen. Wickedness and treachery are so much in vogue, that one cannot be too much on one's guard: and the shepherd who is not vigilant will always be plundered by the sly and crafty wolf."

"It is nevertheless true," observed Dagoucin, "that a distrustful and suspicious person can never be a perfect friend; and many friendships have been broken upon a mere suspicion."

"If you know any example in point, tell it us," said Oisille.

"I know one," he replied, "so true, that you will feel pleasure in hearing it. I am going to tell you, ladies, of what most easily breaks friendship, and that is, when the very security of the friendship itself begins to inspire suspicion. As one cannot do a friend a greater honour than to trust in him, so likewise one cannot offer him a keener insult than to distrust him. The reason is, that one thereby shows that one believes him to be quite different from what one would have him to be; and this causes a breach between many good friends, and makes them enemies, an instance of which you shall see in the tale I am about to tell you."

NOVEL XLVII.

A GENTLEMAN OF THE PAYS DU PERCHE, DISTRUSTING HIS FRIEND, OBLIGES HIM TO DO HIM THE MISCHIEF OF WHICH HE HAS FALSELY SUSPECTED HIM.

NEAR the Pays du Perche there were two gentlemen, who from their childhood had been such perfectly good friends, that they had but one heart, one house, one bed, one table, and one purse. Their perfect friendship lasted a long while, without there having ever been the least dispute, or even a word that savoured of it; for they lived, not merely like two brothers, but like one man. One of the two married, but this did not diminish his affection for the other, or prevent his continuing to live with him as happily as before. When they happened to be in any place where beds were scarce he

made him sleep with his wife and him. It is true that he
himself lay in the middle. All their goods were in common,
so that the marriage, whatever might happen, never altered
this perfect friendship.

But as there is nothing solid and permanent in this world,
time brought about a change in the felicity of a too happy
household. The husband, forgetting the confidence he had in
his friend, became jealous without cause of him and his wife,
to whom he could not refrain from saying some harsh things,
whereat she was the more surprised, as he had ordered her
to treat his friend in all respects, save one, exactly like himself. All this, however, did not hinder him from forbidding
her to speak to him, unless it was in full company. She
made known this prohibition to her husband's friend, who
could not believe it, well knowing that he had not done or
thought anything with which his friend could be displeased.
As he was accustomed to conceal nothing from him, he told
him what he had heard, begging him to disguise nothing, for
it was his earnest desire not to give him, either in that or in
any other matter, the least cause to break a friendship of
such long duration.

The husband assured him he had never harboured such a
thought, and that those who had spread this report had foully
lied. "I know well," said the friend, "that jealousy is a
passion as insupportable as love; and though you were
jealous, and even of me, I should not be angry with you, for
you could not help it. But I should have reason to complain
of a thing which it is in your own power to do or not to do,
and that is, to conceal the matter from me, seeing that you
have never yet concealed from me any opinion or emotion
you have known. On my part, if I were in love with your
wife, you ought not to make it a crime in me, for love is a
fire which no one can master; but if I concealed the fact
from you, and sought means to make it known to your wife,
I should be the worst man that ever lived. Besides, though
you have a good wife and a worthy, I can assure you that
even though she were not yours, she is, of all the women I
have ever seen, the one I should give myself the least concern
about. I pray you, however, if you have the least suspicion,
to tell me so, in order to take measures accordingly, so that
our long friendship may not be broken for sake of a woman;

for even if I loved your wife above all the women in the world, I would never speak to her in that case, because I prefer your friendship to any other."

The husband protested to him with great oaths that he had never had such a thought, and begged that he would continue with him in all respects upon the old footing. "I will do so, since you desire it," replied the friend; "but allow me to tell you, that I never will live with you if, after this, you have such a thought of me, and keep a secret from me, or take it amiss."

They continued then to live together on the same terms as before, until, after some time, the husband's jealous fit came upon him more strongly than ever, and he ordered his wife no longer to show his friend the same fair countenance. She immediately informed the friend of this, and begged him not to speak to her, as she was forbidden to speak to him. The friend, seeing from this and from certain grimaces of his comrade that he had not kept his word, said to him in great indignation, "If you are jealous, my friend, that is a natural thing; but, after the oaths you have sworn to me, I cannot help telling you that I am aggrieved by your having concealed it so long. I had always believed that between your heart and mine there was no medium or obstacle; but I see with regret, and without any fault of mine, that I have not succeeded so well as I had hoped, since not only are you jealous of your wife and me, but you furthermore want to make a mystery of it, in order that your malady may endure so long that it may turn into hatred, and the closest friendship which has been seen in our day be succeeded by the most mortal enmity. I have done what I could to prevent this mischief, but since you believe me to be so wicked, and the reverse of all I have ever been, I solemnly vow to you that I will be such as you take me to be, and that I will never rest until I have had from your wife what you imagine I am striving for; and I warn you henceforth to be on your guard against me. Since suspicion has made you renounce my friendship, resentment makes me renounce yours."

The husband tried to make him believe that it was all a mistake, but the other would not listen to him. The furniture and property they had in common were divided, and this division was accompanied by that of their hearts, which had always been so united. The unmarried gentleman kept his word, and never rested until he had made his friend a cuckold.

So be it, ladies, to all those who distrust their wives without cause. A woman of honour sooner suffers herself to be overcome by despair than by all the pleasures in the world, and many husbands who are unjustly jealous behave so that at last they have just cause for jealousy, and make their wives do what they suspect them of. Some say that jealousy is love: I deny it; for though it issues from love as ashes from fire, just so it kills it, just as ashes smother the flame.

"I am persuaded," said Hircan, "that there is nothing more irritating to man or woman than to be unjustly suspected. For my own part, there is nothing would sooner make me break with my friends."

"Yet it is not a reasonable excuse," said Oisille, "for a woman to say she revenges herself for her husband's suspicions at the cost of her own shame; it is doing like a man who, not being able to kill his enemy, runs himself through with his own sword, or bites his own fingers when he cannot scratch him. She would have acted more wisely in never speaking to the friend, in order to show her husband that he was wrong in suspecting her, for time would have reconciled them."

"She acted like a woman of spirit," said Ennasuite; "and if there were many wives like her, their husbands would not be so outrageous."

"After all," said Longarine, "patience finally enables a chaste woman to triumph, and by it she should abide."

"A woman, however, may be sinless, and yet not chaste," observed Ennasuite.

"How do you mean?" asked Oisille.

"When she mistakes another for her husband," replied Ennasuite.

"And where is the fool!" exclaimed Parlamente, "who does not know the difference between her husband and another man, disguise himself as he may?"

"There have been, and there will be," rejoined Ennasuite, "those who have made such a mistake in perfect good faith, and who consequently are not culpable."

"If you know an instance of the kind, relate it to us," said Dagoucin; "to me it seems that innocence and sin are two very incompatible things."

"Well, ladies," said Ennasuite, "if the stories you have already heard have not sufficiently shown you that it is dangerous to lodge those who call us mundane, and look upon themselves as saints, and as persons much more regenerate than we are, here is a tale which will convince you not only that they are men like others, but that they have in them something diabolical exceeding the common wickedness of men."

NOVEL XLVIII.

A CORDELIER TOOK THE HUSBAND'S PLACE ON HIS WEDDING-NIGHT, WHILE THE LATTER WAS DANCING WITH THE BRIDAL PARTY.

A GIRL having been married in a village in Perigord, the wedding was celebrated at an inn, where all the relations and friends made merry with the best cheer. Two Cordeliers arrived on the wedding-day, and as it was not in accordance with propriety that they should be present at the marriage-feast, they had their suppers served up to them in their chamber. That one of the pair who had the most authority, and also the most villany, conceived that since he was not allowed to partake with the rest at board, he ought to have his share in bed, and resolved to show them a trick of his trade.

When evening came, and the dance was begun, the Cordelier gazed long on the bride from the window, and found her handsome and much to his taste. He inquired of the servant-girls which was the bridal-chamber, and learned, to his great satisfaction, that it was close to his own; and then, in order to arrive at his ends, he took care to watch well till he saw the old women steal off with the bride, as usual on such occasions. As it was still early, the husband would not quit the dance, on which he was so intent that he seemed to have forgotten his bride, which the Cordelier had not done; for as soon as his ears informed him that she had been put to bed, he threw off his grey robe, and went and took the bridegroom's place. The fear of being surprised did not allow him to remain there long. He rose, therefore, and went to the end of an alley, where his companion, whom he had left on the watch, signalled to him that the bridegroom was still dancing. The Cordelier, who had not satisfied his wicked lust, then went back to the bride, and stayed with her until his companion made the signal that it was time to go away.

The bridegroom went to bed, and the bride, who had been so briskly plied by the Cordelier, and wanted nothing but rest, could not help saying to her husband, "Have you made up your mind never to go to sleep, but to worry me all night long?" The poor husband, who had but just lain down, asked her in great amazement how he had worried her, seeing that he had been dancing all the evening. "Fine dancing, indeed," said the poor woman; "this is the third time you have come to bed. You had better go to sleep, I think."

Astounded at these words, the husband insisted on knowing the exact truth. After she had related to him the whole thing just as it had occurred, he got up instantly, making no doubt it was the Cordeliers, and went to their chamber, which, as before mentioned, was not far from his own. Not finding them, he shouted for help so loud, that all his friends came flocking round him. When he had told them the fact, every one helped him with candles, lanterns, and all the dogs in the village to hunt for the Cordeliers. Not finding them in the houses, they beat the country round, and caught them in the vineyards, where they treated them as they deserved; for after having well beaten them, they cut off their legs and arms, and left them among the vines to the care of Bacchus and Venus, of whom they were better disciples than of St. Francis.

Do not be astonished, ladies, if these people, who are distinguished by a manner of living so different from ours, do things which adventurers would be ashamed to do. You may rather wonder that they do not do worse, when God withdraws his grace from them. The habit does not always make the monk, as the proverb says. It often unmakes him, and pride is the cause.

"Mon Dieu!" said Oisille, "shall we never have done with tales about these monks?"

"If ladies, princes, and gentlemen are not spared," said Ennasuite, "it strikes me they have no reason to complain if they are not spared either. They are, for the most part, so useless, that no one would ever mention them if they did not commit some rascality worthy of memory; which makes good the proverb, that it is better to do mischief than to do nothing at all. Besides, the more diversified our bouquet, the handsomer it will be."

"If you promise not to be angry," said Hircan, "I will tell you a story of a great lady so insatiable in love, that you will excuse the poor Cordelier for having taken what he wanted where he found it, the more so as the lady of whom I have to speak, having plenty to eat, indulged her craving for tit-bits in a way that was too bad."

"Since we have vowed to speak the truth," said Oisille, "we have also vowed to hear it. You may then speak freely; for the evil we speak of men and women does not injure those who are the heroes of the tale, and only serves to cure people of the esteem they have for the creatures, and the confidence they might repose in them, by showing the faults to which they are subject, to the end that we may rest our hopes on none but Him who is alone perfect, and without whom every man is but imperfection."

"Well then," said Hircan, "I will proceed boldly with my story."

NOVEL XLIX.

OF A COUNTESS WHO DIVERTED HERSELF ADROITLY WITH LOVE SPORT, AND HOW HER GAME WAS DISCOVERED.

At the court of one of the kings of France, named Charles (I will not say which of them, for the honour of the lady of whom I am about to speak, and whom I shall also abstain from naming), there was a foreign countess of very good family. As new things please, this lady at once attracted all eyes, both by the novelty of her costume, and by its richness and magnificence. Though she was not a beauty of the first order, she possessed, nevertheless, so much grace, such a lofty deportment, and a manner of speaking which inspired so much respect, that no one ventured to attempt her, except the king, who was very much in love with her. That he might enjoy her society more freely, he gave the count her husband a commission which kept him a long time away from the court, and during that interval the king diverted himself with the countess.

Several of the king's gentlemen, seeing that their master was well treated by the countess, took the liberty to speak to her on the subject; among the rest, one named Astillon, an enterprising and handsome man. At first she answered him with great dignity, and thought to frighten him by threatening to complain to the king his master; but he, who was not a man to be moved by the menaces of an intrepid captain, made light of those which the lady held forth, and pressed her so closely, that she consented to grant him a private interview, and even told him what he should do in order to reach her chamber; a lesson which he failed neither to remember nor to practise. To prevent any suspicion on the king's part, he made a pretence of a journey to obtain leave of absence for some days, and actually took his departure from the court, but quitted his retinue at the first stage, and returned at night to receive the favours which the countess had promised him. She fulfilled her promise; and he was so satisfied with his reception, that he was content to remain seven or eight days shut up in a *garderobe*, living on nothing but aphrodisiacs.

During the time he was thus confined, one of his comrades, named Duracier, came to make love to the countess. She went through the same ceremonies with this second wooer as with the first, spoke to him at first sternly and haughtily, softened to him only by degrees; and on the day she let the first prisoner go, she put the second into his place. Whilst he was there, a third came, named Valbenon, and had the same treatment as his two predecessors. After these three came two or three others, who also had part in that sweet captivity; and so it went on for a long while, the intrigue being so nicely conducted that not one of the whole number knew anything of the adventures of the rest. They heard plenty of talk, indeed, of the passion of every one of them for the countess, but there was not one of them but believed himself to be the only favoured lover, and laughed in his sleeve at his disappointed rivals.

One day, all these gentlemen being met together at an entertainment, at which they made very good cheer, they began to talk about their adventures, and the prisons in which they had been during the wars. Valbenon, who was not the man to keep a secret which flattered his vanity, said to the others, "I know in what prisons you have been; but as for me, I have been in one for sake of which I will speak well of prisons in general as long as I live; for I don't believe there is a pleasure in the world equal to that of being a prisoner."

Astillon, who had been the first prisoner, at once suspected what prison he meant. "Under what gaoler," he asked, "were you so well treated, that you were so fond of your prison?"

"Be the gaoler who he may," replied Valbenon, "the prison was so agreeable, that I was very loth to leave it so soon, for I never was better treated or more comfortable than there."

Duracier, who hitherto had said nothing, shrewdly suspected that the prison in question was that in which he had been confined, as well as the other two. "Tell me," said he to Valbenon, "what sort of food did they give you in that same prison you praise so highly?"

"Food? The king has not better, or more nutritive," was the reply.

"But I should like to know, too," returned Duracier, "did not the person who kept you prisoner make you earn your bread?"

"Hah! Ventrebleu!" cried Valbenon, who saw that the mark was hit. "Have I had comrades? I thought myself the only one."

"Well," said Astillon, laughing, "we are all companions and friends from our youth, and all serve the same master. If we all share alike in the same *bonne fortune*, we may well laugh in company. But in order to know if what I imagine is true, pray let me interrogate you, and all of you tell me the truth. If what I suppose has happened to us, it is the oddest and most amusing adventure that ever could be imagined."

All swore they would speak the truth, at least if matters were so that they could not help doing so. "I will relate my adventure to you," said Astillon, "and you will each answer me yes or no, if yours is like it or not."

Every one having agreed to this, "In the first place," said Astillon, "I asked leave of absence of the king, under pretence of a journey."

"And so did we," said the others.

"When I was two leagues from the court, I left my retinue, and went and surrendered myself a prisoner."

"And so did we."

"I remained for seven or eight days hid in a *garderobe*, where I was fed upon nothing but restoratives, and the best viands I ever tasted. At the end of eight days, my keepers let me go, much weaker than I had come."

They all swore that they had been served just the same way.

"My imprisonment ended such a day," continued Astillon.

"Mine began the very day yours ended," said Duracier, "and lasted until such a day."

Valbenon now lost patience, and began to swear. "By the Lord," said he, "I find I was the third, though I thought myself the first and the only one; for I entered such a day, and left such another."

The other three who were at table swore that they had entered and departed successively in the same order.

"Since that is the case," said Astillon, "I will describe our gaoler. She is married, and her husband is away."

"The very same," said all the others.

"As I was the first enrolled," continued Astillon, "I will be the first to name her, for our common relief. She is the countess, who was so haughty, that in winning her, I thought I had done as great a feat as if I had vanquished Cæsar. To the devil with the slut, that made us toil so hard, and deem ourselves so fortunate in having won her. There never was a more infernal woman. Whilst she had one of us caged, she was trapping another, so that the place might never be vacant. I would rather die than not have my revenge."

They all asked Duracier what he thought of the matter, and in what manner she ought to be punished; adding, that they were ready to put their hands to the work.

"It strikes me," said he, "that we ought to tell the facts to the king our master, who esteems her as a goddess."

"We will not do that," said Astillon; "we can revenge ourselves very well without our master's aid. Let us wait for her to-morrow when she goes to mass, every man with an iron chain round his neck, and when she enters the church, we will salute her as is fitting."

This suggestion was unanimously approved. Every one provided himself with a chain, and next morning, dressed all in black, with their chains round their necks, they presented themselves to the countess as she was going to church. When she saw them in that trim, she burst out laughing, and said to them, "Whither go these people that look in such doleful plight?"

"As your poor captive slaves, madam," said Astillon, "we are come to do you service."

"You are not my captives," she replied, "and I know no reason why you should be bound more than others to do me service."

Valbenon then advanced: "We have so long eaten your bread, madam," he said, "that we should be very ungrateful not to do you service."

She pretended not to have the least idea of what he meant, and preserved an unruffled air, thinking thereby to disconcert them; but they played their parts so well that she could not but be aware that the thing was discovered. Nevertheless, she quite baffled them; for as she had lost honour and conscience, she did not take to herself the shame they sought to put upon her; but as one who preferred her pleasure to all the honour in the world, she showed them no worse a countenance for what they had done, and carried her head as high as ever, whereat they were so astounded that they felt themselves as much ashamed as they had meant to make her.*

---

* "The adventure related by Margaret in this novel is

If you do not think, ladies, that this tale sufficiently shows that women are as bad as men, I will tell you others. It strikes me, however, that this one is enough to show you that a woman who has lost shame does evil a thousand times more audaciously than a man.

There was not a lady in the company who, on hearing this story, did not make so many signs of the cross, that one would have thought she saw all the devils in hell.

"Let us humble ourselves, mesdames," said Oisille, "at the contemplation of such horrible conduct, the more so as the person abandoned by God becomes like him with whom she unites. As those who attach themselves to God are animated by his spirit, so those who follow the devil are urged by the spirit of the devil; and nothing can be more brutified than those whom God abandons."

"Whatever this poor lady did," said Ennasuite, "I cannot applaud those who boasted of their prison."

"It is my belief," said Longarine, "that a man finds it as hard to keep his good fortune secret as to pursue it. There is no hunter who does not take pleasure in blowing his horn over his quarry, or lover who is not very glad to proclaim the glory of his victory."

"That is an opinion," said Simontault, "which I will maintain to be heretical before all the inquisitors in the world; for I lay it down as a fact that there are more men than women who keep a secret. I know, indeed, that some might be found who would rather not be so well treated than that

---

most *piquant* in the whole Heptameron. It would be very interesting to know the real names of the persons concerned. Brantôme has not disclosed them; he only says: 'I knew a very great lady, a widow. . . . . Although she was in a manner adored by a very great person, yet she could not do without some other lovers in private, that she might not lose any time, or remain idle. I refer to that lady in the *Cent Nouvelles* of the Queen of Navarre, who had three lovers at once, and was so clever that she managed to entertain them all three very affably.'—(*Dame* Galantes, Discours iv.) As for the principal hero, the name of *Hastillon,* by which he is designated, warrants us in making a conjecture. May he not have been Jacques de Chastillon, chamberlain of Charles VIII. and Louis XII., and lieutenant of the hundred gentlemen of Charles VIII., who was killed at the siege of Ravenna in 1512 ? Brantôme has devoted to him the nineteenth Discours of his work in *Les Capitaines Français.*"—*Bibliophiles Français.*

any one in the world should know of it. Thence it is that the Church, as a good mother, has appointed priests and not women for confessors, for women can conceal nothing."

"That is not the reason," replied Oisille, "but because women have such a hatred of vice, that they would not give absolution so easily as men, and would impose too severe penances."

"If they were as austere in imposing penance as they are in responding," said Dagoucin, "they would render more sinners desperate than they would save. The Church, therefore, has ordained wisely in all ages. I do not pretend, for all that, to excuse the gentlemen who boasted of their prison; for it never was to a man's honour to tell ugly tales of a woman."

"Nay," said Geburon, "for the sake of their own honour even they should never have avowed the fact. The books of the Round Table inform us that it is not glorious for a knight to vanquish another who has no valour."

"I am surprised the poor woman did not die of shame in presence of her prisoners," said Longarine.

"Those who have lost shame can hardly ever recover it," said Oisille, "unless they have lost it through deep love. Of such lost ones I have seen many come back."

"I suspect you have seen them come back as they came," said Hircan, "for deep love is very rare in women."

"I am not of your opinion," said Longarine, "for some I know have loved to death."

"I am so curious to hear a story of one such woman," said Hircan, "that my voice is for you. I shall be very glad to find in women a love of which I have always deemed them incapable."

"You will believe it when you have heard the story," said Longarine, "and you will be convinced that there is no stronger passion than love. As it makes one undertake things almost impossible, with a view to obtain some pleasure in this life, so does it above all other passions undermine the existence of him or her who loses the hope of succeeding, as you shall see from what I am going to relate."

NOVEL L.

A LOVER, AFTER A BLOOD-LETTING, RECEIVES FAVOURS FROM HIS MISTRESS, DIES IN CONSEQUENCE, AND IS FOLLOWED BY THE FAIR ONE, WHO SINKS UNDER HER GRIEF.

It is not a year ago since there was in Cremona a gentleman named Messire Jean Pierre, who had long loved a lady in his neighbourhood; but for all he could do he had never been able to obtain from her the response he longed for, though she loved him with all her heart. The poor gentleman was so distressed at this, that he secluded himself at home, resolving to abandon a vain pursuit in which he was wasting his life. Thinking to detach himself from his cruel fair one, he remained some days without seeing her, and fell into such a profound melancholy, that no one would have known him, so altered were his looks. His relations sent for physicians, who, seeing his face yellow, thought it was an obstruction of the liver, and bled him. The lady who had been so coy, knowing very well that his illness was nothing but grief that she had not responded to his love, sent a trusty old woman with orders to tell him, that as she could no longer doubt that his love was genuine and sincere, she had made up her mind to grant him what she had so long refused; and that to that end she had contrived means to leave home and go to a place where he might see her without impediment.

The gentleman, who had been let blood that morning from the arm, finding himself more relieved by this embassy than by all the remedies of his physicians, sent her word that he would not fail to meet her at the appointed hour, and that she had performed a manifest miracle, inasmuch as by a single word she had cured a man of a malady for which all the faculty could find no remedy. The evening he so longed for being come, he went to the trysting-place with a joy so extreme, that as it could not augment, could not of necessity but diminish and come to an end. He had not long to wait for her he loved more than his soul; nor did he waste time in making long speeches. The fire that consumed him made him rush promptly to the pleasure he promised himself, and which he could hardly believe was within his reach. Too much intoxicated with love and voluptuous delight, and thinking he had found the remedy that would prolong his life, he found that which hastened his death; for heedless of himself in his ardent passion for his mistress, he did not perceive that his arm had come unbound. The wound opened afresh, and the poor gentleman lost so much blood, that he was quite bathed in it. Believing that the excess he had indulged in was the cause of his lassitude, he attempted to return home. Then love, which had too much united them, so dealt with him, that on quitting his mistress, his soul at the same time quitted his body. He had lost so much blood that he fell dead at the lady's feet.

The awful surprise, and the thought of what she lost in so perfect a lover, of whose death she was the sole cause, put her beside herself. Reflecting, besides, on the shame that would devolve on her if a dead body was found in the house with her, she called to her aid a trusty woman servant, and they carried the body into the street. But not choosing to leave it alone, she took the sword of the deceased, and being resolved to follow his destiny, and punish her heart, which was the cause of her calamity, she pierced herself with the sword, and fell dead on her lover's body. That sad spectacle was the first thing that met the eyes of her father and mother when they came out of their house in the morning. After the lamentations due to so tragic an event, they had them both interred together.

This, ladies, was an extreme disaster, which could only be ascribed to a love as extreme.

"That is what I like to see," said Simontault; "a love so reciprocal, that when the one dies the other will not survive. Had I, by God's grace, found such a mistress, I believe that no man would ever have loved more perfectly than I."

"I am sure," said Parlamente, "that love would never have so deprived you of your wits but that you would have taken care to tie up your arm better. Men no longer lose their lives for ladies. That time is gone by."

"But the time is not gone by," retorted Simontault, "when ladies forget their lovers' lives for sake of their own pleasure."

"I do not believe," said Ennasuite, "that there is a woman in the world who would take delight in any man's death, though he were her enemy; but if men choose to kill themselves, the ladies cannot hinder them."

"She, however, who refused bread to the poor famishing man," said Saffredent, "must be regarded as his murderess."

"If your prayers were as reasonable as those of the beggar who asks for bread," said Oisille, "it would be too cruel on the part of the ladies to deny your petition. But, thank Heaven, this malady kills none but those whose time is come."

"I cannot think, madam," replied Saffredent, "that there is any greater need than that one which makes a man forget all others. When one loves well, one knows no other bread than the glances and the words of the beloved being."

"If you were starved for a while, you would tell a very different story," said Oisille.

"I confess," he replied, "that the body might grow weak under that discipline, but not the heart and the will."

"That being the case," said Parlamente, "God has been very gracious to you in making you fall into the hands of women who have given you so little satisfaction, that you must console yourself for it by eating and drinking. You take so kindly to that sort of consolation, that methinks you ought to thank God for that merciful cruelty."

"I am so inured to suffering," he replied, "that I begin to take pleasure in the ills which others bemoan."

"It may be," said Longarine, "that your lamentations exclude you from the company to which you would otherwise be welcome; for there is nothing so disagreeable as an importunate lover."

"Or as a cruel lady, you may add," said Simontault.

"If we were to wait till Simontault had delivered all his maxims," said Oisille, "I see that we should come in for complines instead of vespers. Let us, then, go and thank God that this day has passed without any dispute of more consequence."

She then rose, and was followed by all the rest; but Simontault and Longarine ceased not to dispute, but so gently that, without drawing the sword, Simontault gained the victory, and proved that there is no greater need than a great passion. Thereupon they entered the church where the monks were waiting for them. After vespers they went to table, and conversed during the repast; nor did the conversation end with it, but would have been prolonged far into the night if Oisille had not advised them to go and refresh their spirits with sleep. She added, that she was afraid the sixth day would not pass off so agreeably as the five others, for even if they should have recourse to invention, it would be impossible to produce better tales than those which had been already told.

"As long as the world lasts," said Geburon, "there will every day be done things worthy of memory. The wicked are always wicked, and the good always good: and as long as wickedness and goodness reign on earth, something new will always be taking place, although Solomon says that nothing new happens under the sun. As we have not been called to the privy council of God, and consequently are ignorant of first causes, all things seem new to us, and the more wonderful the less we could or would do them. So do not be afraid that the days to come will not be as good as the past, and think only of doing your own duty well."

Oisille said she commended herself to God, in whose name she bade them good night. And so the whole company retired.

SIXTH DAY.

Next morning, earlier than usual, Madame Oisille went to prepare her exhortation in the hall; but the rest of the company being informed of this, their desire to hear her good instructions made them dress so speedily, that she was not kept waiting long. As she knew their hearts, she read the epistle of St. John, which speaks only of love. This was so palatable to the company, that although this morning's devotion was longer than usual, they all thought it had not occupied more than a quarter of an hour. After it was over they went to mass, and commended themselves to the Holy Ghost. When they had dined and taken a little rest they went to the meadow to continue their novels. Madame Oisille asked who should begin the day. "I call upon you to do so, madam," said Longarine, "for you gave us such a fine lecture this morning, that it is impossible you should tell a story which should not correspond to the glory you acquired thereby."

"I regret," replied Oisille, "that I cannot relate anything to you so profitable as what you heard this morning. What I shall tell you, however, will be conformable to the precepts of the Scriptures, which warn us not to put our trust in princes, or in any sons of man, who cannot save us. For fear you should forget this truth for want of an example, I will give you one that is quite true, and so recent, that those who beheld the sad spectacle have hardly yet dried away their tears."

NOVEL LI.

PERFIDY AND CRUELTY OF AN ITALIAN DUKE.

THE Duke of Urbino, surnamed the Prefect, who married the sister of the first Duke of Mantua, had a son about eighteen or twenty years of age, who was in love with a girl of good family. Not being free to converse with her as he wished, in consequence of the custom of the country, he had recourse to a gentleman who was in his service, and who was in love with a handsome, virtuous young damsel in the service of the duchess. The cavalier employed this damsel to make known his passion to his mistress, and the poor girl took pleasure in rendering him service, believing that his intentions were good, and that she might with honour take upon her to be his ambassadress. But the duke, who looked more to the interest of his house than to his son's pure affection, was afraid that this correspondence would end in marriage; and he set so many spies on the watch, that at last he was informed that the girl had meddled with carrying letters from his son to her of whom he was so passionately enamoured. Burning with rage, he resolved to put it out of his power to do so any more; but as he was not sufficiently careful to conceal his resentment, the girl was warned of it in time. She knew the prince to be malicious and without conscience, and was so terrified, that she went to the duchess, and implored permission to retire until the fit of anger had passed away. The duchess told her that before she gave her leave she would try to find how her husband took the matter. She did so, and found that the duke spoke of it with great bitterness; whereupon she not only gave her young lady permission, but even advised her to retire into a convent until the storm should have blown over; and this she did as secretly as possible.

The duke, however, missed her, and asked his wife, with a countenance of feigned good humour, where the damsel was. The duchess, who supposed that he knew the truth, told it him without reserve. He pretended to be sorry for this, and said there was no need for her to do so, that he meant her no harm, and that the duchess had better make her come back, for it did no good to have a talk made about such matters. The duchess told him that if the poor girl had been so unfortunate as to incur his displeasure, it was better that she should abstain from appearing in his presence for some time; but he would not be so put off, but insisted on her return.

The duchess made known the duke's pleasure to the damsel; but the latter was not satisfied, and begged her mistress would excuse her from running such a risk, knowing as she did that her husband the duke was not so ready to grant forgiveness. The duchess, however, pledged her life and honour that no harm should happen to her; and the damsel, who felt sure that her mistress loved her, and would for no consideration deceive her, trusted to her promise, believing that the duke would never violate a promise made by his wife on her life and honour, and she returned to court. As soon as the duke was aware of this, he entered his wife's chamber: and the moment he set eyes upon the poor damsel, he ordered his gentlemen to arrest her, and take her to prison. The duchess, who had induced her to quit her asylum upon the faith of her word, was filled with horror, and throwing herself at her husband's feet, besought him, for his own honour and that of his house, not to do such an act. But no supplications she could make, no arguments she could urge, had power to soften his hard heart, or turn him from his stubborn purpose to be revenged. Without answering his wife a word, he abruptly quitted the room, and without form of justice, forgetting God and the honour of his house, this cruel duke had the poor girl hanged.

I will not undertake to depict the indignation of the duchess; enough to say that it was such as might have been expected of a lady of honour and spirit, who, contrary to her plighted faith, saw a person whom she would have saved, put to death by her husband. Much less will I attempt to portray the affliction of the poor gentleman, the unfortunate girl's lover. He did all he could to save his mistress's life, and even offered to die in her place; but nothing could move the duke, who knew no other felicity than taking vengeance on those he hated. Thus was this poor innocent put to death by this cruel duke, against all equity and honour, to the great regret of all who knew her.

Here you see, ladies, what a bad heart is capable of when it is united with power.

"I have heard," said Longarine, "that the Italians were prone to all capital vices; but I could never have supposed they would carry vindictiveness and cruelty so far as to put a person to such a miserable death for so slight a cause."

"You have mentioned one of the three vices," said Saffredent, laughing; "let us know, Longarine, what are the other two."

"I would do so willingly," she replied, "if you did not know them; but I am sure you are acquainted with them all."

"You think me, then, very vicious?" said Saffredent.

"Not at all," returned Longarine; "but I believe you know so well the loathsomeness of vice, that you can better avoid it than another."

"Do not be surprised at this excess of cruelty," said Simontault, "for they who have been in Italy relate such horrible things of the kind, that what we have heard is but a trifle in comparison with them."

"When the French took Rivolte," said Geburon, "there was an Italian captain who had the reputation of a brave man, and who, seeing a man lie dead who was not otherwise his enemy than in having been a Guelph whilst he was a

Ghibelline, tore out his heart, broiled it, ate it greedily, and replied to those who asked him was it good, that he had never eaten anything more delicious. Not content with this fine deed, he killed the dead man's wife, who was pregnant, ripped her open, tore out the child, and dashed it to pieces against the wall; and then stuffed the bodies of the husband and wife with oats for his horses to eat. Judge if this man would not have put to death a girl whom he suspected of having done anything offensive to him."

"This duke," said Ennasuite, "was more afraid his son should marry one who was not wealthy enough, than desirous of giving him a wife to his liking."

"There is no doubt," said Simontault, "that the tendency of the Italians is to love more than nature the things that are only made for nature's service."

"Their case is still worse," said Hircan, "for they make their God of things that are contrary to nature."

"Those are the sins I meant," said Longarine; "for we know that to love money beyond what is necessary for our wants is idolatry."

Parlamente said that "St. Paul had not forgotten their vices, no more than those of such as think themselves surpassing in prudence and human reason, on which they count so much, that they do not render to God the honour that is His due. Therefore, the Almighty, jealous of His glory, renders more insensate than the brute beasts those who think they have more sense than other men, and allows them to do acts contrary to nature, which shows evidently that their sense is reprobate."

"That is the third sin," said Longarine, interrupting her, "to which the Italians are addicted."

"In good sooth, I like this remark," said Nomerfide. "Since those who are regarded as having the subtlest wits, and are the best speakers, are punished in this manner, and brutified more than the brutes themselves, it must be concluded that persons who are humble and low and of little reach like myself, are endowed with angelic sapience."

"I assure you," said Oisille, "I am not far from your way of thinking; and I am persuaded that there are none more ignorant than those who imagine themselves knowing."

"I never knew a mocker who was not mocked," said Geburon, "a deceiver who was not deceived, or a proud man who was not humbled."

"You put me in mind of a trick I should like to relate to you if it was seemly," said Simontault.

"Since we are here to tell the truth, tell it, whatever it be," said Oisille.

"Well, since you desire it, madam, I will tell it you," he replied.

NOVEL LII.

A NASTY BREAKFAST GIVEN TO AN ADVOCATE AND A GENTLE-
MAN BY AN APOTHECARY'S MAN.

In the time of the last Duke Charles there was at Alençon an advocate named Antoine Bacheret, a merry companion, and fond of breakfasting o' mornings. One day, as he was sitting before his door, he saw a gentleman pass whose name was Monsieur de la Tireliere. He had come on foot upon business he had in town, and the day being cold, he had not forgotten to take with him his great robe, lined with foxskin. Seeing the advocate, who was much such a man as himself, he asked him how he was getting on, and observed that a good breakfast would not be amiss. The advocate replied that a breakfast would be found soon enough, provided some one could be found to pay for it. Thereupon La Tireliere took him by the arm, saying, "Come along, gaffer, perhaps we shall fall in with some fool who will pay for us both."

There happened to be behind them an apothecary's man, a cunning and inventive young fellow, whom the advocate was perpetually making game of. That moment the thought of having his revenge came into his head, and without going more than ten steps out of his way, he found behind a house a fine big sir reverence, well and duly frozen, which he wrapped up so neatly in paper that it might be taken for a small sugar-loaf. He then looked out for his men, and passing them like a person in great haste, entered a house, and let fall the sugar-loaf from his sleeve, as if inadvertently. The advocate picked it up with great glee, and said to La Tirelière, " This clever fellow shall pay our scot; but let us be off quickly for fear he comes back."

The pair having entered a cabaret, the advocate said to the servant girl, " Make us a good fire, and give us some good bread and good wine, and something nice with it;" for he fancied he had wherewithal to pay. They were served to their liking; but as they grew warm with eating and drinking, the sugar-loaf, which the advocate carried in his bosom, began to thaw, and gave out such a stench that, thinking it came from elsewhere, he said to the servant, " You have the most fetid and stinking house I ever was in." La Tirelière, who had his share of this fine perfume, said the same thing. The servant, incensed at thus being accused of sluttishness, replied, " By St. Peter, my masters, the house is so neat and clean that there is no nastiness in it but what you have brought in with you." The two friends rose from table, spitting and holding their noses, and stood near the fire; and presently, while warming himself, the advocate took his handkerchief out of his bosom, disgustingly smeared with the syrup of the melted sugar-loaf, which he produced with it. You may well believe that the servant made fine fun of them after the insult they had offered her, and that the advocate was sorely confounded at finding himself the dupe of an apothecary's man, whom he had always made the butt of his wit. The servant, instead of taking pity on them, made them pay as handsomely as they had been served; and said that no doubt they must be greatly intoxicated, since they had drunk both by nose and mouth. The poor wights slunk away with their shame and their cost.

They were no sooner in the street than they saw the apothecary's man going about and asking every one if they had seen a loaf of sugar wrapped up in paper. They tried to avoid him, but he shouted to the advocate, " Monsieur, if you have my loaf of sugar I beg you will give it back to me; for it is a double sin to rob a poor servant." His shouts brought many people to the spot out of curiosity to witness the dispute; and the real state of the case was so well verified, that the apothecary's man was as glad to have been robbed as the others were vexed at having committed such a nasty theft. They comforted themselves, however, with the hope of one day giving him tit for tat.

The like often happens, ladies, to those who take pleasure in such tricks. If the gentleman had not wanted to eat at another's expense, he would not have had such a nasty draught at his own. It is true that my story is not very decorous, but you gave me permission to speak the truth. I have done so, to show that when a deceiver is deceived no one is sorry for it.

"It is commonly said that words do not stink," said Hircan; "but those who utter them cannot help smelling of them."

"It is true," said Oisille, "that words of this sort do not stink; but there are others called dirty, which have such a bad odour, that the soul suffers from them more than the body would suffer from smelling a sugar-loaf like that you have spoken of."

"Do tell me, pray," rejoined Hircan, "what words you know so dirty, that they make a woman of honour suffer both in body and soul."

"It would be a fine thing," replied Oisille, "if I were to say to you words which I would not advise any woman to say."

"I understand now what those words are," said Saffredent. "Women like to appear demure, and do not commonly use such language. But I should like to ask those present why they laugh so readily when they are uttered before them, since they will not themselves utter them. I cannot understand their laughing at a thing which is so offensive to them."

"It is not at those pretty words we laugh," said Parlamente, "but by reason of the natural propensity every one feels to laugh either when we see some one fall, or when we hear something said out of place, as it often happens to the best speakers to say one thing instead of another. But when men talk filth intentionally, and with premeditation, I know no honourable woman but feels intense aversion for such people, and, far from listening to them, shuns their society."

"It is true," said Geburon, "that I have seen women cross themselves on hearing that sort of words which seemed more disgusting the more they were repeated."

"But," said Simontault, "how often have they put on their masks to laugh behind them as heartily as they pretended to be vexed?"

"Even that were better than to show that one took pleasure in such language," said Parlamente.

"So, then," remarked Dagoucin, "you praise hypocrisy in ladies as much as virtue?"

"Virtue would be much better," replied Longarine; "but when it is wanting, we must have recourse to hypocrisy, as we use high-heeled shoes to hide our littleness. If we can hide our defects, even that is no little advantage."

"By my faith, it would be better sometimes to let some little defect appear," said Hircan, "than to hide it so carefully under the cloak of virtue."

"It is true," said Ennasuite, "that a borrowed garment dishonours him who is obliged to return it, as much as it did him honour to wear it. There is a lady in the world who, in her over-anxiety to hide a small fault, has committed a much greater one."

"I think I know whom you mean," said Hircan; "but at least do not name her."

"O! you have my voice," said Geburon, "on condition that when you have told the tale, you will tell us the names, which we will swear never to mention."

"I promise it," said Ennasuite, "for there is nothing which may not be said decorously."

NOVEL LIII.

MADAME DE NEUFCHASTEL, BY HER DISSIMULATION, FORCED THE PRINCE OF BELHOSTE TO PUT HER TO SUCH A PROOF AS TURNED TO HER DISHONOUR.

On one occasion, when King Francis I. went with but a small suite to spend some days at a very handsome château, to enjoy the chase and other recreations, he was accompanied by the Prince of Belhoste, as much distinguished for every excellence of mind and person as any at court. He had married a wife who was not of a great family, but whom he loved as much as any husband can love a wife. He put such confidence in her, that when he loved elsewhere he made no secret of it to her, well knowing that she had no other will than his. This lord conceived a strong regard for a widow named Madame de Neufchastel, who was considered the handsomest woman of her time. If the prince was greatly attached to this widow, the princess his wife was no less so, often invited her to table, and thought so highly of her, that far from being displeased that her husband loved her, she was delighted to see that he addressed his attentions to so worthy and virtuous an object. This friendship was of such long duration, and so perfect, that the prince busied himself with Madame de Neufchastel's affairs as much as with his own, and the princess his wife did likewise.

The widow's beauty attracted round her many great lords and gentlemen as suitors, some of whom were actuated only by love, others had an eye to her wealth; for, in addition to her beauty, she was very rich. One gentleman especially, named the Seigneur des Cheriots, was so assiduous in his wooing, that he never failed to present himself at her *lever* and her *coucher*, and spent as much time in her society as he possibly could. The prince, who thought that a man of such mean birth and appearance did not deserve to be treated so favourably, was not at all pleased with his assiduities, and often remonstrated with the widow on the subject; but as she was a duke's daughter, she excused herself, saying that she talked generally to everybody, and that their intimacy would be the less observed when it was seen that she did not talk more to one than another. After some time, this Sieur des Cheriots pressed his suit so much, that she promised to marry him, more in consequence of his importunity than of her preference for him, on condition that he would not require her to declare the marriage until her daughters were married. After this promise, the gentleman used to go to her chamber without scruple, at any hour he pleased; and there was only a femme-de-chambre and a man who were privy to the affair.

The prince was so displeased at seeing the gentleman becoming more and more domesticated with her he loved, that he could not help saying to her, " I have always prized your honour as that of my own sister. You know with what propriety I have always addressed you, and what pleasure I feel in loving a lady so discreet and virtuous as you; but if I thought that another obtained by importunity what I would not ask for against your inclination, I could not endure it, nor would it do you honour. I say this to you because you are young and fair, and have hitherto enjoyed a good reputation; but you are beginning to be the subject of reports greatly to your disadvantage. Though this person has neither birth, fortune, credit, knowledge, nor good looks in comparison with you, it would have been better, nevertheless, that you had married him than have given rise to suspicion, as you are doing. Tell me, then, I entreat, if you are resolved to love him; for I do not choose to have him for a companion, but will leave you wholly to him, and will no longer entertain for you the sentiments I have hitherto cherished."

The poor lady, fearing to lose his friendship, began to cry, and vowed to him that she would rather die than marry the gentleman in question; but that he was so importunate that she could not hinder his entering her room at the hours when every one else visited her. "I do not speak of those hours," said the prince, "for I can visit you then as well as he, and every one sees what you do; but I have been told that he comes to you after you are in bed, which I think so bad, that if you continue it without declaring that he is your husband, I look upon you as the woman most ruined in reputation that ever was."

She assured him with all the oaths she could think of that she regarded the man neither as husband nor lover, but as the most importunate person in the world. "Since that is the case," said the prince, "I promise that I will rid you of him."

"What!" replied the widow, "would you put him to death?"

"No, no," said the prince; "but I will let him know that he must not give occasion in this way for people to speak ill of ladies in the king's residence. I swear to you, by the love I bear you, that if he does not correct himself after I have spoken to him, I will correct him in such a manner that he shall be an example for others."

With these words the prince went away, and on leaving the room he met the Seigneur des Cheriots coming thither, and spoke to him to the same purpose, assuring him that the first time he found him there at any other hour than one in which it was proper for gentlemen to visit ladies, he would give him such a fright as he should not forget as long as he lived, and would teach him not to trifle with a lady whose relations were persons of such consequence. The gentleman protested that he had never been there except like other visitors; and that if the prince found him transgressing in that respect he would give him leave to do the worst he could.

Some days afterwards, the gentleman, fancying that the prince had forgotten what he had told him, went to see the lady in the evening, and stayed very late. The prince told his wife that Madame de Neufchastel had a severe cold, and the good lady begged him to go see her for them both, and apologise for her, as she was prevented from accompanying him by indispensable business. The prince waited till the king was in bed, and then went to say good evening to the widow. He had just reached the foot of the staircase, and was about to go up, when he met a valet de chambre coming down, who swore, in reply to the prince's questions, that his mistress was in bed and asleep. The prince retraced his steps, but presently, suspecting that the valet had told a lie, he looked back and saw the man returning hastily. He stopped, therefore, and walked up and down the yard before the door to watch if the valet reappeared, and a quarter of an hour afterwards he saw him come down, and peer about in all directions to see who was in the yard. The prince entertaining no doubt now that the Seigneur des Cheriots was with the widow, and durst not come out for fear of him, continued his promenade for a long while. Recollecting that one of the lady's chamber windows looked upon a little garden, and was not very high, he called to mind the proverb which says, "Whoso cannot pass through the door let him jump through the window." He therefore called one of his valets and said, "Go into that garden, and if you see a gentleman come down from a window, draw your sword, and the moment he is down, make your sword clash upon the wall, and shout, 'Kill! kill!' but do not touch him." The valet went to where his master ordered him, and the prince walked up and down till near midnight.

The Seigneur des Cheriots hearing that the prince was still

in the yard, resolved to escape by the window, and throwing his cloak into the garden he followed it with the help of his good friends. The valet no sooner espied him than he made a great clatter with his sword, and shouted, "Kill him, kill him!" The poor gentleman, mistaking the valet for the master, was so frightened, that, without stopping to pick up his cloak, he ran off as fast as his legs could carry him, and was met by the archers of the watch, who were greatly surprised to see him running so. He durst not say anything else to them than to beg earnestly they would open the gate for him, or take him to their quarters till the next day; which they did, not having the keys.

Then it was that the prince went to bed. He found his wife asleep, woke her, and asked her to guess what o'clock it was. "I have not heard the clock strike since I came to bed," said she.

"It is past three o'clock," said he.

"Good Heavens! monsieur, where have you been staying so long?" exclaimed the wife. "I am afraid you will be the worse for it."

"Watching will never make me ill, my dear," he replied, "so long as I keep those awake who think to deceive me." And so saying, he laughed so heartily that she begged him to tell her what it was for. He told her the whole story, and showed her the wolf's skin, which his valet had carried home with him. After they had diverted themselves at the expense of the widow and her gallant, they went to sleep with as much composure as the other pair felt fear and uneasiness lest their intrigue should be discovered.

Now the gentleman, reflecting that he could not dissemble before the prince, came to his levee next morning, and besought the prince not to expose him, and to order his cloak to be restored to him. The prince pretended not to understand him, and played his part so well that the poor gentleman did not know what to make of it. But at last he received such a rating as he had not expected; for the prince assured him that if ever he was found there again, he would speak to the king and have him banished from the court.

Judge, ladies, I pray you, if this poor widow would not have done better to speak frankly to him who did her the honour to love and esteem her, than by her dissimulation to reduce him to the necessity of seeking evidence so dishonouring to herself.

"She knew," said Geburon, "that if she told him the truth she would wholly lose his esteem, which she wished to preserve by all means."

"It strikes me," said Longarine, "that since she had chosen a husband to her liking, she had no reason to care for losing the love of all her other admirers."

"I believe," said Parlamente, "that if she had ventured to declare her marriage she would have contented herself with her husband; but wishing to conceal it until her daughters were married, she could not make up her mind to let go so good a means of cloaking her real sentiments and conduct."

"That is not it," said Saffredent; "but the fact is, that the ambition of women is so great, that they never content themselves with one lover. I have heard that the best of them like to have three—one for honour, one for interest, and the third for pleasure; and each of the three believes himself the most favoured; but the first two serve the last."

"You speak of women who know neither love nor honour," said Oisille.

"There are women, madam, of the character I describe, whom you regard as the most virtuous women in the country," replied Saffredent.

"Rely upon it," said Hircan, "that a clever woman will always contrive to live where others would die of hunger."

"But when their slyness is known their case is mortal," said Longarine.

"Nay, they thrive all the better for it," said Simontault. "It is no small glory for them to be reputed more cunning than their companions. Such a reputation brings more lovers under subjection to them than does their beauty. In fact, one of the greatest pleasures known to lovers is to conduct their amours slily."

"You are speaking of criminal love," said Ennasuite; "for lawful love has no need of concealment."

"Put that notion out of your head, I beseech you," said Dagoucin, "for the more precious a drug is the less it should be exposed to the air. Secrecy is necessary whether one loves virtuously or the reverse; and that for fear of false judgment on the part of those who cannot believe a man capable of loving a woman honourably. Such persons judge others by themselves; and as they love their pleasure only they imagine that every one is like themselves. If we were all of good faith, dissimulation would be needless, at least with regard to those who would rather die than harbour a bad thought."

"I assure you, Dagoucin," said Hircan, "your philosophy is so sublime that there is not one person in this company who can compass or believe it. To hear you talk, one would say you meant to persuade us that men are either angels, or stones, or devils."

"I know well," replied Dagoucin, "that men are men, and subject to all the passions; but I know that there are those among them who would rather die than for their pleasure the lady they love should do aught against her conscience."

"To say they would rather die is saying a great deal," said Geburon. "I could not believe it, though I were told it by the most austere monk in the world."

"I am disposed to believe," said Hircan, "there is no one whose desires do not run quite the other way. People pretend, however, not to like grapes when they are too high for them to reach."

"But," said Nomerfide, "I suppose the prince's wife was very glad that he came to know what women are."

"I assure you it was quite the reverse," said Ennasuite; "she was very sorry for it, because she loved the widow."

"She was a match for the woman who laughed when her husband kissed her servant," said Saffredent.

"Decidedly, you shall tell us that story," said Ennasuite.

"It is short," he replied, "but it will make you laugh, which is better than being long."

NOVEL LIV.

A LADY LAUGHED TO SEE HER HUSBAND KISSING HER SERVANT, AND BEING ASKED THE REASON, REPLIED THAT SHE LAUGHED AT HER SHADOW.

THERE lived between the Pyrenees and the Alps a gentleman named Thogas, who had a wife and children, a very fine house, and so much wealth and pleasure that he had great reason to be content. The only drawback to so many sources of enjoyment was a violent pain under the roots of the hair, on account of which the physicians advised him to desist from sleeping with his wife. To this she readily consented, preferring her husband's health and life before all things, and had her bed put at the other corner of the room, directly opposite her husband's, so that they could neither of them put their heads out without seeing each other. This lady had two chamber women. The husband and wife used often to read entertaining books in bed, the servant women holding the candle, the younger for the husband, and the other for the wife. The gentleman finding the servant younger and handsomer than his wife, took such pleasure in contemplating her, that he used to leave off reading to converse with her. His wife heard all, and was not displeased that her valets and her handmaids should amuse her husband, being sure that he loved none but herself.

One evening, after reading longer than usual, the lady looked along her husband's bed, and saw only the back of the servant who was holding the candle to him; whilst of her husband she saw nothing but his shadow projected on the white wall forming the side of the chimney which jutted into the room. She perfectly distinguished the faces of both, and saw by their shadows, as clearly as she could have seen by the substance of each, if they were apart, or met, or laughed. The gentleman, who was not aware of this, and never supposed that his wife could see him, kissed his servant. For that time the wife said not a word; but seeing that the shadows often repeated the same movement, she was afraid there was reality beneath it, and she burst into such a loud laugh that the shadows separated in alarm. The gentleman asked her why she laughed so heartily, and begged she would let him have part in her merriment. "I am such a simpleton, my dear," she replied, "that I laugh at my shadow." Question her as he would, there was no getting any other answer from her. There was an end, however, to that shadowy dalliance.

I have been reminded of this incident by what you said of the lady who loved her husband's mistress.

"In faith," said Ennasuite, "if my servant had served me so, I would have got up and smashed the candle on her nose."

"You are very terrible," said Hircan; "but it would have been a bad business for you if your husband and the servant had turned round upon you and beaten you soundly. What need to make such a pother about a kiss? The wife would have done still better not to say a word, but leave her husband to divert himself. That would, perhaps, have cured him."

"Perhaps, on the contrary, she feared that the end of the diversion would make him worse," said Parlamente.

"She was not one of those of whom our Lord speaks," said Oisille, "when he says, 'We have mourned and you have not wept, we have sung and you have not danced,' for when her husband was ill she wept, and when he was merry she laughed. All good women ought thus to share with their husbands good and evil, joy and sorrow, and should love, serve, and obey them as the Church does Jesus Christ."

"Our husbands, madam," said Parlamente, "ought likewise to behave to us as Jesus Christ does to the Church."

"And so we do," said Saffredent; "and we would do something more if it were possible; for Jesus Christ died only once for his Church, and we die daily for our wives."

"Die?" exclaimed Longarine; "it strikes me that you and the rest of you here are worth more crowns than you were worth sous before you were married."

"I know why," said Saffredent. "It is because our worth is so often proved. Nevertheless, our shoulders feel the effects of having so long worn harness."

"If you had been constrained," retorted Ennasuite, "to wear harness for a month, and to lie on the bare ground you would be very glad to get back to your good wife's bed and wear the harness of which you now complain. But they say that people can bear anything except ease, and that no one knows the value of repose until he has lost it."

"This good woman, who laughed when her husband was merry," said Oisille, "was glad to enjoy her repose under any circumstances."

"It is my belief," said Longarine, "that she loved her repose better than her husband, since nothing could move her, do what he might."

"She took to heart what might be injurious to his conscience and his health," said Parlamente; "but at the same time she was not a woman to make a fuss about trifles."

"You make me laugh when you talk of conscience," said Simontault. "That is a thing about which I would never have a woman make herself uneasy."

"You deserve," said Nomerfide, "to have a wife like her who plainly showed, after her husband's death, that she cared more for his money than his conscience."

"Pray tell us that tale," said Saffredent.

"I had not intended to tell so short a tale," replied Nomerfide; "but since it comes so *à propos*, you shall have it."

NOVEL LV.

CUNNING DEVICE OF A SPANISH WIDOW TO DEFRAUD THE MENDICANT FRIARS OF A TESTAMENTARY BEQUEST MADE TO THEM BY HER HUSBAND.

THERE was at Saragossa a merchant who, feeling his end approach, and seeing that he must quit his possessions, which he had, perhaps, acquired with bad faith, thought to make satisfaction in part for his sins after his death by giving some little present to God, as if God gave his grace for money. After giving orders respecting his house, he desired that a fine Spanish horse, which constituted nearly the whole of his wealth, should be sold, and the money bestowed on the poor Mendicants; and he charged his wife to do this without fail immediately after his death. The burial being over, and the first tears shed, the wife, who was no more of a simpleton than Spanish women are in general, said to the man-servant, who, like her, had heard her husband deliver his last will, "Methinks I lose enough in losing my husband, whom I so tenderly loved, without losing, also, the rest of my property. I would by no means, however, contravene the orders he laid upon me, but would rather improve upon his intentions. The poor man, beguiled by the avarice of the priests, thought to make a sacrifice to God, in giving away after his death a sum, one crown of which he would not have given in his lifetime, however pressing might be the need, as you very well know; it has occurred to me, then, that we will do what he ordered us much better than he could have done it himself had he lived a few days longer, but no one in the world must know a word about it."

The man having promised to keep the secret, she continued: "You will take the horse to the market, and when you are asked the price you will say one ducat. But I have a very good cat which I want to sell also. You will sell it along with the horse, and charge for it ninety-nine ducats, making of the two one hundred ducats, which is the price at which my husband wished to sell the horse alone."

The man promptly obeyed his mistress's orders. As he was walking the horse about in the market-place, carrying the cat under his arm, a gentleman who knew the horse, and had before wished to buy it, came up and asked what he would take for it at a word. "A ducat," said the man.

"I would thank you not to make game of me," said the gentleman.

"I assure you, sir," said the man, "it will cost you more. It is true you must buy this cat at the same time, and I want ninety-nine ducats for it."

The gentleman, who thought it a pretty good bargain, paid him forthwith a ducat for the horse, and then the remainder for the cat, and had his two purchases taken home. The man on his side went off with the money to his mistress, who was delighted to get it, and failed not to bestow on the poor Mendicants, according to her husband's intentions, the ducat for which the horse had been sold, and kept the rest to provide for her own wants and those of her family.

Don't you think she was wiser than her husband, and did she not take more care of the fortune of her family than of his conscience?

"I believe she loved her husband," said Parlamente; "but seeing that most men wander in their wits on their death-bed, and knowing his intentions, she interpreted them to the advantage of her children; and in this, I think, she showed laudable prudence."

"Do you not think it a great fault," said Geburon, "to contravene the last wishes of our deceased friends?"

"A very great one," replied Parlamente, "when the testator is in his sound senses, and not raving."

"Do you call it raving," returned Geburon, "to bequeath one's property to the Church and to the poor Mendicants?"

"I do not call it raving," she answered, "to give to the poor what God has given to us; but to give away as alms what belongs to another appears to me no great proof of good sense. How commonly you see the greatest usurers in the world erecting the finest and most sumptuous chapels, as thinking to make their peace with God for a hundred thousand ducats' worth of robbery by ten thousand ducats' worth of building, just as though God did not know how to count."

"Truly, I have often wondered," said Oisille, "how they think to make their peace with God by means of things which he himself reprobated when he was on earth, such as great buildings, gildings, painting, and decorations. But if they rightly understood what God has said, that the only offering he requires of us is a humble and contrite heart, and another text in which St. Paul says that we are the temple of God in which he desires to dwell, they would have taken pains to adorn their consciences while they were alive, and not have waited for the time when a man can no longer do either good or ill; nor would they have done what is still worse, in laying upon those they leave behind the burden of giving their alms to those they would not have deigned to look upon all through their lives. But He who knows the heart cannot be deceived, and will judge them not according to their works merely, but according to the faith and charity that was in them."

"Wherefore is it, then," said Geburon, "that these Cordeliers and Mendicants talk to us of nothing at death but making great bequests to their monasteries, assuring us that they will put us into Paradise, whether we will or not?"

"How now, Geburon," said Hircan; "have you forgotten the wickedness you have related to us of the Cordeliers, that you ask how it is possible for such men to lie? I declare to you I do not think there are in the world greater liars than theirs. It may be that those among them are not to be blamed who speak on behalf of their whole community; but there are many of them who forget their vow of poverty to gratify their own avarice."

"It strikes me, Hircan," said Nomerfide, "that you know of some such case; if it is worthy of this company, I beg you will tell it us."

"I will do so," he replied, "although I dislike speaking of such people, for methinks they are of that class of whom Virgil says to Dante, 'Pass on, and heed them not.' However, to show you that they have not laid aside their passions with their mundane garments, I will tell a thing that happened."*

NOVEL LVI.

A PIOUS LADY HAVING ASKED A CORDELIER TO PROVIDE A GOOD HUSBAND FOR HER DAUGHTER, HE MARRIES ANOTHER CORDELIER TO THE YOUNG LADY, AND POSSESSES HIMSELF OF HER DOWRY — THE CHEAT IS DISCOVERED AND PUNISHED.

A FRENCH lady who visited Padua heard that there was a Cordelier in the episcopal prison. Observing that every one talked and joked about him, she inquired the reason, and learned that this Cordelier was an old man, confessor to a very respectable and devout lady, who had been some years a widow, and had but one daughter, whom she loved so much that she spared no pains to amass wealth for her and procure

* The opinions expressed in this novel and epilogue were too bold for the first editors of the Heptameron, Boaistuau and Gruget, who altered some passages in the former, and substituted for the latter a much shorter epilogue, containing only common-place reflections on avarice, &c.

her a good match. As her daughter grew up, her whole thought was how to find her a husband who might live happily with them both; that is to say, a conscientious person like herself. As she had heard it laid down by some stupid preacher that it was better to do wrong by the advice of the doctors of the Church than to do right trusting in the inspiration of the Holy Ghost, she applied to her confessor, an aged monk, who was a doctor of theology, and bore a blameless reputation throughout the town, never doubting but that she should secure her own peace and her daughter's through the advice and the prayers of the good father.

She besought him earnestly to choose a husband for her daughter—such a husband as he knew would be suitable to a girl who loved God and her honour. He told her he must first of all implore the grace of the Holy Spirit by fasting and prayer, and then, God lending him light, he hoped he should be able to find what she sought. Upon that he went away to ponder over the affair. As the mother had told him that she had five hundred ducats ready to hand over to her daughter's husband, and that she would maintain both husband and wife, and supply them with lodging, furniture, and clothes, he bethought him of a handsome strapping young brother of his order on whom he would bestow the pretty girl, the house, furniture, board, and clothing, while he himself would keep the five hundred ducats to assuage his burning covetousness. After he had talked with his man and arranged everything, he went to the mother and said to her: "I believe, madam, that God has sent me his angel Raphael, as of old to Tobias, to enable me to find a spouse for your daughter. I have in my house the most respectable young gentleman in Italy, who has seen your daughter, and is deeply in love with her. When I was to-day at prayer, God sent him to me, and he declared how much he longs for this marriage; and I, knowing his family and his relations, and that he comes of a notable race, promised to speak to you on the subject. I know but one inconvenience attending this match, which is, that wishing to save one of his friends whom another man would have slain, he drew his sword to part them; but it happened that his friend killed the other; in consequence of which, though he never struck a stroke, he is nevertheless a fugitive, because he was present at the murder, and had drawn his sword. His parents have advised him to retire to this city, where he wears the dress of a student, and where he will remain incognito until this affair of his is arranged, which it is hoped it will be before long. You see, consequently, that it would be necessary for the marriage to be secret, and that you should not object to his going every day to the public lectures, and coming home in the evening to sup and sleep in your house."

"I see a great advantage to myself in what you tell me, sir," said the mother; "for at least I shall have by me what I desire most in the world."

The Cordelier produced the gallant in very good trim, and with a handsome doublet of crimson satin. He was so well received that the betrothal took place without more delay, and midnight had no sooner struck than mass was said, they were wedded and bedded, and remained together until daybreak, when the bridegroom said to his bride, that, in order to maintain his incognito, he was obliged to leave her and go to the college. After putting on his crimson satin doublet and his long robe, not forgetting his black silk coif, he took leave of his wife, who was still in bed, and assured her that every evening he would come and sup with her, but that she must not expect him at dinner. Thereupon he went away, and left his wife the happiest woman in the world in her own esteem, for having met with so excellent a match. Away went the young Cordelier to the old father, and handed over the five hundred ducats, according to their previous agreement, and in the evening he returned to her who regarded him as her husband; nor did he fail to make himself so beloved by her and by his mother-in-law, that they would not have exchanged him for the greatest prince in the world.

This went on for some time; but as God has pity on those who honestly err, it came to pass that the mother and daughter had a mind to go hear mass at the church of the Cordeliers, and to pay a visit at the same time to the good father confessor through whose instrumentality they thought themselves so well provided, the one with a son-in-law, the other with a husband. Chance so ordained, that, not finding the confessor there, nor any one else they knew, they were content to hear high mass, which was just beginning, whilst they awaited the confessor's arrival. The young wife attending closely to the divine service, was greatly surprised when the priest turned to say *Dominus vobiscum*, for she fancied she beheld her husband, or some one singularly resembling him. She said not a word, however, but waited till he appeared again, when she had a still better view of him than before, and no longer doubting that it was he, "Oh, mother!" she exclaimed, "what do I see?"

"What is it?" said the mother.

"My husband saying mass, or somebody the most like him in the world."

"Pray, my dear," said the mother, who had not taken much notice of the priest, "don't let such a notion into your head. It is absolutely impossible that such pious men should practise such a cheat. It would be a great sin in you to believe any such thing."

For all that the mother did not fail to use her eyes, and when it came to saying *Ite missa est*, she saw for certain that no twin brothers were ever more like each other. Nevertheless, so simple was she, that she would fain have said, "God preserve me from believing my eyes." However, as the matter was one which so deeply concerned her daughter, she determined to sift it to the bottom and know the truth. The husband, who had not perceived them, having returned home, she said to her daughter, "We shall now know the truth about your husband if you choose. When he is in bed I will come in, and you will pull off his coif from behind before he is aware of it. We shall see then if he is tonsured like the one who said mass."

So said, so done. The wicked husband was no sooner in bed than the old lady came in, and took him by both hands as if in play, whilst the daughter lifted up the back of his cap and discovered his fine shorn crown. Appalled at the sight, they instantly called in the domestics, who seized and bound him, and kept him fast till morning, in spite of all his excuses and fine words, which moved no one. Next morning the mother sent for her confessor, under pretence that she had some great secret to communicate to him. He came with speed, and had no sooner entered her doors than she had him seized like the other, upbraiding him with the cheat he had put upon her. After this she committed them both into the hands of justice; and if the judges were honest men, it is not likely that this crime was left unpunished.

You see from this, ladies, that those who take the vow of poverty are not exempt from being tempted by avarice, and this is what leads them to the commission of so much mischief.

"Or rather of so much good," said Saffredent; "for how often did the monk make good cheer with the five hundred ducats which the old woman would have hoarded? Besides, the poor girl who had longed so much for a husband was put by his means into a condition to have two, and to judge the better of all hierarchies."

"You always entertain the falsest opinions I ever heard," said Oisille. "This comes of your believing that the temperaments of all women are like your own."

"By your leave, madam, that is not it," said Saffredent; "and I would with all my heart that women could be as easily satisfied as men."

"That is a bad saying," replied Oisille, "for there is no one here but knows the very contrary, and that what you say is not true. The tale we have heard is a convincing proof of the ignorance of poor women, and the wickedness of those whom we regard as better than the generality of men; for neither the mother nor the daughter would do anything by themselves, but submitted to the advice of those whom they believed to be wise and good."

"There are women so hard to please," said Longarine, "that it seems as if nothing less than angels will suit them."

"Thence it comes," said Simontault, "that they often meet with devils; and especially those of them who, not trusting in God's grace, imagine that by their own good sense, or by that of others, they shall find in this world the felicity which can only come from God."

"Why, Simontault!" exclaimed Oisille, "I was not aware that you knew so much good."

"Madam," replied he, "it is a pity I am not much tried and proved, because, for want of being known to you, I see you have formed a bad opinion of me. I may fairly, however, practise a Cordelier's trade, since a Cordelier has put his hand to mine."

"Then you call deceiving women your trade," said Parlamente; "thus, out of your own mouth, you condemn yourself."

"If I had deceived a hundred thousand of them," he returned, "I should not yet have revenged myself for the woes which one alone of their sex has made me endure."

"I know," retorted Parlamente, "that you complain perpetually of women; yet we see you so merry and in such good case, that there is no appearance of your having suffered as much as you say. But the Fair Lady without Mercy replies that 'it suits well to say so, by way of deriving some comfort from it.' "*

"You quote a notable doctor," said Simontault, "who is not only disagreeable, but makes all those ladies so who have read and followed his doctrine."

"Nevertheless, his doctrine is as profitable to young ladies as any I know," rejoined Parlamente.

"Were it come to that," said Simontault, "that the ladies were without mercy, we might well let our horses rest and our harness rust until the next war, and do nothing but think of household affairs. I pray you tell me, is it to a lady's credit that she should be without pity, charity, love, or compassion?"

"Without charity or love, no," replied Parlamente, "that she should not be, but that word compassion sounds so badly among women, that they cannot use it without wronging their honour. For what is this pity or compassion? It is properly granting the favour one asks for. Now we know well what is the favour men usually crave."

"With your good leave, madam," said Simontault, "some there are so moderate that the only favour they ask is liberty to speak."

"You remind me of one who was contented with a glove," said Parlamente.

"Let us know something about a lover who was so easy to deal with," said Hircan.

"I will tell you the tale with pleasure," she replied.

---

* A passage from Alain Chartier's poem, previously quoted in Novel XII.

NOVEL LVII.

OF A RIDICULOUS MILORD WHO WORE A LADY'S GLOVE ON HIS DRESS-COAT.

KING LOUIS XI. sent Monsieur de Montmorency to England in the capacity of ambassador. He conducted himself so well there that he won the friendship of the king and all the other princes, and they even communicated to him many secret affairs on which they wished to have his advice. One day, when he was at an entertainment given by the king, he was seated beside a milord of high family, who wore, fastened to his doublet, a small glove such as women use. The glove was fastened with golden hooks, and the seams were adorned with such a great quantity of diamonds, rubies, emeralds, and pearls, that the value of the glove was something extraordinary. Monsieur de Montmorency cast his eyes on it so often, that the milord perceived he wished to ask him the reason of his magnificence; and, thinking the explanation would redound to his honour, he said to the ambassador, "I perceive, monsieur, that you are surprised I have so much enriched this poor glove; but I will tell you the reason. I look upon you as a gallant man, and I am sure you know what love is. You must know that I have all my life loved a lady whom I still love and shall love even after I am dead. As my heart was bolder to make a good choice than my tongue to declare it, I remained for seven years without daring even to show any signs of loving her, for fear, if she perceived them, I should lose the opportunities I had of being frequently with her—a thought which terrified me more than death. But one day, being in a meadow and gazing upon her, I was seized with such a palpitation of the heart that I lost all colour and countenance. She having noticed this, and asked me what was the matter, I replied that I felt intolerably sick at heart. Thinking that this sickness was one in which love had no share, she expressed her pity for it; and that made me to entreat that she would put her hand on my heart, and see how it beat. She did so, more from charity than affection, and as I held her gloved hand on my heart, its motions became so violent that she perceived I had spoken the truth. Then I pressed her hand on my bosom, and said to her, 'Receive this heart, madam, which struggles to escape from my bosom and put itself in the hands of her from whom I hope for grace, life, and pity. It is this heart, madam, which now constrains me to declare the love I have long cherished for you in secret, for neither my heart nor I, madam, can longer withstand so potent a god.' Surprised at so unexpected a declaration, she would have withdrawn her hand, but I held it so fast that her glove remained with me instead of that cruel hand. As I never had before or since any other approach to nearer intimacy with her, I placed this glove over my heart as the fittest plaister I could apply to it. I have enriched it with all the finest jewels in my possession; but what is dearer to me than all of them is the glove itself, which I would not give for the realm of England, for there is nothing I prize in the world so much as to feel it on my bosom."

The Seigneur de Montmorency, who would rather have had a lady's hand than her glove, highly extolled his gallantry, and told him he was the most genuine lover he had ever seen, and worthy of better treatment, since he set so much store by such a trifle. "But," said he, "there is some comfort even in ill luck, as the proverb says. You were so much in love, that if you had had something better than the glove you would perhaps have died of joy." The milord admitted this probability, without perceiving that Monsieur de Montmorency was making game of him.

If all the men in the world were of this character, the ladies might trust them, since it would cost them no more than a glove.

"I have been so well acquainted with Monsieur de Montmorency," said Geburon, "that I am sure he would not have been so easily satisfied as the Englishman, otherwise he would not have achieved so many successes as he did in love; for, as the old song says, 'Of a faint heart in love no one hears any good.'"

"You may be sure the poor lady withdrew her hand in great haste when she felt the great agitation of the heart," said Saffredent. "She thought, no doubt, that the milord was about to expire; and there is nothing, they say, which women abhor so much as to touch dead bodies."

"If you had frequented hospitals as much as taverns," said Ennasuite, "you would not say that; for you would have seen women lay out dead bodies for burial, which men with all their boldness were often afraid to approach."

"It is true," said Simontault, "that there is no one on whom penance has been imposed who has not done the reverse of that which afforded him pleasure: witness a lady I once saw in a distinguished house, who, to compensate for the pleasure she had taken in kissing a man she loved, was found at four o'clock in the morning kissing the dead body of a man who had been killed the preceding day, and for whom she had never had any especial love more than for another. Every one was then aware that she was doing penance for her past pleasures."

"That is just the way," said Oisille, "in which men poison all the good acts done by women. My opinion is that we ought to kiss neither the living nor the dead, except after the manner which God commands."

"For my part," said Hircan, "I care so little for kissing any other woman than my wife, that I willingly subscribe to any terms that may be made on the subject; but I pity the young folk whom you would deprive of such a small gratification, annulling the precept of Saint Paul, who ordained that people should kiss *in osculo sancto*."

"If Saint Paul had been a man like you," said Nomerfide, "we should have demanded palpable evidence of the spirit of God which spoke in him."

"To the last you will rather doubt Holy Writ than give up a hair's breadth of one of your petty ceremonies," said Geburon.

"God forbid," replied Oisille, "that we should doubt Holy Writ, though we put little faith in your lies. There is no woman but knows that her proper creed consists in never doubting the Word of God, and always distrusting that of men."

"I believe," said Simontault, "that there are more men deceived by women than women deceived by men. Their want of love for us hinders them from believing the truth;

whilst we, on the contrary, love them to such excess, that we readily believe their falsehoods, and find ourselves their dupes before we have imagined the possibility of their duping us."

"I suppose," said Parlamente, "you have heard some fool complain of having been duped by some light woman. In fact, what you state carries so little weight with it, that it has need of being supported by some example. So, if you have one to adduce, let us hear it. I do not mean to say that we are bound to believe you; but it will not pain our ears to hear you malign us, for we know the truth of the matter."

"Well, that being so," said Simontault, "you shall be satisfied."

NOVEL LVIII.

HOW A LADY OF THE COURT PLEASANTLY REVENGED HERSELF ON HER FAITHLESS LOVER.

There was at the court of Francis I. a lady of lively wit, who, by her beauty, her good breeding, and pleasing tongue, had won the hearts of several gentlemen, with whom she contrived to pass the time very well without exposing her honour, playing with them so pleasantly that they knew not on what to reckon; for the most confident were in despair, and the most despairing were not without hope. However, whilst making sport of most of them, she could not help greatly loving one of them, whom she called her cousin—a name which served as a pretext for a closer intimacy. But, as there is nothing stable in the world, their friendship often turned into anger, and then again became stronger than ever, in such wise that the whole court could not be ignorant of it. One day this lady, in order to let it be seen that she was passionless, as well as to tease him on account of whose love she had suffered much annoyance, showed him a more gracious countenance than ever she had done before. The gentleman, who was not deficient in boldness either in war or in love, began hotly to press the suit he had often before addressed to her. She pretended she could no longer resist, granted what he asked, and told him that, in order to do so, she would go up to her chamber, which was on a garret-floor, where she knew there was nobody, and as soon as he saw her go, he was to follow her; and then, as she said, so graciously was she disposed towards him, that he would find her alone.

The gentleman believed her, and went with great delight to amuse himself with the other ladies, until he should see her depart. His fair one, who was not deficient in any of the sly ways of women, went up to Madame Margaret, the king's daughter, and the Duchess of Montpensier, and said to them, "I will show you, if you like, the finest sport you have ever seen." The princesses, who were no friends to melancholy, begged she would tell them what the sport was. "There is such a one, whom you both know," she said, "a charming man, if there ever was one, but the most audacious in the world. You know how many tricks he has played me; and you know, also, that when I loved him most he quitted me for others; which vexed me more than I suffered to appear. But now God has given me an opportunity to be revenged. I am now going to my room, which is overhead; and if you will watch you will presently see him come up after me. When he shall have passed the galleries, and is about to ascend the stairs, go both of you to the window, help me to cry 'Thief! thief!' and you will see what a rage he will be in. I am sure his anger will not become him badly; and if he does not openly abuse me, I am sure he will not fail to do so in his heart."

This plan was agreed on, not without much laughter beforehand; for there was no gentleman who waged war more on the ladies, all of whom loved and esteemed him so much, that for nothing in the world would they have exposed themselves to his raillery. As soon as the concocter of the plot had left them, the two princesses, who anticipated a large share in the glory which she was to win from the gentleman, set themselves on the watch, and when he went out they followed him into the gallery. There, suspecting nothing, he muffled himself in his cloak to hide his face, and descended the stairs to the court, but, seeing some one by whom he did not wish to be observed, he traversed the court and returned by another way, all the while without perceiving the princesses, who saw all his movements. When he reached the staircase leading to the fair one's chamber, the princesses posted themselves at the window, and presently they heard the lady above crying "Thief! thief!" with all her might. The two princesses repeated the cry so loudly that they were heard all over the château. I leave you to imagine the vexation of the gentleman as he ran away, not so well muffled but that he was known by those who were in the secret. They often rallied him on the affair afterwards; nor did she who had played him the trick spare him, but told him to his face that she had well revenged herself. But he had such ready answers, and defended himself so cleverly, that he would have had them believe he had suspected their design, and that he had only promised to go to the lady to make sport of her in some way, assuring them he would never have given himself the trouble for her sake, for he had long ceased to love her. But the ladies would not own themselves defeated in that way, and the affair is still undecided.

If he really believed the lady, which is not probable, since he was so wary and so bold that few or no men of his age and time surpassed him, whereof his glorious death is good evidence, it strikes me that one cannot help admitting that gallant men who are in love are often the dupes of ladies from excess of credulity.*

"In faith," said Ennasuite, "I applaud the lady for what

* The Bibliophiles Français surmise that the Queen of Navarre has made herself the heroine of this novel. The doctrines she has several times laid down in her epilogues respecting love and the relations of courtesy between the sexes, are quite in harmony with what she there says respecting the *serviteurs* whom a lady may entertain without giving her husband any reason for suspicion. Nothing can be conjectured as to the name of the gallant on whom the trick was played.

In the following novel Margaret returns to the same subject, and relates how the same lady contrived to convict her husband of infidelity, and force him to take her to court, from which he had removed her through jealousy. If we compare this with what is known of Margaret's married life, the conjecture of her last editors appears so much the more plausible.

she did; for when a man loves a lady and quits her for another, she can never revenge herself too much."

"True, if she is loved," said Parlamente; "but some th­ are who love without making sure they are loved; and when they perceive that their gallants love elsewhere, they accuse them of inconstancy. But women of discretion never suffer themselves to be thus deceived. They pay no heed to anything but the truth, for fear of being exposed to the irksome consequences of falsehood; for the true and the false talk the same language."

"If all women were of your way of thinking," said Simontault, "men might box up their supplications. But for all that you and others like you can say, we will never believe that women are as incredulous as they are fair. Under this conviction we will live as content as you would wish to render us uneasy by your maxims."

"As I very well know the lady who played this good trick," said Longarine, "I can have no difficulty in believing any sly things that may be attributed to her. Since she did not spare her own husband, it is not likely that she would spare her lover."

"What, her husband?" said Simontault. "Then you know more than I; so pray tell us what you know."

"I will, since you wish it," she replied.

NOVEL LIX.

THE SAME LADY, WHOSE HUSBAND WAS JEALOUS OF HER WITHOUT JUST CAUSE, CONTRIVES TO DETECT HIM IN SUCH A POSITION WITH ONE OF HER WOMEN THAT HE IS OBLIGED TO HUMBLE HIMSELF, AND ALLOW HIS WIFE TO LIVE AS SHE PLEASES.

THE lady of whom you told the tale was married to a man of good and ancient family, whose fortune was not inferior to his birth. Their marriage was solely the result of their mutual love. The wife, who was of all women in the world

the most ingenuous, made no secret of it to her husband
that she had lovers, whom she made game of, and only
used for her pastime. Her husband had his share in this
pleasure; but in the long run he grew dissatisfied with
this manner of proceeding. On the one hand he took it
amiss that she had long visits from persons he regarded
neither as relations nor as friends, and on the other he was
not pleased with the expenditure he was compelled to make
in attending the court. For this reason he retired to his
own house as often as he could; but he received so many
visits there that his expenses were hardly diminished. Wherever
he was his wife always found means to divert herself,
whether with play, or dancing, or other amusements, to
which young ladies may decorously addict themselves. When
her husband sometimes told her that they spent too much,
she would reply that he might be assured she would never
make him a cuckold, but only a rogue. In fact, she
was so fond of magnificence in attire, that she insisted on
having dresses as rich and fine as any seen at the court, to
which her husband took her as seldom as possible, notwithstanding
her eager desire to be always there. For this
reason she made herself so complaisant to her husband that
it was with difficulty he refused her most extravagant requests.

One day, when she had failed in all her devices to induce
him to take her to court, she perceived that he looked very
wistfully at a chambermaid of hers, and thought she might
turn this circumstance in some way to her own advantage.
She questioned the girl in private, and managed so cleverly,
by dint of promises and threats, that she made her confess
that since she had been in her service not a day had passed
in which her master had not made love to her; but that she
would rather die than do anything contrary to God and her
honour, the more so as the lady had done her the honour to
receive her into her service, which would make the crime
double.

The lady, on learning her husband's infidelity, was at once
vexed and rejoiced. She was vexed that at the very time
when he testified so much regard for her, he was furtively
seeking means to put an affront upon her under her very
eyes, and to quit her for a girl she regarded as greatly

inferior to herself in beauty and attractions. She was rejoiced, because she hoped to surprise her husband in the fact, and to work him in such a way that he would never again reproach her with her lovers or her fondness for residing at court. To this end she begged the girl to yield gradually to her husband's solicitations upon certain prescribed conditions. The girl made some objections; but her mistress having made herself warrant for her life and honour, she promised to do whatever she pleased.

The next time the husband accosted the girl he found her quite changed, and pressed her to comply with more than his usual vivacity; but knowing her part by rote, she represented to him that she was a poor girl, and would become poorer than ever if she yielded to him, because she would be dismissed by her mistress, in whose service she hoped to save enough to get her a good husband. The gentleman replied, that she had no need to be uneasy on that score, for he would settle her better in marriage than her mistress could do; and, moreover, he would manage the intrigue with such secrecy that no one should ever be able to say a word against her. Thereupon the bargain was concluded. When the parties came to deliberate on the place where it was to be sealed, the girl said she knew no better place, or less likely to be suspected, than a little house in the park, in which it happened, fortunately, that there was a chamber and a bed. The gentleman, who would never have made objections to any place proposed, was quite satisfied with this, and awaited with great impatience the day and hour agreed on.

The girl kept her word with her mistress, told her all that had passed between her master and herself, and said that the rendezvous was for the next day after dinner. She would not fail, she said, to give her mistress a signal when it was time for her to keep the appointment, and begged she would not fail to notice it, and be upon the spot in time to deliver her from the peril to which she exposed herself for her sake. The lady vowed she might depend upon her, begged her to have no fear, and assured her she would never forsake her, and would perfectly secure her from her master's resentment.

Next day after dinner the gentleman showed a fairer face to his wife than he had ever done; this was by no means agreeable to her; but she dissembled so well that he never suspected what was passing in her mind. When dinner was over, she asked him how he would while away the time. He said he knew nothing better for the purpose than to play at cent.* The company then sat down to play, but she would not be of the party, saying she would be as much amused looking on. Before he sat down to play he did not forget to tell the girl to remember her promise. The game had no sooner begun than she went out of the room, making a sign to her mistress that she was setting out on the pilgrimage she had to make. The signal was not lost upon the wife, but the husband saw nothing. An hour afterwards, however, one of his valets having made him a sign from a distance, he told his wife he had a headache, and must go into the open air and rest a little. She knew what ailed him quite as well as he did himself, and asked him, should she hold his cards. He begged her to do so, and said he would soon be back. There was no need to hurry himself, she said, for she could play for two hours without being tired. The husband then retired to his chamber, and thence to the park. His wife, who knew a short way, waited a little, and then suddenly pretending to have the colic, she gave up her hand to another.

The moment she left the room she threw off her high pattens, and ran as fast to the place where she did not choose the bargain to be concluded without her, and arrived in good time, almost as soon as her husband. She remained behind the door to hear the fine things he said to her servant, and when she saw that he was approaching the criminal point, she caught hold of him behind, and said, "I am too near for you to take another." It is needless to ask if he was then in a towering passion, both at being frustrated of his expected pleasure, and at seeing that his wife, whose good-will he was afraid of losing for ever, knew more than he would have had her know. Believing, however, that it was a trick played upon him by the girl, he ran at her with such fury, without speaking to his wife, that if the latter had not held his hands he would have killed her. He said, in a transport of rage, that

* *To play at cent.* This probably means the game now called picquet; it is an old game, and is among those enumerated by Rabelais in book i. ch. xxii. of Gargantua.

she was the worst baggage he had ever known, and that if his wife had waited, she would have seen that he only came there to try her and make a fool of her; and that instead of what she expected he would have given her a flogging. But the wife knew better than to accept such flimsy excuses, and rated him so roundly that he was greatly afraid she would leave him. He made her all the promises she desired, and touched by her sage remonstrances, he confessed that he was wrong to take it amiss that she had lovers. He agreed with her that a handsome and respectable woman is not the less virtuous for being loved, provided she say and do nothing contrary to her honour; but that a man is unpardonable who takes pains to pursue a girl who does not love him, and to wrong his wife and his own conscience. He ended by promising that he would no longer prevent her from going to court, nor ever take it amiss that she had lovers, convinced, as he was, that she retained them only for her diversion, not for any regard she had for them.

This language was not displeasing to the lady, who thought she had gained a great point; however, she pretended quite the reverse, saying she did not care to go to court, and that there was nothing dearer to her than his affection, without which all companies were odious to her. A woman, she said, who was loved by her husband, and who loved him as she did hers, carried with her a safe-conduct, warranting her to speak with all the world and be blamed by no one. The poor gentleman took such pains to assure her of the love he cherished for her, that at last they went back good friends. To avoid a recurrence of the mischief, he begged her to dismiss the servant who had caused all this hubbub. She did so; but it was by marrying her well and respectably at the expense of her husband, who, to make his wife forget the prank he had played, took her soon to court with such pomp and magnificence that she had full reason to be satisfied.

This, ladies, was what made me say I was not surprised at the trick she had played on one of her lovers after the one I knew she had played on her husband.

"You have depicted to us a very sly wife, and a very stupid husband," said Hircan. "Since he had gone so far, he ought not to have stopped on so fair a road."

"And what should he have done?" inquired Longarine.

"What he wanted to do," replied Hircan, "for his wife was not less angry at knowing what he had intended to do than if he had actually done it. Perhaps she would have liked him better if he had shown himself bolder and a better fellow."

"That's all very well," said Ennasuite; "but where do you find men who can force two women at once? The wife would have defended her rights, and the girl her maidenhead."

"That is true," said Hircan; "but a strong and bold man will fearlessly attack two weak persons, and be sure to get the better of them."

"I admit that if he had drawn his sword he might have killed them both," returned Ennasuite; "but I don't see how he could have escaped from them otherwise. Tell us, pray, what would you have done, had you been in his place?"

"I would have thrown my arms round my wife and carried her out of doors, and then I would have done what I pleased to the servant by fair means or by force."

"It is enough, Hircan," said Parlamente, "that you know how to do wrong."

"I am sure, Parlamente," he replied, "that I do not scandalise the innocent before whom I speak, or wish to maintain a bad cause. I neither praise the enterprise which was bad in itself, nor the enterpriser who stopped short half-way for fear rather than for love. I applaud a man who loves his wife as God ordains; but when he does not love her, I do not think the better of him for fearing her."

"Truly," returned Parlamente, "if love did not make you a good husband, what you would do for fear would be no great thing, and so I should esteem it."

"The love I have for you, Parlamente," said Hircan, "subjects me as much to your wishes as the fear of death and hell could do."

"You may say what you will," his wife replied, "but I have reason to be content with what I have seen and known of you. As for what I have not known, I have no wish to doubt, and still less to inquire about it."

"It is in my opinion," said Nomerfide, "a great folly in

women to pry so curiously into what their husbands do; but it is no less a one in husbands to want to know every step taken by their wives. Sufficient for the day is the evil thereof, without taking so much thought for the morrow."

"Nevertheless it is sometimes necessary," said Oisille, "to inquire into matters in which the honour of a house is concerned; that is to say, for the purpose of setting things right, and not from a wish to judge ill of persons, for every one is liable to error."

"Many have come to mischief for want of inquiring into their wives' freaks," said Geburon.

"If you know any instance of the kind, pray tell it us," said Longarine.

"I will do so with pleasure," he replied, "since you desire it."

NOVEL LX.

A WOMAN OF PARIS QUITS HER HUSBAND FOR ONE OF THE KING'S CHANTERS, COUNTERFEITS DEATH, AND IS BURIED, BUT SECRETLY DISINTERRED ALIVE AND WELL—HER HUSBAND MARRIES ANOTHER WIFE, AND FIFTEEN YEARS AFTERWARDS IS OBLIGED TO REPUDIATE HER, AND TAKE BACK HIS FIRST WIFE.

There was in Paris a man so good-natured that he would have scrupled to believe that a man had lain with his wife though he had seen it with his own eyes. This poor man married the most profligate woman in the world, but never noticed her licentiousness, and treated her as though she were the best of wives. But one day, when King Louis XII. was in Paris, this woman went and gave herself up to one of that prince's chanters; and when she found that the king was quitting Paris, and that she was about to lose her lover, she resolved to go with him and quit her husband. The chanter had no objection to this, and took her to a house he had near Blois, where they lived long together. The poor husband, not finding his wife, searched for her in all directions, and learned at last that she had gone off with the chanter. Wishing to recover his lost sheep, which he had badly guarded, he wrote her several letters, begging her to return, and promising to receive her, provided she would lead a good life for the future; but she took such pleasure in the chanter's singing that she had forgotten her husband's voice, made no account of his fair words, and snapped her fingers at him. The incensed husband then gave her notice that he would claim her legally through the Church, since she would not return to him of her own accord; whereupon, fearing that if justice meddled with the matter she and her chanter would come badly off, she devised a scheme worthy of such a woman.

She pretended to be sick, sent for some worthy women of the city to visit her, and they came the more willingly as they hoped to make her illness instrumental towards bringing her back from her vicious ways. To this end each of them addressed the best remonstrances she could to her, and the seemingly dying woman listened to them with tears, confessed her sin, and played the part so well, that the whole company had pity on her, believing her tears and her repentance to be sincere. They tried to console the poor penitent, told her that God was not so terrible by a great deal as some indiscreet preachers represented him to be, and assured her He would never withhold his mercy from her; and then they sent for a good man to hear her confession. Next day the priest of the parish came and administered to her the holy sacrament, which she received with so much devotion that all the good women of the town who were present were moved with tears, and praised the divine goodness for having had pity on the poor creature. Afterwards, upon her feigning that she could no longer swallow food, the priest brought her extreme unction, which she received with many fine signs of devotion; for she could hardly speak, at least so it was believed. She lay a long while in the same state; but at last the spectators imagined that she gradually lost her sight, her hearing, and her other senses, whereupon everybody began to cry, "Jesus! Lord! have mercy!" Night being now at hand, and the ladies having some way to go, they all retired. As they were leaving the house, word was brought them that she had just expired. They said a *De profundis* for her, and went away.

The priest asked the chanter where he would have her

buried. He replied that she had expressed a wish to be buried in the cemetery, and that it would be advisable under the circumstances that the interment should take place by night. The unfortunate woman was laid out for burial by a servant, who took good care not to hurt her; and then she was carried by torchlight to the grave which the chanter had caused to be dug. When the body was carried past the houses of those who had seen the deceased receive extreme unction, they all came out and accompanied her to the grave, where the priests and the women left her, but the chanter remained after them. The moment he saw that the company were far enough off, he and his servant woman lifted the pretended dead woman out of the grave more alive than ever, and took her back to his house, in which he kept her long concealed.

The husband, who was bent on recovering his wife, went to Blois to demand justice, and found that she was dead and buried. The fact was certified to him by all the ladies of Blois, who related to him what a fine end she had made; and greatly did the good man rejoice, believing that the soul of his wife was in Paradise, and himself disencumbered of her wicked body. He returned to Paris with a glad heart, and entered into a second marriage with a respectable young woman, a good housewife, by whom he had several children, and with whom he lived fourteen or fifteen years. But at last rumour, which keeps no secrets, informed him that his first wife was not dead, and that she was still with her chanter. The poor man dissembled as much as he could, affecting to know nothing, and heartily wishing that the rumour might be false; but his virtuous wife heard of it, and was so distressed that she almost died of grief. Could she have concealed her misfortune without wounding her conscience, she would gladly have done it; but that was impossible, for the Church took up the matter at once, and began by separating them until the truth should have been ascertained. The fact having been verified, the poor man was constrained to quit his good wife and go after his bad one. He came to Blois shortly after Francis I. became king. He found there Queen Claude and the regent-mother, laid his complaint before them, and demanded of them her whom he would fain not have found; but he was forced to seek her, to the great pity of all beholders.

His wife, on being confronted with him, insisted for a long time that he was not her husband; which he would gladly have believed if he could. Angry but unabashed, she then told him she would rather die than go back to him. The good man was very well satisfied with this declaration; but the ladies, before whom she spoke so impudently, condemned her to return to her husband, and so sharply admonished and threatened the chanter, that he was constrained to tell his ugly mistress he did not want to have anything more to do with her, and that she must go back to her husband. Thus repulsed on all sides, the wretched creature went away with her husband, and was better treated by him than she deserved.

I repeat, ladies, that if the poor husband had taken heed to his wife, he would not thus have lost her; for a thing well watched is not easily lost, and doubtless the proverb is true, which says that negligence makes the thief.

"It is strange," remarked Hircan, "strong love is where it seems least reasonable."

"I have heard," said Simontault, "that one might sooner break two marriages than the love of a priest and his servant."

"I believe it," said Ennasuite, "for those who bind others in marriage know how to fasten the knot so tightly that it is only to be undone by death; the doctors, too, maintain that spiritual language is more persuasive than other, and consequently spiritual love surpasses every other kind."

"I cannot pardon ladies," said Dagoucin, "who forsake a well-bred husband or lover for a priest, however good-looking."

"Leave our holy mother the Church alone, I pray you," said Hircan, "and be assured that it is a great pleasure for poor timid women to sin in secret with those who can absolve them; for some there are who are much more ashamed of confessing a sin than of committing it."

"You speak of such as know not God," said Oisille, "and imagine that secret things will not be revealed before the whole host of Heaven. But I do not believe that it is for sake of confession that such women seek confessors. The enemy has so blinded them that they think much more of settling down upon a place that seems to them the most secret and secure, than of having absolution for the guilt of which they do not repent."

"Repent, indeed!" exclaimed Saffredent. "They think themselves much more saintly than other women, and I am sure that there are some who think it a great honour to them to persevere in intrigues of this sort."

"From the way in which you express yourself," said Oisille, "one would think you know some such person. That being the case, I beg you will begin the day to-morrow by telling us what you know. There goes the last bell for vespers; for the monks went away after our tenth novel, and left us to decide our dispute between ourselves."

So saying she rose, and the company following her example, they went to church, where they found they were waited for. After vespers they supped, and not without talking over several fine tales. After supper they all went, according to custom, to divert themselves in the meadow, and then to bed, to have their memories clearer next day.

SEVENTH DAY.

Madame Oisille failed not to administer to them in the morning the wholesome pasture she drew from the reading of the acts and virtuous deeds of the glorious knights and apostles of Jesus Christ, and told them that those narratives were enough to fill one with the wish to have lived in such times, and make one deplore the deformity of this age compared with that. After reading and explaining to them the beginning of that excellent book, she begged them to go to church in the union with which the apostles addressed their prayers to Heaven, and solicit the grace of God, who never refuses it to those who ask for it with faith. Every one thought the advice very good, and they arrived in church just as the mass of the Holy Ghost was beginning. This was so *à propos*, that they listened to the service with great devotion. Again at dinner the conversation turned on the lives of the blessed apostles, and the subject was so pleasing that the company had nearly forgotten to return to the rendezvous for the novels. Nomerfide, who was the youngest of them, observed this, and said: "Madame Oisille has put us so much upon devotion, that the time for relating novels is passing away without our thinking of retiring to prepare our novels." Thereupon the company rose, went for a short while to their respective chambers, and then repaired to the meadow as they had done the day before.

When all were comfortably seated, Madame Oisille said to Saffredent, "Though I am quite sure you will say nothing to the advantage of women, yet I must remind you that you promised us a novel yesterday evening."

"I stipulate, madam," replied Saffredent, "that I shall not pass for an evil speaker in speaking the truth, nor lose the good-will of virtuous ladies by relating what wantons do. Experience has taught me what it is to be deprived of their presence, and if I were likewise deprived of their good graces, I should not be alive at this moment."

So saying, he cast his eyes on the opposite side to that where sat she who was the cause of his weal and woe; but at the same time he looked at Ennasuite, and made her blush as if what he had said was meant for her. However, he was not the less understood by the right person. Madame Oisille having then assured him he might fairly speak the truth at the cost of whom it concerned, he began as follows.

NOVEL LXI.

A HUSBAND BECAME RECONCILED TO HIS WIFE AFTER SHE HAD LIVED FOURTEEN OR FIFTEEN YEARS WITH A CANON.

THERE lived near the town of Autun a very handsome woman, fair complexioned, very tall, and of as goodly a presence as any woman I ever saw. She had married a respectable man, who seemed younger than herself, and with whom she had reason to be satisfied. Shortly after their marriage he took her to Autun, where he had business. Whilst the husband was engaged as a suitor in the courts of justice, the wife went to church and prayed for him. She continued her visits to that holy place so long, that a very rich canon fell in love with her, and took his measures so well that the poor wretch gave herself up to him; but the husband had no suspicion of this, and was more intent to taking care of his property than of his wife.

When the time came for the husband and wife to return to their home, which was distant seven good leagues from the town, great was the regret on her part. The canon promised to go see her often, which he did under pretence of journeys, in which he always called at their house. The husband was not such a fool as not to understand the canon's purpose, and accordingly, when he next came there he did not see the wife, for her husband had taken good care to prevent it. The wife pretended not to notice this jealousy, of which she was well aware, but she was bent on counteracting the precautions it led to, deeming it a hell to be deprived of the sight of her idol. One day, when her husband was abroad, she gave her men and women servants so much to do, that she remained alone and unobserved in the house. Immediately, taking what was necessary for her, and without any other company than her extravagant love, she started off on foot for Autun, where she arrived not so late but that she was recognised by her canon, who kept her close and concealed for more than a year, in spite of all the monitions and excommunications launched at him at the husband's suit.

Finding all other expedients fail, the husband laid his plaint before the bishop, whose archdeacon, as good a man as any in France, personally visited all the houses of the canons, until he found the woman who was supposed to be lost, committed her to prison, and condemned the canon to a heavy penance. The husband, hearing that his wife had been recovered by the exertions of the good archdeacon, and of several other worthy people, was willing to take her back upon her oath that, for the future, she would behave like an honest woman; an oath which the simple man, who loved her much, readily believed that she would keep. He took her back into his house, and treated her in all respects as before, except that he gave her two old servant women, one of whom was always with her when the other was elsewhere. But for all her husband's good treatment, her extravagant love for the canon made her regard all her repose as a torment. Though she was a very fine woman, and he a man of strong and vigorous temperament, yet she had no children by him, for her heart was always seven leagues away from her body. Nevertheless, such was her dissimulation, that her husband believed she had forgotten the past as he had done on his part; but her heart was too wicked to be capable of so happy and laudable a change.

At the very time when she saw that her husband loved her most and distrusted her least, she feigned illness, and carried on the deception so well that the poor husband was in great distress on her account, and spared nothing for her cure. At last he and all his household believed that she really was sinking to the grave. Seeing that her husband was as much afflicted at this as he had reason to be rejoiced, she begged he would authorise her to make her will; which he freely did with tears in his eyes. Having the power to make a will, because she had no children, she bequeathed to her husband all she had in her gift, beseeching his pardon for the affront she had put upon him. Then she sent for the parish priest, confessed, and received the holy sacrament of the altar with such devotion, that every one wept at witnessing so fine and so glorious an end. In the evening she begged her husband to have extreme unction brought her, and told him she was sinking so fast she was afraid she should not live to receive it. Her husband had it brought with the utmost speed, and she received it with a devotion that excited every one's admiration. After partaking of these fine mysteries she said to her husband, that since by God's grace she had received all that the Church had ordained, she felt her conscience so calm that she wished to repose a little, and begged that he would do the same, seeing what great need he had of it, after having wept and watched so long beside her bed. The husband and the men-servants having gone to sleep, the two old women who had kept guard over her so long while she was in health, having now no fear of losing her but by death, went to sleep likewise. As soon as she heard them snoring soundly, she got up in her shift, and stole out of the room, listening to hear if there was anybody stirring in the house. Finding all quiet, she passed out through a little garden door which was not locked, and walked all night, in her shift and barefooted, in the direction of Autun, to repair to the saint who had hindered her from dying.

The road, however, was so long, that daylight overtook her before she reached her journey's end. Looking round then on all sides, she saw two men on horseback coming towards her at full gallop, and making no doubt that one of them was her husband who was in pursuit of her, she hid her whole body in the mud of a marsh and her head between the rushes, and heard her husband say to his servant as he rode by like a man in despair, "O the wicked wretch! Who would ever have imagined that she would have thought of cloaking such an infamous and abominable act under the holy sacraments of the Church?"

"Since Judas did not scruple to betray his master when partaking of the like food," replied the servant, "can you wonder at a woman's betraying her husband in that manner?"

The husband rode on, and the wife remained among the rushes, more joyous at having duped and baffled him than ever she had been at home in a good bed, where she thought she was held in slavery. The husband searched for her all over Autun, but having clearly ascertained that she had not entered the town, he retraced his steps, and on his way did nothing but inveigh against her and his great loss, threatening her with nothing less than death if he caught her; but she was as inaccessible to fear as to the sense of cold, although the weather and the place might well have made her repent of her horrible journey. Any one who knew not how the fire of hell heats those who are full of it, would have wondered how this woman, coming out of a warm bed, could have endured such severe cold for a whole day. She did so, however, without losing courage, and resumed her journey to Autun as soon as night came. Just as they were about to close the town gates this pilgrim arrived, and went straightway to her saint, who was so astonished to see her in such a trim that he could hardly believe it was she. After turning her about and examining her well on all sides, he found that she had flesh and bones, which a spirit has not; he was satisfied she was not a phantom, and they agreed so well together that she remained with him for fourteen or fifteen years.

For a while she lived secluded, but at last she lost all fear; and what was worse, she prided herself so much on the honour of having such a lover, that she took precedence at church of most of the respectable women of the town, the wives of officers as well as others. She had children by the canon, and, among others, a daughter, who was married to a rich merchant, with so much magnificence that all the ladies of the town were indignant, but had not influence enough to correct such an abuse.

It happened at this time that Queen Claude, consort of King Francis, passed through Autun, accompanied by the regent-mother and her daughter, the Duchess of Alençon. Then came a femme de chambre of the queen, named Perrette, to the duchess, and said to her, "Hearken to me, madam, I beseech you, and you will do as good an act as if you went to hear the service of the day, or even better." The duchess willingly listened, knowing that from her lips would come nothing but what was meet to be heard. Perrette told her how she had engaged a little girl to help her to soap the queen's linen, and that on asking her news of the town, the girl had told her of the vexation felt by the honourable ladies thereof at being obliged to yield precedence to this canon's wife, part of whose history she related to her. The duchess immediately went to the queen and the regent-mother, and repeated to them what she had heard; and without other form of process they immediately sent for that wretch, who did not conceal herself; far, indeed, of being ashamed, she was proud of the honour of being the mistress of the house of so rich a man. Accordingly, she presented herself with effrontery before the princesses, who were so astounded at her impudence, that at first they knew not what to say to her; but afterwards the regent-mother spoke to her in terms that would have drawn tears from any woman of good understanding. Instead, however, of weeping, the wretched woman said to them with great assurance:

"I beseech you, mesdames, not to let my honour be touched; for, thank God, I have lived with the canon so well and so virtuously, that no one can say a word against me on that score. Let it not be supposed that I offend God; for it is three years since the good canon has touched me, and we live as chastely and with as much love as if we were two dear little angels, without there ever having been between us a word or a wish to the contrary. Whoever, then, shall disunite us will commit a great sin; for the good man, who is nearly eighty years old, will not live long without me, who am forty-five."

You may imagine what these ladies said to her, and how they reproved her for her obduracy; but say what they would to her, old as she was, and illustrious and worshipful as were the persons who addressed her, there was no shaking her obstinacy. To humble her the princesses sent for the good archdeacon of Autun, who sentenced her to a year's imprisonment on bread and water. They also sent for her husband, who, in consideration of their good exhortations, promised to take her back after her penance. But finding herself a prisoner, and knowing that the canon was resolved never to take her back, she thanked the ladies for having taken a devil off her shoulders; and her repentance was so great and so perfect that her husband, instead of waiting the year's end to take her back, did not wait a fortnight before he claimed her of the archdeacon, and they have since that lived together in peace and harmony.

You see, ladies, how wicked ministers convert St. Peter's chains into chains of Satan, so strong and hard to break, that the sacraments, which cast out devils, are means of retaining them longer in the consciences of such people; for the best things become the most pernicious when they are abused.

"Truly she was a great wretch," said Oisille, "but no less true is it that she was severely punished in appearing before such judges. In fact, the regent-mother's mere look had such a virtue, that there was no good woman who did not fear to stand before her, thinking herself unworthy of her sight; or who, if regarded by her with gentleness, did not think herself deserving of great honour, knowing that the regent-mother was one who could not look with a favourable eye upon any but virtuous women."

"It would be a fine thing," said Hircan, "that one should stand more in awe of the eyes of a woman than of the holy sacrament, which if not received in faith and charity is received to eternal damnation."

"I promise you," said Parlamente, "that those who are not inspired of God are more afraid of temporal than of spiritual powers. I believe too, that this wretched woman was much more mortified by her imprisonment and by the loss of her canon, than by all the remonstrances and rebukes that could be addressed to her."

"But you forget the principal thing that determined her to return to her husband," said Simontault, "and that was that the canon was eighty years old, and her husband was younger than herself; so the good lady was a gainer on both hands. But had the canon been young, she would never have quitted him; the remonstrances of the ladies would have availed no more than the sacraments."

"I think she did right," said Nomerfide, "not to confess her sin too easily; for one should only tell that sort of offence humbly to God, and deny it stoutly before men, since, though the thing be true, by dint of lying and swearing one throws doubt on its truth."

"It is difficult, however, for a sin to be so secret as never to come to light," said Longarine, "unless God himself conceals it for sake of those who repent of it truly for love of Him."

"What would you say of women," said Hircan, "who have no sooner committed a folly than they go and tell it?"

"The thing seems so surprising," said Longarine, "that it seems to me a token that they do not dislike the sin. I have already said that the sin which is not covered by the grace of God can hardly be denied before men. There are many who take pleasure in talking of such things, and glory in publishing their vices, and others who accuse themselves by self-contradiction."

"That is a very clumsy kind of self-contradiction," said Saffredent, "but if you know any example of it, I beg you will relate it."

"Hearken, then," said Longarine.

NOVEL LXII.

A LADY RECOUNTING AN ADVENTURE OF GALLANTRY THAT HAD OCCURRED TO HERSELF, AND SPEAKING IN THE THIRD PERSON, INADVERTENTLY BETRAYED HER OWN SECRET.

In the time of King Francis I. there was a lady of the blood royal who had honour, virtue, and beauty, and who knew how to tell a story with grace, and also to laugh at a good one when she heard it.* This lady being at one of her houses, was visited by all her dependants and neighbours, by whom she was greatly beloved. Among other visits she received one from a certain lady, who, seeing that every one told the princess tales to divert her, wished to do like the rest, and said, "I have a good story to tell you, madam; but you must promise not to speak of it. It is quite true, and I can conscientiously give it you as such.

"There was a married lady who lived on very creditable terms with her husband, though he was old and she young. A gentleman in her neighbourhood, seeing she had married this old man, fell in love with her, and solicited her for several years, but she only replied to him as became a virtuous woman. One day it occurred to the gentleman that if he could come upon her at a moment advantageous to himself, she would perhaps not be so cruel. After he had long weighed the danger to which he exposed himself, love smoothed over all difficulties, dissipated his fear, and determined him to seek time and opportunity. Keeping good watch for intelligence, he learned that the lady's husband was going away to another of his houses, and intended to set out at daybreak to avoid the heat, whereupon he repaired to the lady and found her asleep in bed. Seeing that the maid-servants were not in the chamber, he got into the lady's bed, booted and spurred as he was, without having had the wit to lock the door. She awoke, and was very much vexed to see him there; but in spite of al_

---

* The lady of the blood royal whom Margaret eulogises so highly was probably her mother, who was very fond of hearing all sorts of court gossip.

nor remonstrances there was no stopping him—he violated her, and threatened, if she made a noise, to tell everybody she had sent for him; which frightened her so much that she durst not cry out. One of the servants came back some moments afterwards into the chamber. The gentleman jumped up with such celerity that she would have noticed nothing, if his spur had not stuck in the top sheet, and carried it clean off the bed, leaving the lady quite naked."

So far the lady had told her story as if of another; but here she could not help saying:

"Never was woman more astonished than I when I found myself thus naked."

The princess, who had listened to the whole tale without a smile, could not then restrain her laughter, and said, "I see you were quite right in saying you knew the story to be true." The poor lady tried hard to mend the matter; but there was no possibility of finding a good plaister for it.

I assure you, ladies, if the act had given her real pain she would have been glad to have lost the recollection of it; but as I have already said, sin is sure to discover itself unless it be covered by the mantle which, as David says, makes man blessed.

"Truly, of all the fools I ever heard of this was the greatest, to set others laughing at her own expense," said Ennasuite.

"I am not surprised that speech follows action," said Parlamente; "for it is easier to say than to do."

"Why," said Geburon, "what sin had she committed? She was asleep in her bed, and he threatened her with death and infamy. Lucretia, who has been so much lauded, did quite as much."

"It is true," said Parlamente, "there is no righteous person who may not fall; but when one has felt at the instant great disgust at one's fall, one remembers it only with horror. To efface its memory Lucretia killed herself; but this wanton chose to make others laugh at it in her own case."

"It seems to me, nevertheless," said Nomerfide, "that she was a good woman, since she was urgently solicited several times, but would not consent. Accordingly, the gentleman was obliged to use fraud and violence in order to succeed."

"What!" said Parlamente, "do you suppose that a woman's honour is spotless when she succumbs after two or three refusals? At that rate there would be many a woman of honour among those who are regarded as having none. Plenty of women have been known for a long time to repulse him to whom their hearts were already given. Some do it because they fear infamy; others to make themselves the more loved and esteemed by a feigned resistance. A woman, therefore, ought not to be held in any consideration unless she remains firm to the end."

"If a young man were to refuse a handsome girl," said Dagoucin, "would you not regard that as a great act of virtue?"

"Assuredly," said Oisille, "if a young man in good health made such a refusal, I should think the act very laudable, but not hard to believe."

"I know some," said Dagoucin, "who have refused adventures which all their comrades sought for with avidity."

"Pray take my place," said Longarine, "and tell us what you know in that way; but recollect that we are pledged to speak the truth."

"I promise to tell it you," said Dagoucin, "without cover or disguise."

NOVEL LXIII.

NOTABLE CHASTITY OF A FRENCH LORD.

THERE were in Paris four girls, two of whom were sisters, so handsome, so young, and so fresh, that they had the choice of all the gallants. The gentleman whom the king then reigning had made provost of Paris, seeing that his master was young, and of an age to desire such company, managed so dexterously with the four, making each of them believe that she was for the king, that they consented to what the provost desired. This was that they should all be present at a banquet to which he invited his master, communicating to him his design, which was approved by the king, and by two great lords of the court, who were not sorry to have a finger in the pie. While they were at a loss for a fourth, in came a young lord, a handsome, well-bred man, and younger by ten years than the others. He was at once invited to the treat, and accepted the invitation with a good grace, though in reality he had no mind for it, for two reasons. He had a wife with whom he was very happy, who bore him fine children; and they lived so tranquilly together, that for no consideration would he have given her cause to suspect him. Besides, he loved one of the handsomest ladies then in France, and esteemed her so much that all others seemed ugly to him in comparison with her; so that in his early youth, and before he was married, there was no means of making him see and frequent other women, however fair, for he had more pleasure in seeing his mistress, and loving her perfectly, than he could have had from all he could have obtained of another.

This young lord went to his wife, told her what the king had in view, and said he would rather die than do what he had promised. "As there is no man," he said, "whom I would not dare to attack in anger, so I would rather die than commit a murder in cold blood, unless honour compelled to it. In like manner I would rather die than violate conjugal fidelity at another's caprice, unless extreme love, such as blinds the best, extorted such a violation from me."

His wife, seeing in him so much virtue with so much youth, loved him more than ever, and asked him how he could excuse himself, seeing that princes often take it amiss that others do not applaud what they like. "I have heard say," he replied, "that the wise man is always ready at a critical moment with an illness or a journey. So I intend to be sick four or five days beforehand; and, provided you play the sorrowing wife, I trust I shall get out of the scrape."

"That is what one may call a good and holy hypocrisy," said his wife. "I will not fail to wear as sad a face as possible; for one is very fortunate when one can avoid offending God and provoking the sovereign's resentment."

So said, so done; and the king was very sorry to hear through the wife of the husband's illness, which, however, was not of long duration. Certain affairs having then supervened to claim the king's attention, he forgot his pleasure to think of his duty, and suddenly quitted Paris. One day, recollecting his unfulfilled project, he said to the young prince,

"We were great fools to quit Paris with such haste as not to have seen the four girls who have been represented to us as the handsomest in my realm."

"I am very glad," replied the prince, "that you have not done so, for I was greatly afraid during my illness that I alone should lose such a good fortune."

The king never suspected the dissimulation of the young lord, who thenceforth was more beloved by his wife than ever.*

Parlamente burst out laughing, and said, "He would have shown his love for his wife much more if he had done it for her sake only; but, in any point of view, such conduct was certainly most commendable."

"It seems to me no such great merit in a man to be chaste for his wife's sake," said Hircan. "He is bound to it by so many reasons that he can hardly do otherwise. In the first place, God commands it; he is pledged to it by his marriage vow; and besides, the satiated appetite is not subjected to temptation like the craving one. But for the free love one cherishes for a mistress whom one does not enjoy, obtaining from her no other pleasure than that of seeing and speaking to her, and often nothing but mortifying replies, when this love is so faithful and so constant that it will not change, happen what may, then I maintain that chastity displayed on occasions of this sort is not only laudable but miraculous."

"It is no miracle," said Oisille, "for when the heart is devoted, nothing is impossible for the body."

"Yes, for angelic bodies," observed Hircan.

"I do not mean to speak only of those who by God's grace are all transmuted into Him," said Oisille, "but also of the most carnal among men; and if you examine, you will find that those who have set their hearts and affections on seeking perfection in the sciences, have not only forgotten the delights of the flesh, but even things which are most

* This novel is wanting in the edition of 1558, published by Boaistuau; it appeared for the first time in that of Gruget in 1559. The king who figures in it is Francis I.; and the gentleman whom the king had made provost of Paris is Jean de la Barre, who is mentioned in Novel I.

necessary to nature, such as food and drink. In fact, as long as the soul is in the body by affection, the flesh remains, as it were, insensible. Thence it comes that those who love handsome and virtuous women take such delight in seeing and hearing them speak, that the flesh then suspends all its desires. Those who cannot experience this contentment are carnal persons, who, enveloped in too much fat, know not whether they have a soul or not; but when the body is subjected to the spirit, it is almost insensible to the imperfections of the flesh, so that the strong persuasions of persons of this character may render them insensible. I knew a gentleman who, to show that his love for his mistress surpassed any other man's, was willing to give proof of this by holding his bare fingers over the flame of a candle. He had his eyes bent on his mistress at the same moment, and he bore the fire with such fortitude that he burned himself to the bone; and yet he said that he felt no pain."

"Methinks," said Geburon, "that the devil to whom he was a martyr ought to make a St. Lawrence of him, for there are few who endure such a great fire of love as not to fear that of the smallest taper. If a lady had put me to so severe a trial, I should demand a great recompense of her; or, failing it, should cease to love her."

"You would then insist on having your hour after your mistress has had hers," said Parlamente. "So did a Spanish gentleman of Valencia, whose story was related to me by a very worthy commander."

"Pray take my place, madam, and tell it us," said Dagoucin, " for I suspect it is a good one."

"The story I am going to relate, ladies," said Parlamente, "will make you think twice before you refuse a good offer, and not trust that the present state of things will last for ever. You shall see that it is subject to change; and that will oblige you to have a care for the future."

NOVEL LXIV.

A GENTLEMAN HAVING BEEN UNABLE TO MARRY A PERSON HE LOVES, BECOMES A CORDELIER IN DESPITE—SORE DISTRESS OF HIS MISTRESS THEREAT.

There was in Valencia a gentleman who for five or six years had loved a lady with so much propriety, that the honour and conscience of neither had suffered any blemish. The gentleman's intention was to marry her—an intention the more reasonable as he was handsome, rich, and of good family. Before engaging in the lady's service, he had an explanation with her on the subject of marriage, respecting which she referred him to her relations. They assembled to consider the question, and resolved that the match was a very suitable one, provided the young lady was willing. But she, whether thinking to do better, or willing to dissemble her love for the gentleman, started so many objections, that the assembly broke up, regretting that they had not been able to bring the affair to a conclusion, advantageous as it would have been on both sides. The most sorely disappointed of all was the poor lover, who would have borne his rejection with patience if he could have persuaded himself that it was not the maiden's fault, but her relations'. But as the truth was well known to him, his affliction was so extreme that, without speaking to his mistress or any one, he went home, and, after setting his affairs in order, retired to a deserted spot to try to forget his love, and turn it wholly towards Our Lord, to whom he was more bound in gratitude than to his mistress.

During his abode there he heard nothing from the lady or her relations, and resolved, after having missed the happiest life he could have hoped for, to choose the most austere and disagreeable he could imagine. In this dismal state of mind, which might well be called despair, he betook himself, with a view to becoming a monk, to a Franciscan monastery, which was not far from the residences of several of his relations. As soon as they were aware of his purpose, they did all they could to dissuade him from it, but his resolution was so fixed that nothing could shake it. As the cause of the mischief was known to them, they sought a remedy at the hands of her who had given occasion to such a precipitate fit of devotion. She was greatly surprised and distressed at this news; and as her intention had only been to try her lover's fervour by refusing him for a while, and not to lose him for ever, as she saw she was about to do, she wrote him a letter, earnestly beseeching him to forego his dismal resolution, and return to her who loved him, and was ready to be wholly his own, as she had always desired to be, even when she affected coyness for the purpose of proving the sincerity of his love, whereof she was now fully convinced.

This letter, conveyed by one of her friends, who was charged to accompany it with all possible remonstrances, was received by the gentleman Cordelier with so sad a countenance, and with so many tears and sighs, that it seemed as though he would fain have drowned and burned the poor paper. His only reply was to tell the bearer that the mortification of his excessive passion had cost him so dear, that it had taken from him the wish to love and the fear to die. That being the case, he begged her who was the occasion of it, and who had not chosen to respond to his passion, to torment him no more now that he had overcome it, and to content herself with the harm she had already done him. "I could find no other remedy," he said, "than the austere life I have chosen. Continual penance makes me forget my grief. I so weaken my body by fastings and castigations, that the thought of death is for me a sovereign consolation. Let her, then, who sends you to me, spare me, I entreat, the misery of hearing her mentioned, for the mere recollection of her name is to me an intolerable purgatory."

The bearer returned with this unwelcome reply, and reported it to her who had sent him. It was with inconceivable regret she heard it; but love, which will not suffer the spirit to be utterly cast down, put it into her head that if she could see him she would effect more by her eyes and her tongue than she had by her pen. She went then to the monastery, accompanied by her father and her nearest relations. She had omitted nothing that she thought could set off her beauty, in the belief that if he once saw her and heard her, it was impossible but that a fire so long cherished should kindle up more strongly than ever. She entered the monastery towards the end of vespers, and sent for him to meet her in a chapel of the cloisters. Not knowing who wanted him, he obeyed the summons, and went to encounter the rudest shock he had ever sustained. He was so pale and worn that she could hardly recognise him; nevertheless, as he seemed to her as comely and as lovable as ever, love constrained her to stretch out her arms, thinking to embrace him; but she was so touched by the sad state in which he appeared, and the idea of it caused such a sinking at the heart, that she fainted away. The good monk, who was not destitute of brotherly charity, raised her up, and seated her on a bench in the chapel. Though he had not less need of aid than she, he nevertheless affected to ignore her passion, fortifying his heart in the love of his God against the present opportunity, and he succeeded so well that he seemed to be unconscious of what was before his eyes.

Recovering from her weakness, and turning upon him eyes so lovely and so sad that they might have softened a rock, the maiden said everything she could think of as most likely to persuade him to quit that place. To all her arguments and entreaties he made the best replies he could; but at last, finding that his heart was beginning to yield to his mistress's tears, and seeing that Love, whose cruelty he had long experienced, had in its hand a gilded arrow ready to inflict on him a new and mortal wound, he fled from Love and from his mistress, as his only means of safety. Shut up, then, in his cell, and unable to let her depart in that uncertainty, he wrote her a few words in Spanish, which appear to me so expressive, that I will not translate them for fear of impairing their grace: *Volved donde veniste anima mi, que en las tristes vidas es la mia.** The lady seeing from this that no hope remained, resolved to follow his advice and that of her friends, and returned home, to lead a life as melancholy as that of her lover in his monastery was austere.

You see, ladies, how the gentleman revenged himself on his rigorous mistress, who, intending only to try him, drove

---

* "Return whence thou camest, my soul, for among the sad lives is mine."

him to such despair, that, when she would have relented towards him, it was too late.

"I am sorry he did not throw off the grey gown and marry her," said Nomerfide. "Theirs, I think, would have been a perfectly happy marriage."

"In faith I think he did very wisely," said Simontault; "for all who have well considered the inconveniences of marriage are agreed that there are none greater than the austerities of the monastic life. As he was already weakened by fastings and abstinences, he was afraid to load himself with a burden he would have been obliged to bear all his life long."

"She did wrong, I think, by so weak a man," said Hircan, "to tempt him by a proposal of marriage, since that is a matter in which the most vigorous and robust find themselves hard bestead. But if she had talked to him of an intimacy free from all but voluntary obligation, there was no knot but would have been untied. But since, by way of drawing him out of purgatory, she offered him a hell, I maintain that he was right to refuse, and make her feel the pain which her refusal had caused him."

"Many there are," said Ennasuite, "who, thinking to do better than others, do either worse, or the reverse of what they had expected."

"Truly you put me in mind," said Geburon, "though the fact is not quite to the point, of a woman who did the contrary of what she intended, which was the cause of a great tumult in the church of Saint Jean de Lyon."

"Pray take my place," said Parlamente, "and tell us the story."

"Mine will be neither so long nor so sad as yours," he replied.

NOVEL LXV.

SIMPLICITY OF AN OLD WOMAN WHO PRESENTED A LIGHTED CANDLE TO SAINT JEAN DE LYON, AND WANTED TO FASTEN IT ON THE FOREHEAD OF A SOLDIER WHO WAS SLEEPING ON A TOMB—WHAT HAPPENED IN CONSEQUENCE.

There was a very dark chapel in the church of Saint Jean de Lyon, and in front of the chapel a stone tomb, with figures of great personages as large as life, and several men-at-arms represented in sleeping postures round them. A soldier walking one day about the church (it was in the heat of summer) felt inclined to sleep. He cast his eyes on this chapel, and seeing it was dark and cool, he went and lay down among the other recumbent figures on the tomb, and fell asleep. Presently up came a very pious old woman, who, after performing her devotions with a candle in her hand, wanted to fix it to the tomb, and the sleeping man being more within her reach than the other figures, she set about sticking the candle on his forehead, imagining that it was stone; but the wax would not stick. The good woman, supposing that this was in consequence of the coldness of the image, clapped the lighted end of the candle to its forehead, but the image, which was not insensible, began to roar. The good woman was frightened almost out of her wits, and shrieked out "Miracle, miracle!" so loudly, that all the people in church ran, some to the bells, others to the scene of the miracle. She took them to see the image which had stirred, which made many laugh; but certain priests, not contenting themselves with laughing, resolved to turn the tomb to account, and make as much money of it as of the crucifix on their pulpit, which is said to have spoken; but the display of an old woman's silliness put an end to the comedy.*

If every one knew what are their follies they would not be deemed holy, nor their miracles true. I pray you then, ladies, take care, henceforth, to what saints you give your candles.

* The end of this novel, and the whole epilogue, were suppressed in the first edition. Gruget restored the epilogue in the second edition, but not the passage relating to the crucifix.

"How strange it is," said Hircan, "that be it in what manner it may, women must always do wrong!"

"Is it doing wrong to carry candles to the tomb?" said Nomerfide.

"Yes," replied Hircan, "when the lighted end is put to a man's forehead; for no good deed should be called a good deed when mischief comes of it. The poor woman thought of course she had made a grand present to God in giving Him a paltry candle."

"God does not look to the value of the present," said Oisille, "but to the heart that offers it. Perhaps this poor woman loved God more than those who gave great torches; for as the Gospel says, she gave out of her need."

"I do not believe, however," said Saffredent, "that God, who is supreme wisdom, can look with favour on women's folly. Simplicity is acceptable to Him, it is true; but the Scriptures inform me that He scorns the ignorant; and if we are there commanded to be simple as doves, we are also enjoined to be prudent as serpents."

"For my part," said Oisille, "I do not regard as ignorant her who carries before God her lighted candle, as making *amende honorable*, kneeling on the ground, and candle in hand, to her sovereign Lord, in order to confess her guilt, and pray with lively faith for His grace and salvation."

"Would to God that every one acquitted herself in this way as well as you," said Dagoucin; "but I do not believe that poor ignorant women do the thing with this intention."

"Those women who are least capable of expressing themselves well," rejoined Oisille, "are often those who have the most lively sense of the love and the will of God; consequently, it is prudent not to judge any but oneself."

"It is no wonderful thing to have frightened a sleeping groom," said Ennasuite, laughing, "since women of as mean condition have frightened great princes without setting fire to their foreheads."

"I am sure you know some story of the sort which you wish to tell us," said Dagoucin, "so take my place, if you please."

"The story will not be long," said Ennasuite; "but if I could recount it to you as it occurred, you would have no mind to cry."

NOVEL LXVI.

AMUSING ADVENTURE OF MONSIEUR DE VENDÔME AND THE PRINCESS OF NAVARRE.

The year when Monsieur de Vendôme married the Princess of Navarre, the king and queen, their father and mother, after having been regaled at Vendôme, accompanied them into Guienne. They visited the house of a gentleman in which there were several ladies, young and fair, and where the company danced so long that the young married pair, being tired, retired to their chamber, where they threw themselves on the bed in their clothes, the doors and windows being closed, and no one remaining with them. They were wakened from their sleep by the sound of some one opening their door from without. Monsieur de Vendôme drew back the curtain, and looked out to see who it might be, supposing that it was one of his friends who wished to surprise him. But instead of that he saw a tall old chamber-woman, who walked straight up to their bed. It was too dark for her to distinguish their features, but she could see that they were very close together, and cried out, "Ah, thou naughty, shameless wanton! 'tis long I have suspected thee for what thou art; but not having proofs to show, I durst not speak of it to my mistress, but now I have seen thy infamy I am resolved to conceal it no longer. And thou, villanous apostate, that hast done this house the scorn to beguile this poor wench, were it not for the fear of God I would beat the life out of thee on the spot. Get up, in the devil's name, get up! It seems thou art not even ashamed."

Monsieur de Vendôme and the princess, to prolong the scene, hid their faces against each other, and laughed so heartily that they could not speak. The chamber-woman, seeing then that they did not budge for her rebuke, or show any signs of rising, went to drag them out of bed by the legs and arms; but then she perceived by their dresses that they were not what she took them for. The moment she recognised their faces she fell on her knees and implored their pardon for the fault she had committed in disturbing them. Monsieur de Vendôme, wishing to know more of the matter, got up at once and begged the good woman to tell him for whom she had taken them. At first she would not do so; but after making him promise on oath that he would never mention it, she told him that the cause of her mistake was a demoiselle belonging to the house, with whom a prothonotary* was in love; and she had long watched them, because she was vexed that her mistress put confidence in a man who offered her such an affront. She then retired, and left the prince and princess shut in as she had found them. They laughed long at the adventure; and though they often told the tale, nevertheless they would never name the persons for whom they had been mistaken.

You see, ladies, how the good woman, thinking to do a righteous act, informed these princely strangers of things whereof the domestics of the house had never heard a word.†

---

* The office of Apostolic Prothonotary was instituted in the early times of the Romish Church by Pope Clement I. There were originally twelve such officers, and their duty was to write the lives of the saints and the other apostolic records. Gradually their number increased, and their functions diminished in importance, so that in the fifteenth century the title of prothonotary was merely an honorary dignity conferred as a matter of course on doctors of theology of noble family, or otherwise of a certain importance. Brantôme says, in the beginning of his 28th Discours on the great captains and illustrious men of France: "Monsieur de l'Escun, brother of M. de Lautrec, was a good captain, but more intrepid and valiant than remarkable for the morality of his conduct. He had been destined for the long robe, and studied for a long time at Pavia in the time of the grand master Chaumont, when Milan was in our peaceable possession. He was called the Prothonotary of Foix, but I think he was what the Spaniard calls *un letrado que no tenia muchas letras*—that is to say, a *literatus* who had little acquaintance with letters; and indeed it was usual in those days with prothonotaries, and even with those of good family, not to have much learning, but to enjoy themselves, hunt, make love, and generally to cuckold the poor gentlemen who were gone to the wars. There was a song in those days in which a lady says:

'Passerez vous tousjours par cy (*bis*)
Prothenotaire sans soucy?'"

† This novel was omitted in the first edition of the Heptameron. It was in 1548 that Antoine de Bourbon, Duke of Vendôme, married Jeanne de Navarre, only daughter of Margaret, and mother of Henri IV., King of France.

"I think," said Parlamente, "I know where the adventure happened, and the name of the prothonotary. He has already governed many ladies' houses, and when he cannot win the good graces of the mistress, he never misses one of the demoiselles; with that exception, he is a well-behaved and worthy man."

"Why do you say with that exception," said Hircan, "since it is for that very thing that I esteem him a worthy man?"

"I see," replied Parlamente, "that you know the malady and the patient, and that if he needed an apology you would not fail to be his advocate. However, I should not like to entrust an intrigue to a man who did not know how to conduct his own without letting it be known even to the chamber-women."

"Do you suppose," said Nomerfide, "that men care whether such things are known or not? Provided they attain their end, that is enough for them. Be assured, that if nobody spoke of the matter they would publish it themselves."

"There is no need for men to say all they know," said Hircan, angrily.

"Perhaps," replied Nomerfide, blushing, "they would say nothing to their own advantage."

"To hear you talk," said Simontault, "it seems as though men took pleasure in hearing women spoken ill of, and I am sure you think me one of that sort. For that reason I have a great mind to say some good of them, that I may not be regarded as a slanderer."

"I give you my vote," said Ennasuite, "and pray you to constrain yourself a little in order to do your devoir to our honour."

"It is no new thing, ladies," said Simontault, "to hear of your virtues. In my opinion, when some one of your noble actions presents itself, far from being hidden it ought to be written in letters of gold, to serve as an example to women, and to give men cause for admiration, to see in the weaker sex what weakness recoils from. It is this that prompts me to relate what I heard from Captain Robertval and several of his company."

NOVEL LXVII.

LOVE AND EXTREME HARDSHIPS OF A WOMAN IN A FOREIGN LAND.

The king having given the command of a small squadron to Robertval for an expedition he had resolved to make to the island of Canada, that captain intended to settle in the island, in case the air proved good, and to build towns and castles there. Every one knows what were the beginnings of this project. In order to people the country with Christians, he took with him all sorts of artisans, among whom there was one who was base enough to betray his master, so that he was near falling into the hands of the natives. But it was God's will that the conspiracy should be discovered; and so did no great harm to Captain Robertval, who had the traitor seized, intending to hang him as he deserved. He would have done so but for the wife of this wretch, who, after sharing the perils of the sea with her husband, was willing to follow his bad fortune to the end. She prevailed so far by her tears and supplications, that Robertval, both for the services she had rendered him, and from compassion for her, granted what she asked. This was, that her husband and herself should be left on a little island in the sea, inhabited only by wild beasts, with permission to take with them what was necessary for their subsistence.

The poor creatures, left alone with fierce beasts, had recourse only to God, who had always been the firm hope of the poor wife. As she had no consolation but in her God, she took with her for her preservation, her nurture, and her consolation, the New Testament, which she read incessantly. Moreover, she worked along with her husband at building a small dwelling. When the lions and other wild beasts approached to devour them, the husband with his arquebuse, and the wife with stones, defended themselves so well, that not only the beasts durst not approach them, but even they often killed some of them which were good to eat. They subsisted for a long time on such flesh and on herbs after their bread was gone. However, in the long run, the husband could not resist the effects of such diet; besides, they drank such unwholesome water that he became greatly swollen, and died in a short while, having no other service or consolation than his wife's, who acted as his physician and his confessor; so that he passed with joy from his desert to the heavenly land. The poor woman buried him in a grave which she made as deep as she could; the beasts, however, immediately got scent of it, and came to devour the body, but the poor woman firing from her little dwelling with her arquebuse, hindered her husband's body from having such a burial. Thus living like the beasts as to her body, and like the angels as to her spirit, she passed the time in reading, contemplation, prayers, and orisons, having a cheerful and contented spirit in a body emaciated and half dead.

But He who never forsakes His own in their need, and who displays His power when all seems hopeless, did not suffer that the virtue with which this woman was endowed should be unknown to the world, but that it should be known there for His glory. After some time one of the vessels of Robertval's fleet passing before the island, those on deck saw a woman, who reminded them of the persons they had put ashore there, and they resolved to go and see in what manner God had disposed of them. The poor woman, seeing the vessel approach, went down to the sea-beach, where they found her on landing. After thanking God for their arrival, she took them to her poor little hut, and showed them on what she had subsisted during her melancholy abode there. They could never have believed it, had they not known that God can nourish His servants in a desert as at the finest banquets in the world. As she could not remain in such a place, they took her straightway with them to Rochelle; and there, when they had made known to the inhabitants the fidelity and perseverance of this woman, the ladies paid her great honour, and were glad to send their daughters to her to learn to read and write. She maintained herself for the rest of her days by that honourable profession, having no other desire than to exhort every one to love God and trust in Him, holding forth as an example the great mercy with which He had dealt towards her.

Now, ladies, you cannot say but that I laud the virtues which God has implanted in you—virtues which appear the greater, the weaker the being that displays them.

"We are not sorry," said Oisille, "that you praise in us the graces of our Lord, for in truth it is from Him that comes all virtue; but neither man nor woman contributes to the work of God. In vain both bestir themselves and strive to do well; they do but plant, and it is God that gives the increase."

"If you have well read Scripture," said Saffredent, "you know that St. Paul says that he has planted and Apollos has watered; but he does not speak of women having put their hands to the work of God."

"You do like those bad men who take a passage of Scripture which makes for them, and pass over that which is contrary to them," said Parlamente. "If you have read St. Paul from one end to the other, you will find that he commends himself to the ladies who have toiled much with him in the propagation of the Gospel."

"Be that as it may," said Longarine, "this woman is worthy of great praise, both for her love for her husband, for whom she risked her life, and her confidence in God, who, as you see, did not abandon her."

"As for the first point," said Ennasuite, "I believe there is no wife present who would not do as much to save her husband's life."

"And I believe," said Parlamente, "that there are husbands such mere beasts that it could be no surprise to their wives to find themselves reduced to live among their fellows."

Ennasuite could not help replying, as taking this to have been said on her account, "If beasts did not bite me, their company would be more agreeable to me than that of men, who are irascible and unbearable. But I do not retract my assertion, and I say again, that if my husband was in the like danger, I would not forsake him though it were to cost me my life."

"Beware," said Nomerfide, "how you love to such a degree that the excess of your love may be mischievous both to you and to him. There is a medium in all things, and for want of a right understanding love is often converted into hatred."

"It seems to me," said Simontault, "that you have not pushed the matter so far without purposing to confirm your principle by some example. Therefore, if you know one, let us hear it."

"Well then, my tale shall be short and gay, as usual," replied Nomerfide.

NOVEL LXVIII.

A WOMAN GIVES HER HUSBAND POWDER OF CANTHARIDES TO MAKE HIM LOVE HER, AND GOES NEAR TO KILLING HIM.

THERE was formerly at Pau, in Bearn, an apothecary whose name was Maître Etienne. He had married a good thrifty woman, with such a share of beauty as ought to have contented him; but as he tasted different drugs, so too he had a mind to taste different women, the better to judge of all. This was so disagreeable to his wife that she lost all patience, for he never noticed her except in Passion Week, by way of penance. The apothecary being one day in his shop, and his wife hid behind the door, listening, in came a woman of the place, who was *commère** to the apothecary, and was sick of the same complaint as the listener behind the door. "Alas! *compère*, my friend," she said to the apothecary, sighing deeply, " I am the most unfortunate woman in the world. I love my husband more than myself. I have not a thought but how to serve and obey him; but it is all labour in vain, and he loves the worst and nastiest woman in the town better than he does me. If you know any drug that can change his constitution, pray give it me, *compère*. If it succeeds with me, and I am well treated by my husband, I assure you I will recompense you to the utmost of my power."

The apothecary, to comfort her, told her he knew of a

---

* In France, the godfather and godmother of a child are called in reference to each other *compère* and *commère*, terms which imply mutual relations of a peculiarly friendly kind. The same usage exists in all Catholic countries. One of the novels in the Decameron is founded on a very general opinion in Italy that an amorous connexion between a *compadre* and his *commadre* partook almost of the nature of incest.

marvellous powder, and that if she made her husband take it in his broth or in his roast meat, like *duc* powder, he would regale her in the best possible manner. The poor woman, wishing to see this miracle, asked him what it was, and if she could not have some of it. He told her she had only to take some powder of cantharides, of which he had good store. Before they parted she made him prepare this powder, and took as much of it as she needed; and subsequently she thanked him for it many times; for her husband, who was strong and vigorous, and who did not take too much of it, found himself none the worse for it, and she all the better.

The apothecary's wife, who had overheard the whole conversation, thought to herself that she had no less need of the recipe than his *commère*. She marked the place where her husband put away the rest of the powder, and resolved to use it when an occasion should offer. She had not long to wait. Her husband, feeling himself incommoded with a coldness of stomach, begged her to make him some good broth. She told him that a roast with *duc* powder would do him still more good, and he begged her to make him one forthwith, and to get some cinnamon and some sugar out of the shop. She did so, and did not forget the remainder of the powder which he had given to his *commère*, without regarding either weight, or dose, or measure. The husband ate the roast, which he found very good, and soon experienced its effect, which he thought to appease with his wife; but it was impossible, for he felt all on fire, so that he did not know on what side to turn. He told his wife she had poisoned him, and insisted on knowing what she had put in the broth. She did not disguise the truth, but told him plainly that she had as much need of that recipe as his *commère*. The poor apothecary was in such torture that he could not belabour her with anything harder than bad words. He ordered her out of his sight, and sent her to the Queen of Navarre's apothecary to beg he would come and see him, which he did, and administered the remedies suitable to the case. The queen's apothecary set the patient on his legs again in a very little time, and censured him sharply for making another take drugs which he would not willingly take himself; adding, that his wife had done as she ought, seeing the desire she had to make herself loved by him. The poor man was obliged to have patience, and own that God had justly punished him in exposing him to the raillery to which he would have subjected another.

To me, it seems, ladies, that this woman's love was not less indiscreet than excessive.

"Do you call it loving her husband," said Hircan, "to make him suffer for the pleasure she expected of him?"

"I imagine," said Longarine, "she had no other intention than to regain her husband's regard, which she thought she had lost. There is nothing women would not do for such a blessing."

"Nevertheless," said Geburon, "in matters of food and drink, a woman ought on no account whatever to give her husband anything of which she is not sure, as well by her own experience as by that of persons of knowledge, that it can do him no harm; but ignorance must be excused. The woman in question was excusable, for the passion which blinds people most is love, and the person most blinded is the woman who has not the strength to carry such a great burden judiciously."

"Geburon," replied Oisille, "you depart from your own good custom to conform to the sentiments of your companions. Yet there are women who have patiently sustained love and jealousy."

"Ay," said Hircan, "and pleasantly too; for the most sensible are those who take as much pleasure in laughing at their husbands' doings, as the husbands in secretly playing them false. If you will allow me to speak before Madame Oisille closes the day, I will tell you a tale about a husband and a wife who are known to all the company."

"Begin, then," said Nomerfide; and Hircan, laughing, began thus.

NOVEL LXIX.

AN ITALIAN SUFFERED HIMSELF TO BE DUPED BY HIS SERVANT MAID, AND WAS CAUGHT BY HIS WIFE BOLTING MEAL IN PLACE OF THE GIRL.

At the château of Odoz, in Bigorre, dwelt one of the king's equerries, named Charles, an Italian. He had married a very good and virtuous lady, who had grown old after bearing him several children. He, too, was not young, and lived on peaceable and friendly terms with his wife. It is true he sometimes talked to his women servants, which his good wife pretended never to observe, but she always dismissed the girls very quietly when she knew that they had forgotten their station in the house. One day she took one who was an honest, good girl, told her what was her husband's humour and her own, and warned her that she would turn off a girl the moment she knew she was not well behaved. The servant, being anxious to remain in her mistress's service and gain her esteem, resolved not to swerve from the path of virtue. Though her master often addressed improper language to her, she never would hearken to him, but told all to her mistress, who laughed with her at her husband's folly.

One day the servant was bolting meal in a back room, with her surcoat over her head after the manner of the country. This surcoat is made like a *crémeau*, but it completely covers the back and shoulders. Her master, finding her in that trim, was very pressing with her; and she, who would as soon have died as done what he wished, pretended to consent, and begged he would first let her go and see whether or not her mistress was engaged in any way, so that they might not be surprised by her. He willingly consented to this, and then she begged him to put on her surcoat and continue to bolt during her absence, so that her mistress might not miss the sound of the bolting machine. This he did with glee, in the hope of having what he desired. The servant, who loved a good laugh, ran to her mistress, and said, "Come and see your husband, whom I have taught to bolt, in order to get rid of him." The wife made haste to see this new servant, and found her husband with the surcoat on his head, working away at the bolting machine, and laughed at him so heartily, clapping her hands, that it was as much as she could do to say to him, "How much a month dost thou ask for wages, wench?" The husband, hearing his wife's voice, and seeing that he was duped, threw away the surcoat and the bolting machine, and darted at the servant, whom he called all sorts of bad names. If his wife had not interposed he would have paid her for her courtesy; however, the storm was at last appeased to the content of all parties, who afterwards lived peaceably together.*

What say you of this wife, ladies? Was she not wise to make sport of her husband's sport?

"It was no sport for the husband to miss his aim," said Saffredent.

"I imagine," said Ennasuite, "that he had more pleasure in laughing with his wife than in half killing himself with his servant at his age."

"I should have been sorely annoyed to have been found with that fine *crémeau* over my head," said Simontault.

"I have heard," said Parlamente, "that it was not your wife's fault that she did not catch you pretty nearly in the same trim; and since that time, they say, she has never known rest."

"Be content with the adventures of your own house," replied Simontault, "without looking after mine. My wife has no cause to complain of me; but even if I were such as you say, she would not notice it, for she is not at all stinted."

"Women of honour need nothing but the love of their husbands, the only persons who can content them," said Longarine; "but those who desire a brutal pleasure will never find it where propriety prescribes."

"Do you call it brutal pleasure when a woman wishes to have from her husband what belongs to her?" said Geburon.

"I maintain," replied Longarine, "that a chaste wife, who loves truly, finds more contentment in being perfectly loved, than in all the pleasures which the flesh can desire."

* This is the same story as Le Conseilleur au Bluteau, the 18th of the *Cent Nouvelles Nouvelles*.

"I am of your opinion," said Dagoucin; "but their lordships here will neither hear of it nor confess it. I believe that if mutual love does not content a woman, a husband will content her no more; for if she does not conform in love to the seemly ways of women, she must be possessed by the infernal lust of the brutes."

"Truly you remind me," said Oisille, "of a fair lady who was well married, and who, for want of contenting herself with that seemly love, became more carnal than swine, and more cruel than lions."

"I pray you, madam, to finish the day by telling us that story," said Simontault.

"I cannot, for two reasons," replied Oisille; "first, because it is long; and secondly, because it is not of our time. It has been written, however, by an author worthy of credit; but we are vowed to relate nothing here that has been written."

"That is true," observed Parlamente; "but as I believe I know the tale you mean, I must tell you it is written in such antiquated language that I do not think any one present, except us two, has heard of it. Therefore it will be as good as new."

The whole company then besought her to tell the story without troubling herself about its length, for they had still a good hour to spare before vespers. Madame Oisille, therefore, yielded to their entreaties, and began as follows.

NOVEL LXX.

THE HORRIBLE INCONTINENCE AND MALICE OF A DUCHESS OF BURGUNDY WAS THE CAUSE OF HER DEATH, AND OF THAT OF TWO PERSONS WHO FONDLY LOVED EACH OTHER.

THERE was in the duchy of Burgundy a duke who was a very agreeable prince and of very goodly person. He had a wife with whose beauty he was so satisfied that it blinded him to her disposition, and he thought only of pleasing her, whilst she, on her part, made a show of responding only to his affection. This duke had in his household a young gentleman so accomplished in all that can be desired in a man, that he was loved by everybody, and especially by the duke, about whose person he had been brought up from childhood, and who, knowing him to possess so many perfections, had the warmest regard for him, and trusted him in all affairs suitable to his years. The duchess, who was not a virtuous woman, nor satisfied with her husband's love and the kind treatment she received from him, often cast her eyes on this gentleman, and found him so much to her taste, that she loved him beyond measure. She was evermore trying to make this known to him by languishing and tender glances, sighs, and impassioned airs; but the gentleman, who never studied anything but virtue, knew nought of vice in a lady who had so little excuse for it; so that the glances, sighs, and impassioned airs of the poor wanton brought her nothing but bitter disappointment. She carried her extravagance so far, that, forgetting she was a wife who ought, though solicited, to grant no favour, and a princess who was made to be adored, yet disdain such servants, she resolved to act like a man transported with passion, and to discharge her bosom of a burden that was insupportable.

One day then, when the duke went to council, to which the gentleman was not admitted, being too young, she beckoned to him, and he came, thinking she had some order to give him. Leaning then on his arm, like a woman wearied by too much repose, she walked about with him in a gallery, and said, "I am surprised that, being as you are, young, handsome, and full of engaging qualities, you have been able hitherto to live in continual intercourse with so many fair ladies without loving any of them." And then, with one of her most gracious looks, she paused for his answer.

"Madam," he replied, "if I were worthy that your greatness should descend to think of me, you would have more reason for surprise, to see so insignificant a man as I am offer his services only to meet with refusal or mockery."

Upon this discreet reply the duchess loved him more than ever, and vowed that there was not a lady in the court but would be too happy to have a lover of his merit; that he might try, and that she assured him he would succeed without difficulty. The gentleman kept his eyes constantly bent on the ground, not daring to look on the countenance of the duchess, which glowed enough to warm an icicle. Just when he was about to excuse himself, the duke sent for the duchess to come to the council upon an affair in which she was interested. She went with much regret. As for the gentleman, he pretended not to have understood what she said, which vexed and confused her so much that she knew not what to impute it to but the silly fear with which she thought the young man possessed. Seeing, then, that he did not understand her language, she resolved a few days afterwards to overleap fear and shame, and declare her passion to him in plain terms, never doubting but that beauty like hers could not fail to be well received. Nevertheless, she would have been glad to have had the honour to be solicited; but, after all, she preferred pleasure to honour.

After having several times again tried the same means she had first essayed, and always with the same unwelcome result, she plucked him by the sleeve one day, and told him she wanted to speak to him on an affair of importance. With all due respect and humility the gentleman followed her to a window recess, where, finding that she could not be seen from the chamber, she resumed the subject of her past conversation with a trembling voice, indicative alike of desire and fear. She reproached him for not having yet made choice of a lady, and assured him that wherever he fixed his affections she would spare no pains to ensure his success. The gentleman, not less distressed than astonished at such language, replied, "My heart is so tender, madam, that if I were once refused I should never know joy; and I am so well aware of my slender merit, that I am sure there is no lady in the court who would accept my services."

The duchess blushed at these words, and imagining that his heart was lost, protested he had only to wish, and she would answer for it that she knew the fairest lady in the court who would receive him with extreme joy, and make him consummately happy. "I do not believe, madam," he replied, "that there is any woman in this court so unfortunate and so infatuated as to have made me the object of her predilections."

Seeing that he would not understand her, she proceeded to give him a more direct glimpse of her passion; and as the gentleman's virtue gave her cause for fear, she spoke by way of interrogation. "If fortune," she said, "had so favoured you that it was myself who was thus well inclined to you, what would you say?"

The gentleman, who thought he was dreaming to hear her speak thus, dropped on one knee on the ground and replied, "When God shall do me the grace, madam, to make me possessor of the good-will of the duke my master, and of yourself, I shall deem myself the happiest of men. It is the sole recompense I crave for my faithful services, bound as I am above all others to sacrifice my life for you both. I am convinced, madam, that the love you have for my lord your spouse is so pure and great, that not even the greatest prince and the most accomplished man in the world, to say nothing of myself, who am but a worm of the earth, could impair the union that subsists between my master and you. As for me, whom he has nurtured from childhood, and made what I am, I would not for my life entertain a thought other than that which becomes a faithful servant as regards either his wife, sister, or mother."

The duchess would not suffer him to proceed, but seeing she was in danger of receiving a shameful refusal, she broke in upon him suddenly, "Wicked and arrogant fool! who requires any such thing of you? Because you are good-looking you imagine that the very flies are enamoured of you; but if you were presumptuous enough to address yourself to me, I would soon let you know that I love, and will love, none but my husband. I have spoken to you as I have done only for my diversion, to sift you, and make you my laughing-stock, as I do all amorous coxcombs."

"I have all along been assured that it was just as you say, madam," replied the gentleman.

She would hear no more, but turned abruptly from him, and to avoid her ladies who followed her into her chamber, she shut herself up in her closet, where she gave way to an indescribable burst of bitter feeling. On the one hand, the love in which she had failed caused her mortal sadness; and on the other, her despite against herself for entering upon so injudicious a dialogue, and against the gentleman for having answered so prudently, put her into such a fury that at one moment she wished to kill herself, at the next she would live to be revenged on him she regarded as her deadliest enemy. After a long fit of tears she feigned indisposition, to avoid appearing at the duke's supper, at which the gentleman was usually in attendance. The duke, who loved his wife more than himself, failed not to go and see her; when, in order to arrive the more easily at her ends, she told him she believed she was pregnant, and that her pregnancy had caused a rheum to fall upon her eyes, which gave her great pain. The duchess kept her bed for two or three hours in so sad and melancholy a mood, that the duke suspected there was something else the matter besides pregnancy. He went to sleep with her that night; but seeing that, in spite of all the caresses he could bestow upon her, she continued to sigh incessantly, he said, "You know, my dear, that I love you as my own life, and that if you die I cannot possibly survive you. If, then, you value my health and life, tell me, I entreat, what makes you sigh thus; for I cannot believe that pregnancy alone can produce that effect."

The duchess, seeing her husband in the very mood she wished, hastened to turn it to her vengeful purpose. "Alas! monsieur," she said, embracing him with tears, "my worst suffering is to see you the dupe of those whose duty it is to preserve your honour and all that is yours." This made the duke wondrously eager to know what she meant, and he begged her to speak openly, without fear or disguise. "I shall never be surprised," she said at last, after repeated refusals, "if strangers make war on princes, since those who are most bound to them undertake to wage such a horrible war against them, that the loss of domains is nothing in comparison with it. I say this, monsieur, with reference to a gentleman" (here she named her enemy) "whom you have fed, reared, treated more like a relation than a domestic, and who, by way of gratitude, has had the impudence and the baseness to attempt the honour of your wife, on which depends that of your house and your children. Though he long laboured to insinuate to me things that left me no doubt of his black perfidy, yet my heart, which is only for you, and thinks only on you, could not comprehend him; but at last he explained himself, and I replied to him as my rank and my honour required. I hate him, however, so that I cannot bear the sight of him; and this it was, monsieur, which made me keep my room and lose the happiness of your company. I beseech you, monsieur, not to keep such a pestilence near you; for after such a crime, the fear of your being made acquainted with it might very likely induce him to do something worse. You now know, monsieur, the cause of my grief, which seems to me most just and most worthy that you should right it without delay."

The duke, who on the one hand loved his wife and felt himself outraged, and on the other hand loved the gentleman, of whose fidelity he had often had practical proof, could hardly believe that this lie was truth. He withdrew to his chamber in great perplexity and anger, and sent word to the gentleman that he was not to appear any more in his presence, but was to retire to his own home for some time. The gentleman, ignorant of the cause of an order so peremptory and so unexpected, was the more keenly affected by it, as he thought he had deserved the very opposite treatment. Conscious of his innocence in heart and deed, he got one of his comrades to speak to the duke on his behalf, and deliver him a letter, wherein he most humbly entreated, that if he had the misfortune to be removed from his master's presence, in consequence of some report to his prejudice, the duke would have the goodness to suspend his judgment until he should have inquired into the truth; and then he durst hope it would be found he had in nowise offended. This letter somewhat appeased the duke; he sent for the gentleman to come secretly to his chamber, and said to him with great gravity, "I could never have believed that after having had you nurtured like my own child, I should have cause to repent of having so highly advanced you, forasmuch as you have sought to outrage me in a manner that would have been worse to me than the loss of life and fortune, namely, by attempting the honour of her who is the half of myself, and seeking to cover my house with perpetual infamy. You may believe that I feel this insult so deeply, that if I was quite sure that the fact was true, you would by this time be at the bottom of the water, to punish you secretly for the affront you have secretly sought to put upon me."

The gentleman was not dismayed by this speech; on the contrary, he spoke with the confidence of innocence, and besought the duke to have the goodness to tell him who was his accuser, the accusation being one of those which are better discussed with the lance than with the tongue. "Your accuser," replied the duke, "has no other arms than her chastity. It was my wife, and no one else, who told me this, praying me to take vengeance upon you."

Amazed as the poor gentleman was at the prodigious malice of the duchess, he would not accuse her, but contented himself with saying, "My lady may say what she pleases. You know her, monsieur, better than I; and you know if I have seen her elsewhere than in your company, except once only when she spoke to me a very little. Your judgment is as sound as that of any prince in Christendom. Therefore, my liege, I beseech you to consider if you have ever seen anything in me which can have caused you suspicion. It is a fire which it is impossible long to conceal in such wise that those who labour under the same malady shall not have some inkling of it. I beg, my liege, that you will be graciously pleased to believe two things of me: one is, that I am so true to you, that though my lady your spouse were the finest woman in the world, love would not be capable of making me do anything contrary to my honour and my duty; the other is, that even were she not your spouse, she is, of all the women I have ever seen, the one I should be least inclined to love; and there are enough of others on whom I should sooner fix my choice."

The duke's anger was somewhat mitigated by these words. "Well," said he, "I did not believe it; so you may go on as usual, with the assurance that if I find that the truth is on your side, I will love you more than ever; but if the contrary appears, your life is in my hand." The gentleman thanked him, and declared his willingness to submit to the severest penalty his master could devise if he were found guilty.

The duchess, seeing the gentleman continue to serve as usual, could not patiently endure it, and said to her husband, "It would be no more than you deserve, monsieur, if you were poisoned, since you have more confidence in your mortal enemies than in your nearest friends."

"Do not make yourself uneasy, my dear," replied the duke; "for if it appears that what you have told me is true, I assure you he has not twenty-four hours to live. But as he has protested the contrary to me on oath, and as, besides, I never perceived anything of the sort, I cannot believe it without good proofs."

"Truly, monsieur," she returned, "your goodness makes my malice greater. What greater proof would you have than that a man like him has never had any amour imputed to him. Be assured, monsieur, that but for the vain and presumptuous idea with which he has flattered himself of becoming my servant, he would not be without a mistress at this time of day. Never did a young man live so solitary as he in good company; and the reason can only be that his heart is set so high that his vain hope stands him in stead of everything else. If you believe that he conceals nothing from you, swear him as to his amours. If he tells you that he loves another, why then believe him; I am content you should; but if not, be assured that what I say is true."

The duke approved of his wife's suggestion, and taking the gentleman into the country, said to him, "My wife continues still to speak to me of you to the same purpose, and mentions a circumstance which gives me some suspicion. To be plain with you, it excites surprise that you, a young and gallant man, have never been known to be in love; and this very thing makes me fear that you entertain the sentiments you have been charged with, and that the hope you cherish is so pleasing to you that you cannot think of any other woman. I pray you then as a friend, and order you as a master, to tell me truly do you pay your court to any lady in this world?"

The poor gentleman, who would fain have concealed his love as carefully as he would have preserved his life, seeing his master's extreme jealousy, was constrained to swear to him that he loved a lady so beautiful that the beauty of the duchess and of all the ladies of her suite was mean in comparison, not to say ugliness and deformity; at the same time he besought the duke not to insist on his naming the lady, because the intimacy between him and his mistress was such that it could only be broken by whichever of the two first disclosed it. The duke promised he would never press him on that point, and was so satisfied with him, that he behaved more graciously to him than ever. The duchess perceived it, and employed her usual artifices to find out the reason; nor did the duke conceal it from her. Strong jealousy was now added to her thirst of vengeance, and she besought the duke to insist that the gentleman should name his mistress, declaring that if he refused to do so, her husband would be the most credulous prince in the world to put faith in so vague a statement.

The poor prince, who was led by his wife as she pleased, went and walked alone with the gentleman, and told him he was in still greater embarrassment than ever, being afraid that what he had told him was only an excuse to hinder him from coming at the truth, which made him more uneasy than before; therefore he besought him most earnestly to tell him the name of her he loved so much. The poor gentleman implored the duke not to constrain him to break the promise he had given to a person he loved as his life, and which he had kept inviolate until that moment. It would be tantamount to requiring him to lose in one day what he had preserved for more than seven years, and he would rather die than do that wrong to a person who was so faithful to him. His refusal threw the duke into such a violent fit of jealousy, that he exclaimed furiously, "Take your choice: either tell me the name of her you love above all others, or quit my dominions on pain of death if you are found in them after eight days."

If ever faithful servant was smitten with keen anguish it was this poor gentleman, who might well say, *Angustiæ sunt mihi undique.* On the one hand, if he told the truth he lost his mistress, should it come to her knowledge that he had broken his word to her; on the other, if he did not tell it, he was exiled from the country where she resided, and could never see her more. Thus pressed on all sides, a cold sweat broke out upon him, as if his anguish had brought him to the brink of the grave. The duke, perceiving his embarrassment, imagined he loved only the duchess, and that his confusion arose from the fact that he could not name any one else. In this belief he said to him sternly, "If you had told me the truth, you would have less difficulty in doing what I desire; but I believe that it is your crime that occasions your embarrassment."

The gentleman, stung by these words, and urged by the love he bore his master, resolved to tell him the truth, assuring himself that the duke was a man of so much honour that he would keep his secret inviolate. He fell on his knees then, and said to him, with his hands pressed together, "My liege, the obligations I am under to you, and the love I bear you, constrain me more than the fear of death. You are possessed with so false a prejudice against me, that, to undeceive you, I am resolved to tell you what no torments could extort from me. The only favour I ask of you, my liege, is, that you will swear, on the faith of a prince and a Christian, never to reveal the secret which you force from me." The duke promised him, with all the oaths he could think of, never to tell his secret to any one, either by word, act, or signs; and the gentleman, relying on the good faith of a prince whom he knew, put the first hand to his own undoing, saying to him, "It is seven years, my lord, since having known your niece, the Lady du Verger, as a widow and disengaged, I tried to acquire her good-will. As I was not of birth to marry her, I contented myself with being received by her as a lover, in which I succeeded. Our intercourse has been conducted hitherto with so much prudence, that no one has come to the knowledge of it except you, my lord, into whose hands I put my life and honour, entreating you to keep the secret, and to have no less esteem for my lady your niece, than whom I do not think there is under heaven a creature more perfect."

The duke was delighted with this declaration, for knowing the extraordinary beauty of his niece, he doubted not that she was more capable of pleasing than his wife. But not conceiving it possible that such a mystery should have been carried on without adequate means, he begged to know how her lover managed to see her. The gentleman told him that his mistress's chamber opened on a garden, and that on the days when he was to visit her a little gate was left open, through which he entered on foot, and advanced until he heard the barking of a little dog, which the lady let loose in the garden after her women had all retired; that then he went to her, and conversed with her all night, and on his departure appointed the day when he was to come again, in which he had never failed, except for indispensable reasons. The duke, who was the most curious of men, and who had been very gallant in his time, begged him, as well to dissipate his suspicions as for the pleasure of hearing so singular an adventure recounted, to take him with him, not as a master, but as a companion, the next time he went thither. The gentleman, having gone so far, assented, and told him his assignation was for that very day. The duke was as glad of this as if he had won a kingdom, and feigning to retire to his *garderobe* to rest, had two horses brought, one for the gentleman and the other for himself, and they travelled all night from Argilly, where the duke resided, to Le Verger, where they left their horses at the entrance of the park.

The gentleman made the duke enter through the little gate, and begged him to place himself behind a large walnut-tree, whence he might see if what he had told him was true or not. They had not been long in the garden before the little dog began to bark, and the gentleman walked towards the tower, whilst the lady advanced to meet him. She saluted him with an embrace, and told him it seemed a thousand years since she had seen him. Then they entered the chamber, the door of which they locked. The duke having seen the whole of this mystery, felt more satisfied; nor had he time to grow weary, for the gentleman told the lady that he was obliged to leave her sooner than usual, because the duke was going to the chase at four o'clock, and he durst not fail to attend him. The lady, who preferred honour to pleasure, did not attempt to hinder him from doing his duty; for what she prized most in their honourable intimacy was that it was a secret for all mankind.

The gentleman quitted the house at one o'clock in the morning, and his lady, in mantle and kerchief, escorted him not so far as she wished, for he made her go back for fear she should meet the duke, with whom he mounted again and returned to the château of Argilly. On the way, the duke never ceased protesting to the gentleman that he would rather die than ever divulge his secret; and his confidence in him was so confirmed, that no one at court stood higher in favour. The duchess was enraged at this. The duke forbade her ever to mention the subject any more to him, saying that he knew the truth, and was satisfied, for the lady whom the gentleman loved was handsomer than herself. These words so stung the heart of the duchess that they threw her into an illness worse than fever. The duke tried to console her, but nothing would do unless he would tell her who was that fair lady who was so devotedly loved. So much did she importune him, that at last he quitted the chamber, saying to her, "If you speak to me any more of these things, we will part." This made her still more ill, and she pretended to feel her infant move; whereat the duke was so rejoiced that he went to bed to her; but when she saw that his passion for her was at the height, she turned from him, saying, "Since you love neither wife nor child, monsieur, I entreat you let both die." These words she accompanied with so many tears and cries, that the duke was greatly afraid she would miscarry; wherefore, taking her in his arms, he entreated her to tell him what she wanted, protesting he had nothing that was not at her command. "Ah! monsieur," she replied, sobbing and crying, "what hope can I have that you would do a difficult thing for me, since you will not do the easiest and most reasonable thing in the world, which is to tell me the name of the mistress of the worst servant you ever had? I thought that you and I had but one heart, one soul, and one flesh, but I see that you regard me as a stranger, since you conceal your secrets from me as if I were an alien. You have confided to me many important secrets, and have never known that I divulged a tittle of them. You have had such proof that I have no will but yours, that you ought not to doubt but that I am more you than myself. If you have sworn never to tell any one the gentleman's secret, you do not violate your oath in telling it to me, for I neither am nor can be other than yourself. I have you in my heart; I hold you between my arms; I have a child in my womb in whom you live; yet I cannot have your love as you have mine. The more faithful I am to you, the more cruel and austere you are to me. This makes me long a thousand times for the day when a sudden death may deliver your child from such a father, and me from such a spouse. I hope it will soon come, since you prefer a faithless servant to your wife, to the mother of a child which is your own, and which is on the point of perishing because you will not tell me what I have the greatest longing to know."

So saying, she embraced and kissed her husband, watering his face with her tears, and sobbing and crying so violently, that the poor prince, fearing he should lose both mother and child, resolved to tell her the truth; but he swore that if ever she mentioned it to any one in the world she should die by no hand but his own. She accepted the condition; and then the poor abused duke told her all he had seen from beginning to end. She pretended to be satisfied, but in her heart it was quite otherwise. However, as she was afraid of the duke, she dissembled her passion as well as she could.

The duke, holding his court on a great feast-day, had called to it all the ladies of the country, his niece among the rest. After the banquet the dances began, and every one did his devoir; but the duchess was too much vexed by the sight of her niece's beauty and grace to enjoy herself, or hide her spleen. Making all the ladies sit down, she turned the conversation on love; but seeing that Madame du Verger said not a word, she said to her, with a heart rankling with jealousy, "And you, fair niece, is it possible that your beauty is without a lover?"

"Madam," replied the Lady du Verger, "my beauty has not yet produced that effect; for since my husband's death I have had no lovers but his children; nor do I desire any others."

"Fair niece, fair niece," rejoined the duchess, with execrable spite, "there is no love so secret as not to be known, nor any little dog so well trained as not to be heard to bark."

I leave you to imagine the anguish of poor Madame du Verger at finding that an affair she had thought so secret was published to her shame. The thought of her honour, so carefully guarded, and so unhappily lost, was torture to her; but the worst was her fear that her lover had broken his word to her, which she did not believe he could ever have done unless he loved some fairer lady, and in doting fondness had suffered her to extort the secret from him. However, she had so much self-command that she did not let her emotion be seen, but laughingly replied that she did not understand the language of brutes. But her heart was so wrung with grief that she rose, and, passing through the duchess's chamber, entered a *garderobe* in sight of the duke, who was walking about. Thinking herself alone, she threw herself on a bed. A demoiselle, who had sat down beside it to sleep, roused herself and peeped through the curtains to see who it might be, and perceiving it was the duke's niece, who thought herself alone, she durst not speak, but remained as still as possible to listen, whilst the poor lady in a dying voice thus began her lamentation:

"Alas! what have I heard! What words of death have smitten my ears! O thou who was loved as man was never loved before, is this the reward of my chaste and virtuous love? O my heart! hast thou made so dangerous a choice, and attached thyself to the most faithless, artful, and mischievous-tongued of all men, mistaking him for the most faithful, upright, and secret? Is it possible, alas! that a thing hidden from all the world has been revealed to the duchess? My little dog, so well trained, sole agent of my long and virtuous friendship, it was not you that betrayed my secret: it was a man, with a voice more piercing than a dog's, and a heart more ungrateful than any beast's. It was he who, contrary to his oath and his word, divulged the happy life we long led without injuring any one. O my friend! for whom alone my heart cherished love, a love wherewith my life has been preserved, has the beauty of the duchess metamorphosed you, as that of Circe did her lovers? Has she turned you from virtue to vice, from good to bad, from a man into a savage beast? O my friend! though you have broken your word to me, I will keep mine, and never see you more after having revealed our intimacy. But as I cannot live without seeing you, I willingly yield to the excess of my sorrow, and will never seek any remedy for it either from reason or from medicine. Death alone shall end it, and that death will be more welcome to me than to remain in the world without my lover, without honour, and without contentment. Neither war nor death has taken my lover from me; my sins and transgressions have not deprived me of honour; nor has my bad conduct bereft me of happiness. It is cruel fortune that has made an ingrate of the most favoured of all men, and has brought upon me the contrary of what I deserved. O duchess, how delighted you were to make that jeering allusion to my little dog! Revel in a bliss that belongs to me alone. Laugh at her who thought to escape derision whilst loving virtuously and concealing it with care. How that word wrung my heart! How it made me red with shame and pale with jealousy! Heart, heart, I feel thou art undone. Ill-requited love burns thee, jealousy and grief turn thee to ice, and forbid thee all consolation. Through having too much adored the creature, my soul has forgotten the Creator. It must return to Him from whom a vain love detached it. Be assured, my soul, thou wilt find a Father more tender than the friend for whom thou hast often forgotten Him. O God, my creator, who art the true and perfect love, by whose grace the love I have borne my friend has been sullied by no vice, save that of loving too much, be pleased to receive in the greatness of Thy mercy the soul and spirit of her who repents of having broken Thy first and righteous command. Through the merits of Him whose love is incomprehensible, forgive the fault which excess of love made me commit, for my trust is in Thee alone. Farewell, my friend, whose unworthiness of that name breaks my heart." So saying she fell backwards, her face ghastly, her lips blue, and her extremities cold.

At the same moment the gentleman she loved entered the reception-room, where the duchess was dancing with the other ladies. He looked round for his mistress, and not seeing her, went into the duchess's chamber, where he found the duke, who, guessing his purpose, whispered him that she was gone into the *garderobe*, and appeared to be unwell. The gentleman asked for leave to follow her, and the duke not only granted it, but urged him to do so. Entering the *garderobe* then, he found her at the last gasp; and, throwing his arms round her, he said, "What is this, my love? Do you want to quit me?" Roused by the well-known voice, the poor lady opened her eyes to look upon him who was the cause of her death; but that look so increased her love and her anguish, that with a piteous sigh she gave up the ghost.

The gentleman, more dead than alive, asked the demoiselle how the lady's illness had begun, and she told him all she had heard. He then knew that the duke had revealed his secret. His grief was so intense, that, embracing the body of his mistress, he wept over it long in silence, and at last exclaimed, "Traitor, villain, wretch that I am! Why has not the penalty for my treachery fallen on me, and not on her who was innocent? Why did not Heaven's lightning blast me the day my tongue revealed our secret and virtuous love? Why did not the earth open to swallow up a wretch who violated his faith? May my tongue be punished as was that of the wicked rich man in hell! O heart, that too much feared death and exile, may eagles tear thee perpetually as they did that of Ixion!* Alas, my dear friend! in thinking to hold you fast, I have lost you. I thought to possess you long alive, with virtue and pleasure, and I embrace you dead, and you have been dissatisfied to your last gasp with me, my heart, and my tongue. O most faithful of women! I denounce myself as the most inconstant, faithless, and perfidious of men. I would I could complain of the duke, whose word I trusted, hoping by that means to prolong our agreeable life; but ought I not to have known that no one could keep my secret better than myself? The duke was more justifiable in telling his secret to his wife, than I in telling mine to him. I am the only guilty one, the only one who deserves to be punished for the greatest crime ever committed between friends. I ought to have suffered him to throw me into the river as he threatened. You at least, dear one, would then be alive, and I should have closed my life with the glory of having observed the rule prescribed by true friendship; but having broken it I live still, and you are dead for having perfectly loved. Your pure heart could not know the baseness of mine, and live. O my God, why didst thou create me with a love so frivolous and a heart so ignorant? Why was I not the little dog that faithfully served its mistress? Alas! my little friend, I used to feel joy at the sound of your barking; but that joy is turned into sorrow, for having been the cause of another besides us two hearing your voice. Yet, sweetheart, neither love of the duchess nor of any other woman ever made me vary, though the wicked duchess has often solicited me to love her; but ignorance has undone me, for I thought by what I did to insure our intimacy for ever. But that ignorance does not make me the less guilty. I have revealed my mistress's secret, I have broken my word, and therefore it is that she is dead before me. Alas, sweetheart, will death be less cruel to me than to you, who have died only for having loved? Methinks death would not deign to touch my faithless and miserable heart. The loss of honour, and the memory of her I have lost through my fault, are more insupportable to me than ten thousand deaths. If any one had cut short your

* The poor gentleman had but a confused knowledge of Greek fable, or grief had muddled his recollection of it.

days through mischance or malice, I should use my sword to avenge you. It is not reasonable, then, that I should pardon that murderer, who has caused your death by a deed more vile than if he had killed you with a sword. If I knew a more odious executioner than myself, I would entreat him to do justice upon your perfidious lover. O love! I have offended thee from not having known how to love; and therefore thou wilt not succour me as thou hast succoured her who perfectly kept all thy laws. Nor is it just that I should make such a glorious end: it must be by my own hand. I have washed your face with my tears; I have implored your pardon; and it now only remains that my arm make my body like yours, and send my soul whither yours is gone, in the assurance that a virtuous and honourable love ends neither in this world nor in the next."

Starting up then, like a frantic man, from the corpse, he drew his poniard, and stabbed himself to the heart; and then, clasping his mistress in his arms for the second time, he kissed her so fondly, that he seemed more like a blissful lover than a dead man. The demoiselle seeing the deed, ran to the door and screamed for help. The duke, suspecting the disaster of those he loved, was the first to enter the *garderobe*, and on seeing that sad couple he tried to separate them, in order to save the gentleman if it were possible; but he held his mistress so fast, that it was impossible to tear him from her until he had expired. Nevertheless, hearing the duke exclaim, "My God! who has been the cause of this?" "My tongue and yours, monsieur," he replied, with a look of fury. So saying he breathed his last, with his face laid on that of his mistress.

The duke, wishing to know more of the matter, constrained the demoiselle to tell him all she had seen and heard, which she did from beginning to end, without forgetting anything. The duke then, knowing that he was the cause of the whole mischief, threw himself on the bodies of the two lovers, and with cries and tears implored their pardon. He kissed them repeatedly; and then rising furiously, he drew the poniard out of the gentleman's body. As a wild boar wounded by a spear runs impetuously at him who has struck the blow, so ran the duke at her who had wounded him to the soul. He found her still dancing in the reception-room, and gayer than usual, because she thought she had so well revenged herself on the Lady du Verger. Her husband seized her in the midst of the dance, and said, " You took the secret upon your life, and upon your life shall fall the forfeiture." So saying he grasped her by her head-dress, and buried the poniard in her bosom.

The astonished company thought the duke was out of his senses; but he had done the deed advisedly; and assembling all his servants on the spot, he recounted to them the glorious and melancholy story of his niece, and the wicked conduct of his wife: a narrative which drew tears from all his hearers. The duke then ordered that his wife should be buried in an abbey which he founded, partly with a view to atone for the sin he had committed in killing his wife; and then he had a magnificent tomb erected, in which the remains of his niece and of the gentleman were laid side by side, with an epitaph setting forth their tragic history. The duke made an expedition against the Turks, in which God so favoured him that he achieved glory and profit. Finding on his return that his eldest son was of age to govern, he became a monk, and retired to the abbey in which his wife and the two lovers were buried, and there he passed his old age happily with God.*

This, ladies, is the story you begged me to relate, and which, your eyes tell me, you have not heard without compassion. It seems to me an example from which you should

---

* " It is probable that the Queen of Navarre has contented herself with turning into prose an old fabliau entitled La Châtelaine de Vergy, which is found in the fourth volume of the *Recueil de Barbasan*, and in Legrand d'Aussy's third volume. Margaret has hardly concealed the fact that she borrowed this novel, since she says in the prologue that it was written in such *old language* that none of the company could understand it except herself and Madame Oisille. The story of the Châtelaine de Vergy has also been told by Bandello (Part IV., Novel V.), and after him by Belleforest, in his *Histoires Tragiques*. It might be supposed that Margaret merely borrowed from Bandello, for it is he who lays the scene in Burgundy, at the period when that province was ruled by a duke. It is to be remarked, however, that at the end of the last epilogue of the seventh day Margaret says that the company talked at supper of nothing but *Madame du Verger*, an evident alteration of *La Châtelaine de Vergy*, the name given to the heroine in the fabliau, whilst Bandello calls her quite differently. Moreover, the Italian writer terminates the tragic story in a different manner."—*Bibliophiles Français.*

profit, so as to beware of fixing your affections on men. However honourable and virtuous be that affection, it always ends badly. You see even that St. Paul would not have married people love to such excess; for the more one is attached to earthly, the more one is detached from heavenly, things; and the more honourable and virtuous love is, the harder is it to break its bonds. This constrains me to beg, ladies, that you will continually pray to God for His Holy Spirit, which will so inflame your hearts with the love of God, that at the hour of death it will not be hard for you to quit the things of the world, for which you have too much attachment.

"The love of these two persons being so virtuous as you represent it," said Hircan, "what need was there to make a secret of it?"

"Because," said Parlamente, "men are so depraved that they can never believe that love and virtue go hand in hand. They judge of the virtue of men and women according to their own passions, and consequently, if a woman has a dear friend other than one of her near relations, it is necessary for her to converse with him in secret if she would converse with him long. Whether a woman loves virtuously or viciously, her honour is alike doubted, because men judge only from appearances."

"But," said Geburon, "when the secret gets vent, the woman is so much the worse thought of."

"That is true, I confess," said Longarine; "and therefore the best course is not to love at all."

"We appeal from that sentence," said Dagoucin; "for if we believed that the ladies were without love, we would rather be without life. I speak of those who live only to win love; and even if it does not come to them, the hope of it supports them, and makes them do a thousand honourable things, until old age changes that fair passion into other pains. But if we thought that the ladies did not love, instead of following the profession of arms we should have to turn merchants, and instead of winning glory, to think only of amassing wealth."

"You mean to say, then," said Hircan, "that if there were no ladies we should be all caitiffs, as if we had no spirit but what they inspire us with. I am of the contrary opinion; and

I assert that nothing is more lowering to the spirit of a man than devoting himself too much to the society of women, and loving them to excess. It was for that very reason that the Hebrews prohibited a man from going to war the year he was married, lest the love of his wife should make him recoil from the dangers he ought to seek."

"I do not think there was much sense in that law," said Saffredent, "for there is nothing that makes a man readier to leave home than being married, the reason being, that no war without is more intolerable than that within. I am convinced, that to give men a taste for going into foreign parts, and not loitering by their own firesides, nothing more need be done than to marry them."

"It is true," said Ennasuite, "that marriage exonerates them from care for the house; for that they commit to their wives, and think only of acquiring glory, relying on it that their wives will attend sufficiently to their interest."

"Be it how it may," said Saffredent, "I am very happy that you are of my opinion."

"But," observed Parlamente, "you do not discuss the most remarkable point—namely, why the gentleman who was the cause of all the mischief did not die of grief as promptly as his mistress who was innocent."

"That was because women love better than men," said Nomerfide.

"Rather," replied Simontault, "because the jealousy of women and the violence of their passion make them give up the ghost without knowing why, whilst men, with more prudence, desire to be informed of the truth. Once they have ascertained it, their good sense makes them show the greatness of their spirit. Thus it was with the gentleman, who, as soon as he knew that he was the cause of his mistress's death, manifested the greatness of his love for her at the cost of his life."

"Nevertheless," said Ennasuite, "the fidelity of her love was the cause of her death; for her heart was so constant and so true, that she could not bear to be so villanously deceived."

"Her jealousy hindered her reason from acting," returned Simontault; "and as she believed the evil of which her lover was not guilty, her death was not voluntary, for she could not help dying; but her lover owned he had done wrong, and died voluntarily."

"Be it as you please," said Nomerfide; "but at all events the love must be great that causes such mortal sorrow."

"Don't be afraid," said Hircan; "you will not die of such a fever."

"No more than you will kill yourself on being conscious of having done wrong," she retorted.

Parlamente, who did not know but that the dispute was at her expense, said, laughing, "It is enough that two died for love, without two others fighting for the same cause. There is the last vesper-bell to separate you, whether you like or not."

At these words the company rose to hear vespers. They did not forget in their prayers the souls of the true lovers, for whom the monks willingly said a *De profundis*. During supper nothing was talked of but Madame du Verger. After amusing themselves a little together they retired to their respective chambers, and so ended the seventh day.

EIGHTH DAY.

The morning being come, they inquired how their bridge was getting on, and found that it might be completed in two or three days. This was not welcome news for some of the company, who would have been glad if the work had lasted longer, in order to protract the pleasure they enjoyed from so agreeable a mode of life. Seeing, then, that they had not more than two or three days left, they resolved to employ them well, and begged Madame Oisille to give them spiritual provender as was her wont. This she did, but detained them longer than usual, because she wished to finish the chronicle of St. John; and so well did she acquit herself of the task, that it seemed that the Holy Spirit, full of love and sweetness, spoke by her mouth. Warmed by that sacred fire they went to hear high mass. After dinner they talked of the past day, and doubted if the present one would be so well filled. They retired to their several chambers for reflection, until it was time to go to the meeting place, where they found the monks already stationed. When they were all seated, the question was asked who should begin. "As you have done me the honour," said Saffredent, "to make me begin two days, methinks it would be unjust to the ladies if any one of them did not also begin two."

"In that case," said Oisille, "we must either remain here a long while, or one of us ladies, or one of you gentlemen, would have to go without his or her day."

"For my part," said Dagoucin, "had I been chosen, I would have ceded my place to Saffredent."

"And I mine to Parlamente," said Nomerfide, "for I am so accustomed to serve that I know not how to command."

The company agreed to this, and Parlamente began thus: "Such good and wise tales have been told on the past days, ladies, that I should recommend our employing this one in relating the greatest follies we can think of, the same being really true. To set you going, then, I will begin in that way."

NOVEL LXXI.

A WOMAN AT THE POINT OF DEATH FLEW INTO SUCH A VIOLENT PASSION AT SEEING HER HUSBAND KISS HER SERVANT, THAT SHE RECOVERED.

There was at Amboise a saddler named Brimbaudier, who worked for the Queen of Navarre. It was enough to see the man's red nose to be assured that he was more a servant to Bacchus than to Diana. He had married a worthy woman, with whom he was very well satisfied, and who managed his children and his household with great discretion. One day he was told that his good wife was very ill, at which he was greatly afflicted. He went home with speed, and found her so far gone that she had more need of a confessor than of a doctor, whereat he made the most doleful lamentations that ever were heard; but to report them properly one ought to speak thick like him; but it would be better still to paint one's face. After he had rendered her all the good offices he could, she asked for the cross, which was brought her. The good man, seeing this, threw himself on a bed howling and crying, and ejaculating with his thick tongue: "O Lord, I am losing my poor wife. Was there ever such a misfortune? What shall I do?" and so forth. At last, there being no one in the room but a young servant, rather a good-looking girl, he called her to him in a faint voice, and said, "I am dying, my dear, and worse than if I was dead all out, to see your mistress dying. I know not what to say or do, only that I look for help to you, and beg you to take care of my house and my children. Take the keys that hang at my side; do everything in the house for the best, for I am not in a condition to attend to such things."

The poor girl pitied and tried to comfort him, begging him not to be so cast down, lest besides losing her mistress she should lose her good master also. "It can't be, my dear," said he, "for I am dying. See how cold my face is; put your cheeks to mine to warm them." As she did so he put his hand on her bosom, whereat she offered to make some difficulty, but he begged her not to be alarmed, for they must by all means see each other more closely. Thereupon he laid hold of her, and threw her on the bed. His wife, who was left alone with the cross and the holy water, and who had not spoken for two days, began to cry out as well as her feeble voice enabled her, "Ah! ah! ah! I am not dead yet!" And threatening them with her hand, she repeated, "Wicked wretches, I am not dead yet!"

The husband and the servant jumped up instantly, but the sick woman was so enraged with them that her anger consumed the catarrhal humour that hindered her from speaking, so that she poured out upon them all the abuse she could think of. From that moment she began to mend; but her husband had often to endure her reproaches for the little love he had shown for her.*

You see, ladies, how hypocritical men are, and how little is needed to console them for the loss of their wives.

"How do you know," said Hircan, "but he had heard it was the best remedy for his wife's case? Not being able to cure her by his care and his kind offices, he wished to try if the contrary would not produce the desired effect. The ex-

* This novel has been imitated by Noël du Fail de la Hérissaye in his *Contes d'Eutrapel*, ch. v.

periment was a happy one; and I am astonished that, being a woman as you are, you have so frankly portrayed the spirit of your sex, who do for spite what they cannot be brought to do by kindness."

"Unquestionably, such provocation as that," said Longarine, "would make me rise not only from my bed but from my grave."

"What harm did he do her in consoling himself, since he thought she was dead?" said Saffredent. "Do we not know that marriage binds only as long as life lasts, and that death gives a man back his liberty?"

"Death releases a man from the obligation of his oath," said Oisille; "but a good heart never thinks itself dispensed from the obligation of loving. It was making great haste to console himself not to be able to wait until his wife had expired."

"What seems strangest to me," said Nomerfide, "is that having death and the cross before his eyes, those two objects were not capable of hindering him from offending God."

"That is a fine idea," said Simontault. "So, then, you would not be shocked at a naughty thing, provided it were done out of sight of the church and the cemetery?"

"Make game of me as much as you will," replied Nomerfide, "but by your leave I maintain that the contemplation of death is enough to chill the heart, however young and fiery it may be."

"I should think as you do," said Dagoucin, "had I not heard to the contrary from a princess."

"That is as much as to say that she told you some tale to that effect," said Parlamente. "Such being the case, let us hear it."

Dagoucin began thus.

NOVEL LXXII.

CONTINUAL REPENTANCE OF A NUN WHO HAD LOST HER VIRGINITY WITHOUT VIOLENCE AND WITHOUT LOVE.

In one of the best towns of France after Paris there was a hospital richly endowed—that is to say, with a prioress and fifteen or sixteen nuns, and a prior with seven or eight monks, who lived opposite in another building. The latter performed service every day, and the nuns contented themselves with saying their paternosters and the hours of Our Lady, because they had enough to do in attending the sick. One day there died a poor man, about whom all the nuns were assembled. After administering all the remedies for his bodily health, they sent for one of their monks to confess him. Then, seeing that he was sinking, they gave him extreme unction, and shortly afterwards he lost his speech. But as he was a long time dying, and it was thought he could still hear, each of the nuns busied herself in saying to him the best things she could. This continued so long that at last they grew tired, and, as it was night and late, they went to bed one after the other. One of the youngest alone remained to lay out the body, with a monk of whom she stood in more awe than of the prior or any other, on account of his great austerity both in life and in conversation. After these two had shouted three hours loud and long into the poor man's ear, they were sure he had breathed his last, and they laid him out.

Whilst performing this last act of charity the monk began to talk of the wretchedness of life and the blessedness of death; and half the night was spent in this pious discourse. The poor girl listened with great attention, and gazed at him with tears in her eyes. This gave him so much pleasure, that, whilst speaking of the life to come, he began to embrace her as if he would fain have carried her in his arms straightway to Paradise; she listening to him always with the same rapt spirit, and not venturing to gainsay one whom she believed to be the most devout man in the convent. The wicked monk seeing this, and talking always of God, accomplished the work which the devil had suddenly put into their hearts (for previously there had been no question of this), assuring her that a secret sin met with impunity before God; that two persons who have no ties can not sin in that way, provided no scandal comes of it, and to avoid any she was to be careful not to confess to any one but himself.

They separated at last, and as she passed through a chapel dedicated to Our Lady, she wished to offer her orison as usual; but when she came to utter the words Virgin Mary, she recollected that she had lost her virginity without violence and without love, but through a stupid fear, and she burst into such a violent fit of tears, that it seemed as if her heart would break. The monk, who heard her sobs from a distance, suspected her conversion, and was afraid he should not again enjoy the same pleasure. To prevent that untoward contingency, he went up to her as she lay prostrate before the image, reproved her sharply, and told her if her conscience reproached her at all, she might confess to him and not repeat the act if she did not think proper, for she was free either to do it or not without sin. The silly nun, thinking to expiate her sin, confessed to the monk, and all the penance he imposed on her was to swear that it was no sin in her to love, and that some holy water would be sufficient to wash out so trifling a peccadillo.

She believed him rather than God, and relapsed some time after. Finally she became pregnant, and her remorse was so great that she entreated the prioress to have that monk expelled, for she knew he was so crafty that he would not fail to seduce her. The prioress and the prior, who agreed together, treated her with contempt, and told her she was big enough to defend herself against a man, and that he of whom she spoke was a most excellent man. Urged at last by her remorse, she earnestly implored their leave to go to Rome, where she believed she should recover her virginity by confessing her sin at the Pope's feet. The prior and the prioress very willingly granted her request, liking better she should be a pilgrim contrary to the rule of her order than cloistered with the scruples she had. Fearing, too, lest in a fit of despair she should reveal the sort of life that was led there, they gave her money for her journey.

Now God so ordered it that the nun arrived in Lyon at the time when the Duchess of Alençon, who was afterwards

Queen of Navarre, was secretly performing a novaine in the church of St. John with some of her women. One evening after vespers, when that princess was kneeling before the crucifix, she heard some one going up the steps, and perceiving by the light of the lamp that it was a nun, the duchess withdrew to the corner of the altar to hear her devotions. The nun, thinking herself alone, knelt down, and, beating her breast, began to weep most piteously, crying constantly, "Alas, my God! have pity on this poor sinner!" The duchess, wishing to know what was the matter, went up to her, and said, "What is the matter, my dear? Whence come you, and who brought you here?"

The poor nun, who did not know her, replied, "Alas, my dear! my misfortune is so great that I have recourse only to God, whom I beseech with all my heart to enable me to speak to Madame d'Alençon; for I can relate my misfortune to no one but her, being assured that if there be a remedy for it she will not fail to find it."

"My dear," said the duchess, "you may speak to me as you would to her, for I am a very great friend of hers."

"Pardon me," said the nun; "none but herself shall ever know my secret."

The duchess then told her she might speak out, for she had found the person she wanted. The poor woman then fell at her feet, and after many tears and cries related her whole story. The duchess consoled her so well, that, without weakening her repentance, she sent her back to the priory with letters to the bishop of the place, ordering him to have that scandalous monk expelled.

I had this story from the duchess herself; and you may see from it that Nomerfide's recipe is not good for all sorts of people, since this pair, who were touching and laying out a dead body, were not the more chaste for all that.*

"Here was an invention," said Hircan, "of which I do not suppose any one ever availed himself before: to talk of death and perform the actions of life."

"Sinning is not an action of life," observed Oisille, "for we know that sin produces death."

* This novel is wanting in the first edition of the Heptameron.

"Rely upon it," said Saffredent, "those poor people did not think of that point of theology. But as Lot's daughters made their father drunk in hopes of perpetuating the human race, so these good people wished to repair what death had spoiled, and to make a new body to replace that which death had taken away. So I see no harm in the matter except the tears of the poor nun, who wept without ceasing, and always returned to the cause of her tears."

"I have known many like her," said Hircan; "weeping for the sin, and at the same time laughing over the pleasure."

"I believe I know the persons to whom you allude," said Parlamente. "They have laughed long enough, methinks, to begin to cry."

"Say no more," said Hircan; "the tragedy which began with laughter is not yet ended."

"To change the subject, then," rejoined Parlamente, "it strikes me that Dagoucin has not complied with the rule we laid down, which was to tell only laughable tales, whereas his is too piteous."

"You said," replied Dagoucin, "that we should relate only follies, and it seems to me I have not been unsuccessful in that way. But that we may hear a more agreeable one, I give my voice to Nomerfide, hoping that she will repair my fault."

"I have a tale ready," said Nomerfide, "which is worthy to follow yours, for it is about a monk and a dead body. Hearken then, if you please."*

* "Here end the tales and novels of the late Queen of Navarre, which is all that can be recovered of them."—*Edition of* 1559, *by Gruget*.

THE END.

www.ingramcontent.com/pod-product-compliance
Lightning Source LLC
Chambersburg PA
CBHW022057300426
44117CB00007B/492